TARGET:
ARCTIC

Men in The Skies at The Top of The World

TAF
ARC

CHILTO
A DIVISION OF CHILTON COMP

ET:
TIC

George Simmons

OOKS
blishers Philadelphia · New York

for "Chickie," my darling wife

PROLOGUE

This story is true. All the people are real; all the events really occurred, nothing is invented and every detail is rooted in history. But history is like a neglected lawn choked by weeds and covered with dead leaves. It, too, must be weeded and raked and on bare patches the seed of truth must be sown.

The theme is ambition, and ambition has many faces. It is mirrored in courageous men who boarded flimsy airships to make the first, faltering steps toward aerial conquest of the Arctic and in others who set out without fanfare to gain the scientific knowledge essential in transforming ice-clogged seas into navigable waters. Most of these pioneers were ordinary, nonheroic men who went to work methodically, purposefully, and with stubborn determination. Some became famous, many remained anonymous.

Today, powerful jet liners shuttle between continents along airways spanning vast ice-covered territories, and ships sail through waters which had remained impassable for centuries. Commercially essential and strategically vital, these routes have sprouted out of efforts made by aerial pioneers in the Arctic.

This is their story. Gathered from books long out of print and from sources not readily available, it was supplemented by reports buried in newspapers brittle with age and rounded out with verbal accounts from some of those who have moved across this page of history.

The whole purpose of this book is to place into historical perspective these achievements, many of which the tide of time has swept into the pool of things forgotten.

ACKNOWLEDGMENTS

More than fifty people have generously co-operated in the preparation of this book, and their assistance is hereby gratefully acknowledged. First among them is my wife, who has spent countless hours on many tasks without losing her patience.

These men and women graciously contributed valuable information through personal interviews:

Capt. U. Baccarani, Rome; Colonel B. Balchen, Chappaqua, N. Y.; the late Mrs. F. Bennett, New York; G. Biagi, Rome; General A. Briganti, Rome; the late N. Cecioni, Rome; Major E. Christell, Stockholm; Colonel B. Chukhnovsky, Leningrad; Major E. Ekman, Stockholm; Professor Y. Gakkel, Leningrad; Dr. D. Giudici, Bergamo; Commander B. Gottwaldt, Oslo; Professor A. Hoel, Oslo; Admiral A. Mariano, Rome.

General U. Nobile, Rome; General H. Riiser-Larsen,* Copenhagen; W. Ross, New York; Colonel M. Slepnev, Moscow; Professor M. Somov, Leningrad; the late Dr. V. Stefansson, Hanover, New Hampshire; the late Dr. C. Tomaselli, Milan; General G. Valle, Rome; Senator J. Van Dongen, Aardenburg, Holland; Admiral A. Viglieri, Monte Carlo; General M. Vodopyanov, Moscow; L. Vorontsova, Moscow; Lady S. Wilkins, New York.

Others supplied useful information by correspondence: Dr. T. Armstrong, Dr. A. Fagersten, the Finnish Ministry of Defense, Lieutenant Colonel C. Glines, Professor G. Liljequist, the Norwegian Ministry of Defense, Lieutenant Colonel D. Shaw, Lieutenant Colonel A. Simpson.

Out of a particularly voluminous correspondence grew a sincere friendship with Dr. F. Trojani, who has gracefully chosen to dedicate to me his book *La Coda di Minosse,* which may well be the definitive story of the *Italia* disaster.

Still others were most helpful with technical advice and in obtaining research material not readily available: W. Briesemeister, Miss G. Carney, Miss N. Felland, W. Field, Jr., T. Hanrahan, B. Koten, Miss A. Lister, O. M. Miller, O. Rosenwald.

Finally, I thank my wife for being a severe but loyal critic and for errors that may have slipped in I assume responsibility and offer apologies.

Many of the maps in this book had as a base map the *Serial Atlas of the Marine Environment,* American Geographical Society, New York.

* My friend Riiser died after a long illness on June 3, 1965, while this book was in production.

CONTENTS

I. PIONEERS
1896-1924   p. 1

II. QUEST
1925-1926   p. 45

III. CONQUEST
1926-1928   p. 81

IV. DISASTER
1928   p. 125

V. MILESTONES
1929-1935   p. 221

VI. TRANSFORMATION
1936-1963   p. 281

MEN OF THE ARCTIC
A GALLERY   p. 339

EPILOGUE   p. 347

APPENDICES

1. TARGET: ANTARCTIC   351

2. EVOLUTION OF ARCTIC AVIATION   354

3. AIRCRAFT USED IN PIONEER ARCTIC FLYING   357

4. GREENLAND-ICELAND TRANSATLANTIC AIR ROUTE   359

5. PURPOSE OF DRIFTING STATIONS IN THE ARCTIC OCEAN   367

6. SOVIET DRIFTING STATIONS, 1937–1965   368

7. U. S. DRIFTING STATIONS, 1954–1965   369

8. RUSSIAN EXPEDITIONS TO ARCTIC DURING POSTWAR PERIOD   370

NOTES   370

BIBLIOGRAPHY   399

INDEX   407

I. PIONEERS
1896-1924

1

WHEN youthful Fridtjof Nansen, already famous for his spectacular crossing of Greenland, presented to the Norwegian Geographical Society a new and quite revolutionary plan for arctic exploration, he met with criticism and incredulity.[1]* Yet the plan was based on logic, clear thinking and confidence in the advance of technology. It had matured after some ice-caked wreckage of De Long's ill-fated ship *Jeanette*, sunk off the New Siberian Islands in 1881, was found on the extreme southwest coast of Greenland a few years later. Nansen said:

> If a floe could drift right across the unknown region, that drift might be enlisted in the service of exploration. If we pay attention to the actual forces of nature as they exist . . . . and try and work with them and not against them, we shall find the safest and easiest way of reaching the Pole.[2]

All he wanted was a ship, slim enough to slip "like an eel out of the embrace of ice." He was confident that in such a vessel he too could drift across the polar basin, just as the wreckage of the *Jeanette* had done.

Conservative arctic explorers voiced strong disapproval. Adolphus Washington Greely, the leader of a disastrous American expedition to the Arctic,[3] said:

> It is doubtful if any hydrographer would treat seriously his theory of polar currents. . . . Arctic exploration is sufficiently credited with . . . danger . . . without Dr. Nansen's illogical scheme of self-destruction.[4]

One expert decried such "amateur nautical expeditions"; others thought that a drifting expedition would run into land, which, they were sure, existed near the North Pole, and Sir Joseph Hooker, a man with vast Antarctic experience, suggested that Nansen "dispose of his admirable courage, skill and resources in the prosecution of some less perilous attempt to solve the mystery of the Arctic Area."

Unruffled, Nansen stood by his convictions. Support for his project came from the Norwegian Government which provided two thirds of the funds needed; the rest was obtained from private individuals, headed by King Oscar. In June 1893 a ship, the *Fram*, especially built for Nansen and commanded by Captain Otto Sverdrup, set out for the Arctic. It carried a thirteen-man Norwegian expedition headed by Nansen himself.[5]

---

* Superior figures refer to Notes beginning on p. 370.

Less than two years later another serious, self-confident man presented to the Swedish Anthropological and Geographical Society a plan of his own for conquest of the Arctic. So far, he said, attempts to penetrate the central polar regions had had only scant success, as ships had proven to be ineffective weapons against ice. True enough, Nansen was experimenting with a new technique, but there was no way of telling whether the *Fram* would succeed in crossing the Polar Sea with the slowly moving ice. Sleds were really the only means by which pack-ice barring the way to the Pole could be conquered, he said, but progress was slow and results few. "Is there no other way?" he asked. "We need not search very long," he went on, "before we find a means, which is . . . created just for such a purpose. This means is the air balloon . . ."[6]

The man who spoke these words was Salomon August Andrée. A Swede, tall, slender and handsome, he had penetrating blue eyes and a mouth hidden behind a drooping mustache. Aged forty-one, he was a sober intellectual, a product of his time, imbued with practical ideas, firm confidence in science, and a powerful drive for reform. He continued:

> I wish . . . to emphasize that the problem of reaching the Pole or to transverse the Arctic wastes of ice in general is not a purely scientific problem but also a technical one . . .

The balloon he envisioned, would have to lift three men, an assortment of scientific instruments, polar equipment, ballast, and a four months' food supply, all this amounting roughly to some 6,500 pounds. Furthermore, it should be able to stay aloft for thirty days and be steerable to a certain extent.

Salomon Andrée knew what he was talking about; he may have envisioned the invention of a dirigible, but in his zeal for progress he was impatient. He may have been aware of Lilienthal's flights in Germany, he may have heard about Santos-Dumont's dirigible, which was soon to create a sensation in France—but whatever was available seemed adequate for the purpose he had in mind. An air enthusiast for some nineteen years, Andrée owned a 37,230-cubic-foot balloon in which he had made eight ascents. He had stayed in the air as long as ten and one-half hours, rising to a height exceeding 13,000 feet and covering on one occasion a distance of 170 miles. Guide lines and an adjustable sail made his balloon steerable to a certain extent. Primitive as this arrangement was, it enabled the pilot to make his balloon deviate by 27 degrees from the direction of the wind.

For his planned expedition Andrée wanted a hydrogen-filled balloon of 212,000 cubic feet, also equipped with a system of sails and guide ropes. According to his carefully worked out estimate the project could be financed with £7,120.

Coming to the end of his speech, Andrée said:

> By means of a single balloon journey we shall be able to gain a greater knowledge of the geography of the Arctic regions than can be obtained in centuries by any other way. And who, I ask, are better qualified to make such an attempt than we Swedes?

Thus, a reserved but confident Andrée declared himself a contender for the conquest of the North Pole. The confidence he showed was based neither on his own arctic experience (he had been a member of the Spitsbergen-based Swedish expedition which conducted scientific research during the International Polar Year of 1882) nor on his skill in ballooning. It was the outgrowth of support he had received two days earlier from Baron Nils A. Nordenskiöld. At that time Andrée had made essentially the same speech in front of the Academy of Sciences, and the renowned explorer who had crowned twenty-one years of work in the Arctic by navigating the Northeast Passage along the coast of Siberia* had said: "It is a long time since I embraced a proposal for a polar expedition with real enthusiasm, but I do so on this occasion. . . ."

The support Andrée received was not unanimous, of course. There were those who predicted that aeronauts taking off for the Pole would freeze to death or suffocate in the rarefied atmosphere; some feared that a balloon might be shot at by savages or pecked at by birds; there were those who called the whole scheme fantastic, visionary, or folly. One Austrian newspaper editorialized, "That Mr. Andrée is simply a fool or a swindler."[7]

But Salomon Andrée was neither a fool nor a swindler. He was a man of vision, or at least those who offered financial support for his expedition thought so. Among his backers were Alfred Nobel, the inventor of dynamite, Baron Oscar Dickson, who had previously supported Nils Nordenskiöld, and the same King Oscar who had made Nansen's expedition in the *Fram* possible. When sufficient funds were available, Henri Lachambre in Paris was commissioned to construct a balloon while Andrée assembled essential supplies, equipment, and instruments. By June 7, 1896, everything was loaded aboard the steamer *Virgo*, which then left Göteborg to the cheers of several thousand people.†

On June 23 the *Virgo* was anchored off Dane Island, Spitsbergen;‡

---

* The Northeast Passage, now known as "The Northern Sea Route," is composed of Barents Sea, Kara Sea, Laptev Sea, East Siberian Sea, and Chukhi Sea.

† Wherever possible, geographical names are spelled to conform with *The Columbia Lippincott Gazetteer of the World,* Columbia University Press, New York, by arrangement with J. B. Lippincott Co., 1952.

‡ Spitsbergen in an archipelago in the Arctic Ocean, approximately 400 miles north of Norway, between Greenland and Franz Josef Land. It is now owned by Norway and has been renamed "Svalbard." For the sake of simplicity, however, the name "Spitsbergen" has been retained.

the construction of a houselike hangar was under way and all equipment was brought ashore. By June 27 the filling of the balloon was completed, and a few days later the expedition was ready to start.[8]

At this time, Andrée noted in his diary:

> Everything has turned out exceedingly well . . . if Nature will only do its share . . .[9]

But nature did not do its share: the right winds never came, and because of a clause in its insurance the *Virgo* could not remain in Spitsbergen beyond August 20. This meant that the time for the start of Andrée's expedition was limited to the first two weeks of August.

After days spent in useless waiting, the expedition was called off. In the early hours of August 14, while preparations were under way to take Andrée's equipment back to the base ship, a vessel became visible on the horizon. It was Nansen's *Fram,* homeward-bound after a unique journey amidst the ice of the Polar Sea.

Disappointment at Andrée's failure was smothered in the worldwide rejoicing over Nansen's extraordinary feat. Remembering the skepticism which had greeted Nansen's plan to allow the *Fram* to become icebound and turn into an ice-based meteorological station, whose course would chart the speed and direction of currents in the polar basin, many of Andrée's critics became silent. If Nansen could do what had been considered impossible, why, it was asked, should Andrée not be able to carry off his plan successfully?

The following year Andrée again left for Spitsbergen.[10] This time he started earlier in the year and his expedition had two ships: the *Virgo*, carrying the equipment, and the *Svensksund,* commanded by Count C. A. Ehrensvärd, which had been placed at Andrée's disposal by the Swedish Government for the transport of personnel. The aerial expedition itself consisted of three men: Salomon Andrée, Nils Strindberg, and Knut Hjalmar Fraenkel. Andrée himself had chosen the other two from a number of volunteers. Both men were in their twenties, and had been to Paris for training in ballooning. Strindberg, a physicist at the University of Stockholm and an accomplished photographer, had full confidence in Andrée's project and, as if to underline his firm belief that he would soon return from a successful aerial expedition to the Arctic, he had recently become engaged. Fraenkel was a slender, quick-witted man with a yen for adventure, whose dexterity and physical strength were the qualifications which had prompted Andrée to take him along. This was a team of three well-qualified and unassuming men who believed firmly that what they were setting out to do could be done and who were prepared to accept the risks involved in a balloon flight over unknown territories. They were also prepared to fight for survival should they be forced down somewhere in the inhospitable Arctic.

On May 30 the expedition arrived at Dane Island. The hangar was repaired, the balloon was placed inside and inflated,[11] Lieutenant Svedenborg, an alternate, was sent to the Seven Islands, in the Archipelago of Spitsbergen, to establish a food depot as far north as possible. By July 1 all tests and preparations were virtually completed. Bearing in mind that the balloon might come down somewhere in the Arctic and knowing that Nansen had found it possible to travel over some 700 miles of ice and water by using sleds and a canoe, Andrée had with him three sledges, a boat, an adequate amount of food, guns and ammunition. Carrier pigeons, provided by Stockholm's newspaper *Aftonbladet,* were to serve as a means of communication with the outside world. In addition Andrée had a number of hollow cork balls, protected by copper netting, each holding a small metal cylinder into which messages could be inserted. He intended to throw these out as buoys at different times, hoping that they might drift toward inhabited land, where they would be found. One of the buoys was larger than the others; this—the "Polar buoy"—was to be thrown overboard at the Pole or at the most northerly point reached by the expedition.

By the beginning of July all equipment and provisions were stored aboard the balloon and a period of anxious waiting for proper weather set in. Early in the morning of July 11 the clouds overhanging Virgo Harbor were seen moving in a northerly direction, the waters of the bay became agitated, and two sealers were seen pulling in to escape the gathering storm. The south wind Andrée had been waiting for had arrived. But Andrée was somewhat dubious as he studied the cloud formations. The force and direction of the wind were quite favorable for an ascent, but there were frequent sudden gusts which could equally well bring sudden disaster. Standing with the others on the roof of the hangar, examining the balloon and conscious of the passing of time, Andrée asked: "Shall we try or not?"

"I think we ought to attempt it," Strindberg said, and Fraenkel agreed. Andrée looked serious and remained silent. He climbed down and, accompanied by the others, walked back toward the *Svensksund.* It was obvious that he was finding it difficult to make a decision which might well determine the outcome of a venture to which he had dedicated so much thought and work.

Once aboard the ship. Andrée turned to Captain Ehrensvärd. "Well," he said, "we have been considering whether to start or not; my companions insist on starting and since I have no absolutely valid reasons against it, I must agree to it, although with some hesitation. . . ."[12]

The word spread quickly and the sailors set out to free the balloon by breaking loose plank after plank of the hangar. Standing by solemnly in the midst of this activity, Andrée was watching and supervising, while Strindberg was busily snapping pictures of what promised to be an historic event. Instruments, supplies and food had already been stored inside the balloon's gondola or stuffed into canvas pockets designed for that purpose; now additional bags of sand were taken aboard to serve as ballast. Freed from the hangar and anchored to the ground only by three straining ropes, the dark balloon swayed gently in the clear air of Virgo Harbor.

There were restrained farewells and Andrée handed Captain Ehrensvärd a hastily written note addressed to the newspaper *Aftonbladet:*

> We began on Sunday, at 10:45, preparations for our ascent, and at this moment, 2:30 P.M., we are ready to start . . .[13]

Then Andrée climbed into the gondola. "Strindberg, Fraenkel, are you ready?" he shouted. Within minutes they too were aboard and there was profound silence, broken only by the whistling wind and by the flapping of canvas.

Eyewitness Alexis Machuron later would say:

> Andrée is always calm, cold and impassable. Not a trace of emotion is visible on his face, nothing but an expression of firm resolution and an indomitable will.[14]

Andrée gave the final command in a quiet, controlled voice: "Cut away everywhere . . ."

Instantly knife-wielding sailors cut the three ropes holding the balloon and with hurrahs from those on the ground the primitive airship, christened *Eagle,* began rising. The time was forty-six minutes past one-o'clock in the afternoon, Greenwich mean time, July 11, 1897.

Jerkily, the balloon rose and slowly floated in a northeasterly direction across Virgo Harbor at a height of less than 300 feet. Hanging inertly below, ropes from the *Eagle* were being dragged along, cutting the waters of the bay. Once away from the sheltering mountain against which the hangar had been built and when halfway across the harbor, the balloon was suddenly caught in a strong air current and pulled downward. Expecting the gondola to hit the water and the well-advertized venture to end ingloriously before it had really got under way, some of the watching sailors rushed to their boats. But the aeronauts aboard the *Eagle* were working fast to lighten the balloon. Emptying eight bags of sand, and thus sacrificing 450 pounds of valuable ballast, Andrée and his men soon regained altitude and continued their journey in a northerly direction at a speed of some twenty miles an hour.

The men on the ground saw the *Eagle* clear a range of hills, at about 300 feet. Suspended in a blue sky, the balloon appeared like a gray speck before vanishing in a cloud over Vogelsang Island at twenty minutes past two in the afternoon.

The *Eagle* was in flight, but somehow the lower two-thirds of three long guide ropes had become detached on takeoff and had been left

Andrée's balloon in flight over Virgo Bay.   © *Swedish Society for Anthropology and Geography.*

behind. This loss deprived Andrée not only of some 1,160 pounds in ballast, but also of the carefully thought-out steering mechanism which was to have transformed his free balloon into one with some, though admittedly limited, maneuverability.[15]

Propelled by a lashing wind from the southwest, the *Eagle* continued its flight at an altitude of some 1,600 feet, passing through layers of cloud and fog. Toward five o'clock Spitsbergen disappeared from view, and as far as the eye could see there was nothing but the gray loneliness of pack ice. The first pigeons were released; hesitating, they opened their wings, settled on the ice for a few moments, then they flew off to the west. They would never reach their destination. Cut off from the outside world, Andrée and his men, the first arctic aeronauts, were on their own.

Warmed by the sun, the hydrogen inside the balloon expanded and the increased pressure opened a valve through which the gas started escaping to the sound of a soft whistling. Aboard the *Eagle* there was silence, only now and then interrupted by the cry of a passing bird, the dull shotlike noise caused by the collision of ice floes below, and the intermittent whistling of the valve.

Leaving Strindberg and Fraenkel on the gondola's roof, Andrée went down to snatch a few hours of sleep. It had been a busy and anxious day for him. Andrée realized that the expedition had assumed a different character from what he had anticipated and for which he had planned.

A log entry made by Strindberg at 8:23 P.M. reads:

> We are now travelling horizontally so finely that it is a pity we
> are obliged to breathe as that makes the balloon lighter of course.
> And so Fraenkel and I went and spit . . .

At ten o'clock in the evening the first buoy was thrown overboard,
carrying this message:

> Our journey has hitherto gone well. We are still moving on at a height
> of 830 feet in a direction which at first was North 10° eastern declination
> but later North, 45° eastern declination. . . . Weather magnificent. In
> best of humors, Andrée Strindberg Fraenkel. Above the clouds since
> 7:45 G.M.T.[16]

Then the *Eagle* was swept into a bank of clouds whose moist and
cooling grip caused the gas inside the balloon to contract. Growing heavier,
the balloon soon lost altitude. Ballast was thrown overboard, but steadily,
though gently, the *Eagle* was coming down, while Strindberg kept watching
a dense cloud at the eastern horizon toward which the balloon was being
carried.[17]

Shortly after midnight the *Eagle* was caught in the shadow of this cloud
and the descent became faster. The short guide ropes touched the ice
below as the balloon continued drifting eastward at a height not exceeding
330 feet and at a speed of barely 1,200 yards an hour. Below them
the men saw wide gaping fissures in the ice and a black bird flying
in the distance seemed an omen of ill luck.

When Andrée returned to the roof of the cabin toward two o'clock
in the morning, much ballast had already been thrown out and there was
no way, of course, to increase the amount of gas. The *Eagle* was low
over the ice, inertly and sluggishly following a wind which had reversed
itself. Slowly, never moving more than 90 yards a minute over a period
of four hours, the balloon kept drifting westward, decidedly away from
the intended course. No land was in sight and the sky was hidden behind
a continuous curtain of gray clouds. The air was heavy with a fine mist,
and the monotony of pack ice was broken only by the occasional appearance of a seal or a small bird.

On a stove, suspended below the gondola to avoid an explosion, the
men made coffee and had their breakfast; more observations on the direction and speed of the drift were made and more pigeons released.

At one o'clock on the afternoon of July 12, almost twenty-four hours
after leaving Virgo Harbor, the *Eagle* was drifting westward at an altitude
of not more than 200 feet. (Before the start Andrée had hopefully anticipated that a helpful wind might by then have carried his expedition
past the North Pole and toward Alaska.) Shortly after three o'clock
the balloon dipped and its gondola hit the ice once and then again.

As the men worked fast, throwing out more ballast, they knew how critical the situation was. Sand, heavy knives, ropes were flung overboard, yet, held down by the fog, the *Eagle* did not rise significantly.

Toward five o'clock the large "Polar buoy" was thrown out—empty—as a wordless admission of defeat.. It was obvious that Andrée would not get a chance to drop this buoy over the North Pole as a messenger of victory. By now it was only another piece of ballast. And even for that its value was somewhat dubious, because a short time later the gondola smashed forcefully into the ice several times in rapid succession.

Hours of fog dragged on, and the slow inert drift to the west continued; again and again the cabin of the *Eagle* bumped into the ice and bounced sluggishly back into the air, like a torn rubber ball whimsically thrown against the pavement.

In the evening Andrée wrote in his diary:

> Although we could have thrown out ballast, and although the wind might, perhaps, carry us to Greenland, we determined to be content with standing still.

Then he added almost like an afterthought:

> It is not a little strange to be floating here above the Polar Sea. To be the first that have floated here in a balloon. How soon, I wonder, shall we have successors? Shall we be thought mad or will our example be followed? I cannot deny but that all three of us are dominated by a feeling of pride. We think we can well face death, having done what we have done. Is not the whole, perhaps, the expression of an extremely strong sense of individuality which cannot bear the thought of living and dying like a man in the ranks forgotten by coming genera-tions? Is this ambition? The rattling of the guide lines in the snow and the flapping of the sails are the only sounds heard, except the whining in the basket.

During the night the drift of the *Eagle* came to a halt. Twisting, rising and sinking, the balloon kept on swaying impotently in the fog-laden air, held captive by a guide rope which had become wedged under a heavy block of ice! The aeronauts could but wait helplessly as the wind changed course once more and the *Eagle* remained suspended above the floes.

In the morning the fog lifted slightly and, as if pushing a gray curtain aside, the sun came through, surrounded by patches of blue sky. Warmed by the sun, the hydrogen expanded again, raising the balloon's lifting power and suddenly, with a frightening jolt, the *Eagle* jerked itself free of the ice which had held it captive for thirteen hours. Had the balloon been free during the night, the steady wind from the northwest might well have blown the *Eagle* back to Spitsbergen, Andrée's cradle of destiny. Then Andrée might have had a chance to gather out of failure the courage and determination for another flight to the North Pole. Instead, this opportunity was lost because a rope had remained freakishly wedged under a piece of ice.

After the *Eagle* had jerked itself free, the aeronauts were carried off to the Northeast, but any hope they might have had of resuming high-level flight under the influence of a favorable wind was soon dashed, as again a curtain of clouds closed out the sun and the *Eagle* floated only a few feet above the ice, never moving faster than 1,000 yards an hour.

The men prepared another meal and Strindberg recorded the menu in his notebook, using euphemistic terms such as "Potage Hotch Potch" and "Chateau Briand."

Another set of four pigeons was released, each carrying, attached to a tail feather, a small paraffin-soaked parchment cylinder with instructions written on the outside:

> Open . . . from the side and take out two letters; of these the one in ordinary hand is to be wired to *Aftonbladet,* the one in shorthand is to be sent by the first post to the paper.

Soon the *Eagle* dropped even lower. Again the gondola started hitting hummocks and scraping noisily along the uneven icy surface. The fog grew denser, bringing with it a fine drizzle which clung to the balloon, dragging it down like the inert body of a drowning man. Strindberg became nauseated from the steady bouncing; Andrée slipped and hit his head violently. Desperate to regain altitude, the aeronauts threw out a medicine chest and various instruments and supplies, whose total weight exceeded 550 pounds. Finally the balloon rose and its sails unfurled, spreading out like the wings of a bird, as it slowly gained speed. "Altogether it is quite splendid," Andrée wrote in his diary, and Strindberg put down in his notebook: "Up in the carrying ring it is confoundedly pleasant."

At 10:30 in the evening of July 13, less than two hours after the sails of the *Eagle* had opened, the balloon was dragged down again and another rope broke off. The situation was hopeless; silence reigned among the men aboard the *Eagle*. Andrée's diary entries became fewer as the aeronauts strained their eyes, hoping to catch a sight of land. But there was no land anywhere, and no sign of life. There were only wide, desolate vistas of gray ice, cut by irregular channels which stretched out monotonously in all directions.

Early on the morning of the following day, a sudden gust of wind swept the balloon up high, but without guide ropes and without adequate supplies, there was no longer any possibility of a high-level flight to the North Pole. Now there could only be a struggle for survival. Tacitly admitting final defeat, the men opened both valves of the balloon and let the gas out. As the hissing sound of escaping gas merged with the whistling of the wind, the balloon came down, hit the ice, and the men jumped out. Andrée's polar journey was over.

Andrée's balloon after descent onto the ice. From a film taken by Andrée in 1897 and developed in Stockholm in 1930. © *Swedish Society for Anthropology and Geography.*

It was nineteen minutes past seven o'clock in the morning of July 14, 1897, when a semideflated dark balloon came to lie helplessly on an ice floe some 216 miles from the nearest land. The balloon had stayed in the air for a total of 65 hours, 33 minutes and had floated 498 miles over the Polar Sea before coming to rest at latitude 82° 56′ north and longitude 20° 52′ east, some 288 miles from the mountain-sheltered hangar on Dane Island. On that July morning the three courageous aeronauts, hungry and utterly exhausted, found themselves on a desolate ice floe adrift in the Arctic.

After seven hours of hard work, during which Andrée and his men unloaded their remaining instruments, supplies and equipment from the deflated *Eagle*, they established their first camp on the ice and took stock of their situation. Some 192 miles to the southwest was the northern fringe of Spitsbergen, while at a distance of 210 miles to the southeast lay Franz Josef Land, where Nansen had wintered two years previously. Andrée and his men found themselves in arctic territory never before invaded by man. Between their floe and the nearest stretch of land there was presumably nothing but pack ice.

Under the low temperatures prevailing most of the year, the surface of the Arctic Sea freezes; then the initial sheet of ice, rocked by sea currents from below and beaten by winds from above, breaks up; channels form and freeze over again, trapping sheets and blocks of the first ice generation. New ice covers old; where blocks are pressed together, some ice melts, the water flows off and channels form. The water freezes again, trapping the remaining ice blocks. Under the impact of freezing, pressing and melting, subjected to the force of currents and winds, these ice blocks assume bizarre shapes; their edges may be smooth or undermined, jagged and rugged; their surface may be deceptively even or grotesquely broken.

Always at the mercy of the wild elements, the ice blocks keep moving, colliding, breaking, and grinding against one another. Toppling over into newly formed cracks and canals, they bob up and down, surface, and then are pressed together again. Thus in the course of a year, pack ice may become six feet thick, and older hummocks may grow to the height of a one-story building.

Under the relentless pounding of the ocean, pack ice softens at its base, and pushed on by the never-ending drift, it eventually enters warmer waters, where it breaks up and melts. Before this happens, channels form which cross and interlace and whose waters keep on battering the surviving floes, chewing their edges and dissolving marginal chunks, while a mild sun, caressing with killing warmth, softens and melts the surface.

Some twenty hours after the *Eagle* had come down on the ice and while Andrée and his men were enjoying their first uninterrupted

sleep since leaving Dane Island, Captain Ole Hansen, skipper of the Norwegian sealer *Alken,* was called on deck to look at a strange bird which
was sitting on the mast with its head buried under the wings. Mistaking
it for a ptarmigan, the captain shot it. The bird fell, missed the deck,
hit the water and floated away.

Only much later in the day did it occur to Captain Hansen that the
bird might have been one of Andrée's pigeons. He turned back and
launched two search boats. Strangely enough, the bird was found and
a small parchment cylinder bearing a message was recovered. Written
in a strong hand, the note read:

> From Andrée Polar expedition to *Aftonbladet,* Stockholm, July 13
> 12:30 midday. Lattitude 82° 2', longitude 15° 5' E. Good speed to East
> 10° S. All well on board. This is the third pigeon post. Andrée.[18]

Andrée's party now found itself confronted with two alternatives: To
drift with the ice in a vague hope that the current might carry them
toward solid land, or to start on a strenuous march for a predetermined
destination. All three men were anxious to salvage a modicum of success
out of their failure, and to return to Spitsbergen may have appeared
to them as a final admission of defeat. They decided to set out for
Cape Flora, in the archipelago of Franz Josef Land, a territory of
great scientific interest, where they knew a food depot existed. They
did not know, however, that to get there they would have to battle a
powerful ocean current.

Preparations for the ice journey took a whole week. The sledges were
packed, the canvas boat was tested; Strindberg became official cook and
astronomer for the expedition; Fraenkel was to keep a record of meteorological data, and Andrée was to note in his diary whatever might be
of scientific significance. At about this time Andrée killed his first bear
and food thus was no immediate problem. However, the floe, engulfed in
fog, drifted imperceptibly southward.

They started out on July 22, each of them panting and perspiring,
for they were pulling heavy sledges over grotesquely broken-up ice. Their
food was adequate: They had bear meat, cocoa, biscuits, pemmican, bread,
butter, and condensed milk, but it was difficult to shut out gloomy thoughts
in this lifeless gray desert of ice. When they stopped, worn out from hours
of exhausting physical labor, Strindberg penned a neat stenographic note
to his fiancée Anna Charlier:

> We have just stopped for the day after drudging and pulling the
> sledges for ten hours. . . . First and foremost I must congratulate you,
> for on this day your birthday begins. Oh, how I wish I could tell
> you now that I am in excellent health and that you need not fear
> anything   for   us . . . round   about   there   is   ice,   ice in every
> direction. . . . Hummocks, walls and fissures in the sea alternating with

melted ice, everlastingly the same. Yes, it is strange to think that not even for your next birthday will it be possible for us to be at home. Here one day passes like another. Pull and drudge at the sledges, eat and sleep. The most delightful hour of the day is when one has gone to bed and allows one's thoughts to fly back to better and happier times, but now their immediate goal is where we shall winter.[19]

It was almost as if the men were on a treadmill, walking as they did against a drift which continuously carried their floe to the south, and not southeast as they wished to go. Despite all their efforts they had advanced only a mile or so in two days. They checked their supplies and abandoned everything not absolutely essential in order to reduce the load of each sledge. Andrée's sled alone was lightened by some 180 pounds. This was duly recorded in his diary and supplemented by the concise remark: "Great indulgence in food on making reductions."

Strindberg killed a bear and Fraenkel got another with a fine shot at a distance of about 125 feet, and the men cheerfully drank a bottle of champagne which had been intended for a celebration at the North Pole.

At this time, Andrée wrote in his diary:

> Champagne, biscuits and honey. I swept the tent with the strawcap of the Champagne bottle. . . . Even Fraenkel complained about fatigue. . . . Terrible under foot to begin with but in the evening magnificent ice and magnificent weather.

They stumbled and broke through treacherous ice; they fell into pools of water; Fraenkel became temporarily snowblind. Steadily the drift kept carrying the floe southward, nullifying the men's efforts to reach Franz Josef Land, but their courage and confidence remained unbroken.

On July 31, a week after leaving their first camp, they found themselves yet farther to the west. (". . . this is not encouraging," Andrée wrote, "but we shall continue our course to the east some time more.") Three days later the floe had drifted more than seven miles to the northwest, and on August 4 Andrée made his decision:

> We can surmount neither the current nor the ice and have absolutely no prospect of doing anything by continuing our tramp to east. We are therefore determined to begin our next wandering with the course of the Seven Islands which we hope to reach in 6–7 weeks.

They made fun of an old bear Andrée had shot, whose meat was "as tough as leather," and invented a little joke of their own. When coming to the edge of a new ice channel, one of them would ask: "Is it easy to get across?" And another would answer promptly: "Yes, it is easy with difficulty."

After two weeks of relentless trudging the men were once more facing defeat. But their spirits were unbroken, and their will to fight was intact.

The dreary prospect of continuing the uneven struggle against currents, winds, ice, and fog for more weeks did not faze them.

Abandoning their previous plan, Andrée and his men set out toward the Seven Islands, in the archipelago of Spitsbergen, where Lieutenant Svedenborg had established a food depot. Meticulously, the leader of the expedition kept on making notes, jotting down the thickness of the ice, sketching its stratification, describing the animal life, and marking in short sentences the progress of the march.

However, the ice moved erratically, and wide lanes of open water, requiring long detours, often separated the floes because it was not yet cold enough for new and useful ice bridges to form. A careful survey of their possessions revealed that their food and equipment, distributed on the three sledges, still amounted to more than 900 pounds. When they determined their position again, on August 11, they found that they had been carried twelve miles off course in a southeasterly direction.

They shot more bears; they experimented by making soup out of algae, and pancakes out of bear blood mixed with oatmeal ("quite excellent"); they ate raw bear meat ("tastes like oysters") and raw bear brain. Clearly the men had not lost their ingenuity, determination, and self-confidence. Andrée himself was still the dedicated scientist to whom nothing lacked interest: a sample of clay, a piece of decaying driftwood, the eye of an ivory gull he had shot, a fish ("about 4″ long, dark gray on the back and provided with a couple of small wide transverse stripes across the back").

Another entry from Andrée's diary:

> Fraenkel fell into the water today and has diarrhea, and Strindberg has a pain in his foot, and I have diarrhea, but we covered a good distance today in any case. The evening I have made fishing hooks of pins and have fished with meat and fat.

Toward the end of August a strong wind carried them in a wide sweep to the southeast. But on August 28 they were barely twelve miles south of the spot where they had been six days earlier. As August merged into September, it grew colder. The polar summer was coming to an end; the days were beginning to grow shorter, and freshly fallen snow made it even harder to pull the sledges. On September 3 luck was with them and they reached a wide channel into which they could lower their boat. Andrée noted:

> We succeeded in loading everything on it [the boat], and then rowed for three hours at a pretty good pace toward the Seven Islands (our goal). . . . Only the shriek of the ivory gulls and the splashing of the seals when they dived, and the short orders of the steersmen broke the silence. We knew that we were moving onwards more quickly than usual, and at every turn of the leads we asked ourselves in silence

if we might not possibly journey on in this glorious way to the end.
. . . Our joy came to an end; we entered a bay in the ice, which
immediately afterwards was closed by a floe, so that we could go neither
onwards nor backwards.

Two days later they worked their way across floes for four hours,
and then rowed for eight more along ice-free water. But on September
6 they could advance by only 165 feet; and on the following day,
struggling for five hours, they were able to move but 1,100 yards. When
they checked their position on September 9, they found that, despite
their efforts of three days to go southwest, they had been carried eighteen
miles in the opposite direction.

On this day Andrée made a lengthy entry in his diary:

> Fraenkel's foot is now so bad that he cannot pull his sledge, but
> can only help by pushing. Strindberg and I take it in turns to go
> back and fetch Fraenkel's sledge. This taxes our strength. We could
> not manage more than six hours' march, especially as the country was
> extremely difficult. Just when we stopped, I happened to fall into the
> water, for an icefloe which, to all appearances and on being tested
> with the boat hook, seemed to be solid, and on which I jumped, proved
> to consist of nothing but a hard mass of ice-sludge which went to
> pieces when I landed on it. I flung myself on my back and floated
> thus until the others reached me a couple of oars, with the help of
> which I crawled up again.

And so, early in September, progress became nil, Fraenkel was exhausted from diarrhea and could barely manage to hobble on his bad
foot, Strindberg, too, was having trouble walking, and all three men had
lost much of their strength. The unremitting fight against ice, water, cold,
and wind had sapped their resistance. They decided to stop. A short
entry in Strindberg's notebook says simply: "Stopped on account of bad
weather and snow." In thirty-six days the drift had carried them eighty-one
miles to the southeast, away from the Seven Islands and toward the waters
between Franz Josef Land and the eastern coast of Spitsbergen.

On September 17 Andrée wrote in his diary:

> Our humor is pretty good although joking and smiling are not of ordi-
> nary occurrence. My young comrades hold out better than I had ventured
> to hope.

This day turned out to be an important one for the men on the floe.
The faint outline of land appeared at a distance of some six miles on
the misty horizon. It was the first time since July 11 that they had
seen land. Land, solid and firm, but uninhabited.

Animal life now became more plentiful. Andrée shot several seals,
and the men continued their drift in the relative comfort of a primitive
hut which they had built on their floe out of blocks of ice. Beckoning
in the distance were the forbidding-looking, ice-covered walls of White

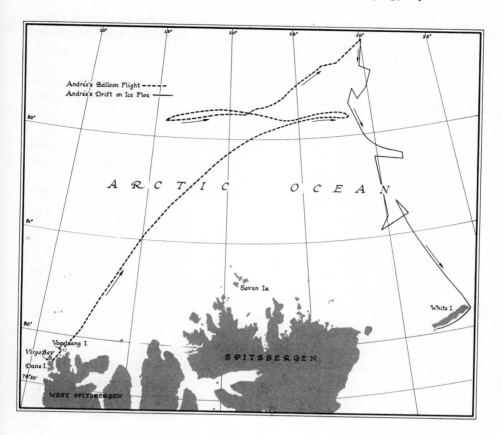

Island. The men remained on their floe for another two weeks, looking for a likely spot where they could land. Then their floe broke with a thundering crash and splintered into small cakes of ice.[20] Somehow, Andrée and his men managed to land on an accessible part of the southwest coast of White Island, but the end of their story was to remain shrouded in mystery for another thirty-three years.[21]

Ill-fated and unsuccessful as it was, the flight of the *Eagle* did foreshadow the coming aerial conquest of polar regions.

2

SCIENTISTS might keep insisting that the North Pole was only an imaginary spot on the globe, and that merely attaining it would not enrich human knowledge, but still there were ambitious men who spent many years of their lives trying to do just that.[22] As the twentieth century came in, two groups of men prepared for a conquest on foot of the North Pole. Robert E. Peary made his first concerted attempt to reach it and failed; Italian Prince Luigi, Duke of the Abbruzzi, tried and was also unsuccessful. Disabled by frostbite, the prince turned command of his exploring party over to young Lieutenant Umberto Cagni. Before Cagni and his men were forced back, they had attained the farthest point north yet reached by men: 86° 34′.[23]

In 1908 Commander Robert E. Peary, a vain, self-centered man of fifty-three, left Etah, a small settlement in northwestern Greenland, on what he felt might well be his last chance to reach the goal he had set for himself.[24] Did Peary really reach the Pole on April 6, 1909? How was he able to sledge at times a daily average of 96 miles over rough ice, when Cagni could do no better than 20, and the great Nansen himself only 37?[25]

It does not matter much whether Peary was ever at the exact geographical Pole or not; he was certainly very close to it and his name must be associated with courage, tenacity of purpose, and perseverance.

Peary's accomplishment brought bitter disappointment to Norway's explorer Roald Amundsen.[26] He had sailed the waters of both the Arctic and the Antarctic, and had been the first to conquer the Northwest Passage in 1903–06. Now he had finally obtained Nansen's *Fram* and was preparing for an assault on the North Pole, when the prize—a spot of desolate white loneliness—was no longer waiting in agelong loneliness. Peary had been there. Amundsen changed his plans, sailed to the Antarctic instead and entered upon an agonizing race to the South Pole.[27] There he succeeded in being first, and on December 14, 1911, raised in triumph the flag of Norway as gallant, heartbroken Robert Falcon Scott became the loser destined never to return alive. Amundsen's conquest of the South Pole was no more significant from the scientific point of view than Peary's like attainment of the North Pole had been. Like Peary, Amundsen wanted a "first." Like Peary, he wanted his name to go down in history as the man who was first to reach a given spot on the globe.

And so, before the twentieth century was a dozen years old, men had finally conquered the ice of both Poles. Yet these conquests were only milestones, though important ones to be sure, on the long road of man's struggle for mastery of the polar regions. Much more work would be needed and different tools would be required before these regions could be fully exploited.

Already in this first decade of the twentieth century these tools were beginning to take shape. In 1900 German Count Ferdinand von Zeppelin, a veteran of America's Civil War, built the world's first airship.[28] It was a gas-filled sausage-shaped bag which carried two gondolas and was powered by two four-cylinder motors. On a memorable day in July the monster stayed in the air for seventeen minutes. Among those who were watching, there were some who believed that the ship had flown under its own power; others just shrugged their shoulders—to them it seemed that another odd-shaped balloon had merely been carried along by the wind. As the control of an awkward sliding weight broke, the ship nosed down, hit a stake in the ground, the envelope tore, and within minutes the balloon had shriveled into formlessness, accompanied by the hissing sound of escaping gas.

A German newspaper, the Frankfurter *Zeitung,* commented:

> Yesterday we experienced a disappointment. The entire countryside was invited to attend a performance to which, as soon became apparent, not even the overture could be played successfully.[29]

But to Count Zeppelin his ship *had* flown. To him those seventeen minutes off the ground spelled the dawn of a new epoch. Overcoming other failures, disappointments, and accidents, he would go on building dirigibles, making them faster and bigger.

In the United States, astronomer Simon Newcomb wrote:

> There are many problems which have fascinated mankind since civilization began, which we have made little or no advance to solving. May not our mechanicians be ultimately forced to admit that aerial flight is one of that great class of problems with which man can never cope and give up all attempts to grapple with it?[30]

Less than two months later, on December 17, 1903, the Wright brothers made several successful test flights in a weird-looking machine of their own design. The first airplane ever to become operational managed to stay in the air as long as fifty-nine seconds and to travel a distance of 852 feet.

The news was duly accorded a seven-column headline in the Norfolk, Virginia, *Virginian Pilot* published the following day. ("Flying machine soars 3 miles in teeth of high wind over sand hills and waves at Kitty Hawk on Carolina coast, no balloon attached to aid it.") And a condensed version of the picturesque, if not overly accurate, account was sent to the larger newspapers over the country, some of which did print it inconspicuously.[31]

The Wright brothers flew again and again, staying in the air as long as thirty-eight minutes, flying as far as twenty-four miles, but for more than four years the world would know nothing of this. Yet these two cousins, the plane and the dirigible, born on different continents, were to inaugurate the coming air age.[32]

The question was no longer whether man could fly. It was, rather, what will man choose to fly in? Plane or dirigible? A period of rapid development now began, as the early planes underwent drastic changes and improvements. All over the world, with the exception of Germany, emphasis was placed on heavier-than-air craft. Farman planes appeared, Bleriots, Fokkers; yet, in Germany, Delag* established an enviable record: During 1,600 Zeppelin flights, covering more than 100,000 miles, there was not one casualty, not one accident.[33] Zeppelin himself was so sure of his dirigibles that in 1910 he went with a commission of German scientists to Spitsbergen to determine whether an airship base could be established there. The commission made a thorough survey, weighing the feasibility of building a hangar and erecting a hydrogen-producing plant. It wound up its work by establishing what was intended to be a permanent weather station, where meteorological conditions would be studied by means of kites and captive balloons equipped with appropriate recording instruments.[34]

In September 1912, short, but wiry and tough, explorer Vilhjalmur Stefansson returned to Seattle from Nome in Alaska. He had completed his second expedition to the Canadian Arctic, in the course of which he had spent four winters among the Eskimos.[35] While the newspapers were still carrying reports on what he had said (or what reporters thought he had said), Stefansson's thoughts were already focused on a new expedition. To be larger in scope than his previous ones, it was conceived as a geographic exploration of the Beaufort Sea, part of the Arctic Ocean, north of the North American continent proper. It was the only major area on the northern fringe of the western hemisphere which had not been explored and where undiscovered land might still exist.

Backed by the Canadian Government, Stefansson set out to organize the new expedition. He bought the steamer *Karluk* to serve as his flagship, and, on recommendation of Admiral Peary, he hired Robert A. ("Captain Bob") Bartlett to become her skipper. Stefansson bought more ships, more instruments, he gathered a staff and asked London's Gaumont Picture Company for a competent photographer to accompany him. The Gaumont Company promptly sent a telegram to employe George H. Wilkins, who had just finished making a film on Trinidad's cocoa industry:

> Would you go important Arctic expedition? Means two or three years absence. Good terms. Excellent opportunity.[36]

George Wilkins was a soft-spoken young man of twenty-four, who had been born in Australia and raised on his father's farm there. As a boy he had watched helplessly as herds of sheep died for lack of water, while the air was laden with clouds of all-penetrating dust. Some 90,000 of his father's sheep died in one summer and their decaying carcasses had spread a nauseating stench of death over the land on which the boy

---

* Abbreviation for *Deutsche Luftschiffahrts Aktien Gesellschaft* (German Air Travel Corporation), the world's first airline, founded by Zeppelin.

had happily hunted rabbits and kangaroos. Tragedies like this, he had thought, would be avoided if weather could be predicted long enough in advance. Then herds could be reduced in size or moved out of a danger zone ahead of a drought period and thus financial ruin would be averted.

A few years later he had started studying engineering. When he was casually called upon to repair a gasoline-powered generator in the tent of a traveling motion-picture show, he had become fascinated with show business, quit his studies, joined a carnival company as a cinema operator and toured Australia. Eventually he became a motion-picture photographer, and the Gaumont Picture Company had offered him a job in England.[37]

Years later, Wilkins would recall:

> It was then that I laid out a plan of action covering forty years. I would travel, study and work in out-of-the-way places particularly the polar regions, for twenty years, and then spend the next twenty years making use of the information gained to build up a comprehensive international weather service from a world point of view.[38]

With such vague long-range plans for forty years' activity already laid out, Wilkins stowed away aboard a ship leaving Adelaide. But instead of going to Sydney, the ship went to Algiers, in Africa. There the young Australian let himself unwittingly be hired by the Italian secret police, at the time tracking down gun smuggling to hostile Arabs threatening Italy's North African colony in Libya. In the best tradition of a movie thriller the unsuspecting youth was quickly exposed, drugged and kidnaped. An Arab girl helped him to escape and join a caravan heading for Algiers. He arrived there a few weeks later, dirty, hot, and nauseated from the monotonous swinging motion of his camel.

British authorities started him off for England. There he took flying lessons, once again not bothering with the formality of a final examination and a diploma. As a passenger, sitting astride the fuselage of a single-seater plane with his camera strapped to the bracing wires, he was the first to take motion pictures from a flying plane. When war broke out in the Balkans, Wilkins was sent there in a dual capacity: As a movie photographer for the Gaumont Company and as a reporter for the *Daily Chronicle*.

Before the war was over, he had learned how to avoid censorship and, suspected of spying, had faced a firing squad on three successive mornings, only to be reprieved each time.

When Wilkins received the telegram from his London home office, old dreams of a trip to the South Pole came up again. Half-buried plans for polar weather stations were reborn and, convinced that he was to join Sir Ernest Shackleton on an antarctic expedition, Wilkins accepted the offer readily.[39] Only later did he realize that he had agreed to go to the Arctic and not to the Antarctic. Only when he arrived in London did he learn that the expedition was not to be led by Shackleton, but by a man called Vilhjalmur Stefansson.

In June 1913 Wilkins arrived in British Columbia, neatly dressed in a topper, striped pants and spats, to become Stefansson's official photographer. Stefansson's sixteen-man expedition was to consist of two sections: A northern party headed by Stefansson himself and a southern group in charge of the second-in-command, zoologist and arctic veteran Rudolph M. Anderson.[40] Stefansson planned to travel light; the parties would live like the Eskimos and subsist mainly on seal and whatever other animals they might shoot.

In July a flotilla of three ships left Nome, Alaska: Stefansson's flagship *Karluk*, commanded by Capt. Bob Bartlett[41]; the *Alaska*, carrying Dr. Anderson's group; and the *Mary Sachs*. While the *Alaska* put in at Teller to have an engine repaired, the other two ships passed through Bering Strait, rounded Point Hope and headed for Herschel Island. The skipper of the *Mary Sachs* kept his ship close to shore; self-confident Bob Bartlett, on the other hand, took his *Karluk* out into the open sea. Some thirty miles from Point Barrow the *Karluk* became icebound. Floes closed in from all sides, the ship became solidly frozen in the ice, some fifteen miles off shore, and drifted helplessly.

Wilkins said later:

> The emotional effect of that immense solitude was overpowering and awe inspiring. There was something terrifying in the way the ice had gripped the *Karluk* and now held it. Our party seemed abandoned in the empty world.[42]

Heading a six-man group which included photographer Wilkins, Stefansson left the *Karluk* on September 20 to go ashore and hunt wild game in order to replenish the dwindling supply of fresh meat aboard the ship. On that same night a howling storm swept the northwestern tip of Alaska and the seas beyond. The storm lasted for two nights and two days, with the screaming of the wind merging with the crunching of ice into a rhapsody of terror. When the storm was over, Stefansson's men found themselves on a broken-off ice floe with the *Karluk* nowhere in sight. They were never to see her again. (Crushed by the ice, the ship went down in the Arctic Ocean, carrying to the bottom almost all Wilkins's photographic equipment.)[43]

By eating the meat of foxes and seals, and sleeping in shelters built out of ice blocks, Stefansson and his men managed to live on their floe for a week, until a lead froze over and they could make their way to the mainland. Slowly and painfully they walked along the coast, hoping to catch a glimpse of their ship. Turning eastward, they headed for Point Barrow and its trading post run by a man named Charley Brower, where they got rest, food and proper clothes. They set out eastward again and after an over-ice march of several hundred miles arrived at Collinson Point by Christmas. Here, they joined up with Anderson's section.

Stefansson had now lost a ship, equipment, and men on whose assistance he had counted, but he nevertheless decided to carry on exploration of the Beaufort Sea by foot. He hired more men along the Alaskan coast, gathered more supplies and bought a small schooner—the *North Star*. Among those who volunteered to go with him, without equipment, was adventure-loving photographer George Wilkins.

Stefansson's party set out for Banks Island, separated from the mainland by ice-covered waters. The group was caught in a blizzard; sleds broke down; fuel was lost; and some dogs became exhausted. Stefansson sent Wilkins back to the base to get more supplies and deliver instructions to Dr. Anderson. These instructions called for the *North Star* to be sent to Banks Island by the end of the summer.

When Wilkins returned from Collinson Point to the site on which he had left Stefansson, he saw only water. There was no trace of Stefansson and his men. Wilkins vainly scanned the horizon in every direction and finally returned to Anderson's camp. Stefansson's party doubtless were marooned on a drifting floe, their food and supplies limited, their fate uncertain.

Stefansson was indeed on a floe some fifty miles off shore. He had sent most of his party back, and with two men, six dogs, and a sled weighted down by about twelve hundred pounds of supplies, he had proceeded on an exploratory ice journey to Banks Island.[44] Soon word spread on the mainland that Stefansson was dead.

Summer came, and Wilkins was ready to take the *North Star* to Banks Island, but Dr. Anderson refused to part with the vessel. He was sure that Stefansson was dead and felt that the *North Star* could be used to better advantage for his own exploratory work in Coronation Gulf. Instead, he gave Wilkins the *Mary Sachs*, a vessel which was larger and equipped with twin screws, but also more vulnerable to damage by ice. However, the crew of the *Mary Sachs* turned rebellious. They, too, believed that Stefansson was dead and therefore did not care to go on a dangerous trip, which they considered useless. With the help of two reliable shipmates, explorer Wilkins, now turned skipper, plied his mutinous crew with liquor and took the *Mary Sachs* out to sea.

In September, some four months after leaving Collinson Point, the *Mary Sachs* finally was limping toward Banks Island. One engine was useless, the shaft of one propeller was broken, and all Wilkins could do was beach the ship.

Stefansson recorded in his diary:

> I got to the top of a hill from which I saw the tips of two masts. I could hardly believe my own eyes—somehow it seemed unnatural to find a ship in Banks Island where it ought to be.[45]

But Stefansson's joy was flawed when he realized that Wilkins had brought the *Mary Sachs* instead of the *North Star*. He noted in his diary:

> It seemed to me that as he [Wilkins] had his orders from the Commanding Officer direct, he should have obeyed them irrespective of countermanding orders from any officer of inferior rank.

3

Soon after his return from the Antarctic, the celebrated Roald Amundsen set out to prepare a new expedition.[46] This time he wanted to cross the polar ocean on a scientific mission. He saw the North Pole as the weather-maker whose air currents determined the temperature of the northern hemisphere, in New York, Seattle, and Paris no less than in Kalamazoo or Nizhne Novgorod. This time Amundsen's goal was to study polar geography and polar meteorology. Nansen had revolutionized arctic exploration by using light sledges and dogs; now Amundsen saw in aircraft a new tool that could be used. He bought a plane and was all set to inaugurate arctic flying. Once again the *Fram* was to go on a history-making voyage. Only this time the ship, again in the charge of Roald Amundsen, would carry a Farman plane, with which the explorer planned to penetrate still deeper into the unknown.[47] Then World War I broke out, Amundsen postponed the expedition and donated his plane to an embryonic Norwegian Air Force.

Unknown to Amundsen, however, arctic flying had already been inaugurated by a Russian, Lieutenant Nagursky,* who had arrived on Novaya Zemlya with his French-built Farman plane aboard the ship *Pechora*. After two preliminary test flights he took off with his mechanic Kuznetsov on August 7, 1914, and flew north along the western coast of Novaya Zemlya.

Nagursky was flying in search of the *Saint Anne*, a vessel aboard which an explorer named Brusilov had left the Russian capital two years earlier in an attempt to navigate the Northeast Passage. The *Saint Anne* had not been heard from since. Nagursky's first flight lasted four hours and twenty minutes and covered a distance of some 420 miles over the pack ice of the Barents Sea. During that same month he made four more search flights before returning to the mainland without having sighted a trace of the *Saint Anne*. Nor did he sight the *Saint Foka,* still another ship lost in the Arctic at that time, which had aboard the poorly equipped expedition of the explorer Georgi Sedov.[48] Nagursky's mission

---

* An adapted version of standards established by the Library of Congress is used for the spelling of all Russian names, except where otherwise noted.

was a failure, but nevertheless he managed to enter the history books as the first man to fly in a plane over arctic territory.

The year of 1914 was just another year of roaming for a man who more than a decade earlier had changed his first name from Linn to Lincoln as a gesture of independence. At the turn of the century, Lincoln Ellsworth had been a twenty-year-old who hated organized acquisition of knowledge; schools to him were prisons. He wanted adventure and uninhibited life in wide-open spaces where he could escape from the domination of an autocratic father in whom he had come to see the symbol of dull comfort and dreary routine existence. He had dropped out of school to go on a survey expedition for the Grand Trunk Pacific Railway in Canada as an axeman, earning forty dollars a month. Wading through swamps and riding across prairies, he was happy that he had found his own individuality. The survey lasted five years. After that it had taken him two weeks to travel from Seattle to Nome in Alaska, where he became an engineer for the Kaugarock Mining Company. At the nearby trading post of Teller, he ate his first caribou steak.[49]

Then, in the wake of Peary's triumph and Amundsen's victory at the South Pole, Lincoln Ellsworth was caught up in the general enthusiasm for polar exploration. Donald MacMillan and George Borup, members of Peary's supporting parties in his last attempt to reach the North Pole, were planning a new expedition to the Arctic. They wanted to set out in search of Crocker Land. Nobody knew whether it really existed, but Peary had reported sighting it, somewhere west of Cape Columbia. Still trying to find himself, thirty-two-year-old Ellsworth wanted to be a part of this expedition and made an appointment to see George Borup. Young Borup, who had been catapulted suddenly into the position of being an authority on the Arctic, thought Ellsworth's proposal over and then accepted him as a participant. But this opportunity was lost when, one day later, Borup was drowned. Later, Ellsworth tried to join Stefansson's expedition, but on that occasion his determination crumbled in the face of stern opposition from his own father.

On the tomb of Captain Robert Falcon Scott, Ellsworth had seen a three-word epitaph: "A gallant gentleman." To him, this embodied all that could be said about a man, and was evidence that even defeat and failure can bring fame and glory. In Ellsworth's mind, a vague wish was growing into fierce determination: He too would become an arctic explorer. He wanted to head an "Ellsworth Arctic Expedition," but once again his determined will clashed with the determined opposition of his father. Without his father's support he could do nothing, as he had no funds of his own and lacked a reputation which would justify others entrusting to him the leadership of an expedition.

In Washington Ellsworth had an interview with Admiral Peary; they talked about the Arctic, about the scope of future explorations, about the use of airplanes. The man who had spent so much of his life trying to reach the top of the world liked Ellsworth. Peary told his daughter, "Keep your eye on that young man. He has not only youth and courage but ability and imagination. He will go far."

But in 1914 the road to the Arctic and to fulfillment of ambition was barred to Ellsworth. The best he could do was to go as a field assistant on the U. S. Biological Survey to study the distribution of animal life in North America. For three years he roamed the country from California to Alaska, studying mountain sheep and hunting caribou, moose and deer.

World War I did not extend to the Arctic, where Vilhjalmur Stefansson was planning an over-ice journey to Patrick Island with soft-spoken Australian George Wilkins. Airminded Wilkins was finding arctic exploration methods outdated. How much faster and more comprehensively could such work be done from the air! Halfheartedly, expedition chief Stefansson agreed; even submarines could be used, he suggested. By traveling under the ice and surfacing at suitable spots, the submarine crews could collect scientific information which now was gathered so slowly and so painfully.

Stefansson needed more supplies and once more Wilkins was sent back, with written orders for Dr. Anderson to release the *North Star*. When Wilkins arrived at Anderson's headquarters, he heard for the first time of the war in Europe. Eventually he took the *North Star* to Stefansson, and the two talked more about the use of planes and submarines in the Arctic. But for Wilkins the current arctic venture was over. His next project was to take part in the war. Released by Stefansson, he soon found himself in London again, wearing the uniform of a lieutenant in the Royal Australian Air Force.

Stefansson remained in the Arctic for three more years. He discovered new land, and his party amassed a wealth of scientific information, but one of the most significant exploits of the Canadian Arctic expedition was the establishment of a drifting ice station.[50] Stefansson himself was ill at the time, and Storker Storkerson, accompanied by four others, established a camp on a floe some seven miles wide and fifteen miles long, on which they allowed themselves to drift for 184 days. During this six-month period, they drifted more than 400 miles in a northwesterly direction from Barter Island, conducting regular scientific observations, incidentally anticipating by approximately twenty years what a party of Russian scientists would do near the North Pole.[51]

As the war in Europe dragged on, and dirigibles were defeated in English skies by the faster and more maneuverable airplanes, the whole world became air-minded. George Wilkins became official photographer for Australia's war historian and covered every major action fought by his countrymen in France. Repeatedly buried by shell bursts, he was wounded nine times, mentioned in dispatches twice, and was awarded the Military Cross with bar for exceptional bravery.

At the same time, in neutral Norway, Amundsen was prospering in wartime shipping business, and a young, totally unknown, handsome naval lieutenant, Hjalmar Riiser-Larsen, was trying to become a pilot.[52] While still on duty aboard a torpedo boat, he made an application for admission to the newly established Flying School in Horten. The new service had some reservations about accepting the ruddy-faced lieutenant—he was too tall and too heavy—but once he reported for training, Norway found no reason for regret. (Among the planes he flew in training was the one donated by Amundsen.)

As the war progressed, indignation over German ruthlessness swept the neutral countries. An angry Roald Amundsen returned to the acting German Minister in Oslo the medals and decorations which had been conferred upon him by the Kaiser. He was not the only one in Norway to be appalled and angry. There was Hjalmar Riiser-Larsen, who by then had become Norway's outstanding test pilot, and also youthful Bernt Balchen, a champion boxer and expert marksman, who was restlessly waiting to be called for military service in Norway's army.

In 1917 a British lieutenant named Rutland was gathering intelligence on the strength of the Norwegian air force. His host was Riiser-Larsen, especially detailed by the Norwegian command for this purpose. "We need fighters," he told Rutland. "It is not enough that you have such planes ready for us should Germany attack Norway. We must have them now, to train our pilots." The Englishman nodded and said nothing, but shortly thereafter Norway received ten Sopwith fighters from England.

The war in Europe also affected the lives of many men in the United States, which so far had remained neutral in action, if not in emotion. For many months a young, and ambitious naval officer named Richard Evelyn Byrd had been stymied in his attempts to become a pilot. His naval career had come to sudden end before it had really begun when he had fallen from the flying rings in the gymnasium of the Naval Academy and broken a leg. As a result of this, he was placed on the retired list. In the fall of 1917, he was finally recalled to active duty and sent to Florida's Pensacola Naval Air Station to learn how to handle a plane.[53]

Automobile mechanic Floyd Bennett sold his share in the People's Garage at Ticonderoga, New York, and enlisted in the Navy just one day before he was due for the draft.[54] He also was assigned to duty at Pensacola. At the same time, a young North Dakotan named Ben C. Eielson was being trained by the Army to become a pilot.[55]

For Ellsworth, a frustrated would-be explorer, the war in Europe was a new opportunity. He resigned from the Biological Survey and tried to join the Lafayette Escadrille. But, at the age of thirty-seven, Ellsworth was fourteen years beyond the limit set for combat pilots. However, the Escadrille's representative in America held out hope that an exception might be made if Ellsworth got to France on his own. Enlisting in a Red Cross Hospital Unit, Ellsworth sailed across the Atlantic and landed in France two days after America had officially entered the war. He left his hospital unit and joined the French Air Service. Too old to become a pilot, he was accepted for training as an "aerial observer" and sent to a camp in Tours, where the French instructors promptly set out to teach him how to fly.

When the field at Tours was taken over by the American Army, the case of Sergeant Ellsworth became an annoying problem. His file showed that he was an aerial observer, yet he was actually sitting at the controls of training planes. Rightly the sergeant belonged in a camp for observers. But there was no such camp in France. This matter could apparently be resolved only one way: Ellsworth had to be transferred to a desk job. Such an assignment was found at aviation headquarters in Paris, where Sergeant Ellsworth had to make out reports, as well as dutifully stand at attention and hang up the cap of his commanding officer, a Philadelphia banker turned Army major.

Invited by the Allies, Roald Amundsen came to tour the war zone in France. At the Hotel Meurice in Paris he received a request for an interview from an American sergeant wearing the airman's insignia of a silver wreath enclosing a single wing attached to a star. Sergeant Ellsworth was ill at ease in the presence of the great man. He talked about his travels, about his experience, advancing them as qualifications for acceptance on a polar expedition. He wanted escape from the boring routine of Army life, he said, and influential people could effect his discharge if only Amundsen would consent to take him along on his forthcoming expedition.

How often had Amundsen heard such requests? How many men were seeking escape or looking for glamour, excitement or adventure? For a moment he remained silent; then, obviously not having even considered the matter seriously, he answered with a short question which carried in itself the finality of a decision. "Isn't it a bit late?" he asked.

Whatever slim hope there might have been was dashed with this short question, and for Sergeant Ellsworth the future seemed to be a drab routine of paperwork. However that might have been, things worked out differently for Ellsworth. He caught influenza, developed pneumonia, and was returned to the United States.

For others the war had not even started. In Norway a restless Bernt Balchen, anxious to become a soldier, was seeking help from his uncle, Major General Olaf Dietrichson.[56]

"I'm glad to hear that you want to be a soldier," the old man said, "and I want you to be a good one." Critically he eyed the blond youth, who in the past had shown traits of unconventional independence and rebellion against authority. "I can help you to enter the Foreign Legion." That was not quite what Balchen wanted, but he was not afraid. Let it be the Foreign Legion, then; anything to get into a real fight! Armed with a letter of introduction, he was on his way to Marseilles a few days later. And soon he, too, was swallowed up in the stifling routine of a rear-echelon training camp.

And at the Pensacola Naval Air Station in Florida, Byrd was getting restless too. He wanted to see excitement and action, but a galvanized nail in his fractured leg kept him from being sent to Europe. He remained in Florida, an unhappy member of a committee investigating plane accidents. He heard that the NC-1, the largest seaplane hitherto planned in the United States, was under construction. In July of 1918 he requested duty aboard the NC-1 on its projected transatlantic flight. Two weeks later Lieutenant Byrd was summoned to Washington . . . to be assigned to an as yet nonexistent air station in Nova Scotia!

War has the face of frustration. Lieutenant Byrd knew it, Sergeant Ellsworth knew it, and legionnaire Balchen was soon to find out. Summoned before his commanding officer, Balchen heard him say: "There is a military threat to Scandinavia; I have to return you to Norway immediately." Balchen, standing at the threshold to adventure, did not quite understand—he had come to fight a war and now he was being sent home again. "I have to," the captain insisted. "If you were a thief or a murderer, I could keep you, but as it is . . . ." Back in Norway, Balchen was sent to an artillery school, but World War I was over before he had graduated. The best he could do was to enlist under an assumed name in a volunteer brigade, fighting for Finland in the civil war which had broken out in Russia. In a cavalry charge, Balchen's mount was killed under him and he himself was left for dead on the battlefield. Somehow he managed to make it back to his own lines.

4

In the wake of war came a period of readjustment and search for "normalcy." But there was no "normalcy" for Ellsworth, recuperating after several attacks of pleurisy; there was no "normalcy" for Byrd, who was back in Washington while orders were being prepared reassigning him to Pensacola, and there was no "normalcy" for lanky twenty-three-year old Ben Eielson. The Army had trained him to be a pilot, but then came the armistice. Eielson found himself a bored clerk in his native

Hatton, North Dakota. The only thing he wanted to do was to fly, but aviation was still in its infancy; the Air Force was being reduced. Its planes were being sold as surplus goods, and there were too many pilots, mass-produced during the war, who found themselves without a mission.

Ben Eielson founded the Hatton Aero Club, which acquired a Curtiss Standard Model J aircraft. He started making exhibition flights until he wrecked the plane, and was once again at the end of a flying career.

Back from the war in Finland, Bernt Balchen, now a lieutenant, was restless. He liked to tinker with farm equipment, watches, motorcycles, guns and automobiles, but what he really wanted was to get his hands on an airplane. Flying would be a real challenge. However, at that time there was no civil aviation in Norway; all military planes belonged to the Navy and Balchen was in the Army. He resigned his commission and with the help of his cousin, Leif Dietrichson, he joined the Navy instead, determined to become a pilot.[57]

Among the men scattered around the world who had linked their future to aviation, Norway's Riiser-Larsen was a flying instructor; Australia's Wilkins was compiling a pictorial history of the war, and America's Byrd was relegated to a desk job. These men—and others—were looking for a new challenge. One such challenge was the aerial conquest of the Atlantic, and it attracted numerous contenders. The United States Navy had three large seaplanes of the NC class, readied too late to make the war. Now they belonged to the new "Transatlantic flight section of the Bureau of Aeronautics," to which Byrd managed to get himself assigned as a navigator.

The planes flew from Rockaway Beach to Trepassey Bay in Newfoundland. While they were there, new orders arrived from Washington: Byrd was not to continue aboard the NC-1. Instead, he was transferred to the small semidirigible C-5, in charge of Lieutenant Commander Emory Coile, which was also scheduled to attempt an Atlantic crossing. But a heavy gust of wind tore the C-5 from her moorings, and, unmanned, she disappeared drifting away into cloud-hidden skies. Gloomily, Byrd stood by as the three NC planes took to the air. (One of them would reach Horta, in the Azores, and then proceed to a triumphal welcome in Lisbon.) Lieutenant Commander Byrd had to return to Washington.

A few weeks later Britain's Major George Scott crossed the Atlantic in both directions with the dirigible R-34. The prestige of the dirigible soared, and the United States Navy ordered a big airship from Britain. Then Captain Alcock and Lieutenant Brown made the first successful nonstop crossing in an airplane. Rivalry for mastery of the sky continued between plane and dirigible. Count Zeppelin had said: "The future of my ships lies in long distance passenger transportation." In fact, Germany's small dirigible *Bodensee* was already maintaining a regular service between Berlin and Friedrichshafen.[58] (Soon pilot Riiser-Larsen would make the trip as an observant passenger, and there would be plans to establish a commercial airship service between England and Scandinavia.)

There were other aerial challenges: the London *Daily Mail* offered a prize of 10,000 British pounds to the crew of the first plane to fly from England to Australia in thirty days or less. To compete for the prize, a Blackburn *Kangaroo* airplane, carrying four men and 270 gallons of gasoline, took off from Hounslow Airport. Its commander and navigator was war hero George Wilkins. Retarded by bad weather and mechanical difficulties, Wilkins's plane hopped across France and Italy. Over the Adriatic, some eighty miles off Crete, an oil pipe broke and the *Kangaroo* made it limpingly to the island. It came down for an emergency landing, dropped into a ditch, bounced out, nosed over, and came to a jolting stop a few feet from the walls of an insane asylum, with its tail pointing toward the sky.[59]

Still other men were finding a challenge in the conquest of unknown arctic regions. To some of them this was only a part of their quest for individual fullfillment, but to others it was an effort geared to national necessity.

Aboard a sturdy wooden vessel, called *Maud* in honor of the Queen of Norway, built to his own specifications and paid for with his wartime profits in the shipping business, Amundsen was headed eastward along the northern coast of Siberia. The route carried him along an ice-clogged seaway which links the Barents Sea with the Bering Strait and which only three ships had ever traversed before.[60] Passing along this waterway, the *Maud* skirted a huge arctic territory of virgin forests and hidden mineral wealth, only sparsely populated by primitive nomadic tribes.

Exploited by wealthy merchants, at the mercy of ruthless tax collectors, cheated and maltreated by irresponsible priests and foreign traders, these natives had never received any help or protection from the czarist regime. The Bolshevik Government had at once realized the potential importance of these vast territories, as well as the significance of a Northern Sea Route linking the European and Asian ports of Russia. In a memorandum dated Jauary 17, 1919, Professor Rudolf Samoilovich, who in prerevolutionary days had been staking out claims in Spitsbergen for a czarist coal-mining enterprise, asked Commissar of Commerce Krassin:

> Has the question of an expedition to the Pechora territory for . . . exploiting its natural resources been settled in principle? If so, can an expedition be organized without delay and when?[61]

Secretary Krassin scribbled his answer on the margin of this letter: "Yes—next week," and asked Samoilovich to telephone him. Less than two weeks later a Commission for the Study of the North was established, with geologist Rudolf Samoilovich as its secretary. Within five days, plans for an expedition to the Pechora territory, in the western part of the Soviet Arctic, were drawn up. The next summer a group of geologists went there and discovered valuable coal deposits.

The Siberian Revolutionary Council established a committee on the Northern Sea Route, called *Komseverput*," whose scope was defined as

> all-around equipment, completion and study of the Northern Sea Route with the objective of turning it into an artery of constant practical communication.[62]

It was an ambitious program. In time new vessels would be acquired, ice breakers diverted, and weather stations established along the route. Improved weather forecasts and ambitious hydrographic studies eventually would make the route navigable. Ten years later, in 1930, forty-six freighters would carry 125,000 tons of raw material from Siberia along northern waterways as compared with 10,000 tons carried by ten freighters in 1920.[63]

Captain George Wilkins* was again thinking about resuming exploratory work. Once more he was thinking about establishing meteorological stations in both the Arctic and the Antarctic. He presented a plan to the Royal Meteorological Society of England, but it was rejected as impractical; he tried to obtain a surplus Zeppelin (in order to make a flight to the North Pole) but failed. However, John Lachlan Cope was organizing an expedition to the Antarctic and he gladly accepted Wilkins as his second-in-command.[64] Physician-biologist Cope had a grandiose plan: He wanted to use twelve planes for an aerial survey of the last unknown continent.

After many delays Cope's Antarctic expedition arrived in Montevideo, Uruguay. When Wilkins joined the expedition there, its scope and plan had been changed. There were to be no aircraft at all, and, in addition to Cope and Wilkins, there were only two other men, both inexperienced. The expedition was so deeply in debt that even its equipment was attached by creditors. A whaler took the group to Graham Land, that long, horn-shaped stretch of land which juts out from the Antarctic continent toward South America. For four months they remained there, succeeding only in mapping thirty miles of coast. Then the group split up and Wilkins went to the United States, obsessed with the idea of buying planes to inaugurate aerial exploration of the South Polar regions.

---

* Wilkins is usually referred to as Sir Hubert, but he was not knighted until 1928.

By this time Sir Ernest Shackleton was also planning another expedition to the Antarctic; he too wanted to use an airplane. While Wilkins was in New York, he received an offer to join Shackleton. He accepted eagerly, but this venture also failed. Shackleton died and the expedition was called off.

5

The British were building dirigible R-36 for the proposed regular commercial air service between England and Scandinavia. News of the project came to Norway in a short article carried by an Oslo newspaper and did not escape the attention of Lieutenant Riiser-Larsen. He was a military man, but first and foremost he was a patriot. Oslo, he felt, must be included in the projected itinerary. A fast, reliable air-mail service would help revitalize the economy of his seafaring country, which just at that time was going through a depression. Riiser-Larsen applied to Britain's Air Ministry for airshipman's training. Only as a qualified dirigible pilot could he establish contact with British policymakers, and thus hope to make Norway a partner in the project. His application was accepted and Riiser-Larsen was given an intensive training course at the Naval Air Station at Howden.[65] Among his teachers was Major George Scott, hero of the first transatlantic crossing by dirigible. When he returned to Norway, Riiser-Larsen was well qualified to pilot planes as well as dirigibles. For him airships were not just tools for destruction, and flying not just an end in itself. He saw clearly that the future lay with commercial aviation and he realized the importance of a regular airline between Norway and other nations.

Roald Amundsen, too, was thinking in terms of commerce and economy. Passing along the coast of Siberia, his *Maud* had mastered the Northeast Passage and had arrived in Nome after a long voyage.[66] The ship twice had to winter in the ice, and now, with her supplies exhausted and her crew thinned out, she had to undergo repairs in Seattle. Amundsen was restless; he needed more money, and his scientist, Professor Sverdrup, wanted an assistant for the work which was to begin once the *Maud* started her drift. The Norwegian Government had voted additional funds for the expedition, and a grateful Amundsen returned to Norway while the *Maud* was being repaired. There a young meteorologist, Finn Malmgren, was suggested to him as an assistant. Amundsen nodded, but his thoughts were wandering. A drift with the *Maud* was no longer the summit of his ambition. More than ever he was thinking of planes. Exploration is the mother of exploitation, and the future of both was linked to aircraft. Wilkins, Nansen, Shackleton, Peary, Stefansson, and Ellsworth all thought so. And Roald Amundsen was convinced of it. Aviation was growing fast. A new Junkers plane had just established a world record by staying in the air for twenty-seven hours! There, all but in his grasp, Amundsen saw a chance to fly from continent to continent. Across the Polar Sea* would be the shortest intercontinental route. In the light of new technical developments this was a logical step for the man who had been first to find and navigate the Northwest Passage linking the Old World with the New. The world is a sphere, yes; but for practical purposes it had remained a cylinder. Fog and ice still rendered the top of the world impassable, and traffic could move only from east to west or from west to east. By bridging the 2,200 odd miles across the Pole, Amundsen planned to turn the cylinder into a sphere.

There were still other men, concerned with the exploration and exploitation of the Arctic. In Russia, on March 10, 1921, Lenin signed a decree ordering a comprehensive study of the Soviet north.[67] Hydrologists were to chart its waters, meteorologists were to study its weather, geologists were to investigate its mineral wealth. The resources of the north were to be exploited for the benefit of the whole country. But before that would be possible, a route had to be found by which men and machinery could be brought to the north and raw materials from the Arctic could be exported. First in the ambitious program was the exploration of Novaya Zemlya, a poorly known archipelago in the western part of the Northeast Passage.

At the head of an expedition charged with surveying and charting the west coast of Novaya Zemlya was Professor Rudolf Samoilovich. He knew the potential wealth of the Soviet north, but he also knew that before it could be exploited, Russia's northern seas must be made navigable. He knew, too, that a northern waterway could be developed only after the seas had been charted, and facilities established to report (and eventually predict) weather and ice conditions.

Not unlike Riiser-Larsen, the "retired" explorer Vilhjalmur Stefansson anticipated the rapid growth of commercial aviation. In a letter to a Canadian Government official he wrote:

> The distance from England to Japan . . . through the Polar Ocean is not much more than a third . . . the distance . . . by way of Montreal and Vancouver. . . . As naval bases for submarines and as way

---

* The terms "Polar Sea," "Polar Basin," and "Arctic Ocean" are used here interchangeably to indicate the body of water, approximately 2,000 miles across, which is bounded by three continents: North America (Canada and Alaska), Asia (U.S.S.R.), and Europe (U.S.S.R. and Norway). The Arctic Ocean communicates with the Atlantic Ocean via Baffin Bay, Davis Strait and the Labrador Sea (all west of Greenland) as well as via the Greenland Sea and Norwegian Sea (east of Greenland). Bering Strait connects the Arctic and Pacific Oceans.

stations for aircraft, we need a chain of islands across the Polar Basin. About the most strategically situated island possible on such a route is Wrangel.[68]

Wrangel island is a small piece of land off the northern coast of Siberia. Near it, Stefansson's flagship *Karluk* had gone down, and three of her survivors had been rescued on the island some time later. This uninhabited land was covered in an official territorial claim made by the defunct Czarist Government.

Stefansson received no satisfactory answer to his letter to the Canadian Government and decided to act on his own by sending four men to occupy the island. With the help of Eskimos, the little party was to set up a colony on Wrangel and support itself by fishing and hunting. Eventually, the island would be claimed for Great Britain on the ground that it had been colonized.

When Stefansson's men arrived aboard their schooner, they received no co-operation from the Siberian natives, and only a lone Eskimo woman, Ada Blackjack, was willing to join the small group of adventurers. The would-be colonizers established themselves on the island and prepared to wait for a relief party sent by Stefansson. (It would be two years before such a relief party arrived.)[69]

While Amundsen, Samoilovich and Wilkins were making their attempts to explore polar regions, other men were still in the grip of frustration. Among these was Ben Eielson.

Reluctantly having enrolled in Georgetown University Law School, Eielson was working as a part-time guard at the House Office Building in Washington, D. C. There he met Alaskan Dan A. Sutherland, who talked wistfully about salmon streams and herds of caribou roaming endless plains, about moose whose antlers spread over eighty inches, about blue glaciers and cool fjords—all to be found in his native Alaska.[70] It was the land of adventure, America's last frontier; a huge territory thinly populated. It was a land so underdeveloped that travel time was not measured in hours but in weeks or even months.

If Eielson was interested, Sutherland said, he could get him a job in Alaska. Indeed, Eielson was very much interested. Abandoning the study of law after only one semester, he started out for Alaska, where he became a high-school teacher in Fairbanks. He was quite willing to become a basketball coach and, incidentally, also to teach English and science.

On August 24, 1922, the dirigible R-38 which had been commissioned in Britain by the United States, broke up in flight and crashed, burning, into the Humber River. In the worst air disaster the world had yet known, forty-four of the men aboard the ship died, including Commodore Mait-land and Lieutenant Emory Coile, one-time skipper of the ill-fated C-5. Two men who had originally been scheduled to participate in this fatal flight were not aboard, and so missed the rendezvous with death. They were Lieutenant Commander Byrd and Captain Wilkins. In the wake of this tragedy, enthusiasm for dirigibles died in England; none would be built there for several years to come, and Riiser-Larsen's carefully made plans for a commercial airline linking England and Norway collapsed.

Roald Amundsen had now returned to the United States. He bought a Junkers plane from the Curtiss Airplane Company in Garden City, and its president gave him a small *Oriole,* suitable for shorter flights, as a gift.[71]

When the *Maud* was repaired and provisioned for seven years, she headed for Bering Strait, commanded by the co-conqueror of the South Pole, Oscar Wisting, who had with him Professor Harold Sverdrup, meteorologist Finn Malmgren, the *Oriole* and Its Pilot Odd Dahl. Out on the lonely Arctic Ocean, the men celebrated their first Christmas around a tree thoughtfully sent by President Harding. They would remain on their ship for more than two years, but the drift would not carry them across the Pole as they had hoped.

Amundsen himself stayed behind, determined to start flying in the Arctic. He was preparing for an extended arctic flight. His plan was to fly across the Arctic Ocean from Point Barrow, Alaska, to the archipelago of Spitsbergen.[72] The fuel which Amundsen's plane could carry was insufficient for this flight of some 2,000 miles. The solution: Establish a secondary aerial expedition in Spitsbergen which would fly gasoline and supplies to an advanced base on the ice. Once Amundsen reached this depot, he would have enough fuel to complete the inter-continental flight.

During the long cold winter in Wainwright, Alaska, Amundsen's pilot-mechanic, Oscar Omdal, worked on the Junkers plane, adjusting it for arctic flying. In Europe, Amundsen's friend, Consul Hammer of Seattle, was preparing the supporting expedition. It was to be a seven-man group, which included Hammer, pilot Neumann, and Lieutenant Mittelholzer of the Swiss Air Force.

When Amundsen's plane was ready, Omdal took off on a first trial flight. He circled, came down for a landing, and hit uneven ice. The plane's left ski broke, crumpling "like a piece of cardboard." Amundsen's hopes and dreams were shattered in the snow of Alaska that day. Studying the wreckage, he realized that repairs were impossible; a new landing gear was needed. But what reason was there to believe that a replacement would hold up any better? The plane would have to be redesigned, he thought, or perhaps he should get a seaplane. But Amundsen had no money to buy a seaplane or any other plane, for that matter.

The Spitsbergen-bound auxiliary expedition was notified of the disaster and Hammer changed the original plan. Now his lone Junkers hydroplane would make a few reconnaissance flights off Spitsbergen.[73] After three such flights, during which the small craft (affectionately called *"Icebird* D 260") stayed in the air for a total of eleven hours and forty-two minutes, engine trouble forced the group to give up and return home.[74]

In those days of gloom and discouragement, Hammer offered help. He was ready, he said, to provide seaplanes. Not one but three of them. How about money? Hammer had the answer all wrapped up in an ingenious promotion scheme: He would have thin postcards printed. Bearing special stamps, to be issued by Norway, these cards could be carried on the first polar flight in history and funds collected from the sale of cards and stamps would certainly be sufficient to buy seaplanes!

Shrewd but trustful, Amundsen listened. He was no businessman; he had trained himself to be an explorer and there had always been others to handle his finances. Yes, he was quite willing to give Hammer his power of attorney. Armed with this document, Hammer, who had no more than $10,000 at his immediate disposal, ordered three Dornier sea-planes, each costing $40,000 while Amundsen set out for Norway to solicit the special stamp and to gather personnel, supplies, and equipment for a three-plane arctic expedition.

It was only logical for Norway's outstanding active explorer to consult Norway's outstanding airman about pilots and mechanics for what promised to become the most difficult aerial undertaking yet attempted.

Riiser-Larsen was attracted by the fascination radiating from a determined and courageous Amundsen. He volunteered to go, and Amundsen was only too glad to have him on the team.

Other would-be explorers, throughout the world, were still floundering. Ellsworth was still battling with pleurisy; Byrd was bogged down organizing training stations for naval reserve fliers; Wilkins was on an expedition to tropical Australia sponsored by the British Museum, and Eielson was hiding his restlessness behind a façade of serenity. Watching the blue sky over the endless Alaskan land, Eielson talked to Bill Thompson about bringing an airplane to Alaska. Bill Thompson was editor of the Fairbanks *Daily News-Miner* and he knew Dick Wood, President of the Fairbanks First National Bank. Soon teacher, editor and banker got together to found the Farthest-North Airplane Company, whose assets included one Curtiss plane (purchase price, including transportation charges, $1,500) and pilot Ben Eielson. Soon he would be billed in the *News-Miner* as "the greatest living flyer" and "an aerial daredevil able to make an airplane eat out of his hands."

Two weeks later, on July 15, 1923, a group of dignitaries, headed by President Harding, arrived in Fairbanks to celebrate completion of the Alaska railway. In three days of stunt flying, the Curtiss plane paid for itself. After 145 flight hours and a total of some 12,000 miles, Eielson stored the plane in a warehouse and went to Washington to put in a bid for the first Alaska air-mail contract.

In September 1923 dirigible fever gripped the United States as a Philadelphia-built airship made her maiden flight. Christened *Shenandoah*—"Daughter of the Stars"—she was a copy of the German LZ-49, captured during the war. The disaster of the R-38 and that of the *Roma* were forgotten.[75] Americans were proud of their own airship, and their enthusiasm was boundless. What would be a feat worthy of the *Shenandoah?* The plan of a polar flight was advanced and eagerly endorsed by explorer Vilhjalmur Stefansson. Byrd was recalled to the Navy Department in Washington to assist in preparing an expedition which would take the "Daughter of the Stars" from Point Barrow, Alaska, across the Arctic Ocean to Spitsbergen. The *Shenandoah* would carry out Amundsen's plan of the previous year. While final plans were being worked out in Washington, the ship would make a transcontinental flight across the United States as a general preliminary test. Mooring masts were erected at strategic spots across the country and advance parties were sent out. Senator Dill proposed that any new territory discovered during the forthcoming arctic expedition be named Coolidgeland, and Pathé News dropped negotiations with Amundsen for pictorial rights to his expedition, preferring a photographic record of the *Shenandoah's* projected flight to the North Pole.[76]

6

The year of 1923 drew to a close. It had brought some progress for Eielson; the promise of a new beginning for Amundsen and Riiser-Larsen, and the vision of an adventure eagerly anticipated to Byrd. Other men had found it a year of gloom and disappointment.

Heading a relief party sent out by Stefansson, Harold Noice had arrived on Wrangel Island, only to find nobody there to be rescued. One of the original four would-be colonizers had died of scurvy and the other three had abandoned Ada Blackjack and vanished. They had left, presumably, in an attempt to cross the hundred-odd miles of ice to the Siberian mainland. (They would never be found.) Once more the north had proven itself to be unfriendly, and Stefansson found himself in precarious remote control of an island which neither the British nor Canadian Government was willing to claim. In fact, re-asserting Russia's sovereignty over Wrangel Island, the Soviet Government sent notes of protest to both the Canadian and British Governments.[77]

Early in 1924 the Fairbanks *News-Miner* ran a triumphant headline: "Mail Service For Kuskokwim Through Air." The U. S. Post Office Department had granted an experimental air contract to Eielson. The contract called for ten biweekly flights from Fairbanks to McGrath—a 600-mile round trip.[78]

Starting out in a ski-equipped DeHavilland plane on February 21, Eielson delivered the first airmail to McGrath about three hours later, and returned to Fairbanks the same day. Progress and speed had come to Alaska on the wings of a plane, aided by the U. S. Post Office Department. The progress was appreciated by editor Bill Thompson, who pointed out that local mail delivery was being speeded up by some twelve to sixty days.

Eielson's eighth flight ended with an accident, and the airmail superintendent in Seattle sent a telegram to Fairbanks:

> Airmail Alaska plane not considered safe for further operation. Return plane to Seattle at once.

Encouraged by what he had seen and anticipating a profitable venture, one Jim Rodenbauch founded the Alaska Aerial Transportation Company and Eielson went again to Washington with a bid for another mail contract. Washington postal officials, however, were somewhat less than enthusiastic about resuming air service in Alaska. When the bid was definitely rejected, the disappointed Eielson became a bond salesman in Minneapolis.

Ellsworth meanwhile had recovered from pleurisy and set out on an expedition to Peru; a few months later, Amundsen, accompanied by pilot Riiser-Larsen arrived in Italy's Marina di Pisa to inspect the planes ordered by Hammer. The planes were ready, their silvery bodies glistening in the warming rays of a friendly sun. But was Mr. Hammer ready? Mr. Hammer was not; it seems he had no money!

Saddled with debts incurred over his signature scrawled on a power of attorney, a humiliated Amundsen, planeless and once more hopeless, sadly set out on the return trip to Norway with Riiser-Larsen. (Between the two of them they did not have enough money to buy a meal on the long way home.) The future looked bleak. The press was merciless: Was it not a fact that once before Amundsen had slipped off in the dark of night to escape creditors? And could the bankruptcy he had just declared be a clever scheme to defraud new creditors? And how about the two Eskimo girls Amundsen had living in his house? Was it not *barely* possible that they were really his illegitimate children?

Dragged through the mire of distorted publicity, Amundsen, yesterday's hero, became a has-been. Once again he returned to the United States to give lectures. He talked about aviation in polar regions and suggested dirigibles as the most suitable tools for exploration; but the lecture halls got emptier, the newspaper notices scantier, and the lonely road he was traveling looked like a dead-end street.

At the same time, in the Soviet Arctic, work on development of a Northern Sea Route was progressing.[79] Slowly, ploughing through the ill-charted waters of the Kara Sea, ships made their way from Archangel to the mouths of the Ob and Yenisei Rivers. Scattered groups of scientists mapped the land, studying terrain, water, ice, and weather. *Komseverput,* the original committee set up by Siberia's Revolutionary Council, was absorbed by the Office of the Commissar for Trade, which was presumably in a better position to co-ordinate the widely scattered, many-faceted activities.

In July 1924, two ships left the docks of Vladivostok on the Pacific—the gunboat *Krasny Oktiabr* and the steamship *Stavropol,* commanded by Captain Milovzorov. Their immediate goals were different; their over-all mission was the same; secure the Arctic. From Wrangel Island, the gunboad evacuated members of Stefansson's second party of would-be colonizers, and the flag of Soviet Russia was raised on the uninhabited land as a symbol of possession. Protected by a detachment of fifty soldiers, the *Stavropol,* sailing westward along a Siberian coast still roamed by counterrevolutionary bands, reached the Kolyma River—the first Soviet vessel to arrive from the Pacific. The ship had taken forty days to make the trip and deliver a minute cargo of some 24 tons, but with this achievement the eastern end of the Northern Sea Route became a commercially usable waterway. From the west, ships were sailing as far as the Yenisei; only the central portion—a barely-explored stretch extending from the Yenisei to the Kolyma—was still closed to navigation.

More ships were needed, more ports, more weather stations, and more research. A young, frail-looking navy pilot named Chukhnovsky suggested the use of an airplane as an aid to faster development of the Northern Sea Route. His idea was adopted, and a year later he made twelve flights, totaling some thirteen hours, in support of a hydrographic detachment working on Novaya Zemlya.

In the United States, President Coolidge was waiting for an undecided Congress to approve the polar flight of the *Shenandoah.* Pending such approval, further preparations were stopped, and Navy Secretary Denby reluctantly recalled the advance party. Once more it seemed as if Lieutenant Commander Byrd's trail to adventure had come to an end. (Less than a year later the proud "Daughter of the Stars" died piecemeal over an agonizing three-hour period. With her death died the dirigible program of the United States.)

Disappointed and thwarted, Byrd once more mused: How about that so-called Crocker Land Peary once reported seeing? Nobody had ever confirmed its existence. And how about that vast uncharted area of a million square miles around the Pole? Was all this to be left for Amundsen to explore? If the Government was afraid to jeopardize a dirigible, how about using a plane? Others were talking about flying in the Arctic; why shouldn't he be sent on such a mission?

Navy men shrugged their shoulders; some considered the plan sound, others thought it visionary. But there was hardly any room for discussion, because a tight Navy budget could not absorb the expenditure for such an undertaking.

Others were, in fact, thinking about an exploratory flight to the Arctic. Fridtjof Nansen, President of Aeroarctica, an international society for aerial arctic studies, received a telegram from Russian pilot Rossinsky:

> . . . my plan of an airplane flight to the North Pole with you as Arctic expert, representative of Science and friend of the Russian people was enthusiastically received by public opinion of the Soviet Republic. Communicate soonest your decision regarding participation in scientific expedition to North Pole. . . .[80]

Nansen's answer was disappointing:

> Regret unable accept kind invitation go North Pole.[81]

Byrd considered asking for public support, but why would such support be forthcoming? Who was Byrd? Undaunted, Byrd kept on talking about an arctic flight, its feasibility, and its potential benefits. He had spoken to Admiral Peary about it and the old man had nodded approvingly. Now Byrd talked to Captain Bob Bartlett, former skipper of Stefansson's *Karluk* and Peary's *Roosevelt*. After years of struggling with icebound schooners, Captain Bartlett was eager to start exploring from the air.

The idea was born, the men were available, and a general plan was soon drawn up: The mountain-locked Bay of Etah in northwestern Greenland would serve as a base.

Etah-based planes would establish advance depots beyond the rim of the Arctic for further flights into unexplored regions. Planes could be obtained from the U. S. Navy, and Captain Bartlett knew where he could get a mother ship for the projected expedition. All they needed was money.

Edsel Ford would promise $15,000; so would John D. Rockefeller, Jr., and Captain Bartlett could scrape up $10,000. Yet, unknown to the main actors, the road to high adventure in the Arctic would once more be barred.

II. QUEST

1925-1926

1

In New York's Waldorf-Astoria, a gloomy Amundsen was taking stock. At the rate he was going, he would be one hundred and ten years old before he could repay his debts, he had decided, but was interrupted in his thoughts as the phone rang.

"Mr. Amundsen?"

"Yes."

"I met you several years ago in France, during the war." It was a cheerful young voice, but Amundsen sounded gruff as he answered with a short, "Yes." (There were many people he had met in France and also there were many process servers who used the telephone.)

"I am an amateur interested in exploration and I might be able to supply some money for another expedition."

It was the voice of Lincoln Ellsworth, the son of a rich father. Everyday thrills had no appeal for him. "He could not stand civilization," his sister has said. Since childhood he had always wanted to be under the open sky, to look for something no one ever found before. He hated everything hinting of ease or luxury. "He wanted to battle for his life, for his food and for warmth."[1]

If he were permitted to share command of an expedition, Ellsworth said, he would provide funds for the purchase of two seaplanes. Amundsen listened. Disappointment and despair were suddenly thrust aside, and the future once again was illuminated by a ray of hope. Acclaim and honors were by-products of success which he could well share with an apprentice. What counted was the deed, the thrill of achievement, conquest and victory. Yes, he was quite willing to have a younger man share leadership of a new expedition.

Within a short time the elder Ellsworth, vacationing in Italy, received a letter in which his son pleaded for funds and the opportunity to "serve with such a man as Captain Roald Amundsen," adding, ". . . it is my wish in life to accomplish solely through my individual efforts something noteworthy for science."[2]

When he returned to the United States, the elder Ellsworth was unyielding and noncommittal. Would he at least see Amundsen, his son asked.[3]

"Bring him, then," the elder Ellsworth said in an irritation-choked voice, "bring him."

On Sunday, November 9, 1924, Amundsen sat facing the self-made millionaire in his palatial New York home at 603 Park Avenue.

"I suppose you have something to tell me, Captain Amundsen." James W. Ellsworth said, in a voice which betrayed impatience.

"What do you want to know?"

"About your experience, what this business is like."

Slowly, haltingly, in a heavily accented English, Amundsen spoke.

"What about the danger?" The old man interrupted.

The chief dangers, Amundsen said, were foreseeable and could be discounted. The unexpected ones were not unlike those encountered in everyday life.

There was a glint in the eyes of the old man as he cut in sharply:

"Suppose I don't help you, what will you do?"

Slowly, not turning his head, Amundsen replied:

"Well, Mr. Ellsworth, I will do what I have always done. I will get along some way."

James W. Ellsworth, wealthy, determined and stubborn, capitulated. What good was a villa in Florence if his son preferred adventure on the rugged ice of the Arctic? Of what use was the luxury of Lensburg castle in Switzerland, if his son wanted to sleep in a wind-swept tent? What good was wealth if it did not back up his authority in breaking down the independent will of his son? Out of defeat he tried to salvage a minor concession: "Lincoln," he said, "if I give this money, will you promise never to touch tobacco again?"[4]

At the price of a promise which he resolved not to keep, the clash ended in a victory for Lincoln Ellsworth.

Shortly afterward, Lieutenant Riiser-Larsen, in Norway, received a telegram from Amundsen:

"Eighty-five thousand dollars deposited to your account. Go ahead."

Riiser-Larsen wasted no time. Considering the German-built, duraluminum Dornier-Wal seaplanes best suited for arctic flying, he ordered two of them in Marina di Pisa.[5]

Once again at the threshold of achievement, Amundsen returned to Norway. He drew up plans, procured personnel, supplies and equipment and chartered the *Hobby* to become base ship of his expedition. Norway's government placed the naval transport vessel *Farm* at his disposal and arranged for an issue of special postage stamps, the proceeds from which were to go toward meeting additional expenses in connection with the new undertaking. The Norwegian Navy granted leave to Lieutenant Riiser-Larsen and two fellow officers he had chosen: Leif Dietrichson and Oscar Omdal.

The year of 1925 approached. In Alaska, Nome was struck by a severe diphtheria epidemic, and it took five and one-half days for a twenty-pound box containing three million units of life-saving serum to arrive. The nearest railhead was only 655 miles away, but an 80-mph blizzard raged, dropping temperatures to fifty degrees below zero and delaying the arrival of the serum. Editor Bill Thompson wrote a blistering editorial in his *Daily News-Miner* in which he said:

> Had a trained arctic flier, such as Ben Eielson, been in Fairbanks, the stricken and isolated people of Nome would have soon had the precious antitoxin serum which would have meant life to many . . .

On a mild day in March 1925, Lincoln Ellsworth took leave of his old father, whom he was never to see again, and boarded the liner *Oscar II* for Europe.

Lieutenants Riiser-Larsen and Dietrichson, on their way from Norway to Marina di Pisa, stopped in Rome and visited amiable Lieutenant Colonel Umberto Nobile, builder of Italy's dirigible N-1—*N* for Nobile. Riiser-Larsen immensely admired the dirigible. Of no further use to the Italian Army, the ship, he heard, was for sale and could be had for $75,000. "Riiser-Larsen speaks little," Ellsworth said later. "But when he does, it is best to listen." The Norwegian giant looked, listened and remained silent.

In Marina di Pisa Riiser-Larsen took possession of the two planes. They were to be called N-24 and N-25, and the *N* in this case would stand for Norway. Thriftily, he arranged to have the planes shipped to Narvik, free of charge, aboard a steamer returning from Trapani with a cargo of salt.

In the United States, Donald B. MacMillan, a former member of Peary's North Pole party who was being backed by the National Geographic Society, was also planning an Arctic expedition to be based on Greenland, and asked the U. S. Navy for the loan of two planes.

Secretary of the Navy Curtis Dwight Wilbur found himself in an embarrassing situation: Byrd wanted two planes and MacMillan wanted two planes, but only three suitable craft were available. Byrd might have priority of request, but how could the Secretary rule against an experienced, proven explorer backed by the National Geographic Society? Clearly a compromise was essential. Both expeditions would be merged, with over-all command going to MacMillan. Byrd, the Secretary ruled, would be in charge of a naval flying unit, consisting of eight men, to "accompany and cooperate with the 1925 polar expedition of Donald B. MacMillan."[6]

Buried in the carefully worded directive Byrd saw his mission spelled out: "To investigate and explore territory lying between the North Pole and Point Barrow and Axel Heiberg Land."

True, he would not be in complete charge of the expedition and there would be no Capt. Bob Bartlett to accompany him, but . . . lying between the North Pole and . . . implied the possibility of a flight to the summit of the earth, in Byrd's mind the greatest of achievements.

In Narvik Amundsen's planes were stored aboard the *Hobby,* and supplies and equipment were loaded on the *Farm.* Riiser-Larsen told Amundsen about Nobile's dirigible. An airship was preferable to a plane, they agreed. A dirigible was more self-contained, and could carry more equipment, and also it could drift with the wind. But to change plans was impossible. Had they only known earlier that a dirigible within their means was available. . . . With initial preparations completed, the airplane expedition could not be postponed.

They would fly as far as they could, sticking to the original plan of a reconnaissance. An intercontinental flight across the Arctic Sea in a dirigible could be the next stage in their quest for mastery of the Polar Regions.

When the *Hobby* lifted anchor at 5 A.M. on April 9, 1925, another insecure first step was taken toward aerial conquest of the North Pole.[7] The ship arrived at its destination of April 16 and Amundsen's men started unloading the crated planes and assembling them at Spitsbergen's icy Kings Bay. Amundsen and Ellsworth were co-leaders, Riiser-Larsen and young Leif Dietrichson were to be the pilots, while Omdal and a German named Feucht were the mechanics.

There was a ground party also, among whom were a German, Schulte-Frolinde, supervising the assembly, a photographer, Berge, busily taking pictures, a newspaperman named Ramm scribbling dispatches, and reserve pilot, Lieutenant Horgen, who was on leave from the Norwegian American Line.

The two planes were assembled and tested—two silvery metal birds, each loaded with skis, guns, canoe, sled, 200 pounds of food—enough to keep each crew of three alive for a month—and 750 gallons of gasoline. Meteorologist Bjerknes studied weather reports and consulted his charts. Any day now, atmospheric conditions would permit a takeoff. Slowly, the monotonous days stretched into long weeks of waiting.

Finally the great day came. May 21 dawned as a brilliant crisp day with only a slight breeze blowing from the fjord. At five o'clock in the afternoon the motors of both planes roared and a thick cloud of fine snow rose in the air, as if swept up by an invisible broom.

In the cockpit of N-25, seemingly emotionless, sat Amundsen, the navigator. Behind him, scanning the ice, was Riiser-Larsen; Feucht was busy in the tank room. There were last-minute farewells with those staying behind—reserve pilot Horgen whose services were not needed, Ramm, Berge . . .

Riiser-Larsen opened the throttle and the plane taxied. It was 5:15 P.M. Thursday, May 21, 1925. Through the roar of the motors, clearly perceptible to the trained ears of Riiser-Larsen, came the sound of cracking ice, breaking under the six-ton weight of his overloaded plane. The engines were gunned, the motors howled as the ship glided over the ice. Under the moving aircraft the ice stopped breaking as the plane gathered speed, bounced, swerved, and was finally airborne.

The N-24, propellers whirling, was hidden from view in a spray of snow as Dietrichson, the pilot, heard a sickening noise. He knew that a row of rivets at the bottom of the plane had sprung. His decision came quickly: he would take off anyway.

For the first time in history the monotonous drone of engines pierced the oppressive silence of the Arctic. Moving at 75 miles an hour above a blanket of fog now and then pierced by holes through which the waters of the Arctic Ocean became visible, the planes flew northward. A cold wind cut the men's skin like a knife.

After two hours the fog ended abruptly and, as Amundsen would say later, beneath them was "the most spectacular sheet of snow and ice ever seen by man from an aerial perspective."[8]

During every hour of flight the men gazed over more than 9,000 square miles of unknown and unexplored territory. Ellsworth thought of Andrée and Wellman,[9] first to attempt the aerial conquest of the Pole; he thought of Peary who had given twenty-three years of his life to reach the earth's summit . . .

Intently, Riiser-Larsen was watching. His powerful hands were on the throttle, his blue eyes on the ice below. Every vibration of the plane must be evaluated, every sound of the motors must be interpreted. Above all, however, he was watching the ice floes below. Were any big enough for a landing? Like a good general, he not only had one plan but an alternative as well. The first plan, of course, was to fly across the Pole and to land somewhere in the New World. But simple arithmetic showed that only under the most favorable conditions would their gasoline supply be sufficient for this. The alternative might have to be chosen: fly as far as possible, land with both planes, transfer men and gasoline to one of them, abandon the empty plane and take off again.

Time passed to the steady roar of the propellers and the whistling of a cold wind. Eight hours stretched into a lifetime as the gasoline supply shrank.

Out on the ice a lake appeared. But setting a plane down on it was too dangerous. The ice might close in, gripping the fragile man-made bird in its vicious clutch. As Riiser-Larsen circled, fate forced the issue. One engine coughed; there was no more time; instinctively, Riiser-Larsen cut both engines. Tilting the plane, he avoided the ice hummocks and brought the craft to rest on the water. Rocked by man-made waves, the surrounding pack ice broke loose and drifted toward the N-25. The ice would soon surround the craft.

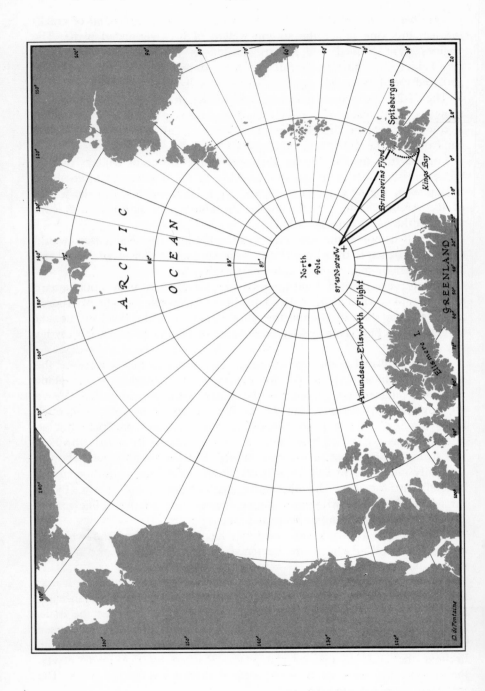

Dietrichson saw the descent. He, too, circled and came in low, looking for a stretch of open water. Taking a chance, he set his plane down on the water, in the midst of cakes of jagged ice.

The men of the N-24 climbed out. On stiffened limbs they hobbled around. Ellsworth laughed, the lips of the others moved—but they heard nothing except the persistent roaring in their ears. They looked around, but their field of vision was cut off by high, irregular walls of ice. Where was Amundsen? Where was the N-25?

It was one o'clock in the morning of May 22 and a red sun hung low over the horizon like a giant orange. Their position was 87°43′ North, 10°20′ West—about 136 nautical miles from the Pole. At the altitude they had been flying they were able to see to within ninety miles of the earth's summit.

One ship, the N-24, was crippled. A propeller was out of commission, there was a leak where the rivets had sprung, and the plane was in danger of sinking. Separated by high hummocks, the two groups of men could not see one another. Ellsworth's men were bailing; using pieces of underwear, they plugged leaks, and then limped about over the ice, occasionally falling into the icy water. Finally, exhausted, they pitched a tent and went to sleep.

A few hours later, Amundsen climbed a tall hummock and saw, about three miles away, the Norwegian flag waving from a bamboo pole over Ellsworth's tent. Using the Morse code, Riiser-Larsen signaled with his arms: "Frozen in twenty meters from the lead . . . working to get free. If your position hopeless, come here. Bring food, axe, drift indicator. Our plane O.K."

Dietrichson answered: "Suppose we can get off. Plane very leaky. Long stay in water impossible . . ."

On May 24 Ellsworth and his men tried to join the crew of the N-25: Amundsen, Riiser-Larsen, and Feucht.

The two groups were not far apart, but in more than two hours of steady trudging through deep snow and over mountainous hummocks, dragging their loaded sled, Ellsworth's party barely reached the halfway mark. They gave up and started back for their disabled plane. The futile round trip had taken seven and one-half hours.

Twice the Ellsworth group tried to reach Amundsen, and twice their attempt failed. Then, shifting ice brought the two camps closer together. The initial distance of three miles shrank to six hundred yards, and, with each man carrying an eighty-pound pack, Ellsworth's party tried once more.

Sagging under their weight, some newly formed ice broke; Omdal and Dietrichson found themselves in the water, desperately trying to cling to the edge of a crumbling ice sheet. Stretched out on his stomach,

Ellsworth pushed a ski up to Dietrichson, grasped his pack with a free hand and hauled him out. Omdal, still in the water, was growing weaker. Through chattering teeth he yelled: "I'm gone! I'm gone!" He could not support himself any longer; his bruised hands slipped off the ice, the heavy pack pulled him down and undercurrents threatened to sweep him away. The combined efforts of the other two saved him. Cold and shivering, he lay on the ice, panting, his face smeared with blood oozing from his ice-battered face.

Shuffling through waist-deep snow, they now resumed their march. Crawling, clinging to hummocks, they finally reached Amundsen's party. It was their fifth day on the ice.

The immediate goal was rescue of the N-25. Precariously perched on a big floe, its nose pointing skyward, its tail under water, the plane looked like a wounded bird.

Amundsen established an orderly camp routine. Food was rationed carefully: A cup of chocolate made with milk powder and melted snow, three biscuits twice a day, and a cup of pemmican soup for dinner—this had to supply energy for a daily fifteen hours of hard work.

The choice lay between two alternatives: Abandon both planes and try a march over 400 miles of ice toward Greenland, or save the N-25, pool the gasoline and hope for the right combination of weather and ice to make a takeoff possible.

Toward evening of the sixth day, the plane was hauled out of the water and rested on a moving floe, continuously showered with large chunks of ice falling from neighboring hummocks.

In Spitsbergen time hung heavily. Correspondent Ramm was disturbed. While scanning the horizon, he also strained his ears for the welcome drone of approaching planes, but a gray speck in the distance turned out to be an iceberg and two moving objects were wild geese, flying southward.

The fliers were overdue. The six men—if still alive—must be in distress. But where? The *Farm*'s radio operator intercepted messages from America which were heavy with anxiety and pessimism.

"The fear that we have all sought to hide," Ramm wrote in his diary "now rises. . . . The first uncomfortable thoughts are thoroughly discussed. . . ."[10]

In the United States, Donald MacMillan was also disturbed. He was afraid that his expedition might have to be abandoned and that he would have to go in search of Amundsen's party instead.

Meanwhile, at 88 degrees north, life went on. The fliers stood watch for five hours at a time. They were cold and some became snowblind but the will to live remained unbroken. With a pocket axe, three wooden shovels, and knives tied to ski poles for tools, they shoveled more snow, cut and leveled still more ice.

On May 26 they took a sounding of the ocean. As Dietrichson, stop-watch in hand, listened, Riiser-Larsen set off an explosive, a detonating cartridge of *trinol*. It took exactly five seconds for the sound of the explosion to reach the bottom of the ocean and to return to the surface. This meant the ocean was 12,500 feet deep at that spot. It also indicated that there was not likely to be land on the European approach to the North Pole. (An eminent geographer, Breitfuss, would later say that this finding alone more than justified the expedition.)

Amundsen's men took stock of their gasoline and food. There was enough fuel to fly them back to Spitsbergen if they could get the plane into the air; on reduced rations they could stay where they were until June 15 and still have enough food for a march south, where they might find some seals or bears to shoot. Beyond that, there was only hope for a painless death—or a miracle.

Amundsen made a command decision: June 15 was to be the final day. Until then, efforts would go on to take to the air, but thereafter every man would have to decide for himself.

When May 31 came, Ellsworth and his two men had salvaged more gasoline and food from the abandoned N-24, but Amundsen's party had found no level stretch of ice suitable for a takeoff. No leads of open water had appeared and the chances for launching the plane were no better than they had been ten days earlier.

An 800-yard runway was needed for the takeoff. Before such a stretch could be cleared, the ice, yielding to pressure from neighboring floes, crumbled, and all the work of the six exhausted men was wiped out. On the tenth day, however, the floe was firmly stuck to eight-inch thick ice located six feet lower down. Laying heavy blocks of ice and covering them with snow, the men set out to build a slip. It took two more days and three nights to finish.

On June 2, with everyone aboard, Riiser-Larsen taxied the plane across the floe, down the slip, and started a run on the lake ice. If the plane could gather enough speed to rise, and if the ice held, deliverance might be at hand.

The ice bent, sagged and broke. The plane promptly stalled. It was five o'clock in the afternoon, and in a narrow channel between masses of floating ice, the N-25 was abandoned.[11]

During the night more ice surrounded the plane and its framework groaned under the increasing pressure. Gripping the wings, five men shook the craft up and down to prevent the plane from freezing in, until moving ice could settle under the floats. Big Riiser-Larsen jumped high in the air to come down on stiffened knees, breaking big hunks of ice into smaller ones which could drift under the plane. Again and again he pounded the chunks of ice until, lifted out of the water on floating ice, the plane was momentarily saved.

Dense fog descended and held the men in its clammy grip. Under the savage pressure of the ice, the body of the N-25 again started to crumple and at the same time the nose of the plane split open.

As one nightless day merged into another, the six haggard, bearded men followed a set pattern for survival in an atmosphere of silence born out of strain and only weakly supported by hope. They became very irritable. Ellsworth resented Feucht's defeatist gloominess, while Amundsen objected to Ellsworth's sighing in his sleep. But the will to survive was still there and hope lingered as Amundsen, recalling an eventful past, said: "When it is darkest, there is always light ahead."

On June 7, Riiser-Larsen and Omdal started out on reconnaissance and they were lucky. When the fog lifted, they saw a large floe, 500 yards long, the biggest they had yet seen. If they could get the plane to it and then smooth the ice, they might be able to take off even before June 15.

On returning to camp they saw the Norwegian flag hoisted atop the N-25. It was Norway Day, and also the thirty-fifth birthday of Riiser-Larsen.

Once more the men started cutting a passage through the fifteen-foot hummocks. Then they taxied the plane to the new floe which was covered with a deep layer of loose snow. A trial run failed as the N-25 dug its nose deep into the snow, which made the engine stall. After that, the men shoveled snow for another whole day. Progress was slow and the fatigue became unbearable.

They finally tried stamping the snow down, and it worked. Under the weight of the six men, the loose snow packed into a hard surface, and, at the end of the first day of steady tamping, a section of 100 yards—one-eighth of the needed length, was firmly packed. For six full days they continued tamping snow while their sweat-covered bodies ached and their weary joints creaked.

The Norwegian Defense Department, meanwhile, announced plans for a relief expedition to be conducted with two seaplanes. On June 8, eighteen days after Amundsen's takeoff from Kings Bay, two small low-winged seaplanes were disassembled and loaded on a tramp steamer in the harbor of Horten in Norway for an irritatingly slow journey to Advent Bay in Spitsbergen. Aboard was Riiser-Larsen's classmate, Flight Lieutenant Lützow-Holm, commanding a task force which included Lieutenants Balchen and Styhr.

Gloom had settled over Spitsbergen. Berge, whose camera stood on the *Farm's* bridge ready to film Amundsen's return, left his post. Ramm, who had slept in his clothes, ready to make a victory broadcast, told the coastal radio station that it was no longer necessary to keep it open. Bjerknes sadly gathered his meteorological instruments, as he and other members of the ground party prepared to return home aboard a vessel which just arrived with several bags of mail addressed simply to "Roald Amundsen, The North Pole."

Reflecting futility and hopelessness, entries in the diary of correspondent Ramm had gotten progressively shorter:

"Saturday, June 13: Weather fine, calm and clear with slightly blurred sky."[12]

"Sunday, June 14: Same as yesterday."

That day Lützow Holm's rescue party arrived in Advent Bay. Amundsen's *Farm,* needed for a scientific expedition, had left Spitsbergen and was replaced by the naval patrol vessel *Heimdal.*

On June 15, Lützow-Holm's planes were readied for their mission, but a paralyzing cold front, bringing snow and high winds, made flying impossible.

On their floe 130 miles from the North Pole, six tired, bearded men had finished building a runway and Riiser-Larsen was pacing its length. He stopped abruptly, before reaching the end—his initial measurement of the floe's diameter has been wrong! Instead of being 400 yards the runway was actually 500 yards long.

"If somebody offered me a million kroner for these extra hundred meters," Amundsen said, "I would not accept."

Low-lying clouds hid the sky over Amundsen's camp, which was also in the grip of subzero weather. Engines of the N-25 were warmed up; all but the most essential supplies were abandoned, and the men piled into the plane. At the controls again was Riiser-Larsen. He opened the throttle and there was the ominous grating of the fuselage against ice, as the plane started to move. With increasing speed came an increase of jolting and bumping while six exhausted men lived through interminable seconds of suspense.

A few yards from the edge of the floe, the pilot gently pulled back on the stick. The bumping stopped and hesitatingly the plane rose, its hull skimming the snow. The N-25 was airborne once more. Deliverance had come with those extra 100 yards of runway!

Back they flew through fog and cloud alternating with patches of blue sky. After six hours of flight they spotted a beautiful sight: The snow-covered, black cliffs of Spitsbergen. But, now, jammed controls made a forced landing necessary, and with their gasoline supply down to a half hour's flying time, Riiser-Larsen pointed his ship into the wind and ditched the N-25 in a rough sea.

They taxied to the coast, where they were spotted by a sealing ship which accidentally sighted them while in chase of a wounded walrus. Aboard the foul-smelling vessel, appropriately called *Siøliv* (*Sealife*), they found warmth and food. Seal steaks smothered in onions and eider-duck omelets tasted better than anything they had ever eaten before, and Riiser-Larsen soon forgot the resolution he had made on the floe to never touch coffee again. Taken in tow, the disabled N-25 was hauled to a safe spot in Brandy Bay.*

Three days later, on June 18, a rescue force, composed of Captain Hagerup's *Heimland* and the two planes carrying Lieutenants Lützow-Holm, Balchen, and Styhr, was in Kings Bay ready to start operations, when Ramm, the correspondent, noticed a man running along the pier, shouting hoarsely, "Amundsen has arrived!" Then he saw people on shore waving their hats and yelling joyfully at the *Siøliv*, which was pulling into the harbor.

And so, twenty-eight days after they had left, Amundsen and his men came back to Kings Bay. Soon Amundsen's group, his repaired plane, and Lützow-Holm's rescue party were aboard a freighter headed for Horten, in Norway. From there the N-25 flew to Oslo. Amundsen and his men were met with all the honors a proud and grateful nation could show at the return of pioneers who had made history: Bells pealed, riverboats whistled, guns from Oslo's forts and assembled warships boomed a salute, and everywhere there was a cheering, waving mass of humanity, as the N-25 landed and taxied up the fjord.

There were receptions, banquets and speeches. Dietrichson and Riiser-Larsen were made Knight Commanders of the Order of St. Olav; the two leaders received honors, and the gold medal for life-saving—the highest award Norway had to offer—was bestowed by the Norwegian parliament on Lincoln Ellsworth.[13] But these tributes only fanned a desire for total victory in Amundsen, Ellsworth, Riiser-Larsen, and Omdal, who saw in the flight of the N-25 merely a prelude to greater achievement.[14]

Soon Amundsen sent a telegram to the Italian engineer, Umberto Nobile, inviting him to a meeting in Oslo. Nobile, handsome in his Army uniform, was the director of Rome's *Stabilimento di Costruzioni Aero-nautiche* (The Institute for Aerial Construction) which Riiser-Larsen had visited earlier in the year. He had a brilliant mind, but above all he loved giving orders. He had escaped from the narrow confines of a poverty-stricken village in the mountains of Naples where he was born, and become an engineer in the Italian Civil Service. When war had come, he had been rejected for military service and thus was free to start designing dirigibles; with peace restored, he found himself firmly entrenched as Director of the *Stabilimento*. During Italy's postwar period of economic

---

* Brandy Bay is now known as Bennevings Fjord.

and political uncertainty, Nobile, a socialist, went with the political tide. When Mussolini's newly established government created *The Genio Aeronautico* (the Corps of Air Force Engineers), Nobile, backed by politically powerful forces, managed to be commissioned a Lieutenant Colonel. This annoyed the regular Army men, who wondered why such a high rank should go to a civilian who had never seen a day's fighting.

Nobile was an acknowledged authority in the field of dirigible construction, although not all the ships he built were happy ones. In collaboration with others he had designed the T-34, which later was called the *Roma*. She was the biggest airship hitherto built and was sold to the United States Army. Although a state-employed engineer, Nobile got a handsome share of the profit from the transaction. On a trial flight over Langley Field a stabilizing fin collapsed, the ship took a dive, hit a high tension wire and exploded, taking to their deaths thirty-three of the men aboard. (In the rescue party on the ground was an obscure mechanic named Floyd Bennett.) Now Nobile had another ship for sale, and when he went to Oslo he had a fairly good idea what Amundsen wanted. He also had his mind made up as to what he himself wanted.

Shrewdly, Nobile offered his N-1 free of charge on condition that the airship should fly under the Italian flag; coldly, Amundsen rejected the offer.[15] His boldest venture, climaxing years of exploratory work for the glory of Norway, was not going to go down in history as an Italian undertaking. When Nobile then asked for $75,000, Amundsen accepted, and it was agreed that the dirigible was to be delivered "in perfect condition," with a rebuilt nose suitable for mooring at masts and generally adapted for requirements of a north polar flight. It was also agreed that the crew would include Nobile himself as the pilot, plus five experienced Italian mechanics.

On September 1 of the same year, Premier Mussolini signed a contract for the sale of an airship of the N class. It was Mussolini's first official act as Ministro dell'Aeronautica (Secretary of Aviation), and the dirigible sold was to be known as the *Norge*.

2

On June 20, 1925, two schooners left Wiscasset, Maine, bound for Greenland. Aboard the *Bowdoin* was the five-man scientific complement of an arctic expedition headed by Commander Donald B. MacMillan; the *Peary* was carrying a naval unit of eight men, in charge of Lieutenant Commander Richard E. Byrd. This group included two pilots, three chief machinist mates, and, as mechanic, Chief Petty Officer Floyd Bennett. It would take the ships forty-two days to complete the 3,000-mile trip.

Off Cape Mokkovik the *Peary* ran aground; a smashed propeller of the *Bowdoin* had to be repaired at the cost of five valuable days; both ships found themselves at times helplessly immobilized in thick ice. Icebergs, looming mountainlike in the gray mist, constantly threatened them. Richard Byrd was finally on the road to adventure—and failure. (A few years later Byrd's ghost writer, Hugh Fitzgreen, would describe the trip in fifteen words: "After an uneventful voyage of 3,000 miles we reached, on August 1st, Etah, North Greenland."[16])

MacMillan's plan called for start of the homebound trip not later than September 1, and his expedition carried food for only three months. Byrd had therefore thirty days for exploration. But sea gulls were flying south already, and the Eskimos expected no more than fifteen more days of summer. As it turned out there would be only six good flying days.

At 5:30 in the morning of August 2, Byrd's men started unloading their planes. Working in cold and snow, sometimes waist-deep in water, they rowed the wings and fuselages ashore, smoothed a rocky beach and built a runway (which later turned out to be useless).[17]

The three Loening planes were assembled, and two days later the NA-1 (*N* for Navy, *A* for Amphibian) was test-flown to Cape Sabine, thirty miles from Etah. But the beach was too small and the ground too rough, so the original plans had to be changed. Since the planes were equipped with both wheels and pontoons, Byrd decided to start his flights on water, and the aircraft were moored to buoys dropped several hundred feet offshore. Full load tests, made on August 5, were unsatisfactory: food, other supplies, and ammunition had been stored in the tail sections and this threw the planes off balance. Storage space was needed up in the nose of the planes and to provide it, the emergency gasoline tanks had to be removed.

On the following day a dense fog descended, smothering ships, planes and men alike in a wet blanket. The motor of NA-1 did not perform well and had to be changed. Tied up alongside the *Peary,* the plane bobbed up and down like a rubber ball, while a 900-lb. engine was jerkily lowered from a creaking boom and installed by mechanics Bennett and Sorensen. Then, in the wake of the fog, came rain lasting a night and a day, followed by a gale which soon turned into a snowstorm.

At 7 o'clock on the evening of August 8 the air was calm over the northwest coast at Etah, and at 9:10 two of Byrd's planes took off for Canon Fjord on Ellsmere Island, barely missing a herd of walrus. If a depot could be established there, it would serve as a take-off place for a 200-mile flight to Cape Thomas Hubbard, where Peary had reported seeing the distant peaks of an unknown land.

Smith Sound was filled with floating ice, only here and there broken by narrow leads. In thirty minutes the planes covered an area which Isaac Israel Hayes had struggled for thirty days to cross some fifty years earlier. Past Cape Sabine, MacMillan, aboard as a passenger, saw the forsaken spot on which he had left a crude memorial to seventeen of

General Greely's men who had died there of starvation and exposure some forty years previously.

But nowhere in the desolate snow-covered loneliness was there a place suitable for landing. They flew on over uncharted mountains enveloped by low-lying clouds.

MacMillan said later, in an article written about the trip:

> I looked down from a height of 5,000 feet upon big hills over which we had laboriously pushed our sledges in 1914–1916. . . . Stripped down to underwaists and reeking with sweat, we had wallowed in snow thigh-deep, yelling at our dead-tired dogs until our throats were raw and our voices gone. At that time I looked up into the deep-blue sky of a beautiful May day and said to myself: "Some day the aviator will laugh at this." The dream has come true, as dreams generally do if one persists in them.[18]

The weather worsened, dark clouds were beginning to obscure the landmarks. Trying to outrace the oncoming storm, the planes turned back and headed for Etah, their first mission a failure.

Still another storm hammered Etah. The whistling of furious winds fused with the mournful creaking of taut cables, as ships and planes pitched and rolled in a stormy sea. Pushed by the gale, an iceberg weighing possibly 500 tons barely missed crushing one of the aircraft.

On August 10, one third of the allotted time had elapsed, and with every passing day hope for success was becoming dimmer. The plan called for establishment of a supply depot on the northwestern tip of Ellsmere Island. Byrd thought of crossing the mountains farther to the south and then flying northward to Axel Heiberg Land. When the storm subsided, a reconnaissance flight was made, but Ellsmere Island was found to be tightly enveloped in fog and thickly blanketed with snow.

On the following day the air was clearer, visibility was better, and all three planes took off. Their destination was Bay Fjord. They flew for two hours, winging over mountain peaks hidden in gray clouds, over glaciers, fjords, and wide headlands cut by black ravines. Eureka Sound, on the western coast of Ellsmere Island, was shut off by fog hanging like a heavy curtain. The NA-3 turned back and the NA-2 was hidden in low clouds. With Bennett piloting the NA-1, Byrd reached Bay Fjord. But there was no chance for a landing and the plane returned to Etah after a flight of some six hours.

Fighting against time, Byrd was anxious to try anew. Checked and refueled, all three planes were again in the air three hours later. How about Beistad Fjord? Maybe a depot could be established there.

Beset by engine trouble, the NA-2 turned back; the other two planes arrived at their destination. But once more Byrd saw that no landing was possible. Both aircraft turned and headed back toward their base. The western end of Hayes Sound was icefree, but a high wind made a landing dangerous. Tired and wet, the fliers returned to Etah.

August 13 was not a Friday but it brought mishaps and near-disaster to the inexperienced party. Under the pounding of the rough sea, the NA-2 sprang a leak and filled with water. Nose-heavy and with its tail in the air, the plane appeared ready for a fatal dive to the bottom of Etah Bay. Hurriedly, the cargo was thrown out, pumps were started, and the plane was saved. Hoisted aboard the *Peary,* the crippled NA-2, its water-drenched motor irreparably damaged, would do no more flying in the Arctic.

Then thick black smoke was seen rolling over the forward deck of the *Peary,* which was loaded to the gunwales with gasoline. Somebody succeeded in throwing overboard some oil-soaked rags which had caught fire, before there was an explosion. Just then an ice floe was seen bearing down on the NA-3. Crawling onto the plane's wing, machinist's mate Rocheville firmly planted his legs against the ice. Straining and pushing, he warded off a collision, and the small berg, crunching and scraping along the hull of the *Peary,* was carried out to sea by the wind.

The following day Byrd, tired but stubbornly determined, was flying again. The NA-1, with pilot Bennett and navigator Byrd and followed by the NA-3, flew toward Flagler Fjord, one hundred and seven miles from Etah. There they found open water, and the planes came down some fifty feet from shore. Through icy waters the men waded ashore, carrying two hundred pounds of food, oil, rifles, ammunition, and one hundred gallons of gasoline. The first subdepot was established, even though it was small and only some one hundred miles from the main base. An ugly ice-floe was now seen drifting straight toward the NA-1. To avoid destruction, the planes quickly took off and were Etah-bound again. With their cargo of oil and gasoline replenished, they returned some fifteen hours later, only to find the fjord packed with jagged blocks of ice which made another landing impossible and rendered all their previous effort futile.

Wherever he had looked, Byrd had found defeat and failure. Once more he tried to push toward Canon Fjord; once again the fog proved impenetrable and the planes were beached in Sawyer Fjord, where they remained stranded for six hours before they could start the return flight to Etah. Flying at an altitude of five thousand feet, Bennett maneuvered his NA-1 over rugged unexplored Grinnell Land. Fighting fog, winds, and fatigue, Byrd's planes returned after an absence of nine hours which had been anxiety-filled for Donald MacMillan.

Commander MacMillan knew the difference between stubborn determination and determined stubbornness. In the face of such adverse conditions, courage, ambition and perseverence were proving nothing but senseless daring, the price for which could well be death. And death, MacMillan knew, was too high a price to pay for vanity.

That night, carried on a film of gasoline spreading from the *Peary,* fire caught the NA-3, which was tied to the ship's stern. Before the plane was cut loose and saved, its wings were burned and the motor ruined. Only the NA-1 was still airworthy, and Commander MacMillan would not permit the lone NA-1 to take off. Even if the edge of the Arctic Ocean was reached, he argued, nothing could be accomplished by a single plane in the short time remaining.

In a telegram to Washington he said:

> I am convinced that far Northern Arctic work is extremely hazardous in heavier-than-air planes. . . . The lighter-than-air machines can do the work. . . . If the officials of the Navy could see the conditions from the air, I am sure that orders would have been issued to stop all work at once.[19]

The long-suffering MacMillan, recognizing inexperience, amateurishness and senseless persistence, had rendered his judgment. Secretary of the Navy Wilbur answered promptly with an order addressed to Lieutenant Commander Byrd:

> Withdraw with MacMillan and make such flights in secondary exploration, as expedition returns South, as you deem practical.[20]

The arctic venture of Richard E. Byrd was at an end. Its mission, even as spelled out in the restrained directive of the Navy, had not been accomplished; two high-priced amphibian aircraft were ruined; the planes had flown only a total of 500 miles; they had sighted no new land and had not even come near taking off for the North Pole. For all practical purposes Byrd's expedition was a failure.

As Byrd set out for home, he could only say that he had tried—and tried hard. But in Floyd Bennett, Byrd had found a pilot who would make it possible for him to turn initial defeat into final victory. Within himself, Lieutenant Commander Byrd felt that he had acquired the experience which justified a more ambitious undertaking.

3

At the time of Byrd's Greenland venture, George Wilkins was back in London after a two-year-long expedition to northern Australia, and was as anxious as ever to resume arctic exploration. He had been to the Canadian Arctic with Stefansson; he had gone on two abortive antarctic expeditions, and now he was ready to start on his own.[21] Wilkins had faith in aviation and was sure that it had its place in exploration.

Aviation had advanced rapidly since the day, some fifteen years back, when he had first learned how to handle an aircraft.[22] Now planes were available which functioned well even under worse conditions than those prevailing in the arctic spring.

Wilkins went to the United States, and the North American Newspaper Alliance added $25,000 to his own capital of $15,000, part of the fee he had received from the British Museum for the expedition to Australia. The American Geographic Society endorsed his plan, which envisioned a small expedition consisting of three men and one plane. The goal of such an expedition would be the discovery of new land in the Arctic on which weather stations could be established. Such meteorological posts, Wilkins thought, would greatly facilitate arctic flying and would eventually make intercontinental transarctic flights possible.[23]

Wilkins wanted an aircraft with a flying radius of about 1,200 miles, suitable for exploration of the unknown regions north of Alaska's Point Barrow. A group of important Detroit citizens, including Edsel Ford, William Mayo, and Edwin Denby, was willing to make a substantial financial contribution and a Wilkins-led arctic expedition became a definite possibility. The *New York Times* even reported that an Army lieutenant, James Doolittle, might join it as a pilot.

However, the Detroit group approached the project in a strictly businesslike manner and was not inclined to accept Wilkins's plan of a small organization. A Board of Control was appointed, to be in charge of plans and management. A special committee of aviation engineers was chosen to select equipment, and to handle the affairs of what was now being called the Detroit Arctic Expedition. There was a manager, an assistant manager, a finance committee, a treasurer, and a secretary. It was a cumbersome organization which threatened to stifle individual initiative. And then there were differences in principle. The Board of Control was primarily interested in a flight from Alaska to Spitsbergen, whereas Wilkins wanted to explore unknown arctic areas. On December 22, newspapers throughout the United States carried the story of a projected transpolar flight of Captain George H. Wilkins.

At the same time, basic plans for Amundsen's expedition aboard the *Norge* were completed, as the airship was being rebuilt. Designed along criteria adopted for German Zeppelins, the 653,000-cubic-foot dirigible, known as the N-1, had a luxurious passenger cabin which had to be stripped. Additional gasoline tanks must be installed, the nose rebuilt, and numerous other details attended to.

Nobile's satisfaction was flawed. His government had signed an amended contract with Amundsen, from which the clause appointing Nobile skipper of the airship had been deleted.[24] As an engineer, Nobile had a solid reputation, but his prowess as a pilot was the subject of heated debates in aeronautic circles. With only a license to test-fly dirigibles, engineer Nobile was lacking a fundamental prerequisite; other pilots were available who were much more experienced. However, maneuvering cleverly and insistently, Nobile succeeded in being appointed skipper of the *Norge*. The King of Italy signed a temporary license, authorizing Lieutenant Colonel Nobile to pilot the dirigible for the duration of the transpolar flight.

Conscious of a historic mission and projected into the limelight of publicity, Nobile, unaccustomed to military regulations, was overbearing and fanned intraservice jealousy. On military Ciampino Airfield, where his dirigibles were being tested, he established a state within a state. Only his men were permitted to enter a certain part of the dirigible hangar. The Airfield's commanding officer, Lieutenant Colonel Giuseppe Valle, resented this order. Colonel Valle, a regular Army man, an airship-man and a much decorated veteran of two wars, was fed up with the highhanded attitude of a conceited civilian dressed in an Army uniform. He reported to his commanding officer, General Prandoni, that Nobile's attitude was inconsistent with proper discipline, and no amicable co-opera-tion could be maintained if his men were considered outsiders, to be treated like servants. Valle also was not too certain of Nobile's political reliability. Prandoni ordered Valle to submit his complaints in the form of a memorandum, and the matter became subject of an official inquiry.[25]

Lincoln Ellsworth, who had contributed $100,000 to Amundsen's new expedition, was in New York winding up his father's estate. But more funds were needed and Amundsen took off for a lecture tour in the United States. The Aero Club of Norway was empowered to negotiate further details with Nobile during the absence of both expedition leaders. The club was headed by Dr. Rolf Thommessen, owner-editor of Norway's largest daily, the rightist *Tidens Tegn*.

Amundsen started his American tour with an inaugural address in Washington which was attended by Ellsworth. Chairman of the meeting was Lieutenant Commander Byrd. After the lecture these three got to-gether, and Byrd announced a vague plan of his own to head an aerial expedition in search of the legendary Crocker Land in the following spring.

"Would you object to my using Kings Bay as a preliminary base from which to fly to the north coast of Greenland?" he asked.

"We will welcome you with open arms," Amundsen said.

Byrd wanted to use a three-motored plane designed by Anthony Fokker. He asked and received financial support in the form of a $20,000 contri-bution from Edsel Ford, himself a plane builder. John D. Rockefeller, Jr., gave a like amount. Now, Byrd had sufficient funds to prepare a new expedition. Next, he obtained a six months' leave of absence from the Navy for himself and Floyd Bennett.

Thus, by January 1926, three men had their sights set on aerial exploration of the Arctic: Amundsen, who had a ship and a pilot; Byrd, who had a pilot, and Wilkins, who had neither a plane nor a pilot.

Stefansson had a suggestion for Wilkins: How about that man Eielson, who had once run a short-lived air-mail service in Alaska? Wilkins was agreeable and Eielson eagerly accepted the invitation to come to New York for an interview. Eielson was a man of few words and Wilkins liked him. Now that he had a pilot, Wilkins figured he would need only a reliable plane, one good mechanic, and a minimum of financial assistance to carry out his plan.

But lengthy discussions went on in Detroit. The flying season in the Arctic is short and, disgusted with the long delays, Wilkins was about ready to proceed independently. Airplane designer Anthony Fokker, who had attended a meeting of the Board of Control, met Wilkins.

"We are building a new large-wing monoplane in Holland," he said. "With that machine I believe you can do all you want to do in the Arctic. . . . We will bring the plane at once from Holland, and," he added in his sputtering heavily Dutch-accented English, "if those Detroit people won't stand behind you, I will provide the machine." Shrewd Anthony Fokker well knew the value of publicity.[26]

Wilkins accepted and while the committee of Detroit engineers kept on debating, a dismantled Fokker was stored aboard a vessel leaving Holland for New York.

The Detroit Committee wanted Wilkins to have an American-built plane but no suitable aircraft could be found and discussions went on endlessly. The plane Anthony Fokker was so anxious to supply arrived in New York and on that very day the purchase of two such aircraft was approved in Detroit.

The Finance Committee had pledged to raise upward of $80,000. Appeals for public support were made, and more than 80,000 individual donations were received. But among the donors were many schoolchildren whose contributions were limited to five cents and thus the total collected fell short of the sum needed. Some of Wilkins's most enthusiastic supporters made up the difference.

April and May are the best flying months in the Arctic. If the Detroit Arctic Expedition was to get under way, supplies and equipment had to be in Point Barrow by March. By the end of January, two Fokker planes were transported by rail from New York to Seattle, and a few days later the Detroit *News* carried an article by Vilhjalmur Stefansson, predicting success for Wilkins's venture.

Two pilots were under contract: Major Thomas C. Lanphier, commander of the U. S. First Pursuit Squadron stationed at Selfridge Field, and Ben Eielson.[27] Should new land be discovered, the Detroit newspaper reported, the major was empowered to claim it for and in the name of the United States.

Eielson, without fanfare, left for Fairbanks two weeks before the rest of the expedition to form an advance party, while Wilkins, shy and retiring, had to endure the ordeal of a final fund-raising drive complete with luncheons, dinners, and banquets. Only after a final public speech, by the Mayor of Detroit at City Hall, was Wilkins's party, which by then included two newspapermen, escorted noisily to the railroad station by a brass band.

The Australian Wilkins was finding the American way of doing things somewhat odd, but he bowed to the dictate of publicity men. Dutifully he attended more banquets, dinners and luncheons. He made speeches and stood by while "high-pressure salesmen" unloaded his autographed picture for anything from fifty cents to one hundred dollars in towns along the way from Detroit to Seattle.

After a boat trip to Seward, Alaska, Wilkins's men and planes set out on a two-day train ride for Fairbanks, where both a hangar and an airfield were available. There the craft were unloaded in weather 52 degrees below zero. It then took two days before all the equipment was safely inside the hangar and assembly of the planes could begin.

When the work was completed, journalist Palmer Hutchinson, looking for newsworthy copy, arranged an official christening for the planes of the Detroit Arctic Expedition.

In the presence of three clergymen and most of Fairbanks's inhabitants, the mayor's wife and a little girl drew flags from the nose of each craft and satisfied eleven special photographers by smashing two bottles of gasoline against the propellers. When speeches and prayers were over, the three-engined plane became known as the *Detroiter* and the mono-plane as the *Alaskan*.

With the field cleared and people continuing their celebration in town, Palmer Hutchinson was secretly summoned to witness the first trial flight of the *Detroiter*.

Major Lanphier was at the controls. The propellers whirled and the plane moved, but after a few yards its wheels stopped in a bank of soft snow. The field was inadequate and snow had to be pressed down to provide a firm surface. When a makeshift runway was ready, Lanphier opened the throttles but, as the plane was beginning to move, there was a heavy thud. A propeller had struck Hutchinson, who was standing too close to the aircraft, and the only newsworthy story from Fairbanks on March 12, 1926, was his obituary.

A better runway was needed. Using tractors, shovels and snowplows, Wilkins, Eielson and some nameless Eskimos set out to clear a stretch twenty feet wide and two thousand feet long. A week later the job was done, and the next step was to test-fly the single-engined *Alaskan*. The plane taxied down the runway, turned, gathered speed and was airborne. Pilot Eielson and navigator Wilkins enjoyed the soft rhythmic purring of the motor. Satisfied, and with the engine well tested, they prepared to land after a flight of forty minutes. Flying over the field at an altitude of some two hundred feet, Eielson throttled down. The engine promptly coughed, and fifty feet from the end of the runway the *Alaskan* crashed. Thrown clear, both men fell through space, broke through a fence, rolled over for twenty yards and buried themselves in deep snow.

Eielson's crash had been caused by an erroneous maneuver. The men were not injured, but the *Alaskan's* undercarriage was smashed, the propeller bent and twisted and, all in all, it would take a long time to make repairs.

One day later, on March 19, the *Detroiter* was tested. As it gathered speed, there was an awkward pull to the left which carried the plane toward a high snowbank lining the runway. A crash seemed unavoidable. Lanphier opened the throttle, brought up the tail and at the last second the plane rose, clearing the snow by a few inches. The plane's performance was not satisfactory, as one engine kept on vibrating suspiciously. The pilot circled and returned for a landing. Exactly over the spot where the *Alaskan* had stalled, Major Lanphier cut the side engines. The third motor choked and the *Detroiter* crashed from an altitude of almost one hundred feet. The plane quivered, its tail shot up, while the engine frame crumbled on impact. Both men escaped injuries, but the landing gear and central engine mount of the *Detroiter* were beyond repair and it would take weeks to get spare parts.

Wilkins was thus without a serviceable plane. In the wreckage of his two machines he could see the end of his ambitious undertaking. He had planned to use both planes for establishing a gasoline depot at Point Barrow. When sufficient fuel was at the new base, the *Detroiter* was to have made reconnaissance flights east and west of Point Barrow, while the *Alaskan* continued building up supplies until enough fuel was on hand to try for a dash to Spitsbergen. As things stood, the flying season might well be over by the time repairs were completed. With both planes disabled, the original plan had to be abandoned, and the best that could be expected was to have one plane, the smaller of the two, available in a couple of weeks to ferry gasoline from Fairbanks to Point Barrow.

4

There were many details to be worked out in connection with the projected transpolar flight of the *Norge*. It was not practical to transport a dismantled dirigible to Spitsbergen and reassemble it there; it was much simpler and easier to fly the ship to Kings Bay, Nobile argued. His plan was accepted and a flight route was selected and facilities available for intermediate landings on the way from Italy to Spitsbergen were investigated. There were many other details which required attention and which the Aero Club of Norway was empowered to handle while Amundsen and Ellsworth were away.

One of the details was the pilot's fee. In the presence of Riiser-Larsen a contract was signed, granting Nobile the 40,000 kroner he had demanded.* On the way from the Aero Club's office to Oslo's Grand Hotel a pensive Nobile stopped and scratched his head. "I should have asked for more," he said, as an amazed Riiser-Larsen remained embarrassedly silent. The following day Nobile was back at the Aero Club to cancel his signature on the contract and to demand an additional 15,000 kroner as well as a free life insurance policy. Riiser-Larsen, whose hopes of seeing dirigibles sailing the skies of Oslo on a regular schedule had been shattered after the crash of the R-38, recommended acceptance of the demands on condition that the *Norge* fly via Oslo.[28]

Other requests were forthcoming from Nobile. He wanted permission to write an account of the "technical part" of the expedition and when the final agreement was signed, it included—unknown to Amundsen and Ellsworth—permission to write about "technical and aeronautical" aspects of the flight. The word "aeronautical," Nobile knew well, could easily be stretched to include every phase of the expedition. Amundsen and Ellsworth had a contract granting the New York *Times* exclusive rights to stories concerning the first transpolar crossing of the Arctic Ocean, but the Aero Club's president Rolf Thommessen had thus given Nobile written permission to write and to lecture independently.[29]

Back in Italy, the popular Nobile, enjoying the benevolent support of a friendly Duce, was accorded good publicity. The inquiry precipitated by Lieutenant Colonel Valle was conducted by Nobile's friend Guidoni, Major General in Italy's *Genio Aeronautico*. The general did not find the accusations substantiated, and at a humiliating ceremony in the presence of fellow-officers Valle was sentenced to a month's detention in a fortress, while the expression of official regret went to Nobile.[30]

In the meantime, work preliminary to the *Norge* flight was going on in many places. A hangar was needed in Spitsbergen. Designed by Nobile's engineer Trojani, it was erected by a Norwegian crew under the command of a Lieutenant Höver, especially chosen for this assignment by Riiser-Larsen. In freezing weather and deep snow almost 22,000 cubic feet of timber brought from Norway was put together, making a wooden skeleton which looked like an open oyster. To enclose this, some 12,000 square yards of canvas were needed—enough to cover a field of two

---

* A sum close to $10,000 at the 1926 rate of exchange.

and one-half acres. Mooring masts were erected in Vadso and Oslo, and the hangar at Gatchina Airfield, near Leningrad, was reconditioned by the Soviet Government at no cost to the expedition.

The *Norge* itself was being adapted to its new mission. Every bit of space had to be utilized, every pound of weight had to be calculated. Gone from the main cabin were the comfortable chairs and the large chandelier, as the ship neared completion.[31]

Fighting time and men, Nobile actually accomplished a great deal. Vague mutterings of the soldier-poet D'Annunzio, suggesting that he, D'Annunzio, be sent on an arctic flight in a dirigible piloted by Lieutenant Colonel Valle, had died down and his wish to be dropped at the North Pole to become "part of the earth's axis" had remained what it always had been: the dream of a mystic.[32]

Work on the *Norge* went forward, even though the dirigible was deemed inadequate by many and Italian General Crocco had proposed construction of another, bigger airship. The N-1 was being ridiculed in some quarters, and in the midst of a public controversy the New York *Times* correspondent had withdrawn his request to participate in the flight. Selected among volunteers from the *Stabilimento,* the Italian contingent of the crew was ready. Norwegian members of the expedition were to arrive shortly, and the first trial flights were scheduled for the end of February.

Nobile had built other ships before, but none of them, he felt, had the grace and majesty of the *Norge,** which in his mind would always remain the dirigible of the N-class, *N* standing for the first letter of his own name. Ships of his had been bought by the United States and Spain, but each time a dirigible was sold, the pride he felt contained sadness, the sadness of a father seeing a child take off for a distant country and an unknown destiny.

But this time there was no sadness. The great Amundsen himself had not only chosen Nobile's ship but also had accepted him as the pilot. Nobile already saw himself as the real hero of a historic undertaking. He was going to fly to the North Pole. Where Andrée had failed, he would succeed; where Wellman had blundered, he would not. After a successful polar flight there would be no limit to his further opportunities.

True, he would have to share the honors, because Amundsen, too, would be there, but the great man's functions would be merely those of an observer. Ellsworth would be there, but only as a passenger; Riiser-Larsen would be there, but only as second-in-command. To Nobile the expedition was but a feat of aviation, and who, after all, deserved the credit? The pilot, of course. And how much more credit does a pilot deserve if he happens to be the builder of the ship as well?

The first trial flights of the reconditioned N-1 were satisfactory. Supplies

* *Norge* means Norway.

had already been sent to Spitsbergen, Italy's king was to inspect the dirigible on March 26, and the Duce himself wanted to see it off. But not content with being both builder and skipper of his dirigible, Nobile wanted to be a co-leader of the expedition. He wanted all the participants to take an oath of personal allegiance to him, and, disregarding the reasons for the flight, demanded for himself the right to decide whether to continue or return once the Pole was reached. Nobile wanted the venture to become a stunt, an impressive proof of the worthiness of his dirigible. He wanted the dramatic propaganda value which the first aerial attainment of the North Pole would bring, while for Amundsen the Pole was incidental. For him the objective remained the pioneering of the shortest intercontinental air route.

There was, of course, a clash. The rigid authority of an experienced and purposeful Norseman collided squarely with the ambition of the glory hunter from Italy. Calling Nobile "a hired pilot," Amundsen made it quite clear that he reserved for himself and Ellsworth the right to decide whether the flight should be interrupted before a transarctic crossing was completed and Alaska reached.[33] Amundsen was disgusted. Never before had anyone tried to usurp his authority, never yet had anybody dared question his ability to make command decisions.

After all preliminary arrangements had been completed and after insurance for the dirigible had been obtained,[34] a ceremony took place on March 29, 1926, at Rome's Ciampino Airport, which had once been commanded by Lieutenant Colonel Valle. The Duce himself took the Italian flag as it was lowered from the dirigible N-1, and, handing it to Nobile, he said: "This, Colonel, you will drop at the Pole. . . . You'll succeed," he added. "I have no doubts."[35]

Nobile, recently promoted to full colonel, was standing at the threshold to fame, firmly supported by Pope Pius XI, Italy's King Victor Emanuel III, and Benito Mussolini. The man with the bulging eyes who himself had risen from squalor to the splendor of absolute power may have felt akin to Nobile, who had managed to escape the poverty of a little mountain village to find himself standing in the limelight. Both of them were representatives of a newly resurrected Italy.

On that same day hasty repairs on the *Alaskan* were all but completed in Fairbanks, and, in New York, preparations for Byrd's expedition entered the final stage. Byrd had obtained a three-engined Fokker plane with air-cooled Wright motors and a wingspread of sixty-three feet. The tanks could hold more than 600 gallons of gasoline, and it could fly as fast as 120 miles an hour. The *Chantier*, a base ship, to transport the expedition, was available, volunteers were coming in, and above all, there was pilot Floyd Bennett, calm, reliable, and efficient. To Byrd, like Amundsen, the flight was an expedition, and who deserved credit for the success of an expedition? The leader of course, the man who made the plans, who took the risks and who was willing to bear responsibility for success or failure. After many frustrated attempts and false starts, Lieutenant Commander Richard E. Byrd, at thirty-seven, saw a road leading to fame.

Wilkins was anxious to be off. The "Snow Motor Section" of his expedition, traveling by land, was supposed to have reached Barrow, there to establish a radio station. But it was only halfway through the mountains; Point Barrow had no radio, and no weather reports were available. Loaded with 3,000 pounds of supplies, the *Alaskan* took off from Fairbanks on March 31. Climbing to an altitude of 5,000 feet and flying at a speed of 130 miles an hour, Eielson headed for the Endicott Range, while Wilkins surveyed the unknown terrain lying below. Mountains, marked on the map as being 5,000 feet high, were visible in the distance and the *Alaskan* climbed higher. Vibrating, panting, the plane reached its maximum height of 9,000 feet, yet mountain peaks ahead loomed still higher. Carefully threading his way between peaks, Eielson broke through the mountain range and came to a wide white plain not even charted on the map. Here, they met a sea of gray cloud stretching out endlessly and completely hiding the ground. Slow minutes stretched into long hours. Were they on course? Where were they?

"Keep on going," Wilkins shouted. "We should take at least five hours to get to Barrow and we have been in the air not much more than four. We cannot be there yet."

Then there was ice below. Ugly, rough, it was piled up in high ridges. Wilkins and Eielson flew over it for an hour. Then they realized this was pack ice! They had lost their way and were now flying somewhere over unexplored arctic territory. Leaning forward, Wilkins shouted into Eielson's ear: "If you look around, you will see a hundred miles farther north than any man has seen until today. We are a hundred miles out over the Arctic Sea. What do you say to going a half an hour longer—just to make it good measure?"

"Whatever you think best."[36]

And so they flew on. There was no land anywhere, only angry-looking broken-up ice. They turned around and again faced the gray blanket of rolling clouds. Point Barrow was nowhere to be seen. They turned and climbed, they twisted and came lower. It was a long time before they saw a low Eskimo house, the spire of a church, and a two-story building dimly visible in the snow. Wilkins recognized the settlement as Point Barrow. Now for the landing. Could a plane on wheels land on an ice-covered surface? Would the plane turn turtle?

Eielson brought the plane down. Gently the wheels touched snow, quickly and smoothly the *Alaskan* came to a stop without turning over.

They had landed amidst drifting snow in the heart of a blizzard. There were high winds and a temperature of forty degrees below zero.

Curious natives poured out of their huts to have a look at the first plane they had ever seen, while the two men in flying suits were grateful for the warmth inside the trading post. The storm held them prisoner for five days, but when it finally subsided, Wilkins and Eielson prepared for the return flight to Fairbanks. Three attempts to take off failed before they were in the air. Flying through fog and clouds, they became lost and somewhere on an ice-covered river they made an emergency landing, to spend a cold night huddled in the cabin of their plane, trying vainly to sleep. Then they scrambled out and started building a runway. After a smooth takeoff the *Alaskan* arrived back at its base in Fairbanks.

Covering a distance of nearly 1,000 miles, venturing some 100 miles north of Point Barrow, Wilkins and Eielson had made the longest nonstop arctic flight to date, and Dr. Isaiah Bowman, president of the American Geographic Society, called it "a remarkable achievement." But there was no time for rejoicing, no time for celebrations; Wilkins was still only at the threshold.

On April 5, the 3,500-ton steamer *Chantier,* on loan to Lieutenant Commander Byrd at a cost of one dollar a year, left the Brooklyn Navy Yard, accompanied by the shrieking whistling of assembled river craft.[37] Extensively reconditioned, she had 1,500 tons of coal in her hold and was manned by forty-six volunteers, all amateurs. Among them were West Point graduates and Army reserve officers without any seafaring experience who had signed on as ordinary seamen. They were ready to work hard and their wage requirements were fairly reasonable—nothing.

Even though a great part of the supplies and equipment had been donated or sold at cost, Byrd was unable to raise the $100,000 needed, and the expedition started out with a deficit exceeding $20,000 for which the commander was personally responsible. (Fees for newspaper stories and pictorial rights later put the expedition in the black.) Many doubted the soundness of Byrd's plan to make an arctic flight in a plane. The craft to use, they said, was a dirigible, needing neither skis nor runway, drifting with the wind and able to stay aloft for days. True, there had been dirigible disasters, and even the *Shenandoah* had crashed. Still, was Amundsen not preparing to fly in the *Norge?* And had there not been talk of an especially designed dirigible capable of flying across the North Pole to China?

As the *Chantier* moved out into the ocean, boatswain Jim Madison noticed a mudcaked anchor chain. "Get a fire hose started," he yelled, "and shake a leg, you there," pointing at Roy Bryant, ex-army officer turned volunteer seaman. Believing the ship to be on fire, Bryant raced

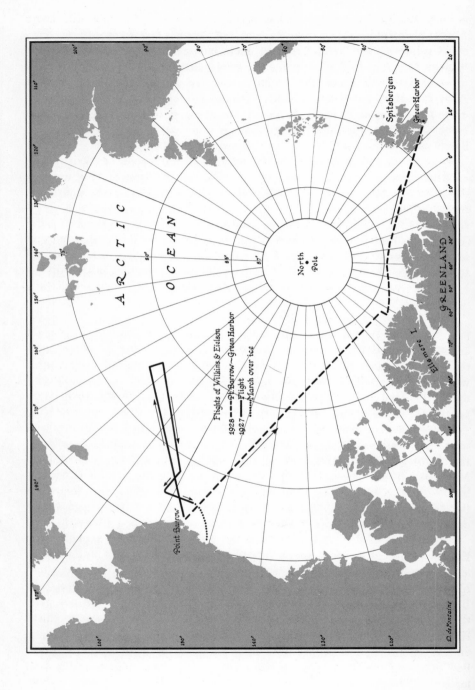

Flights of Wilkins & Eidson

1928 ---- Pt. Barrow~Green Harbor
1927 —— Flight
•••••• March over ice

North Pole

ARCTIC OCEAN

Point Barrow

Spitsbergen

Green Harbor

GREENLAND

Ellesmore I.

D. de Fontaine

off and returned on the double, carrying a fire extinguisher. A shocked Madison, speechless in disbelief, could not even curse as he threw the contraption in the general direction of the retreating Bryant. West Pointer Winston Ehrgott, assigned to a dishwashing detail, single-handedly managed to break so many dishes that he had to be shifted to other duty. Around midnight, a lookout reported a mysterious beacon which turned out to be a star. Captain Brennan, the skipper, was frankly worried. How was he to make a 10,000-mile voyage with a crew so totally inexperienced?

Progress was painfully slow as the ship, steered by untrained, inexperienced helmsmen, time and again slid off course and headed in a wrong direction. Standing on deck, Byrd gazed out into the dark sky of a peaceful night. Barely audible above the rhythmic breaking of waves against the ship's hull, he heard steps and saw a human form trying to steal past. Turning on his flashlight, Byrd saw the dejected face of Malcom P. Hanson, a stowaway. (At Trondheim he would be disembarked and returned to the United States, his hopes of being an eyewitness to history crushed.) Making eleven knots an hour, the *Chantier* ploughed on.

At 9:32 in the morning of April 10, the *Norge* left Rome on the first lap of a historic mission, amidst the pealing of church bells and accompanied by the cheers of an emotional crowd. Absent at takeoff time was Premier Benito Mussolini. His nose grazed by the bullet of would-be assassin Violet Gibson, and covered by adhesive, he had shown up a few days earlier. At that time, however, an unfavorable wind had caused the departure of the *Norge* to be postponed.

Aboard were twenty-one men and Nobile's terrier bitch Titina. There were two journalists, three radiomen (only two would be needed for the trip from Spitsbergen to Alaska), two meteorologists (only one—Finn Malmgren—would be needed for the polar flight). Throughout the trip from Rome to Kings Bay, inadequately clothed Norwegian members of the crew were shivering from cold. Their special flying suits, Nobile had decreed, were too heavy and had to be left behind.[38]

Avoiding the Alps, the *Norge* was to fly via France to Pulham in England, then proceed by way of Oslo, Leningrad, and Vadso to arrive at the point for departure in Spitsbergen. French Lieutenant Colonel Mercer was to act as pilot over France, and, on insistence of Riiser-Larsen, British Major Scott, famed skipper of the R-34, was to help with mooring the *Norge* in Pulham.[39] The leaders of the expedition, Amundsen and Ellsworth, did not take part in the flight, which promised to become an exhibitionist spectacle. Traveling by train and boat, they reached Kings Bay ahead of the *Norge,* to complete preparations for what really mattered: the crossing of the Arctic Sea.

In an uneventful flight the *Norge* crossed France. When the airship reached Pulham, the first leg of a long journey was all but completed and skipper Nobile confidently approached the mooring mast without releasing gas.

"Trim the ship," Major Scott said, raising his voice. "You must trim the ship, sir." The mooring maneuver failed.

Again Nobile tried, and again he failed. A disgusted George H. Scott went to the rear of the cabin in utter frustration. Prevailed upon by Riiser-Larsen, Nobile finally turned command of the dirigible over to Major Scott. With two cables uselessly dangling in the air, Major Scott took the ship up to an altitude of 3,000 feet, and then brought the dirigible smoothly down to a mooring in the manner of an artist.[39]

Usually calm and controlled, Riiser-Larsen, himself an airship pilot, was cursing freely—drawing on the rich vocabulary of a navy man. He was no longer sure of pilot Nobile's ability and wanted Major Scott to stay on with the ship, but this request was denied by Britain's Minister of Defence. Regretfully shaking his head, Sir Samuel Hoare said: "Sorry, but England cannot afford to lose Scott."[39]

The *Norge* flew on to Oslo and an enthusiastic welcome by a jubilant crowd, then proceeded to Gatchina, near Leningrad. There were receptions, festivities, lectures and speeches in Leningrad; thousands of people, including a detachment of Russian cavalry, came to see the airship. Departure of the *Norge* from Leningrad was delayed because an Italian ground party did not arrive in Spitsbergen until April 25.

Wilkins and Eielson completed their second ferrying trip to Point Barrow, where they now had a 200-gallon supply of gasoline, but much more was needed. When the *Alaskan* was readied for a return flight to Fairbanks, Wilkins caught his right arm in the spokes of a wheel and, freeing it, felt a sudden snap at the wrist. Wilkins climbed aboard the plane, and as it took off, he became painfully aware that his arm was broken.

On the third trip to Point Barrow—Wilkins's plane carried a load of 4,750 pounds. Again flying through fog and dense cloud, Wilkins and Eielson hoped their advance base would now have sufficient fuel to allow the big plane, the *Detroiter,* to make at least one arctic reconnaissance flight. Hoping to find the *Detroiter* repaired, they took off for Fairbanks once more, but impenetrable fog closed in from all directions, and they were forced to turn back. At the price of four hours' worth of precious fuel they somehow managed to make their way to Barrow where bad weather again kept them prisoners—this time for two days.

When the skies cleared, the *Alaskan* was made flight-ready again. His fractured arm was in a sling, but holding the propeller with his other hand, Wilkins brought his full weight down on it. The motor started and the plane took to the air, once more headed for Fairbanks. However,

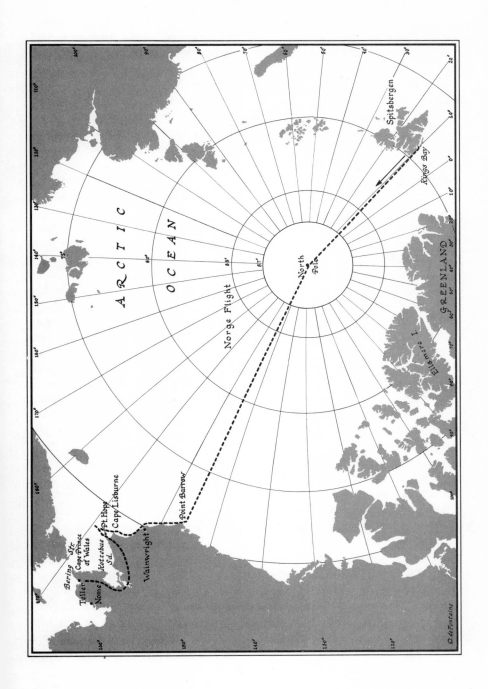

as soon as it was airborne, there was an unusual noise. The propeller started clattering and the plane began to vibrate. Hurriedly, Eielson turned the ignition off and banked steeply, gliding to a standstill on a frozen lagoon not far from Point Barrow. The warped propeller of the *Alaskan* was all but coming apart, and seemed hopelessly beyond repair. By wire, Wilkins asked Major Lanphier to speed repairs on the *Detroiter* and to bring a spare propeller. There was nothing else he could do but wait.

Wilkins and Eielson waited impatiently for two days to get an answer from Lanphier. When the answer came, it was bad news: The *Detroiter* performed poorly, the major wired, and the engines consumed too much gasoline. Just to make a trip from Fairbanks to Barrow and back, the plane would have to draw on the fuel stores painfully built up at the advanced base.

Working against time, the two men now set out to repair the damaged propeller as best they could with materials on hand. Filing the rough edges and binding the blades with strips of brass, they worked in the icy cold for more than three days.

On April 30 Wilkins was back in Fairbanks, only to find his big *Detroiter* useless. Improvising, he decided to attempt another exploratory flight with the *Alaskan*. The propeller was changed, more gasoline was taken on, and once again the plane taxied down the runway. Eielson opened the throttle and the engine strained, but the craft did not become airborne. The new propeller, it turned out, was also inadequate! In a desperate effort to salvage something out of a chain of disappointments and heartaches, the old brassbound propeller was reinstalled and the plane again tested. Before the *Alaskan* got off the ground, its right wing broke and the plane slid on, once more coming to rest with its tail high in the air.

Some thirty loose gasoline cans pinned a helpless Wilkins against the doorway while fuel from the wing tanks poured over the hot exhaust pipe. "Hurry up and get out," Eielson yelled. "She will surely catch fire." But Wilkins could not move, and his body blocked escape for Eielson. The two resigned men held their breaths and waited for the explosion. Once more they were lucky: There was no fire or explosion. With a great sigh of relief, Wilkins started pushing the gasoline cans aside, then both crawled out and inspected the damage. With its wing beyond repair, the crippled plane was useless.

Again hope faded. All these narrow escapes seemed to have been in vain. What good to them was all the gasoline in Barrow which had been carried there with so much effort? But Wilkins still refused to accept defeat. He wanted to try once more. Maybe the *Detroiter* could be used after all, despite its high consumption of gasoline. Within an hour the runway was cleared of wreckage and the three-motored plane was wheeled out of the hangar.

Quickly taking off and climbing to an altitude of 11,000 feet, the *Detroiter,* manned by Wilkins and Eielson and carrying a load of 700 gallons of gasoline as well as 45 gallons of oil, dodged the fog, crossed the high mountains and finally landed in Point Barrow.

But when the new day dawned, the air was filled with clammy fog which was to linger on for days, now and then disappearing for a short time only to reappear before the engines of the *Detroiter* could be warmed up. The year of 1926 was not to bring arctic victory for Wilkins and Eielson.

III. CONQUEST

1926-1928

1

THERE was animated activity in Kings Bay.[1] The upper sections of a mooring mast were being riveted; hydrogen cylinders, crates and boxes were being moved from the dock up a hill and across a snow-covered field one and one-half miles long. Loaded on sleds, they were being pulled by men, using an ancient tractor which often broke down and one sad-looking pony. Nobile had done a remarkable job of assembling and sending some two thousand tons of supplies, meticulously crated and labeled. He had forgotten nothing. There was even a huge searchlight, useless in a land that never sees the darkness of night during spring.[2]

At the small dock, her steam shut off, Amundsen's supply ship the *Heimdal* was being coaled while her boilers were repaired. On her deck, working purposefully, men were lifting boxes and uncrating supplies.

About ten o'clock that morning a sailor was first to spot a dark smudge on the horizon. "Hey, look," he yelled, pointing a stubby finger toward the smudge in the distance. Others straightened up, squinted, cupped their hands, and the yell "a ship" went out, losing itself in the immense whiteness. All morning long they paused now and then to look at a small smoking funnel which slowly grew larger. It might be a sealer or a ship bringing supplies for the coal mine.

By noon miners and members of Amundsen's party knew that it was the *Chantier,* inching her way toward Spitsbergen. By two o'clock, the ship's outline could be seen clearly against the brillant ice; at four o'clock in the afternoon the *Chantier* came to a stop in the midst of floating ice, some nine hundred yards off shore, and Commander Byrd radioed for permission to use the pier.

Regretfully the *Heimdal's* skipper, Captain Tank-Nielsen, had to decline. In anticipation of the *Norge's* arrival work on his ship could not be interrupted. Besides, at this critical time the little *Heimdal* could not be exposed to the danger of being smashed by ice, which any sudden shift of the wind might swing into deadly motion. "Our ship was nearly lost a few days ago," Tank-Nielsen said, "drifting ice caught her and carried her toward land. I'm sorry, sir, I cannot move her."

In the face of such determination Byrd had to capitulate. Assembling staff members of the expedition in his cabin, he explained the situation: "We cannot use the dock, but we must land the plane. It is dangerous, but it can be done." His plan was audacious and risky, but the flying season was nearing its end and Byrd was impatient.

Moving closer, the *Chantier* dropped anchor three hundred yards off shore. A boat was lowered, and, carrying four men, it approached the dock. A handsome young officer, meticulously dressed in U. S. Navy uniform, was first to come ashore. "I'm Commander Byrd," he said. "Can anyone tell me where I can find Captain Amundsen?"

Flying Lieutenant Bernt Balchen casually wiped his greasy hands on a ball of waste. "Up the hill," he said and set out to lead the way over crunching snow to Amundsen's headquarters in a cabin belonging to the Kings Bay coal mine.

When they entered the cabin, Amundsen rose from behind a table covered with charts and papers. "Welcome to Spitsbergen, Commander," he said.

Byrd was formal and reserved. He shook hands with Amundsen and introduced his party, which included Floyd Bennett, a lanky young man with a friendly face. Then the leaders of two "rival" expeditions sat down to discuss the serious business of exploration.

"Where would you suggest we make our takeoff?" Byrd asked. "There is a flat area in front of this house," Amundsen replied. "You can level it off and use it as a runway."

There was the flicker of a smile around Byrd's mouth. "Thank you," he said, "you are being very generous."[3]

Amundsen nodded. He respected men with courage and there was no need for him to withhold assistance because there was no real rivalry between him and the American. Wanting to make aviation history, Byrd hoped to be the first man to fly to the Pole; intent on crossing the Arctic Ocean, Amundsen wished to lay the foundation for an intercontinental air bridge, linking the Old World with the New.

A telegram from Amundsen informed Nobile in Leningrad that all preparations in Kings Bay would be completed within five days. The *Norge* was to leave Gatchina Airport on May 2.

Thus, as April drew to a close and the time available for arctic flying diminished, three teams hoped for success: In Alaska, Wilkins and Eielson still saw a chance for one exploratory flight. In Spitsbergen, Byrd and Bennett were getting ready for a dash to the North Pole, and Amundsen, waiting for the *Norge,* was eager to cross the Arctic Ocean.

There was great activity aboard the *Chantier.* Her four whaleboats were lowered into the water and heavy planks were placed across their gunwales. Under a gray sky spewing snow and in raw and biting air, Byrd's carpenter, Gould, transformed the boats into a raft.

Amundsen and Ellsworth made a courtesy visit to the *Chantier.* Veterans of the fight against ice, they knew danger when they saw it. To them, Byrd's plan to bring his plane ashore on an improvised raft appeared extremely risky.

First mate Frank De Lucca had the fuselage of Byrd's dismantled Fokker hoisted from the ship's hold. Winches growled and through a swirl of snowflakes the fuselage was gently swung overside and lowered

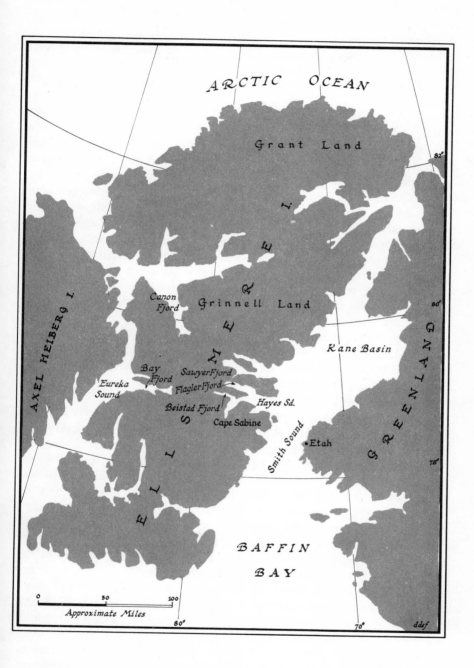

Ellsmere Island.

onto the makeshift raft. Byrd gripped the railing tightly. He knew the gamble he was taking: If a wind sprang up, both raft and plane might be either crushed or blown out to sea.

Moving cautiously over heaving slippery planks, the crew gently lowered the fuselage and secured it to the raft. Then the wind rose, and a sixty-mile-an-hour gale suddenly hit the *Chantier*. The plane's wing, ready to be hoisted overside, was caught in a frightful impact which threatened to wrench it loose from the derrick. Ice appeared and a large floe was sighted heading straight for the rudder of the *Chantier*. The amateur sailors, carrying explosives, rushed forward to plant dynamite charges. Ripped by the ensuing explosions, the floe was reduced to a mass of jagged pieces of ice just in time.

For twelve hours the storm raged. Time and again both raft and plane were violently thrown against the ship, while supporting cables snapped, but the shivering, water-drenched men held out. When the storm finally swept out to sea, an undamaged raft still held the plane with its wings now firmly attached. The Fokker was ready to be taken ashore. Next a narrow channel was hacked in the sheet of land ice and the raft was started moving, rowed by men who had never held an oar in their hands before. When the raft bumped the shore, to the cheers of the assembled Norwegians, Byrd had won his first gamble.

The big three-motored craft, with the name "Josephine Ford" written in bold letters on her sides, was pulled from the boats to the shore, where her wheels promptly sank deep into the fresh snow.[4] A meticulous Bernt Balchen, conscious of history in the making, recorded the time in his diary: It was 3:30 P.M. on April 30.

Skis were quickly substituted for the wheels on the "Josephine Ford," and the plane was pulled through deep snow up a mile-long incline. The temperature in wind-swept Kings Bay remained around fifteen degrees below zero. In addition, tons of supplies, food, gas and oil had to be taken off the *Chantier* and stored near the plane. A field kitchen was set up and food was served in the open; over a fire built in a dugout, oil was heated while a funnel-equipped pressure stove warmed the plane's engines. For eighteen hours Byrd's men flattened snow to prepare a runway.

On May 3 there was whirling of propellers and roaring of engines on the snow-covered hill overlooking Kings Bay. With Bennett at the controls and Byrd beside him, the "Josephine Ford" was ready for her first trial flight in the Arctic. Gathering speed, the plane moved down the slope, but in a snowdrift near the end of the runway a ski broke, the landing gear bent and the trial run ended almost before it had started.

Disregarding rules set up by publicity-minded leaders of both expeditions, Amundsen's photographer Berge snapped a picture of the disabled "Josephine Ford" lying helplessly in the snow.

The weather in Russia was bad. Violent storms were sweeping Leningrad, and to the disappointment of a bored crew, eager to go, Nobile had to postpone departure of the *Norge.*

While meteorologist Malmgren was studying weather reports, Nobile made some last minute changes in his crew. Having caught up with the *Norge* after a long train ride, Renato Alessandrini, a rigger, resumed his place aboard the dirigible. An atmosphere of expectancy mixed with boredom prevailed. Gathered in their smoke-filled quarters, the men played cards and made limp jokes; once in a while one of them would step up to a window and look out on a gray sky, only to turn around again, half-muttering a curse.

It had been a long night for carpenter Gould and Mulroy, chief engineer of the *Chantier,* but they had managed to repair the landing gear of the "Josephine Ford." Now, kneeling in the snow, Lieutenant Oertell, Byrd's supply officer, was busily applying shoe polish to the newly installed ski.[5]

A young Norwegian, his dark flannel shirt open at the neck, ambled up and stopped to watch. "What are you doing?" he asked. Oertell barely looked up. "Waxing the ski," he said. "What do you think?"

"No good," the man said and smiled. His name was Balchen, he volunteered, and he was with Amundsen. He had experience with skis; a mixture of paraffin and resin burned right into the wood would work much better, he suggested.

Once again the "Josephine Ford" was ready for a trial flight. Again, with Bennett at the controls and carrying the lightest possible load, she glided down the runway. Halfway down, a ski collapsed, the plane pitched forward and the roar of her engines became muffled as she buried her nose in a bank of snow. No spare skis were available.

Amundsen saw the crash from a distance. Turning to ski expert Balchen, he said: "Byrd is in trouble, see what you can do for him."[5] Soon Gould and Mulroy were building new skis in Amundsen's workshop under Balchen's supervision. Over the objections of Captain Brennan, the *Chantier's* heavy lifeboat oars, the only hard wood available in Kings Bay, were cut up, and holes were drilled in their long shafts. With these improvised supports bolted to repaired skis, the "Josephine Ford" was once more ready for another start.

In the hangar at Gatchina an anxious crew, weary of waiting, assembled at 4:30 in the morning of May 5. Ground parties were ready, the ship was ready. Would they take off? Silently big Riiser-Larsen walked up and down the hangar.

At nine o'clock the decision was made. The *Norge* was hauled out, her motors were started, and the ship gently lifted into the sky. Passing over Leningrad before proceeding northward toward Vadso, the *Norge* was a graceful sight against the leaden sky.

The flight to Vadso was rough. Buffeted by unpredictable gusts, the *Norge* tossed up and down like a ball. One hour before estimated time of arrival in Vadso the left motor sputtered, coughed, and went dead. The idle right engine was started, and at 6:50 on the morning of May 6 the airship was finally moored near Vadso. With fuel tanks replenished, she would set out again at three o'clock in the afternoon. Destination: Kings Bay.

On that same day, the "Josephine Ford" was rapidly moving down a lengthened runway, on skis waxed in accordance with the suggestions of Bernt Balchen. Gracefully, the plane rose into the air and started on a two-hour test flight. The plane's performance was good, gasoline consumption remarkably low, Commander Byrd was satisfied and so was Floyd Bennett.

There was no time for sleep in Amundsen's camp during the night of May 7. Telegrams kept coming in, reporting the steady movement of the *Norge*. When the dawn came, it was beautiful, with a clear sky, crisp air and hardly a breeze.

At 6 A.M., the dirigible appeared in the sky, an unimpressive dot. The alarm for the ground crew was sounded, and excitement mounted as the dot grew to the shape of a silvery whale.

Looking out from his cabin, Nobile could see the hangar, the *Heimdal,* the *Chantier,* and pulled by hundreds of strong arms the *Norge* gently descended. After a total flying time of one hundred and three hours, passing over nine countries and five seas, through winds, fog, and snow, the airship had finally arrived at the point for departure.

Dressed only in ordinary street clothes and shivering from the cold, Riiser-Larsen and the other Norwegians stood stiffly at attention with the others, as, one by one, four national anthems—Norwegian, American, Italian, and Swedish—were played by the *Heimdal's* little band. Released from the narrow confinement of the crowded gondola, Nobile's dog Titina frolicked in the snow.

One of the *Norge's* motors now had to be replaced, fuel and supplies were to be taken aboard, and plans called for the substitution for some ballast-carrying water tanks, with others holding additional gasoline. It was estimated that three days would be required to complete the work. But Nobile had seen the "Josephine Ford"; to him this clumsy heavier-than-air craft was a deadly rival and Byrd a competitor. Nobile proposed to hurry up the departure of the *Norge*.

Amundsen's voice, the voice of authority, was calm. "Nothing doing," he said. "We are not in a race with Byrd. I do not care. . . whether he reaches the Pole ahead of us or not. Our job is to cross the Arctic Ocean."[6] But to Nobile the flight was still a headline-grabbing aeronautical feat, a stunt.

2

BYRD was ready. Haines, the United States Weather Bureau's meteorologist, forecast favorable atmospheric conditions. The "Josephine Ford" was fully loaded, with instruments checked, and engines warmed up. As the door to the cabin slammed shut behind them, Byrd and Bennett were set for their flight to the North Pole. Men gathered in small groups to watch the plane as it glided down the hill. Those who were conscious of history checked their watches: It was ten minutes past twelve on May 8, 1926.

The skis dragged over the icy surface as the plane struggled to get off the ground. It failed to rise and overshot the runway. Bounding over the rough hummocks, the Fokker careened and once again smashed into a snowbank. To the men watching from the top of the hill this looked like the end of a gallant beginning. Sick at heart, some of them rushed toward what looked like a total wreck.

Byrd and Bennett emerged unhurt and plowing through waist-deep snow they circled the plane in disbelief: Balchen's skis had not collapsed and the plane had taken the pounding without apparently suffering much damage. Byrd was still confident: Lighten the load, and success would come on the next attempt. But one more crack-up would mean disaster, as no spare skis were on hand and the material from which to improvise them was exhausted.

Dug out of the snow once more, the "Josephine Ford" taxied up the hill. Some gas cans were thrown out and all equipment not strictly essential was discarded. Included in the mass of articles left behind was a weird collection of souvenirs smuggled aboard the plane by Byrd's enthusiastic shipmates, weighing a total of some two hundred pounds.[7]

With the sun fixed in the sky, "night" descended on Kings Bay. In wooden barracks the men slept, exhausted from a day of heavy labor.

Byrd and Bennett were ready once more. An engine backfired, propellers turned, a dull roaring filled the air and surprised faces appeared at the windows of Amundsen's barracks. Wearily rubbing sleep out of their eyes, men in long underwear opened doors and Berge, halfdressed, stumbled over the snow, carrying his tripod.

One more wave, one more handshake, then the cabin door of the "Josephine Ford" was once again shut. Engines throbbed and the plane quivered, lurched forward, moved downhill and near the end of the runway gently rose into the air. The ear-splitting roar faded into a gentle drone as it turned and headed into the distance. The time, as recorded by Balchen, was 37 minutes past midnight, May 9, 1926.

Byrd's course was due north. He had abandoned the plan of an intermediate landing at Cape Morris Jesup; his goal was the Pole itself and a safe return to Spitsbergen. There was enough food aboard the plane to last ten weeks, along with a rubber boat, rifles and ammunition, fur clothes and smoke bombs, and, stored in the fuselage, a hand-made sled donated by Roald Amundsen. Should mechanical difficulties force a landing and make it impossible to take off again, their only hope for survival would lie in a march toward Etah, Greenland. In such a case, these supplies would make the difference between life and death.

Relieving Bennett at the controls, Byrd fingered some good-luck charms in the pocket of his flying suit. Among them was a coin once carried by Peary on his way to the Pole. As fuel was consumed, the five-gallon gasoline cans were emptied into wing tanks and then thrown overboard. The plane held to its northerly course, nearly ten thousand square miles of unknown regions coming into view every hour. This was the same area seen by Amundsen and his men one year previously, but nowhere was there land, only ice.

Toward eight o'clock, after some seven hours of flight, oil was seen leaking from the starboard motor. On a piece of paper, Bennett scribbled "That motor will stop" and, handing the message to Byrd, suggested an emergency landing. Byrd looked at the leak. Anxiously he watched the oil pressure gauge, studying it helplessly as the oil kept dripping. With the instinct of a gambler Byrd made his decision: If a landing had to be made, it would be as near the Pole as possible. With the prize in sight, he had reached a mental point of no return.

At Kings Bay, Lieutenant Balchen took a group of reluctant Italians up a hill for training on skis. Most of them had never seen snow before and the skis they were standing on were cumbersome. Closing their eyes and awkwardly twisting their bodies in futile attempts to maintain a precarious balance, the men threw their hands up and one by one came down on the snow with a dull thud.[8] Wearily, Bernt Balchen shook his head. What were these men going to do if forced to land on pack ice? Disgusted, he took off in a spray of snow for another hill. There, he pulled a box of water colors from his pocket and started painting a landscape.

Balchen was actually a member of Lieutenant Höver's ground party, which had been sent to Spitsbergen in support of Amundsen's expedition. Hand-picked by Riiser-Larsen, his teacher in aeronautical theory, who knew his qualifications, he was also part of a special reserve force considered necessary because of Nobile's attitude. No sooner had the Italian got the official name of the expedition changed by the addition of his own name to become "The Amundsen-Ellsworth-Nobile Expedition," than he had asked once more that the *Norge* fly under the flag of Italy.

Riiser-Larsen's reaction had been an unequivocal: "Never! That's out of the question!" After thinking the matter over for a while, Nobile next wanted to know what would happen if he and the other Italian crew members were to go ashore at one of the intermediate landing sites and refuse to continue the flight unless their demands were granted. "Sir," Riiser-Larsen had answered, "I am an airship pilot myself and we will carry on."[10]

"I had to be prepared for such an eventuality and let Nobile understand that I was prepared," Riiser-Larsen said later. "The only place where his threat was serious was Spitsbergen. I therefore engaged Norwegian reserves to be sent to that place; one of them was Balchen."[10]

When Balchen returned to camp on that May 9, he met a serious Amundsen who asked: "How are they making out with those skis?" Balchen shrugged. "The only thing you can do, is to tie one ski to each man's back and another to his belly."[11]

"At 9:02 A.M., May 9, 1926, Greenwich civil time, our calculations showed us to be at the Pole!"[12] Commander Byrd would write. "The dream of a lifetime had at last been realized." What he saw at 9:02 A.M. on May 9 was nothing but an immense solitude, a frozen ocean covered with irregular floes and cakes of ice, extending in every direction to the distant horizon. "We headed to the right to take two confirming sights of the sun, then turned and took two more. After that we made some moving and still pictures; then went on for several miles in the direction we had come, and made another larger circle to be sure to take in the Pole. . . ."

From the diary of Floyd Bennett:

> We continued on until we had been out eight hours and thirty-five minutes. . . . At the end of this period Byrd came forward and shook hands with me in a matter-of-fact way. I knew that we had reached the Pole. . . . It was impossible to speak for the roar of the engines. We saluted the memory of Peary. . . . We dropped nothing upon the snow below us, for Peary had dropped a flag there . . . [13]

The "Josephine Ford" headed back for Spitsbergen, as Bennett and Byrd headed straight for the safety of Kings Bay. The starboard motor kept working; the oil dripped more slowly, and finally the leakage stopped altogether. This happened when the oil dropped below the level of a loose rivet, they would discover later.

Exhilaration was over and fatigue set in. The temptation to doze became overwhelming. "We felt no larger than a pinpoint," Byrd said later, "and as lonely as a tomb, as remote and detached as a star. . . . The smallness of life fell from our shoulders. What wonder that we

Byrd and Bennett in Kings Bay before their polar flight. *The Bettmann Archives.*

felt no great emotion of achievement or fear of death that lay stretched beneath us but instead, impersonal, disembodied."[14]

Toward four-thirty in the afternoon a group of subdued men assembled for dinner in one of the wooden barracks at Kings Bay. Suddenly there were shouts outside. An Italian soldier pushed the door open and gesticulatedly wildly, yelling: *"Arriva, Arriva . . . una machina . . ."* Chairs were pushed back and electrified men, suddenly snapped out of sullenness, stampeded for the door. There was a low humming sound, and, clearly visible above the snow-covered mountain peaks, there was a small moving speck.

At the same time, the little village of Ny Alesund, near Kings Bay, seen from an altitude of 4,000 feet, was the most beautiful sight Byrd had ever seen. The "Josephine Ford" was coming for a landing, but she was returning too soon; the men of the *Chantier* were on their ship and even the official photographer was missing.[15]

Roald Amundsen was one of the first to greet Byrd. His weather-beaten face was illuminated by a warm smile. In a rare display of deep-felt emotion he embraced both men while tears rolled down his cheeks. Also present were a smiling Ellsworth, a grinning Riiser-Larsen, and a happy Balchen. A few feet away, the ubiquitous Berge filmed the authentic version of Byrd's and Bennett's return.[15]

Soon sailors from the *Chantier* came running, and a cheering, yelling, back-slapping crowd carried the two dazed and tired men toward the bay. Correspondent Russell Owen flashed the news to the world. Spread over the front page, the New York *Times* of May 10 carried the blazing headline news:

> Byrd and Bennett circle Pole, return to Kings Bay; made trip in 15 hours 51 minutes . . . President Coolidge's message of congratulation . . . Tributes by nation's leaders . . .

The following day there was a celebration aboard the *Chantier,* and members of the Norwegian team toasted the new polar heroes with the contents of two cases marked "Medicinal," thoughtfully sent the Prohibition-weary Americans by Amundsen. Amid the clinking of glasses there was mixed laughter and speechmaking. In an exchange of gifts, Ellsworth got Byrd's polar bear pants and sealskin mittens, which he would later wear on the *Norge.* No expression of doubt or suspicion, no calculated questions marred the exuberance of the festivities.

On his return, to New York, Byrd would submit to the National Geographic Society his record and the broken sextant with which he allegedly had made determinations of his position during the flight. In due time, Secretary of the Navy Wilbur would receive a report from the Society: ". . . it is the opinion of your committee that at very close to 9 hours 3 minutes Greenwich civil time, May 9, 1926, Lieutenant-Commander Richard Evelyn Byrd was at the North Pole, insofar as an observer in an airplane, using the most accurate instruments and methods available for determining his position could obtain."[16]

Had Byrd really reached the goal he had set for himself? His account was poetic rather than factual, his data scant and his sextant was broken.

3

ON May 10 the weather forecast was favorable. Work on the *Norge* was completed and the departure of Amundsen's expedition was scheduled for one o'clock in the morning. At that time, with the sun at its lowest point, the air would be coldest. In this cold, the hydrogen gas fed into the dirigible would contract; thus the cells could be filled to capacity and the airship's lifting power would be greatest. By midnight, however, it became obvious that the departure would have to be postponed, as a strong wind was hammering the cliffs of Spitsbergen.

Tense hours of waiting and watching followed for Nobile. Time also passed slowly for Roald Amundsen's young nephew, Gustav. If the ship could take off with the maximum amount of gas, he stood a good chance of being taken along. But with every passing hour the air grew warmer and the expanding hydrogen had to be released to prevent the gas cells from bursting. The less gas there was, the smaller would be the lifting capacity of the *Norge* at takeoff time. With a lump in his throat, Gustav waited, while Amundsen and Riiser-Larsen slept. Both knew the strain that long wakeful hours of the following days would bring.

In the early morning the wind subsided, and by seven o'clock the ground party started dribbling in. But Nobile remained hesitant. By 9:40 the *Norge* was fully manned. A silent Gustav Amundsen looked sadly at Nobile. "Wait a minute, there is still a chance," the colonel said.

Vacillating, caught in the grip of paralyzing indecision, Nobile still refused to take the ship out of the hangar against the prevailing wind. Confronted by Riiser-Larsen, he threw his hands up and shouted: "If you want to take the responsibility, then take her out of the hangar yourself!" Assisted by Lieutenant Höver, Riiser-Larsen did exactly that, while Nobile stood aside.[17]

Hauled out of the hangar, the *Norge* came to life, the motors were started, and at 9:50 in the morning of Tuesday, May 11, 1926, the proud airship, propellers whirling gently, rose into the blue sky. From the ground Gustav Amundsen sadly waved. For a long time he stood there, in front of the empty hangar.

At first, the *Norge* was not alone. The "Josephine Ford" took off, and in a gesture of comradeship Byrd and Bennett escorted the dirigible on her mission. One hour later, with the wave of a hand and the dipping of wings, Byrd turned back. Except for the radio, the last link with civilization was now broken and the *Norge* was on her own, flying northward.

The small cabin of the airship was crowded. In the front section was Lieutenant Horgen, Amundsen's disappointed reserve pilot of 1925, whose hands on the wheel of the side rudder held the ship on course. Oscar Wisting, ex-captain of the *Maud* and co-conqueror of the South Pole, was at the altitude rudder. Bent over his maps, Riiser-Larsen charted the flight and determined the ship's position. Pilot Riiser-Larsen was aboard in the dual capacity of navigator and second-in-command, alternating with Nobile in the over-all supervision of the flight.

Moving purposefully among his instruments, the meteorologist, young Finn Malmgren, made notes in a small black book. Near a window, sitting motionless and silent on an uncomfortable aluminum container, Roald Amundsen watched the panorama unfolding below. Co-leader Ellsworth relieved the helmsman and made himself useful in other ways. Standing silently, scribbling notes, some of which he passed now and again to the radio operator, was the journalist, Ramm.

Overlooking all, checking, observing and supervising was Nobile. His tenseness was hidden behind an appearance of calm as he gave orders in Italian and English, while his brown melancholy eyes darted from corner to corner of the cabin.

To the rear of the cabin Gottwald and Storm Johnson, last-minute substitutes for ailing Olonkin, were at the radio.[18] The other six men were scattered in different parts of the dirigible: Pomella was in the rear-motor gondola; Caratti in charge of a seldom used left engine, and at the right, taking turns, were Arduini and Norway's resourceful Omdal. Gray-haired mechanical wizard Cecioni was in over-all charge of the motors.[19] The rigger Alessandrini was hopping about the ship checking gas valves, examining the envelope, climbing, feeling, testing, watching. Of course, there also was Nobile's mascot, the terrier Titina, ill at ease in the crowded cabin.

News of the *Norge's* departure spread over the world and soon was received in Rome, where the skipper's wife, devout Carlotta Nobile, prayed in a little local church. It was received in Oslo, Leningrad, and New York. Anxious people, glued to their radios, waited impatiently for new reports.

Clear skies alternated with heavy layers of clouds as the *Norge* advanced, and Amundsen kept his eyes fixed on the never-changing sheet of ice he had come to know so well.

When they reached 87° 30′ northern latitude, a special message was received: Norway's King Haakon had conferred the Gold Medal for Meritorious Services on Birger Gottwald, radioman. The cheers, loud and heartfelt, were short-lived as the *Norge* approached 87° 43′, the terminal point of Amundsen's previous expedition. For twelve members of the crew this was just another lonely spot in an immense and forsaken icy desert; but the four who had fought for their lives there felt a sense of triumph mixed with gratitude. "We do not know whether we shook our fists or not," Amundsen said later, "it is most probable we took off our hats to our worthy opponent. Certain it is that we looked out on the humpy ice field with endless relief, knowing that we were over it and not on it."[20]

At midnight there were more cheers and handshakes, this time accompanied by toasts made with eggnog thoughtfully produced by Nobile. The occasion was the forty-sixth birthday of Lincoln Ellsworth.

One hour later, kneeling at an open window, sextant in hand, Riiser-Larsen followed the sun. "Ready with the flags," he said. Then, conscious of the impact of his words, he added simply: "Now we are there." It was 1:25 in the morning of May 12, 1926.

Fastened to an aluminum staff, the Norwegian flag was first to go down. As if saluting the men above, it unfolded in the light breeze before hitting the ice. There was no need for words as Amundsen clasped the strong hand of Oscar Wisting. The arms that had raised Norway's colors triumphantly on the South Pole had now dropped them at the opposite end of the world.

Ellsworth dropped the Stars and Stripes. Nobile disposed of a handful of flags: The colors of Italy, the pennant of the city of Rome, that of the Italian Aero Club and the *Stabilimento*.²¹

On they flew. Straining his eyes, Amundsen was on the lookout for new land as well as observing ice conditions, but there was no land, only the familiar fields of ice.

In the morning dense gray fog appeared. Its moisture penetrated clothes, chilling the men. As it settled on the ship's body, it condensed into ice. Under the growing weight chunks of ice broke loose, and the whirling propellers threw them violently against the canvas envelope of the dirigible.

For most of the day the *Norge* flew in this sea of fog. Visibility was poor, and time and again there came the sound of ice hitting the ship's body, slamming into it with vicious force. Coated with a thick layer of ice, the aerial snapped, and radio contact with the outside world was broken. Attempts at repairs failed—within fifteen minutes five spare aerials broke under the weight of the ice. Concern mounted in the anxious outer world and the New York *Times* spread headlines over four columns:

> Last report from Norge was sent from just beyond Pole, Norway asks naval vessels to stand by for Norge.

After an uninterrupted flight of almost two days, land was sighted at last. The coast of Alaska came into view. The *Norge* had reached her goal.

Shouting, waving people could be seen on the ground. Amundsen recognized the little town of Wainwright, Alaska, which once had held such a great disappointment for him. Omdal, too, recognized the tiny village.

Next day's edition of the New York *Times* had this to say:

> Broken message heard at St. Paul, Alaska, is thought to come from Norge, overdue at Nome. Contact not established.

Soon Wainwright was swallowed in the fog again and a rising gale buffeted the helpless ship, carrying her off course, over the invisible ocean. Navigation was extremely difficult as, caught in the grip of furious winds, the *Norge* rolled and pitched. By eleven o'clock in the evening, the ship was back over the coast, but the northerly gale had increased in strength and the ice-covered dirigible drifted with the wind, weakly pushed on by her straining motors.

Next day the New York *Times* headlined this story:

> Speculation as to whereabouts of Norge. Byrd makes ready for possible rescue expedition.

Through a break in the cloud cover over Point Barrow, Captain Wilkins saw a small moving object in the sky. He knew that it was the *Norge* and felt sadness at seeing others fly the trail he himself had confidently expected to blaze. Yet one thought was comforting: He had been right all along. The Arctic could be conquered by air.

At 3:30 in the morning of May 14, the *Norge* was over Cape Prince of Wales. Bouncing about, she was unexpectedly pulled down by strong air currents and started drifting sideways. Numb with cold, weary from strain, fatigue, and sleeplessness, the men aboard had reached the limit of their endurance. Their basic mission had been accomplished; if they could only land somewhere before a heavy wind carried them out into the Bering Strait!

Except for the motormen, the crew anxiously crowded into the main cabin. At seven o'clock Amundsen spotted a few houses along the coast. Could this be Nome? The houses were too few, there was no telegraph mast, and the coast did not look familiar. It was not Nome, but, still, they must land. "There is plenty of help," Riiser-Larsen said, "I see a whole lot of cavalry down on the shore."

Looking down once more, Amundsen shook his head. What Riiser-Larsen saw were some irregular brown furrows along the coast which his tired brain had mistakenly transformed into cavalrymen.[22]

The men braced themselves and the ship descended. Then something close to a miracle took place. As if giving up a losing fight, the wind suddenly stopped, and the air became calm as the *Norge* nosed gently down. People were running from all directions and grabbing the ropes which had been lowered from the dirigible. The *Norge* had arrived in Alaska at last. The door of the gondola opened and one by one the men jumped. "Where are we?" someone asked. "In Teller. This is Teller."

The seventy-two hour flight was at an end. For the first time in history, the polar ocean had been crossed. The earth had become truly round.

Some sixty miles away, Nome's population was still anxiously waiting for Amundsen. With the passing of time, the festive mood had become dampened, and gay banners reading "From Rome to Nome" decorating cobblestoned streets hung limp and forlorn. There had been no news from the *Norge*. Around the globe anxious men and women waited. They were waiting in Kings Bay, in Oslo, New York, in Rome and Stockholm.

With the landing in Teller the job of the leaders—Amundsen and Ellsworth—was done. There remained only the obligation to write a comprehensive account of the flight for the New York *Times*. Captain Gottwaldt finally succeeded in making himself heard by Nome's radio operator and therefore the next day's headline of the *Times* read:

Norge safe in Alaska after 71-hour flight. Forced down at Teller, found no new land.

Deflated, lying on ice-covered ground, the once-proud *Norge* resembled a beached whale. Looking at his ship, Nobile felt a faint sadness. It was his job to dismantle the dirigible. Bought back by the Fascist Government for $35,000, the Norge was to be *sent* back to Italy.[23]

In the small mining community of Kings Bay, life acquired aspects of normalcy again. Gone were the newspapermen and photographers; the men of Amundsen's support party had departed; the *Chantier* had sailed. Only a deserted hangar and the disused mooring mast remained as mute and abandoned relics.

4

Returning in triumph, two groups of brave men converged on the United States in June 1926. Both had a taste of public acclaim already, both knew that more was to come. Congratulations from all parts of the world had already reached Byrd. Six days, filled with receptions, speeches and banquets in London, had already passed. Now the *Chantier* was headed for New York, her crew enlarged by the addition of one man: Flight Lieutenant Bernt Balchen, on leave from the Royal Norwegian Navy. A grateful Byrd had offered him free passage and the promise of work in the New World. Standing on the deck of the ship, Balchen, newly appointed quartermaster, had all his possessions in a rucksack and confidently looked forward to life and work in the land of opportunity.

In the Pacific, the southbound steamship *Victoria* carried Amundsen and his party to Seattle. In anticipation of receptions and banquets Riiser-Larsen had wired the Norwegian consul, ordering new suits for all members of the expedition. Asked to supply measurements of the Italian crew members, Colonel Nobile had just shrugged his shoulders. His men did not need new suits, he said.[24]

Proceeding uneventfully across a stormy Atlantic, Captain Brennan brought the *Chantier* into New York Harbor ahead of schedule, catching the city's welcoming committee unready for a reception. Unrecognized, the little ship had to remain offshore for several hours before a tug brought the official representatives, senators and congressmen, journalists and photographers.

All that occurred during the following hours remained somewhat clouded in the minds of Byrd, Bennett and other members of the expedition, who found themselves submerged in a wave of fanfare and emotionalism. Mayor Jimmy Walker was there and so was Grover Whalen; there was the whistling of river boats, and ticker tape as an emotion-choked parade moved up Broadway to City Hall, past a mass of humanity which was waving, shouting and yelling enthusiastically. Left behind on the *Chantier* was one Bernt Balchen, an alien.

That same evening, in a ceremony attended by high-ranking officers, lawmakers and diplomats, Byrd received from President Coolidge the Hubbard Medal voted him by the National Geographic Society, an honor bestowed on only six men before him: Peary, Amundsen, Stefansson, Shackleton, Gilbert,²⁵ and Bartlett. (A special gold medal went to Floyd Bennett.)

The future held more honors in store, more oratory and more hero worship. Byrd's picture appeared in windows of delicatessen stores and groceries all across the country from New York to California. Winchester, Virginia, his home town, declared a special holiday, and a New York clergyman called the flight "a spur to religion" and an incentive to "the conquest of the spiritual poles."

There were five successive receptions in New York alone. No fewer than fifteen million people would see Byrd and Bennett in person, and on the twenty-third anniversary of the Wright brothers' first flight, the U. S. Senate passed a bill, awarding each man the Congressional Medal of Honor for "distinguishing himself conspicuously by courage and intrepidity at the risk of his life."

Advanced by special congressional action to the rank of full Commander, already talking of a flight to the South Pole, and with the memory of Spitsbergen growing dimmer, Byrd soon became used to hearing the ever-recurring refrain: "you are a national hero."

Without waiting for the cumbersome machinery of his Parliament to go into action, Premier Mussolini promoted Umberto Nobile to the rank of General. The New York *Times,* reporting wrongly, captioned a human interest story:

Nobile to head Italian Air Service. In command of all operations.²⁶

The old steamship *Victoria* which had once had Amundsen as a passenger before, and on which an unknown Ellsworth as well as a hopeful Wilkins had traveled north, was approaching Seattle.

Only this time some of the men aboard the vessel were no longer in quest of achievement. They were now men who had done what they had set out to do. Dressed in rough Alaskan suits, woolen shirts, and heavy shoes, Ellsworth and the group of Norwegians stepped to the rail to acknowledge cheers coming from crowded launches as the ship entered the harbor at Seattle.

Strangely the cheering crowd did not seem to notice them. Their waving and jubilant greeting was directed to another part of the deck. There, the stunned Ellsworth saw Nobile, wearing the "resplendent uniform" of an Italian officer, proudly lifting his arm in a well-executed Fascist salute to greet boatfuls of co-nationals, thoughtfully sent by the local Italian consul to greet him.²⁷

At the dock a crowd including representatives of the city had gathered, and a gaily-dressed little girl held a large bouquet of flowers. There was no doubt in her mind that the handsome officer was the leader of those daring men who were to be honored, and without hesitation she handed the flowers to Nobile, who accepted, convinced that all this tribute was his alone.

In Seattle, too, there were receptions and speeches, climaxed by an official banquet presided over by Mayor Landes, a woman. After that the *Norge* team split up. Ellsworth and the Norwegian contingent proceeded to New York in time to board the *Bergensfjord,* scheduled to sail for Norway. On orders received from Premier Mussolini, General Nobile embarked on a lecture tour in the United States.[28]

Triumphantly and with the most elaborate fanfare, Nobile passed through San Francisco, Los Angeles, Chicago, Cleveland, and Rochester. With a Fascist salute he acknowledged the cheers of more than three thousand Blackshirts in New York, where he proudly presented himself as a symbol of reborn Italy "marching to new glory under the leadership of Benito Mussolini"[29] to twelve thousand enthusiastic Italians crowding Manhattan's Lewisohn Stadium.[30]

This public acclaim was sweet to Nobile, while bitterness grew in Amundsen, who saw his chances of recouping financial losses incurred by the expedition steadily shrink as Nobile continued writing, lecturing, and pushing himself into the limelight. There were mutual accusations and recriminations which expanded into an ugly personal feud between the two. After all, Amundsen thundered, who is this newcomer, this General Nobile? Was he not a subordinate of Amundsen's? By what right did he try to push into anonymity such men as Ellsworth and Riiser-Larsen?

On July 19, the day Amundsen and his party were received by Norway's King Haakon, General Nobile told reporters at the Ritz-Carlton Hotel in New York: "I tried to be nice to Mr. Ellsworth, but I cannot help but feel that he was only a passenger whom I took aboard at Spitsbergen and left off at Teller." The general was confident and sure of himself. "We could have been successful without the contribution of Mr. Ellsworth," he added, "but without me the expedition would not have taken place and would not have been successful."[31]

Fast learning the technique of distortion, the man about to be carried to the summit of adulation by Mussolini's regime lost no time in rewriting history. In his speeches, books and articles he never mentioned that on two occasions the *Norge* had been kept from crashing, while he was at the controls, only by the intervention of his second-in-command, Riiser-Larsen. In a letter to the editor of the New York *Times,* Nobile even claimed that it was he who, in 1925, had conceived the idea of a dirigible flight to the North Pole and that plans were "well advanced" by the time Amundsen had approached him.[32]

Getting bolder, he later declared in a speech at a New York theater: "It was Mussolini who ordered the flight. The idea of using a dirigible in crossing the Pole originated with Italians, and the greatest responsibility for success or failure of the flight rested with Italians. Amundsen and Ellsworth and the others should have their share of the credit, but first of all it should go to Mussolini."[33]

The feud grew between the Norseman and the vain Italian.[34] Never again would the two men speak to each other, although their individual destinies would be fused forever in a great tragedy.

Amid the wailing of sirens and hooting of whistles, the gaily decorated liner *Conte Biancamano* brought the Italian contingent of the *Norge* to a hero's welcome in Naples on August 2. Honors were heaped on Nobile from all over the world. Twenty-four cities—including New York and Rome—made him an honorary citizen; France bestowed the Legion of Honor, Italy gave him her highest decoration—the Military Order of Savoy—and the main square of a mountain village near Naples was re-named "Piazza Umberto Nobile" to honor a native son who had made good. Mussolini embraced this man who had captured the imagination of millions and made him an honorary Fascist. Personified in handsome young General Nobile with those dark melancholy eyes, the world saw an Italy reborn to leadership and glory. At forty-one, Umberto Nobile, engineer, pilot, explorer and national hero, was at the summit of success.

To other men, the road to success was still barred; admitting defeat, Wilkins had stored his planes and equipment in Fairbanks and his expedition had returned to the United States. There were no banners to welcome the men on their return to Detroit. In the eyes of the world and their financial backers they were failures. The expedition was dissolved. In return for available equipment, Wilkins assumed responsibility for the $30,000 deficit. Having learned from mishaps and disappointments, he hopefully started planning resumption of work in the Arctic during the following year. The *Norge* had not sighted new land north of Point Barrow, but vast areas to the northeast and northwest were still unexplored, and a wide field for future activity still remained for Wilkins and Eielson.

A few months later a verbose but eloquent tribute to the heroes of May 1926 was inserted into the *Congressional Record*.[35] In it Amundsen's and Byrd's feats were put on the same level as the accomplishments of such explorers as Marco Polo, Columbus and Magellan. But in the midst of oratory and jubilation one vital and unasked question remained. Did Byrd's plane really reach the Pole?

Thirty-four years later, a Swedish investigator said: The "Josephine Ford" did not reach the North Pole on the famous flight in May 1926. Wind conditions and the plane's performance were such that Byrd could not have made the trip from Kings Bay to the North Pole and back within fifteen and one-half hours. Concluding his thorough study, Gösta H. Liljequist, Professor of Meteorology at the University of Uppsala continued:

> Commander Byrd's flight in the "Josephine Ford" gave inspiration to a generation of men interested in polar work. However, it would seem appropriate that a committee of aeronautical and meteorological experts be given access to the flight log and all available data to study the question whether in actual fact he did reach the Pole.[36]

This proposal, which amounted to an actual challenge, remained unanswered.

Soon after his return to Italy, Nobile initiated the construction of a new dirigible, designed to be three times as big as the *Norge*. Then, seeing a bright future ahead, he left for Japan to join an advance party headed by a young engineer named Trojani, which was assembling the airship N-3, recently bought from Italy by the Japanese Government. Before leaving, Nobile attended a reception in Milan. Mayor Belloni promised that his city would provide whatever financial support was needed, should Nobile ever want to make another expedition. Ernesto Belloni did not know that one day soon he would be called upon to keep his promise.

On his way to Japan, still accompanied by his dog Titina, Nobile again passed through the United States as an ambassador of good will for Benito Mussolini. Il Duce wrote:

> To General Nobile . . . I entrust the task of bringing to the Italians in America my own greetings and those of the new Italy. . .[37]

Nobile was received by President Coolidge. And once again there were speeches and an occasional hostile demonstration by anti-Fascists.

Aviation now held out promise of still more conquest and fame for Richard E. Byrd, triumphantly touring the United States. He was thinking of an expedition to Greenland, of a spectacular transatlantic flight, maybe even a flight to the South Pole.

The United States had a face of eager anticipation for Bernt Balchen. His first job was to go on display, together with the "Josephine Ford." It was a publicity stunt arranged by Byrd's promoters for Wanamaker's stores in New York and Philadelphia. Among his first big thrills was a dinner given by the Quiet Birdmen, an exclusive organization of aviators. There he met men still unknown to the world at large, Captain Spaatz, Lieutenant Doolittle, Major Arnold. He also met airplane designer Anthony Fokker and the court-martialed General Billy Mitchell, dressed in civilian clothes. When Balchen shook hands with him, Billy Mitchell asked: "You are with Byrd, are you not?" Balchen nodded. "Yes and no," he said; he had talked with the commander several times. Mitchell smiled faintly: "He is very well known," he said, "but nobody knows him very well . . . ."[38]

Next Balchen went with Bennett on a cross-country flight on the "Josephine Ford" to prove the safety of flying. In November the trip was over. The "Josephine Ford" had flown nine thousand miles, stopping at fifty American cities, in each of which Balchen had to sit through banquets, dinners, or lunches with the inevitable chicken à la king and green peas. The plane, built by Fokker, was delivered to Detroit, to become part of a permanent exhibit at the Ford Museum, and Bernt Balchen got himself a job as a test pilot for Anthony Fokker.

For the other men the end of the year 1926 brought toil, boredom, and disappointment: To recoup financial losses incurred by the *Norge* flight, Amundsen and Riiser-Larsen lectured. But most of the cream had been scooped off by Nobile; the famous flight had passed into history and people were more interested in the future.

5

On February 11, 1927, all but one member of a new arctic expedition headed by Wilkins left Seattle for Fairbanks. The second pilot, Alger Graham, accompanying two new Stinson planes, was to start out a week later. This time there was no cumbersome organization, no Board of Control, no committees of experts. Funds had come from the Detroit *News* and were supplemented by Wilkins himself.[39]

In Fairbanks it took two weeks to assemble the planes, equip them with skis and ready the necessary supplies. In a seven-hour flight, the plane called "Detroit I," piloted by Eielson and with Wilkins aboard, reached Point Barrow, which once more had been chosen to become the gateway to success—or failure. (The "Detroit II," with Alger Graham at the controls, would be following.)

In Italy, Premier Mussolini appointed bearded Italo Balbo as Undersecretary for Aviation. Balbo set out immediately to revitalize the Italian Air Force. He, like Valle, saw no future for slow-moving, bulky dirigibles. They required a small army of ground personnel for landing; too often they went up in flames, were torn from their moorings, or else broke up in flight. Mastery of the air belonged to heavier-than-air craft. Within a few weeks, Italo Balbo ordered suspension of work on Nobile's new dirigible.

In Canada, gold had been discovered. Enterprising prospectors and engineers were in a great hurry to transport men and equipment to sparsely

populated areas in northern Ontario. Western Canadian Airways provided
Fokker Universal planes for what might be called the first airborne gold
rush. The planes were equipped with skis, especially designed by Bernt
Balchen to withstand rough landings. With the coming of spring, floats
would be needed to replace the skis. Even before the floats were finished,
some of the planes met with accidents, and Balchen set out for Canada
with three mechanics. There, in the cold wilderness which to him was
home, he spent several weeks locating, repairing, and salvaging Western
Canadian Airways planes which had crashed in almost inaccessible places.
In March, Western Canadian hired Balchen as a pilot to transport fourteen
men and eight tons of material from Cache Lake to Fort Churchill.
Balchen's new mechanic was one Al Cheesman. By the middle of April
the contract was fulfilled.

From a Government report on Canada's civil aviation in 1927 the
following:

> . . . the operation was an unqualified success. . . . The decision during
> 1927 as to selection of Fort Churchill as the ocean terminus of the
> Hudson Bay Railway was made possible by these flights. There has
> been no more brilliant operation in the history of commercial aviation.[40]

On March 29, Wilkins's plane had been checked and tested. An extra
stove was placed under the engine, the oil was warmed and the engines
started. At six o'clock in the morning Wilkins and Eielson saluted three
companions left on the ground by dipping a wing, then circled and headed
north, disappearing in the hazy mist of a cold day. Their plan was to
fly northeast in search of new land. If there was no land, they would
look for a suitable floe to set the plane down on and take soundings
of the ocean. Shallow waters might indicate presence of nearby land.
(*See map on p.* 74.)

Aboard the plane there were 225 gallons of gasoline, ten pounds of
biscuits, twenty pounds of chocolate, and a thermos bottle of black coffee.
The men had a fish net, rifles, an axe, an ice pick, spare parts for
their engine, some tools, and extra clothes. There was also a short-wave
transmitter with a hand-driven generator.

They flew at an altitude of a thousand feet and at a speed of 82
miles an hour. As observer, Wilkins continually made notes. After all,
new land might be sighted at any minute.

> 8 A.M.: All O.K. Eielson seems happy and I have every confidence in
> him and everything else on board.[41]

Then the engine started kicking, knocked, and began to miss. Gently,
Eielson brought the plane down on three-foot-thick ice.

Through holes hacked in the ice, Wilkins and Eielson took a sounding.

Depth of the ocean: 16,400 feet—which meant that there was no land nearby.* For two hours both men worked in the minus-thirty-degree temperature, taking the engine apart and putting it together again. Four attempts to take off from the uneven ice failed, but on the fifth try they were airborne and headed back toward Barrow.

Clouds had gathered, and the wind was rising. The engine kicked again and stalled. Once more, there was nothing to do but to land. Again the motor was taken apart and reassembled. Eielson was working with the tips of four fingers frozen. One hour passed and the snow kept falling. Nevertheless, the plane was repaired and took to the air, rising through the howling of a biting wind. The steady roar of the engine had the sound of music for Wilkins and Eielson. It was twenty minutes past two o'clock in the afternoon and their fuel was sufficient for eight more hours of flight.

Wilkins noted:

> The food tastes good, everything O.K., but speed over the ice is painfully slow.[42]

The weather thickened. Sun, sky, and ice were hidden by a dense gray curtain, and toward seven o'clock ground observation became impossible. Wilkins scribbled:

> All gas now in top tanks. We should have enough for three hours.[42]

With gas dwindling and no visibility, Wilkins and Eielson were now flying at 5,000 feet, and all too conscious of dangers lurking below. At two minutes past nine o'clock their single engine stopped cold. There had been no warning sputter, no cough. The rhythmic vibrations simply stopped. Except for the howling of the wind there was silence, as Eielson tried to maintain the glide of the pitching plane.

Both men braced themselves, as the "Detroit I" sailed through a blanket of snow, headed downward, hit the invisible ice, bounced, and came to a standstill.

In the all-enveloping darkness a howling wind drove the snow wildly, piling it up in hillocks as high as a one-story building. Over the transmitter whose current meter failed to register, Wilkins tried to send a message:

> Went out 550 miles. Engine trouble. Forced landing three hours. . . . 65 miles N.W. Barrow.[43]

Weak and exhausted, the two men huddled in the cabin of their useless plane and attempted to sleep.

---

* Wilkins determined the greatest depth to be 17,850 feet, at 77° 45′N, 175° W, approximately 400 miles north of Herald Island.

On the following day, the snow still fell heavily and a cold thirty-mile-an-hour wind raced over the ice floe on which Wilkins and Eielson were caught. The order of the day was survival. The men had food and shelter, and with the half gallon of gasoline they had drained from the plane's tank, they lighted an improvised stove, using as wicks slats torn from the roof of the plane. For two days and two nights the wind howled and the snow continued. Their only hope of survival lay in marching toward land, a hike over eighty-odd miles of irregular ice, cut by treacherous leads, to the trading post at Beechey Point.

When, on April 3, they started their march the world had had no news of Wilkins and Eielson for almost six days. They moved out, pulling food and equipment on crude sleds made of cowling and corrugated duraluminum from the cabin of the cannibalized plane. They trudged for five hours, through waist-high snowdrifts, before they stopped and built a snow house. Eielson's hands were almost useless, his frostbitten fingers numb and the blistering skin turning black. They rested and then stumbled on, crawling and scrambling over ice blocks, crossing high, irregular hummocks and slushy leads, hidden by thin ice which gave menacingly under their feet. Wilkins's experience paid off. Their advance was purposeful and methodic, their morale high and their comradeship remained unbroken.

Five days later the ice became too rugged. Crushed, broken hills and piles formed impassable ridges and the sleds had to be abandoned. Discarding their normal clothes, Wilkins and Eielson dressed in Eskimo fashion. Carrying only essential supplies on their backs, they kept on with painful slowness. Breaking through snow-covered ice, Wilkins found himself up to the waist in freezing water before he could seize a solid ledge and pull himself out. Almost instantly his drenched clothes froze, becoming stiff and solid. However, stumbling, slithering, and crawling, Wilkins and Eielson continued their fight for survival against the cold and fatigue. On April 14, after twelve days, they came to a ridge higher than any they had encountered previously. Eielson's face mirrored discouragement, but arctic veteran Wilkins recognized the barrier for what it really was: The edge of shore ice, packed hard and forced up by the constant pressure of shifting sea ice. Beyond it should be land. With luck, they might see a wooden house in a day or two.

When they managed to cross the ridge, they saw before them a vast, unbroken plain of ice. There were no more hummocks and no more leads. Wilkins and Eielson were back on solid land. There was no longer any question of drowning, but only of losing strength and endurance. Then, there appeared a small house with a dog trail leading toward it. . . . When they reached the trading post of Beechey Point, they still had five pounds of food and a quarter of a gallon of gasoline.

It was noon of April 15, eighteen days after the plane had ventured out to probe the secrets of the Arctic. Wilkins and Eielson were back in the comfort of warmth, security, and human companionship. They learned that efforts to find them had been made: Graham had flown in search of them; radio operator Mason had been listening tirelessly for any sound coming from the frozen Arctic Ocean. He *had* received the faint messages Wilkins first dispatched, but then followed sixteen days, heavy with silence, during which waiting, listening and hoping had fused into frustration and helplessness.

Within a few hours after Wilkins and Eielson had reached the safety of Beechey Point's trading post, an Eskimo, Takput, was racing his dog team toward Barrow, carrying on his person a message for pilot Alger Graham.

On April 22, a week after setting out, Takpuk reached Point Barrow and delivered his message to Graham, who then flew his "Detroit II" to Beechey Point and returned with Wilkins and Eielson. At the price of an eighteen-day ordeal on the ice, the two had determined that for several hundred miles northwest of Point Barrow there was no land. The price was high and the results not spectacular, but any conquest of the unknown is the sum total of individual efforts.

Viewed from a historic perspective, however, most events of 1927 were overshadowed by what became known as "the great air derby." Commander Byrd was making preparations for a transatlantic flight in the "America," a big three-motored Fokker plane. But there were several other men who had the same objective.

On April 20 Byrd's "America" crashed during a test flight and Floyd Bennett was seriously injured; on May 12 Balchen flew Byrd's repaired plane to Roosevelt Field for final tests. That same day Charles Lindbergh arrived in New York.

Then, Lindbergh made his spectacular flight across the Atlantic and Commander Byrd postponed his flight to let the wave of enthusiasm subside before trying for headlines again. Preparations had cost his backers more than a quarter of a million dollars and the project could not be abandoned altogether.

On June 29, 1927, with the weather neither better nor worse than it had been on many previous days, the "America" finally took off on the much delayed transatlantic flight. At the controls was Bert Acosta, next to him relief pilot Balchen, only vaguely aware that his first papers did not make him an American citizen, or that he had left the country without permission from the State Department. It was Balchen who grabbed the stick from the fumbling Acosta, unfamiliar with instrument flying and saved Byrd's plane in a fog over the Atlantic. It was Balchen who piloted the "America" most of the way and finally ditched the plane with stoic calmness near the French coast.[44] There were celebrations, banquets and speeches in France. In the midst of all this, Balchen slipped off to Fokker's factory in Holland, to discuss essential modifications on a plane being built especially for use in the Antarctic.

When Byrd's group arrived back in the United States, there was a ticker-tape parade in New York, a reception in Washington headed by President Coolidge, and a ceremony in New York's Commodore Hotel at which Navy Secretary Wilbur pinned the Distinguished Flying Cross on the crisp white uniform of Commander Byrd.

Balchen, who had salvaged a measure of success out of the affair, got no medal. Not being an American naval officer, he was ineligible for a decoration. . . .[45]

On a summer day of the same year, Nobile was returning to Rome. His work in Japan was finished and he had added more honors and decorations to his collection. In Rome, however, he found himself surrounded by indifference. There was a saying at the *Stabilimento* that Nobile attracts enemies like "honey attracts bees."[46] Under the leadership of Italo Balbo, Italian aviation had been firmly committed to airplanes and Nobile was a "Dirigibilista." The general liked the power of command, the glare of publicity, he liked applause and adulation. He wanted to do something spectacular again. What about another expedition to the North Pole? He had mentioned such a plan to Riiser-Larsen in Teller already. Polite Riiser-Larsen had listened but said nothing. Why should not General Umberto Nobile—a man at the summit of success—lead an expedition of his own? Such a new expedition could place more emphasis on scientific work. What if he was not a scientist himself? What if he knew nothing about meteorology and radioactivity? He could easily gather a group of scientists willing to go with him. On such a new expedition there would be no one to challenge his leadership. Let the world see that he did not need Amundsen, that the Norseman had really only been a passenger aboard the *Norge!*

The general talked about a new polar expedition to engineer Trojani. "Would you be willing to come along?" he asked. Yes, loyal Felice Trojani was willing. But even he was not too enthusiastic at first. "You would make a mistake," he said, "by going on another such expedition. If it goes well, it will cheapen the first one by making it appear that a flight to the Pole and back is easy; if it does not go well, it will make people think that the success of the first was due to luck."[47] Felice Trojani would have liked to see Nobile do something new . . . such as a photographic survey of the Himalayas with a specially constructed dirigible. But he knew how stubborn the general was. And Nobile's mind was made up.

When Nobile submitted his proposal to Il Duce, he found Mussolini much less agreeable than he had been two years earlier. "I do not under estimate the merits of your proposal," Mussolini said, "but maybe it would be better not to tempt fate twice—let us talk about it again next week."[48] (Benito Mussolini had read Amundsen's accusations against Nobile, even though he had not permitted their publication in Italy.)[49] For Mussolini's purposes, another polar flight was useless. A repeat performance never brings the thrills of the original performance.

The two did not talk about this subject again, at least not for a year, and by then many things had changed. Instead, Nobile was referred for further discussion to Undersecretary for Aviation Italo Balbo, who just then was busy gathering funds for a larger air force.

In August, Bernt Balchen sailed for Norway on a mission for Commander Byrd to consult Amundsen about a projected expedition to the Antarctic and to obtain personnel as well as equipment.

In the Officers' Club at Horten Air Base a beaming Bernt Balchen was welcomed by his fellow pilots. There was Commodore Von der Lippe, chief of the naval air force, instructor Riiser-Larsen, former commanding officer Höver, Balchen's cousin, Dietrichson, former squadron mate Oscar Omdal. The Aero Club had a medal for him, and King Haakon invited him to the Royal Palace.[50]

In Bundefjorden, ten miles outside Oslo, stood the small house of Amundsen, the man known all over the world as "The White Eagle of Norway." There, in the presence of Omdal, Balchen discussed Byrd's plan for an expedition to the Antarctic. The *Samson*, Amundsen said, could well be used as a base ship. Amundsen knew the old sealer well; some thirty-four years earlier she was called *Viking* and had carried him on his first trip to the Arctic.[51]

When Balchen returned to the United States, he heard that Byrd had changed his plans: The F-7, a plane especially designed in Fokker's Dutch factory, was not to be used in the Antarctic. Instead, Byrd had decided on a three-motor metal aircraft, which was being built in the factory of financial backer Ford. Soon Bennett and Balchen went to Detroit to test the Ford plane, while the F-7 was sold to Amelia Earhart.

In Italy, Nobile was organizing his second expedition to the North Pole. Although declining to sponsor the plan outright, Mussolini's Government had promised co-operation for a privately financed expedition conducted under the auspices of a scientific organization. Nobile obtained backing from the Royal Italian Geographic Society, and across the letter in which the project was outlined to him, Mussolini wrote in bold letters: "No objection on my part."[52] Mayor Belloni remembered his promise, and the city of Milan raised needed funds.[53] Undersecretary Balbo released a sister ship of the *Norge* for another North Pole expedition, insisting, however, that the dirigible first be properly insured.

Wilkins too, wanted to go north again, to reach the goal he had set for himself. But he had no supporters or financial backers. He had only his own determination and the remnants of two previous expeditions: one Stinson and two Fokker planes—good aircraft, but not quite suitable for his purpose. Becoming his own financier and business manager, he sold two of his planes and purchased a new Lockheed *Vega,* the third ever built. Wilkins himself could act as mechanic, navigator, radio operator and publicity agent, but he did need a pilot. For the third time, Ben Eielson would go with Wilkins.

From a letter of George Wilkins:

> So with our new machine which is being built on the West Coast at Los Angeles, we expect to start out again next March and make a flight from Barrow toward Greenland, and will continue to Spitsbergen if new land is not found. . . . The new machine . . . will have a range of 3,500 miles and will fly at 140 miles an hour. I am choosing it because of its speed, its perfect streamline and its lightness. It weighs only 1,600 pounds empty.[54]

The Lockheed *Vega* was undergoing modifications. Extra tanks were installed, additional windows built, and all metal parts likely to interfere with the compass were eliminated from the navigator's cabin. The axles were strengthened and special skis constructed. Out of loyalty, Wilkins called his new venture the Detroit *News*–Wilkins Arctic Expedition, and the words were painted in dark blue letters on the deep-orange-colored fuselage of his plane. Gracious in its acceptance of this tribute, the Detroit *News* acknowledged Wilkins's good will, but stressed that it assumed no responsibility, financial or otherwise, for the new expedition.

6

When the year of 1928 came in, concerted work was going on in several cities. In Detroit, the metal Ford plane chosen by Commander Byrd for antarctic flying was undergoing modifications proposed by Bennett and Balchen after an initial series of test flights.[55] Target date: March.

In Berlin, the "Bremen," a Junkers monoplane was being readied for another attempt at an east-west crossing of the Atlantic.[55] Target date: March.

In Rome, feverish activity centered around preparations for an arctic flight by the dirigible N-4, a modified sistership of the *Norge.* Cigar-shaped, her silvery body bearing the name *Italia* in big black letters, the ship rested for the time in a hanger. The skeleton, made of steel, was a strong triangular strip running from bow to stern, with vertically placed girders separating airtight compartments, some for hydrogen, others for air. The skin was formed of overlapping panels of rubberized, aluminum-coated canvas.

At the tapered-down tail there were two horizontal fins, controlled manually from the control center of the ship. Air currents traveling along the body and encountering the resistance of these fins, would move against them, forcing a downward tilt of the ship's nose. Similar moveable fins, placed vertically, controlled the lateral movements of the dirigible. The brain of the ship was underneath: a cabin, open on top and suspended from the body by steel cables. In its front section there were the indicators and regulators of the ship's vital functions: manometers, speedometers, altimeters, rudder controls. The rear held a small radio compartment and a collapsible navigating table covered with maps, compasses, and charts. A narrow gangway ran the length of the ship and power was generated by motors housed in smaller cabins, also suspended under the main body of the dirigible.

Looking at the airship with a professional eye, Nobile's assistant, bespectacled engineer Trojani, did not like what he saw. The tail construction was similar to that of the N-3, which had been sold to Japan, but the canvas was lighter. Felice Trojani remembered how the tail section of the N-3 had once broken apart; he also did not care for the canvas envelope, which, he felt, should have been redesigned.

Nobile, however, was proud of the dirigible. Some one and a half tons lighter than the *Norge,* the *Italia* was capable of a maximum speed of seventy miles an hour, and Nobile considered her one of the best airships ever built.

Nobile was very busy assembling supplies and equipment, selecting a crew, fixing the flight route, and supervising reconditioning of the *Italia.*[56] In Norway he discussed with the veteran explorer Nansen what sleds and furs to use; Professors Sverdrup and Hoel helped him obtain clothes, sleds and sleeping bags. In Denmark, he ordered a food concentrate—pemmican—consisting of a mixture of dehydrated meat, vegetables and fat, compressed into individual one-half pound cakes and wrapped in aluminum foil.[57]

The crew was selected from volunteers among employees of the "Stabilimento," five of them veterans of the *Norge* flight. Arduini, promoted after the transpolar crossing, was made chief motor mechanic. Veterans Pomella and Caratti were joined by Nobile's chauffeur, Ciocca. Rigger Alessandrini was there, as was the master mechanic Cecioni, who would also assume the functions of a helmsman.

Officer personnel were recommended by Undersecretary for the Navy Sirianni. Nobile accepted two *Capitani di Corvetta* (Lieutenant Commanders.)* Round-faced Mariano and Zappi, energetic, somewhat self-righteous

---

* Foreign titles and their English equivalents are given only once; hereafter only the English equivalent is given.

and strongly religious. Both men had been friends for a long time, and for both the experience was to be the climax of their Naval careers since they had jointly applied for transfer to the Diplomatic Service.

Tall and handsome, *Tenente di Vascello* (Senior Lieutenant) Viglieri twenty-eight years old, was the youngest member of the expedition. The scientific complement had been recruited from three nations: Malmgren a Swede; Behounek, a Czech,[58] and Pontremoli, professor of physics a the University of Milan.[59] The Italian Navy loaned radiomen Biagi and Pedretti and also provided a base ship for the expedition, an old German vessel, renamed for the occasion *Città di Milano*. The skipper, *Capitano di Fregata* (Commander) Romagna-Manoja, had been especially detached from his post as Director of Genoa's Hydrographic Institute to assum command.

Felice Trojani signed a contract with the Royal Italian Geographi Society to participate in the expedition and in its preparation. Paragraph 3 of the contract bound him to strictest silence, prohibiting the writing of articles and granting of interviews for three years after his return to Italy. Nobile was not going to have Trojani do to him what he had done to Amundsen![60]

On March 19, 1928, there were twenty-eight people aboard when the *Italia* was hauled out of her hangar for a trial flight. Over the Mediterranean, an ingenious device was tested. It was a basketlike contraption which would permit the lowering of a man from the dirigible. Proudl Trojani entered it, but he soon looked ridiculous, for he found himself holding a squirming Titina, thrust upon him at the last minute by the whimsical Nobile. The test was a failure. A rope holding the device had to be cut, and the basket itself was abandoned to the calm water of the Mediterranean.

On a whim, Nobile flew the *Italia* to Milan, where no arrangement had been made to receive the dirigible. There the ship was left, while the men returned to Rome for a round of official visits with Fascis dignitaries and Pope Pius XI.

Deep in Canadian bush country, Balchen and Bennett were testing the Ford trimotor plane in subfreezing weather. Bernt Balchen found the plane wanting. To reach the altitudes required in antarctic flying new motors were needed, and to support the heavier engines, change in the basic design of the plane had to be made. Armed with their meticulously kept notes, Balchen and Bennett would go to Detroit to discuss the matter with Ford's unhappy engineers.

On March 19, while the *Italia* was flying to Milan, Wilkins and Eielson took off for Point Barrow in their overloaded plane. They did so without the glare of publicity and without speeches. This time they crossed the

Endicott Range with a comfortable margin of safety at an altitude of 11,000 feet. They landed, taxied their plane to the trading post, and were welcomed by old friends. They stayed for three weeks, waiting while suitable clothes were made, equipment tested, supplies sorted and stored aboard the plane, and the proposed course of flight from Alaska to Spitsbergen was charted.

Finally, after a three-day snowstorm, thirty Eskimos began shoveling snow from an ice-covered lagoon. Gasoline was taken on, and plans were made for an early start on April 7. But on that day, fighting strong head winds, the plane did not get off the ground. At the end of the icy runway it bounced off, careened sideways, and ploughed through a high bank of snow, finally coming to rest on a broken ski. It took four days to repair the plane and lengthen the runway. When this was done, the plane again failed. Hitched to a team of dogs, the plane was finally towed to nearby Elson Lagoon. There Wilkins, Eielson, and the Eskimos started on the backbreaking job of shoveling yet more snow to prepare a new and longer runway.

On April 12, 1928, Wilkins and Eielson were still clearing a runway on frozen Elson Lagoon. Bennett and Balchen had completed their test flights and were taking a yet unnamed Ford plane back to Detroit. In Milan, where unfavorable weather forecasts had forced Nobile to postpone departure of the *Italia,* the hours were filled with pompous speechmaking, redolent with chauvinism:

> *Italia,* child of Italian genius, imbued with the strength of a multithou-sand-year-old tradition, blessed by God, protected by the Cross of Christ, by the colors of a mighty nation, reborn under the sign of Fascism. . ."[61]

The modest Trojani recoiled from such pompous verbosity; he would have liked to see deeds precede speeches, but the hangar was crowded with visitors and well-wishers. Among them was Trojani's beautiful blond wife, Marta, who was aghast when she saw the dirigible. "Gee," she said, "this is only a paper balloon with heavy motors and a smell of pharmacy!"

On the same day, a Junkers monoplane took off from Dublin's Baldon-nel Airport. It was the "Bremen," with a crew of four, setting out on a second attempt to cross the Atlantic from East to West.

When Balchen and Bennett, their mission in Detroit completed, arrived in New York, they saw big newspaper headlines announcing that the 'Bremen" fliers had come down in Labrador. The landing had not been quite according to plan and receptions scheduled in New York had to be postponed, but at least no lives had been lost this time. Bennett shrugged his shoulders and headed for his home in Brooklyn.

Nobile's base ship, *Città di Milano,* was on her way to Spitsbergen, while the *Hobby,* chartered from the Norwegian Government, was taking additional supplies and men to Kings Bay. Weather conditions caused delays everywhere; twice the crew of the *Italia* was alerted and twice the departure was canceled. In the dead of night, at 1:55 A.M., April 15, the dirigible finally became airborne, when only a few people were at the airport to see the flight off. Hardly anybody knew that Nobile was taking the *Italia* on a hazardous journey without insurance. Contrary to what he told Balbo, Nobile had deliberately omitted taking out insurance for the airship loaned by the Italian Government.[62]

Rising over a sleeping Milan, the small airship, carrying twenty men and a dog, set a northerly course. The first destination was Stolp, Germany. The *Italia* flew over Venice and crossed into Jugoslavia, where she sailed into a storm. Hidden in black clouds, the craft was tossed about violently and under the impact of the ferocious winds a vital metal structure of the airship's base broke. Located at an inaccessible point, the damage could neither be repaired in flight nor its extent estimated. There was sun over Hungary and strong counterwinds with torrential rain over Austria. As she passed into Czechoslovakia, closed in by heavy clouds, the *Italia* was tossed about in a thunderstorm. Miraculously dodging flashes of lightning, the airship, full of inflammable hydrogen, skimmed over the mountain peaks. In the afternoon a battered and bruised *Italia* was cruising aimlessly over wide flat country, somewhere in Central Europe, having eluded both storm and lightning. The navigator had lost his bearings, and Nobile did not know where he was. The question arose: Had the ship crossed the Sudeten mountains or drifted south toward Venice? If the dirigible was past the mountains, more flat country was ahead and she could proceed to Stolp. If not, it would be an inglorious limp back to Milan. At Katowice, Poland, the radio station informed Nobile of his position and a weather report assured him of favorable meteorological conditions. Anticipating no further difficulties in reaching Stolp, the exhausted general retired to sleep, while the *Italia* flew on.

Meanwhile a mild wind blowing from the North gently rippled the Elson Lagoon near Point Barrow, Alaska. Wilkins and Eielson carefully poured warmed oil into the preheated tanks of their plane, which bore license number X 3903. The sky was overcast, but the barometer was holding steady. When all preparations were finished, Eielson climbed into the cockpit and turned on the ignition. Wilkins swung the propeller around, the engine coughed and then filled the air with a steady roar. Wilkins hurried inside the plane, which began gliding over the uneven surface. Soon the plane raced along at a speed of seventy miles an hour, its swaying tail barely missing high snow banks piled up on each side of the fourteen-foot-wide runway. The plane rose, bounced once and gracefully climbed into the air.

"Wonderful takeoff. How's everything?" Wilkins scribbled on a piece of paper.

"Everything great!" Eielson yelled back. "She handles fine . . ."

On they flew, over broken shore ice and drifting pack, at an altitude of 500 feet, ground speed 100 miles per hour, anxiously watching for signs of new land. Their destination: Spitsbergen.

Like a huge wall a dark cloud bank came up, blotting out an area of at least 100 miles, while the X 3903 continued on her course, rising to an altitude of 3,000 feet. Then, as the clouds opened up, there was still more ice, cut by open leads. "We felt certain then and believe now that no mountainous land exists between Grant Land and the North Pole," Wilkins later wrote.[63]

Fuel consumption was high. Eielson passed a note to Wilkins: "We are using approximately eighteen gallons an hour. Now about forty gallons left in wing tanks." Wilkins knew that at the start there had been enough gasoline for a total flying time of twenty-four hours. If they were to succeed, there could be no detours and navigation had to be accurate.

After thirteen hours of flight, Grant Land was sighted. The exploratory part of their mission was over and only the end of the flying remained. If they could reach Spitsbergen, the feat of the *Norge* would be equaled; a single-engine plane would have proven to be as good as a dirigible.

The exhilarated Wilkins, flying over the area from which Peary had left for the Pole, poured himself a cup of coffee and munched on a piece of pemmican. Ominous black clouds now rose skyward in their path, indicating a storm over Greenland.

In a note to Eielson, Wilkins wrote: "There are two courses open. We are above storm now. Down there we can land and wait until it's over. Can we get off again? If we go on, we will meet storm at Spitsbergen and perhaps never find the land. Do you wish to land now?"

Pilot Eielson's answer came promptly: "I'm willing to go on and chance it."

A mountain on the northernmost tip of Greenland disappeared in the mist and the ashen grayness which now covered the horizon was recognized by Wilkins for what it was: an arctic storm. Clouds raced in the sky as the small orange-colored plane turned, twisted, and climbed in a desperate effort to escape the hostile elements.

Eielson climbed to 8,000 feet, but impenetrable clouds reached still higher. There were still 200 miles between disaster and safety, 200 miles of water and ice, covered by the cloud mass reaching high into the sky.

Through a break in the cloud blanket, two sharp mountain peaks appeared. Dangerous and forbidding, yet they were part of land and somewhere behind them was the fulfillment of their hopes. Violent winds rocked and tossed the plane, threatening to smash it against the mountains, as Eielson came down to within a few feet of the ice-covered water.

Fuel was running low and the windshield was frozen over. There had to be a landing. But where and how? A snow-covered spot apparently smooth enough to land on came into view, but the instant Eielson saw it, he was past it and the plane was heading straight toward a mountain wall. Swerving sharply, Eielson avoided a crash, turned, circled, leveled out and blindly went down into a sea of swirling snow.

Miraculously, the X 3903 came to a smooth landing, and both men climbed out into a raging blizzard which limited visibility to a few feet.[64] They were deafened from the plane's steady, monotonous droning and their limbs were stiffened from cramped positions in the narrow cabin. They had work to do and it had to be done fast: Tanks had to be drained before the oil froze and snow had to be packed against the skis before the wind hurled the plane over on its side. When this was done, the two weary men climbed back into the cabin. "Thank God, the machine's safe!" Wilkins yelled. Eielson nodded. There was no need for talk.

It was Monday, April 16, 1928. For Wilkins and Eielson the shortest distance had been a straight line leading over unknown regions, from Point Barrow to an uninhabited island in the archipelago of Spitsbergen. Sleep came to both men; it came not as an escape from fear, but with the warmth of a well-earned triumph. Shifting direction and stopping at times, only to start again with renewed violence, the storm lasted for four days and five nights, keeping the men prisoners, while the world had no word from Wilkins.

On that same Monday of April 16, 1928, the battered semideflated *Italia,* her canvas covered with ice, was finally hauled into the Seddin hangar near Stolp by the strong arms of some German soldiers, on their third attempt. For the *Italia* the margin between defeat and victory had been a 1,200-mile course from Milan to Stolp, which had led over mountains and valleys and through very bad weather.

Welcomed by German and Italian authorities, General Nobile was proud of the trip. Satisfied with his ship and with himself, he was whizzed off for a round of official receptions.

A mission was under way to bring relief to the "Bremen" fliers downed on Greenly Island, Labrador. The men were safe where they were, it was just a question of saving the plane. The editor of the New York *World* was anxious to get a first-hand interview with the stranded men. Ever conscious of publicity, Commander Byrd offered his Ford plane and Floyd Bennett, weak with influenza, insisted on flying it. With him as copilot was Bernt Balchen, also sick. On April 16 both men arrived in Detroit to take possession of the aircraft and were ordered at once to the hospital. Two days later a weak Balchen was at the controls

Some crew members of the *Italia*. Standing, front row, from right: Zappi, Mariano, Nobile, Behounek, Viglieri. Sitting, extreme left, Trojani.

of the plane which carried fuel, spare parts and a reporter, Bennett riding beside him.

It was cold and drizzling, but Bennett was hot and perspiring, his thin body convulsed by violent coughing, his head spinning as he kept on dozing off. In Murray Bay, he had to be carried off the plane in a semiconscious state; influenza had caused pneumonia. The following day Balchen flew on alone.

It was not possible to repair the *"Bremen"* on blizzard-raked Greenly Island and the plane was pulled to the mainland, there to be left for the time being. On April 25, toward eleven o'clock in the morning, Warrant Officer Floyd Bennett, wearer of the Congressional Medal of Honor, died of pneumonia in a small hospital near Murray Bay.

On Saturday, April 21, there still was no news of Wilkins and Eielson. For more than a week there had been no word about them in the newspapers, which were still busy headlining the rescue of the *"Bremen"* fliers.

That day, the weather improved in the Spitsbergen region. Strong winds subsided and blinding snowdrifts turned into a soft white carpet. Climbing out of their plane, Wilkins and Eielson started shoveling snow and hacking ice, freeing their aircraft and building a runway. After six hours of work, the engine was started and the whirling propeller began humming once more. But the plane would not move. Even though there were only two men and twenty gallons of gasoline aboard, the X 3903 simply would not budge.

Wilkins jumped out, and bringing his full weight to bear against the tail of the plane, he started pushing, while Eielson opened the throttle. Slowly the plane began inching forward, gradually gaining speed. Clinging to the open door, Wilkins tried to climb in, slipped and fell, as Eielson took to the air alone. The surprised pilot circled and came down to a landing again. They had to try some other way. Next time, after pushing the plane, Wilkins was to grab a rope fastened to the cabin door and pull himself into the moving aircraft. Straining hard, Wilkins pushed again, the engine roared and the plane once more started moving. Wilkins's hands were numb with cold and he could not maintain a firm grip; grabbing the rope with his teeth, he tried to pull himself into the plane which was jerking along on the uneven surface. Once again he slid, fell, and, struck by the tail of the aircraft, was hurled into waist-deep snow, where he remained, stunned and half-buried.

Again Eielson turned around and landed. Once more fragile skis hit the rough ridges of an ice-covered ground; the plane jumped, swayed and finally came to a stop, undamaged. The engine had been running for close to an hour and most of the fuel was used up. There was time for only one more attempt. If that failed, Eielson would have to fly on alone and Wilkins would have to wait for rescue at a later time.

With one leg in the cabin door, holding on to the wall and straining every muscle of his body, Wilkins pushed down against a piece of driftwood, ramming it hard against the ice. In the freezing weather his body was covered with perspiration. Stirred up by the propeller, a fine mist of snow blew back and the motor was roaring, but the plane did not budge.

There was an unending minute of extreme physical effort, then suddenly the quivering, straining plane lurched forward and, gliding along, gained speed and became airborne. Pulling himself up, the utterly exhausted, bruised and panting Wilkins dropped to the floor, while the monotonous drone of the engine cut the silence of the Arctic. Soon Wilkins saw, from 3,000 feet, the welcome sight of two tall radio masts rising out of a group of small houses in the distance.

"Must be Green Harbor, go over and land where you think best," he scribbled and passed the note to Eielson. Now there was only a five-mile stretch of open water and a mountain, until the plane circled and came down on smooth ice, over which two Norwegian flags waved in the cold breeze. It was the moment of triumph. The Arctic Ocean had been spanned and the first flight from Alaska to Spitsbergen was over.

Shortly Wilkins sent out his first telegram:

> Reached Spitsbergen after 20½ hours flying. One stop account bad weather. . . .

Within three hours, messages started pouring in at Green Harbor. There was a wire from the U. S. Secretary of State, congratulations from the Secretary of War, telegrams from kings, premiers, ambassadors and greetings from friends.

In newspaper offices all over the world headlines were being composed. The New York *Times,* featuring a map and a photograph, devoted most of the first two pages of its Sunday edition to what it called in a subcaption "the greatest feat of all aviation," and printed glowing tributes from Ellsworth, Byrd and Stefansson. Amundsen was quoted as saying: "No flight has been made anywhere, at any time, which could be compared with it."

Comfortably settled in the wooden house of Mr. Ihlen, manager of Spitsbergen's Government Radio, Wilkins and Eielson exchanged toasts with newly made friends. For both a dream had finally become reality as some 1,300 square miles of the earth's surface, never before seen by man, were spanned by air, even if no new land had been sighted on which weather stations could be established.

Wilkins said:

Whatever else we may have accomplished through our efforts, we will learn only as time goes on. Eielson and I have learned, at all events, the sincerity of friendship.[65]

The ambition of a lifetime seemed satisfied, and Wilkins again started thinking of an antarctic expedition. But before he could do anything else, he had to stop and accept awards which enthused individuals and organizations were ready to bestow on him and Eielson.

Nobile is said to have praised Wilkins warmly, although expressing himself "guardedly in regard to the scientific value of the enterprise." In an interview he reaffirmed his faith in dirigibles, which he still considered preferable to planes.

Marooned in ice-locked Green Harbor, Wilkins and Eielson waited for the *Hobby,* which at that time was still discharging Nobile's cargo in Kings Bay. But awards were already being announced. Wilkins was given the Samuel Finley Breese Morse gold medal, the highest recognition the American Geographic Society could offer. In a characteristically modest gesture, he cabled:

Am more than honored by your announcement and sincerely appreciate this acknowledgment of work done by Eielson and myself.[66]

By the end of the month, the *Italia* was flight-ready again. In Ny Alesund the *Norge's* hangar and mooring mast were already repaired and an advance party was on the spot. This included the general's brother, meteorologist Amadeo Nobile, and peppery Captain Gennaro Sora from Italy's crack Sixth Alpine Regiment. Still missing was the *Città di Milano,* baseship of the expedition, whose skipper Romagna-Manoja waited for Kings Bay harbor to become icefree.

Bad news came from Russia. Professor Eredia, sent to Leningrad to make arrangements for transmission of weather reports, brought back the unanimous opinion of Russian meteorologists: Chances for good weather in polar regions during May and June were extremely poor. No news came from Kings Bay. The radio station there was unmanned.[67]

Nobile grew restless. The flying season was short and in his exposed position he could not afford to miss it. In urgent telegrams he asked Commander Romagna to proceed without delay for Kings Bay. On May 2 a pompous bulletin was released aboard the *Città di Milano,* finally near its destination:

Yesterday at eleven in the morning after having forced for itself an opening in steadily thickening ice, the strong stern of the ship has become firmly wedged in at 1100 meters from the small coal pier. Repeated attempts to break through . . . have permitted to gain only

50 meters in ice 1½ meters thick. Anxious hearts and strong arms wait to see the dirigible *Italia* "resplend in the sky amidst the budding crown of surrounding snow-covered peaks . . ."[68]

At 3:28 in the morning of May 3, after two false alarms and some farewell broadcasts, the *Italia* was finally off, on her way to Vadso. Flying lazily over the Baltic, the dirigible was met by an honor escort of three Swedish planes.[69] Over Stockholm's suburb of Appleviken, Malmgren dropped a letter for his mother. Passing over Finland, the *Italia* reached Vadso, where she was moored to a mast, her nose badly crumpled from an awkward maneuver.

General Nobile was not the man to let a chance for publicity slip through his fingers. According to the Boston *Herald* he invited Wilkins and Eielson to participate in the exploratory flight of the *Italia*. Declining gracefully, Captain Wilkins is quoted as having said: "I do not quite understand why he intends performing what Amundsen and he have already completed."[70]

After some delay caused by bad weather, the *Italia* finally left Vadso on the evening of May 5 and some fifteen hours later appeared in the sky over Kings Bay. There, a fickle wind made hangar entry impossible, and the ship, one of her motors out of commission, had to remain precariously moored at her mast. Quite unconcerned, most members of the ground party went aboard the *Città di Milano* for dinner, abandoning the dirigible to the whim of the powerful wind. The distance from Ny Alesund to the dock in Kings Bay was not great, but without skis it could have taken two hours to cover it.

When the wind subsided, a shrill emergency whistle summoned the local miners to help, and their strong Norwegian arms (rather than those of Romagna's Italian sailors) pulled the *Italia* down to safety. Her nose again broken, the ship finally came to rest in the roofless hangar.[71] Utterly fatigued Felice Trojani finally threw himself on a bed in the house of the mine's physician. He had been unable to get anything but occasional snatches of sleep for more than one hundred and fifteen hours . . .

On May 10, repaired and checked, the *Italia* was once more airworthy. These days Nobile was nervous, irritable and given to making irrational statements. "I don't need anybody," Trojani had once heard him shout in a fit of anger, "my will is sufficient!"[72] He now assembled his men for the first of three exploratory flights.

It took fifteen hours of tiresome waiting in the hangar until the flight was finally on. Leaving behind scientist Behounek, Nobile took off with fourteen men and his dog, to explore the territory of Severnaya Zemlya.

Passing over Dane Island, Trojani quietly took off his cap in a salute to the three pioneers of the Arctic who had once started from there, never to come back. He well remembered the story of Salomon Andrée, Nils Strindberg and Knut Fraenkel.

About eight hours after takeoff the *Italia* was back in her hangar at Ny Alesund. From a telegram of meteorologist Finn Malmgren:

> . . . happy home after unsuccessful flight in heavy wind with snow and ice. . . . We are ready for a new trial. . . .[73]

Largely responsible for the failure was a badly frayed cable leading to the directional rudder.[74]

Next, heralded by strong winds, a blizzard swooped down on Ny Alesund and a gray sky poured down snow. It came like a heavy curtain, obliterating visibility, hiding supplies piled up along the hangar and accumulating on the *Italia* at the rate of one ton an hour. Ballast was removed and more gas was fed into the dirigible, but the snow kept falling. The ship, straining and groaning, was in danger of being squashed into the ground like a bug. Wielding brooms, sticks and other improvised devices, over a hundred men—soldiers, sailors and miners—climbed over the *Italia,* sweeping and shoveling steadily.

The snow fell for two days and the men shoveled for two days. A tired, tense Nobile, still largely inexperienced in the ways of the Arctic, toyed with the idea of seeking escape from the wrath of the elements by taking his ship into the air, there to ride out the storm.

When the storm was over, the envelope of the dirigible, bruised and scuffed by hundreds of heavy feet, was inspected. Damaged areas were patched and again the general waited.

On the morning of May 15, the *Hobby,* on her way south and carrying Wilkins and Eielson, docked at Tromso. At the same time, Nobile's men, again assembled in the hangar at Ny Alesund, waited for repairs of an oil line to be completed. There were twelve hours of tedious waiting before the *Italia* was airborne. Aboard were sixteen weary, tired men, the dog and also some 2,500 gallons of gasoline, an abundance of food, equipment, supplies and instruments—the latter including a motion-picture camera which nobody knew how to operate. One journalist had been scheduled to come along and the choice was determined by the flip of a coin. A journalist named Lago had won, but General Nobile reversed the verdict of fate. In a dictatorial manner he gave the nod to Cesco Tomaselli, representative of the *Corriere della Sera.*[75]

The flight plan envisioned exploration of a triangular area between Spitsbergen, Franz Josef Land and Severnaya Zemlya. The estimated distance was 4,350 miles; flying time, perhaps two days.

Heading north, the *Italia* flew again over Dane Island and Virgo Bay, with their memories of Andrée's ill-fated expedition; following the coast of Northeast Land, Spitsbergen, she had on her right the two small islands Broch and Foyn; then the airship entered a fog-shrouded, unexplored area. The men aboard the dirigible kept searching for the nonexistent Gillis Land.[76] Within sight of Franz Josef Land, the ship turned southeast and entered still another unexplored zone.

Fatigue rode heavily on Nobile's shoulders after three sleepless nights. However, journalist Tomaselli was excited. "Think how we will be able to talk about all the things we have seen!" he said, turning to Trojani.

"As far as I am concerned," Trojani, then at the helm, answered dryly, "I'll be able to say that I have seen the altimeter most of the time."

There was no new land anywhere, only ice and intermittent fog. Fighting a strong head wind, the dirigible was consuming far more gasoline than had been anticipated, and turning back toward Spitsbergen, Nobile had to abandon his plan to survey Severnaya Zemlya from the air. He thus missed his chance to make an actual geographic discovery: Severnaya Zemlya is not an unbroken stretch of land, as then current maps showed, but a group of islands.

For Tomaselli the flight was too smooth; he would have preferred it to be spiced with excitement and adventure. For Trojani it brought a sense of exhilaration as he steered the dirigible over unexplored territory. General Nobile was both tired and dejected. He was also worrying about the landing maneuver.

"Well," Trojani asked Tomaselli, as the dirigible approached Ny Alesund, "how did you like the flight?"[77]

"Wonderful, but too quiet. Almost like a bus ride. . . ."

"True," said Trojani, "but didn't you notice that we almost broke our necks?"

Journalist Tomaselli had not noticed what Trojani knew: something was wrong with the dirigible. Returning with only some 350 gallons of gasoline, the ship was lighter than it had been on departure and thus should have been rising. But it did not. So, there must be a heavy layer of ice, a hydrogen leak or both. Nevertheless, Trojani was still content. After the sixty-nine hour flight he was proud of the aeronautical feat, and his pride was only slightly marred by the lack of any geographical discoveries. This time he felt no pang of fear, as he usually did at the end of a flight and always did before each start. He felt only the glow of contentment.

IV. DISASTER

1928

1

By May 22 preparations for the final phase of Nobile's expedition, which had been going on for two days, were all but complete.[1] The polar flight had been built up to appear to the public as the climax to a daring venture; yet everybody connected with it knew that it was only another aeronautical display, complete with ceremonial dropping of flags and dispatching of triumphant messages, undertaken primarily for its publicity value. To be sure, there was a plan to have some members of the crew descend on the ice, but Trojani, for one, did not believe that it would be attempted.[2] Such a descent indeed would have been a revolutionary feat, and might have made possible the gathering of important scientific data, but the crew of the *Italia* had been given no training for this, and the single attempt to lower a man-bearing basket from the dirigible—not on ice but into the calm water of the Mediterranean— had been a flat failure.

The weather was tricky. Wind and fog followed clear beautiful days during which a blue sky hung serenely over the *Italia*. Nobile, the man in command of the expedition, slight, intense and nervous, wearing his gold-braided general's uniform, kept on moving about relentlessly, while waiting for favorable flight conditions.

Tromso's meteorological station forecast good weather for May 22, and Nobile made up his mind. Barring unforeseen developments, he would start within a few hours. The crew was sent to sleep, with orders to report, ready for flight, at eleven o'clock in the evening.

But sleep did not come to Trojani, caught in the grip of fear, this time stronger and more oppressive than ever. Nor did it come to Nobile, busy checking the roster of his crew. The jovial radioman, Biagi, was essential and so were naval officers Mariano and Zappi. The rigger, Alessandrini, motor mechanics Arduini, Caratti, Ciocca and Pomella were absolutely indispensable, and so was Trojani and chief mechanic Cecioni. The expedition leader had decided that all three scientists were to participate in the flight. After all, this had been billed as a scientific undertaking! Of course, for propaganda purposes the general considered the presence of journalist Lago essential. (The man represented the Duce's own newspaper *Il Popolo d'Italia*.) Yet, it might be necessary to reduce the load of the dirigible. Gasoline, oil, rations and equipment could not be cut down. There was one possibility only: Lieutenant Viglieri might have to be left behind. The pleasant, handsome six-footer, youngest among the crew of the *Italia,* had been taught photography in a few easy lessons so that he could double as official photographer as well as being navigation aide. Nobile shrugged his shoulders. It is important to lessen the load, so Viglieri stays behind.

A white night descended over Ny Alesund, as local miners and men from the expedition's base ship milled around on the snow-covered field in front of the hangar, waiting.

As had been foreseen by Mussolini, the world at large showed little interest in another flight to the North Pole, and only a few papers had made arrangements for direct coverage. The May 23 edition of the New York *Times* devoted fifty-eight lines of the second column on page six to three news items: Twenty-nine lines were needed to report on attempts being made to save the Irving House; the fatal accident of one Patrick J. O'Connor, killed by an elevator in New York's McAlpin Hotel, rated fourteen lines. Sandwiched in between was a fifteen-line story, headlined: "*Italia* set for polar flight. Nobile, despite unfavorable weather, sticks to his plan."

At 10:30 in the evening, and again some three hours later, Tromso's meteorological institute reported that weather conditions along the proposed flight route remained favorable. By 2:30 in the morning the general had made up his mind and forthwith ordered the gas chambers of the *Italia* to be fed more hydrogen. After this was done, a hissing sound was clearly audible in the hangar. Through a tear near the stern, gas was escaping, causing still another delay. The hole was patched and once more the ship was inspected. Finally, one by one, the members of the crew climbed aboard.

Toward four o'clock in the morning the *Italia* was pulled out of her hangar. There she stood, her silvery body glistening under the open clear sky. The chaplain of the expedition recited a prayer. Hands crossed, head bowed, Nobile stood solemnly near the priest and next to Romagna, skipper of the *Città di Milano*. A few paces away was young Viglieri, the picture of dejection. The general changed his mind: "All right, Viglieri," he said, "get in."

The lieutenant did not waste any time, his long legs carried him fast, and the hands of his companions pulled him in. He was inside the ship, in exchange for five cans of gasoline which had to be thrown out. Nobile was lifted into the cabin. Remaining at the open door, he looked around and then gave the command: "All clear . . . let her go."

The general saluted, the door was closed, lines were released, there was waving and shouting as the *Italia* ascended into the blue sky. Moving slowly, the ship looked like a huge silvery fish. It was twenty-eight minutes past four o'clock in the morning of May 23, 1928.

For two hours they flew northwestward, seeing nothing below but water; then they headed toward Greenland. Shortly before seven o'clock they were over an endless desert of pack ice. Winds increased, fog descended and, staying at an altitude of some 600 feet, the ship flew on for more

The *Italia* in flight.

than six hours above a smothering sea of gray clouds. To Professor Behounek, the fog looked like a mass of huge cotton balls, which, illuminated by the rays of a weak sun, reflected the shadow of the slowly moving *Italia.* Then the clouds thinned and heavy winds began lashing the ship from the rear. At three o'clock in the afternoon, the men sighted the snow-covered coast of Greenland, rising out of the ocean under a blue sunny sky. Nobile now changed course and headed for the North Pole.

Viglieri was on the steering rudder; at the chart table round-faced Mariano and intense Zappi traced the ship's course. Trojani and Cecioni were taking turns at the elevator controls. On a chart fixed to the wall of Biagi's radio compartment, meteorologist Malmgren kept on recording weather data. Behounek and Pontremoli watched their instruments. Over narrow gangways leading from the main cabin to the motor gondolas, Arduini made his rounds, checking and inspecting the motors—oil pressure, gasoline consumption. Pomella was nursing the rear motor, Ciocca was in charge of the right, Caratti was handling the left. The journalist, Lago, was staring out of a window. There was little to see. Only now and again he made some notes. The man in command stood in the front section of the main cabin, watching.

Time dragged on slowly as the men worked in silence, their hands growing numb from cold. Tea froze in thermos bottles and was consumed in solid chunks, and hamburgers, which had turned into cold rocks, had to be warmed in trouser pockets to become edible. All around there was the howling and hissing, the whistling and moaning of the fierce wind all but drowning out the monotonous drone of the motors.

The flight continued. Toward ten o'clock dark and menacing clouds appeared on the horizon. A half hour later the Italia crossed the 88th parallel. The general was worried about the wind. True, it was now coming from the rear, but once they reached the Pole and headed back, they would be facing it. This would retard their flight, and they would have to use more gasoline . . . Perhaps they should take an alternate route and go on to Alaska or Novaya Semlya . . . .

"What do you think, Malmgren?" he asked.*

The meteorologist was confident. "This wind will not last long," he said, "It will turn, and when we fly back to Kings Bay we will have it in our rear again."

"Still," Nobile insisted, "should we not play it safe and fly with the wind?"

Malmgren shook his head and the troubled Nobile remained silent.

---

* Conversations quoted throughout this account are all authentic. They are quoted faithfully from printed accounts of participants, except where otherwise indicated.

His instinct had collapsed when confronted with the opinion of an arctic expert.

As the ship flew on, the men became more intent and their tiredness fell away. All of them, from Trojani down to Biagi, felt victory in their grasp.

"We are close" someone said.

Animation became agitation. Agitation grew into excitement and the loud whistling of the wind was merged with the soft, relentless ticking of the clock.

"This is it," Mariano said finally, looking up from his map. "We made it."

Cold, fatigue and tiredness were forgotten as pent-up emotions broke loose. They had crossed the top of the world at twenty minutes past midnight of May 24, a date which happened to be the anniversary of Italy's entry into World War I and was officially considered a national holiday.

Nobile ordered the motors slowed and, passing through a thick layer of dense fog which hid the Pole itself, the *Italia* descended in a long spiral. There was laughter and backslapping. The cabin door was opened and the Papal Cross, as well as some flags, were thrown out, to disappear from view in the fog below. From a portable record player came the brassy sounds of the Fascist anthem.

"See," Nobile cockily told Trojani, "one *can* tempt fate twice after all . . ."[3]

As the dirigible kept circling, a bottle of eggnog, lovingly prepared by Mrs. Carlotta Nobile, passed from mouth to mouth, and the phonograph was shifted to a popular Neapolitan song. Gathered around their leader in the cabin of the airship, the men looked at one another through tears born of pride. Customary messages were dispatched to the Pope, the King, and the Duce. The scientist Pontremoli proudly announced that he had measured something called the "vertical component of the earth's magnetism."

That same day Nobile made headlines in the New York *Times:* "Reaches Pole—Circles over it an hour—Starts back to King's Bay." A bigger news story of the day, however, was Coolidge's veto of a farm bill, described by the President as "a deceptive and price-fixing scheme."

At 2:30 in the morning, after having circled the Pole for two hours while vainly waiting for the wind to subside, Nobile set course for Spitsbergen. Ice soon began to form on the ship, and heavy pieces thrown off the whirling propellers crashed against the envelope of the dirigible. The *Italia,* like all dirigibles, was a fragile ship, her steel skeleton covered only by aluminum-painted canvas, and every man aboard knew that one of these flying missiles could tear a hole too big to be patched during flight. Each man also knew that under the heavy beating the ship was taking, even a steel girder might break at any minute, causing total disaster.

Malmgren, the weather man, was nervous. "We have to leave this area as soon as possible," he insisted. His confidence was gone and so was Nobile's plan, vague as it may have been, to change course and cruise on an alternate route. Gasoline stores had dwindled and the *Italia* was past her point of no return. The men aboard were silent. Drowned in gloom and anxiety, the exhilaration of success had gone as suddenly as it had come. The third motor was started, and with all engines turning at maximum power the dirigible flew against the violent wind.

By midnight, the flight had already lasted close to forty-two hours and nobody aboard the *Italia* knew the position of the airship. It was somewhere in the Arctic, possibly some 350 miles from Kings Bay. Minutes became hours as the storm grew stronger, and the fuel supply shrank rapidly. At a prohibitive cost in gasoline, the *Italia* flew on, but never at more than twenty-seven miles an hour.

Nobile reduced speed and kept only two motors running. Malmgren became agitated. "No," he said, "it's dangerous to stay here, the weather may become even worse, we must leave here as fast as we can." Nobile increased the speed again. By then the *Italia* had been fighting head winds for at least thirty hours. Like a wild horse, the ship bucked, shook and quivered, drifting off course as much as thirty degrees. There was no land in sight, only dense fog, driven by the vicious wind.

The movement and senses of the men aboard were slowed by fatigue; their eyes were red from lack of sleep, and the wet cold had penetrated their clothing.

Two men, Lago and Pontremoli, were useless in this fight against nature, and were upstairs, inside the ship's body. Huddled in sleeping bags, they were catnapping on the narrow gangplank among gasoline containers, hydrogen chambers, valves, and boxes crammed with supplies, while Behounek still watched the instruments. Ugo Lago had his notes and his impressions; Aldo Pontremoli had his figures; for both the work of the trip was already over.

In the main cabin men moved purposefully; there were only short commands and equally short reports. Conversation had stopped long ago. Nobile moved from the navigator's desk to the altimeter and back again. Occasionally he looked out a window, hoping to see a solid landmark. But everywhere he saw nothing but a sea of fog. Every so often he dropped a small dye-containing glass sphere and measured with a stopwatch the time it took for the sphere to hit the ice and to break, spilling the dye, which then appeared for an instant like a drop of blood on an immense white sheet. By computing the time it took for the sphere to hit the ice, he could determine the altitude at which the *Italia* was flying. Every once in a while he asked Biagi to request from the *Città di Milano* a new report on the flight direction of his dirigible.

Slowly, ever so slowly, the night passed. At 9:25 in the morning of May 25, Nobile was standing at the door to the radio cabin again while Biagi listened to the *Città di Milano*. Radio contact was established every 25th and 55th minute of each hour, at which time the base ship notified Nobile of the direction in which his dirigible was flying, as determined by the deflection of the *Italia*'s radio beam. There was no way, however, to determine the actual distance of the dirigible from the ship. As the general was standing at the door, he heard the voice of the helmsman, Trojani: "The elevator," the man said, "it's bewitched . . ." Whirling around, Nobile saw that the nose of the dirigible was pointing downward and that Trojani was unable to level the ship out. "Stop the motors," he yelled.

In the face of danger every man reacted differently. Trojani tightened his grip on the jammed elevator controls. In an impulsive gesture and without orders from the skipper, one of the naval officers, Zappi, started hurling ballast out of the cabin. There was no sense to this action because the four cans of gasoline he threw out did not lighten the ship significantly but their loss consituted a considerable decrease in the amount of available fuel.

The motors were at a standstill, but the ship continued to lose altitude. Nobile waited. It was just a question of seconds, but these seconds became indelibly impressed on the minds of those who lived through them. Four seconds, five seconds, six seconds . . . 250 feet above the ice, the fall was arrested and the *Italia* was stabilized again, though still battered by steadily increasing winds.

With two quick steps, Viglieri came forward. Pushing Trojani away, he gripped the elevator control and hit it with the palm of his right hand. Under the impact of Viglieri's blow the controls were freed and the ship began rising again. "Where angels fear to tread . . ." Trojani thought, conscious of a delicate mechanism being slapped violently.

Aware of the commotion and still in contact with the *Città di Milano*, radioman Biagi tapped out a private message to his buddy Pedretti aboard the base ship: ". . . you are lucky . . . if I'm late answering, there is a reason . . ."[4]

Being light, and with motors stopped, the *Italia* kept on rising through layers of clouds until Nobile released some gas to arrest her ascent.

"General," Mariano asked, "don't you think we should take advantage of the situation to go above the clouds to get a fix with the sun?"

"Yes," Nobile said, "let's do that."

Again they rose. Above the clouds, at 2,800 feet, they saw the sun, suspended from a blue sky like a huge orange. Muttering his favorite curses, master mechanic Cecioni removed the casing of the elevator, while Mariano and Zappi were busy calculating their position. Viglieri was still holding the controls. Trojani, standing next to him, kept his eyes glued to the dials of manometers indicating pressure in the gas chambers. Nobile himself had taken the altitude rudder and Behounek was back at his instruments, while Malmgren peered out a window.

Cecioni came back. He had traced the wires all the way to the tail of the ship and had checked the rudder itself; everything seemed to be in order. Some ice must have been blocking the mechanism.

At five minutes before ten o'clock, Biagi was again in radio contact with the *Città di Milano,* but Nobile did not bother to report the mechanical difficulty, nor did he consider it necessary to notify the base ship that they had determined their position—180 miles from Kings Bay. The situation seemed to be under control. With the wind unchanged, the *Italia* should reach Spitsbergen in approximately five hours. The general ordered two motors started again, and the dirigible slowly descended from an altitude of some 3,500 feet.

The flight continued. Malmgren had taken over from Nobile; Cecioni was at the elevator controls, and, next to him, Trojani still watched the manometer dials.

At twenty-seven minutes past ten o'clock, as Biagi was again talking to the *Città di Milano,* Nobile went to the right front window and strained his eyes to pierce the fog before dropping another of his dye markers. Before he could see its impact on the ice he heard Cecioni's voice which was hoarse, as if strangled by fear. "We are heavy . . ." the man was yelling.

The nose of the dirigible pointed upward by some eight degrees, but the rear part was sagging. The *Italia* was falling, and she was falling at a speed of more than a foot per second.

The ship still had considerable altitude and Nobile tried to bring about a dynamic arrest of her fall. "All motors full speed ahead," he shouted. Trojani promptly transmitted the order via the intercom system to the mechanics and almost instantly the roar of the engines grew. But a nagging, fear-inspiring question remained: Why should the ship fall? Was a gas chamber torn? Was a valve out of commission?

Sharp orders, spoken in crisp, short words sent Alessandrini upstairs into the envelope of the *Italia* to make a check. Cecioni was ordered to drop the ballast chain, which was attached to the nose of the dirigible. The fall, however, accelerated; now every second brought the dirigible three feet nearer the pack ice.

A crash was inevitable as the ice came nearer at frightening speed.

"Stop the motors!" This order was an admission of defeat, designed to avoid any explosion on impact. A dazed Cecioni was still fumbling with a rope tied to the ballast chain. "Shall I cut it?" he asked.[5] "Just drop the chain," Nobile yelled back, "fast, fast. . . ." His darting eyes were staring with all their intensity, his body was moving, his mouth half open.

Kneeling, Cecioni kept on fumbling, his shaking hands seeking a knife, which he did not have. The heavy chain, weighted down by a massive anchor, remained tied to the falling ship.

Zappi had taken Cecioni's place at the elevator. Through a window, Nobile saw one propeller still turning. "Stop the motor," he yelled, and Mariano's voice senselessly echoed the command against the wind: "Stop the engine." This was the last command given aboard the *Italia*. The engine stopped.

Malmgren's hands slipped off the side rudder and, his face contorted with fear, he took one or two staggering steps toward the rear of the cabin, as if trying to escape what by then was inescapable.[6] Nobile saw it and instinctively reached for the controls. With a thundering noise, like a collapsing building, the cabin of the *Italia* crashed onto the ice.

It was 10:33 on the morning of Friday, May 25, 1928.

The rear motor was first to hit the ice; a second later the main cabin smashed, cracking like an egg, and in its continued forward motion, the remnants of the walls scooped up snow and ice like a huge shovel.

But none of the men from the *Italia* saw that. Nobile felt himself hit from the rear, and fell. "This is it," he thought, "the end. . . ." His thought was not completed and there were no more words only unconsciousness. Seconds before the impact, Behounek had looked out the window. Incredulously he had seen the ice coming up toward him. He had tried to turn, grasped the railing, felt two jolts and lost his footing. Then he, too, had been knocked unconscious.

Viglieri saw the ice, and he understood the inevitable. Instinctively he bent his knees, leaning slightly forward, the way he would have had he seen a big wave come rushing over the bridge of a naval vessel. Blinded by snow, he brought up his hands to protect his face, as he was dragged over a hard surface.

Still kneeling, still trying to release the chain, Cecioni felt a violent pain in his right leg, crushed by the massive stand of a compass falling under the heavy tilt of the cabin. For him, too, there was short but merciful darkness.

And so it went. Scattered on the ice as if thrown like dice by the mighty hand of destiny, ten men (and a dog) were lying in various attitudes, unconscious or uncomprehending for several seconds.

Viglieri was first to open his eyes, just in time to see the ship pass on a yard or so above him. The breakup of the main cabin had lightened the dirigible by at least two tons, and the *Italia* was rising slowly and drifting eastward, her tattered envelope dragging remnants of the ruined cabin. Viglieri saw Arduini standing on the narrow gangway leading to the left motor. Wide-eyed and staring in horrified disbelief at the men on the ice, he was being lifted higher and higher. Behounek, too, saw the man and so did Biagi. They would remember his eyes, paralyzed in terror. Through glasses covered with snow and blood, Trojani saw the *Italia* in flight for the first and last time; dazed, he was gripped by the frightening thought that he was the only one left alive on this deserted floe.

Slowly, the doomed *Italia* moved eastward and disappeared in the gray fog; her disappearance forever shrouded in mystery. The fate of the men left aboard—Lago, Pontremoli, Carratti, Ciocca, Alessandrini, and Arduini—would remain unknown and their bodies would never be recovered.

Meanwhile from Rome a special correspondent wired:

> Nobile's dropping of the flag and cross over the Pole has caught the popular imagination as has nothing else recently. It caught Italy in a festive mood . . .

The Corriere d'Italia said:

> Catholics and Italians, we salute with joy this great event wherein we see Italian hearts and wings as bearers of the message of the Pope and the message of the Cross.

And Mussolini's *Il Popolo d'Italia* shouted:

> Nobile with his genial audacity not only brings new laurels to Italian aviation but a great conquest for civilization and history.

2

Lieutenant Commander Mariano, Nobile's navigator, was the first to stand. Dazed, he brushed snow off his clothes; bracing himself against the wind, he planted his feet on the ice firmly, looked around and saw human forms moving, trying to get up. "All right," he shouted, "all right, we are all here . . . where is the general?"

Nobile opened his eyes; his hazy mind perceived a sharp pain from the right leg and he could not move his right arm. There was Mariano's voice: "Where is the general?" Nobile raised his head. To his right, two yards away he saw Malmgren, and behind him he heard the plaintive voice of Cecioni, crying out in pain. Farther off there was Zappi, lying on his back; Nobile saw Behounek and Trojani getting up. A few paces beyond them was the tall figure of Viglieri and the squat one of Biagi, already on their feet and looking around. A mass of twisted and crushed remnants of the main cabin was scattered over an area of approximately 200 yards and a wide red streak caused by squashed dye-containing glass spheres smeared the ice.

Mariano approached the general, but Nobile waved him away. "Boys," he said in a voice that did not carry far, "we have to accept our fate. Lift your souls skyward and trust in God. Long live Italy." It was hard to speak and still more difficult to say something. What does one say to a group of men, suddenly thrown empty-handed on an ice floe?

"General, are you all right?" Mariano asked.

Wearing only a sweater and thin trousers, Nobile, with an arm and leg broken, was lying on the ice. "I'm hurt," Nobile said. "I'm going to die. Take care of the others, promise me that you will do everything to save them. Our country cannot afford to lose men like you." The words came out slowly, with effort. "Take care of the others," he repeated.

"I will," Mariano answered. "I will."

Biagi, Trojani, Viglieri and Behounek were moving slowly about. Zappi, still sitting, held the right side of his chest. Malmgren, standing next to Behounek, was supporting his left arm with the right hand. Mariano walked over to big Cecioni, who was lying immobile in the snow, moaning with pain. His right leg was broken and an ugly piece of bone protruded through the torn flesh. There was nothing Mariano could do for him. "Courage," he said, "we will take care of you; just be patient."

Biagi stretched his limbs; he was not hurt. He was glad to feel something solid under his feet, even though it was only pack ice.

Biagi was the first to see a thick black cloud rising lazily on the foggy horizon. "Look," he yelled. "Smoke!" The others, too, saw the smoke, which appeared like a smudge on gray wallpaper. Could nearby hunters be signaling to them? Could that be a sign from the men left aboard the *Italia?* Those on the floe talked about these things, but neither on this, nor any subsequent day would they see smoke again. What they saw was almost certainly the last of the *Italia,* going up in flames.

Cecioni kept on mumbling: "Courage. They will be looking for us . . . they are going to send planes. . . . Wilkins is in Green Harbor, he could be here in three hours . . ." Condemned to inactivity, big Cecioni was trying to see hope where there was none. As a matter of fact, Wilkins was in Oslo and there were no planes in Spitsbergen.

Except for Nobile and Cecioni the others had sustained only minor injuries or none at all. Zappi had a bad bruise on his chest, Trojani was bleeding slightly from a scalp wound, and Malmgren had a dislocated shoulder.[7]

Mariano, the new leader, surveyed his men and their situation. Behounek had found a big sack containing a collapsible tent, a sleeping bag and some food.[8] Among the scattered debris, Malmgren had spotted some boxes of pemmican. Everything useful had to be salvaged at once before it was covered by snow or fell into one of the leads in the ice.

Nobile took the sleeping bag, pulled it over his head and closed his eyes. He still thought he was going to die.

"All right, you men, let's go and collect whatever food we may find," Mariano said. He and four others set out, moving slowly. They stumbled and fell, sometimes breaking through the deceptive ice and sinking knee-deep into freezing water.

On an iceblock next to Nobile, sat Malmgren, his face gray, his eyes filled with bitter despair. He was the only man on the floe who really knew the Arctic. He was the only professional in a group of inexperienced amateurs, whose nominal leader was hiding his head in a sleeping bag.

There was no Amundsen, no Sverdrup, no Riiser-Larsen. Feeling Malmgren's presence, Nobile looked out. "There is nothing we can do . . ." he said.

"No, nothing," Malmgren answered. "All we can do is die . . . my arm is broken." With that he got up, took a couple of painful steps forward and turned around. "General," he said, "thanks for the trip. I'll go and drown myself . . ."

"Malmgren," Nobile shouted, "you have no right to do that: we will die when the time comes." The Swede stopped in his tracks and sat down again, silently.

Biagi had wandered off by himself. Suddenly he saw something familiar-looking, a small box. Then he remembered—his emergency radio! He had wanted to store it in the body of the *Italia,* but his superior, Baccarani, chief communication officer of the *Città di Milano* had made him take it into his small radio cabin, where it had remained all through seventy hours of flight, serving as a footrest. At the moment of impact, Biagi now remembered vaguely, he had gripped it firmly, for no particular reason he could recall. He had still clutched the box, while falling head first into a patch of soft snow.[9]

Now he picked it up, held it to his ear, shook it and then opened it. Everything seemed to be in order (even the bottle of cognac hidden inside was intact). "The radio," he yelled, "I have found the radio. . . ." His words, drowned by the wind, remained unheard.

Walking near Mariano, Behounek was collecting cans of pemmican and dropping them into the cap which he had tied to his belt. "Step aside, Behounek," Mariano said. Following Mariano's look, the Czech saw Biagi, standing some 100 yards away, signaling with widespread arms.

"The radio, Biagi has found the radio . . ." Even Mariano's calm voice was filled with excitement. Biagi held the link between two worlds, between despair and hope.

Soon the sailor holding a small mahogany box with dials and knobs was surrounded by Viglieri, Behounek and Mariano. "Can you transmit with it?" Mariano asked. Then Biagi remembered. Without answering, he put the box carefully on the ice and knelt. With his hands he started going through the snow, digging and pushing, looking for something else. With beads of sweat on his forehead, Biagi searched in an ever-widening circle, oblivious of those who were standing around him. Finally his numbed fingers lifted still another box out of a mass of lumber, twisted wires and water-soaked debris. "The transmitter," he said. "It's unbelievable; here is the transmitter . . . and it seems to be all right."

The situation had changed. Suddenly there was hope. There was some food, there was shelter, and now there would be communication. Perhaps defeat could be reversed.

Mariano reported to Nobile and hope revived the general's confidence. All at once, he felt ready to assume command.

Twenty yards from where the main cabin had crashed, Biagi saw a human form sitting on an iceblock. It was the motor mechanic Pomella. He had only one shoe on and was leaning forward, apparently trying to remove the other. "Hey, Pomella," Biagi called out. His words lost themselves and there was no answer. "What's the matter? Don't you feel well?" Still there was no response. "Here, have some cognac." Under Biagi's gentle touch, Pomella's body swayed, fell sideways and lay face-down, silent and motionless.

Only then did Biagi realize that he had been talking to a corpse. There was a trickle of dried blood at the left corner of his mouth. Young Pomella was dead. Picking up small blocks of ice, Biagi used them to cover the body.[10]

On a fifty square yard floe, a tent was erected. The floe was three feet in thickness and its borders were lined with blocks of ice three to five feet tall. On it were nine living men and a dog.

The sleeping bag was slit lengthwise and put on the ice inside the tent; then Nobile was carried in and placed on it against the wall. Next to the general lay Cecioni.

Back on the *Città di Milano,* chief communications officer Baccarani was worried. There had been no word from the *Italia* for four hours. Captain Romagna-Manoja was frowning. "What's the matter with them?" he asked. Baccarani shrugged his shoulders and ordered his radioman Pedretti to keep on sending the same message: "Do not receive you since 10.27 A.M. Listening with long wave of 900 and short wave . . . repeat: Do not receive you . . ." Nobile had sent his last position report at three-thirty in the morning, at which time the *Italia* was thought to be about a hundred miles from Moffen Island, and her estimated time of arrival in Kings Bay had been given as eight in the morning.

Leaning over a map spread out on his navigating table, Captain Romagna let his pudgy fingers wander over an area between the west coast of Northeast Land and Wijde Fjord. "Here . . . he should be here somewhere . . ." But what if the last position report of the dirigible was incorrect? What if the *Italia* had actually been 150 or 200 miles from Moffen Island at three-thirty in the morning?

Zappi and Viglieri bound crude splints, made of lumber salvaged from the wreck of the cabin, to the broken limbs of the two wounded men. Biagi was assembling the radio. An aluminum tube was set up as an aerial; a ground wire was stretched out over the ice, and connections were tightened. The batteries had enough life in them to last for sixty hours of transmission. Anticipation rose among the men as Biagi put on his earphones and started transmitting the distress signal: Three dots, three dashes, three dots. "SOS, SOS, *Italia,* Nobile, we crashed . . ." It was four o'clock in the afternoon of May 25.

For the men standing around the little mahogany box there was nothing but Biagi's moving fingers, nothing but the monotonous repetition of the signals. "I get nothing," Biagi said after a while, removing his earphones.

Only 220 miles away, the radio of the *Città di Milano* worked overtime. Plenty of messages were received, still others went out, including a long "on-the-scene" report of the reporter, Tomaselli.[11]

Hungry and cold, the men entered the tent. There was no need for words. Mariano distributed carefully measured rations of pemmican and each man stuffed it into his mouth, but no one could swallow it. Even Titina, the general's dog, just sniffed at it. Somebody remembered to tell Nobile that Pomella was dead; but it made no difference. Squeezed into the small square tent were nine men and a dog, covered with one blanket, which Viglieri came to call "the cloak of divine mercy.[12] Lying and sitting next to each other or across each other, they tried to sleep. Their eyes were closed, their bodies were tired, but their minds worked and sleep would not come. The hours dragged on and the wind continued. Cecioni started crying. Some dozed off, others stayed awake and only Trojani was fast asleep, dead to the world.

The late edition of the New York *Times* was now on the stands, carrying on its front page an item about the *Italia:* ". . . radio stops amid arctic gale. Some fear aroused . . ." The paper carried a reassuring dispatch from London and a wire from Kings Bay which asserted that ice had probably broken the ship's aerial, making communication impossible, that there was no reason for concern because the dirigible had plenty of gasoline aboard and carried a food supply sufficient for a month. On page 3 of the same edition were featured the first pictures of George Wilkins, taken on his arrival in Oslo.

At ten o'clock in the evening, with the *Italia* overdue and silent for twelve hours, Romagna wired the Italian Ambassador in Oslo, suggesting that an aerial rescue operation might have to be considered.

By morning of the following day, Mariano and Viglieri had determined the position of their floe. It was 81°14′ North, 25°25′ West, some thirty miles off the island of Charles XII. The order of the day was the business of survival. Every additional can of food salvaged could mean another day of life. While the four injured men remained in the tent, the other five went out to look for whatever might be useful. They found a pistol and two axes. Behounek found his instruments (they were still ticking) and his little red notebook. It was water-drenched, but the notes were still legible.

"Here," Viglieri said, "Here's another one." This notebook was black and it belonged to Malmgren. Inside the tent Behounek handed it to the Swede who stared at it in disbelief. "Where did you find this?" he asked.

"On the way to Pomella's body."

With a shrug of his uninjured shoulder, Malmgren threw it into a corner of the tent: The notebook was the past and the past had no place in the present.

Biagi, Cecioni and Zappi took the transmitter apart. A defective condenser was located, a new one was somehow found and the set was reassembled and tested. Once more Biagi tried to re-establish contact with the *Città di Milano*. Following a prearranged pattern, he sent his distress signals every fifty-five minutes, but every fifty-five minutes hopes were dashed by answering silence. To be sure, the *Città di Milano* kept on sending messages to the crew of the *Italia* and Biagi heard them: "What happened to you? Why don't you answer? If transmitter does not work, use emergency set . . . ." But the base ship did not seem to be receiving the signals sent from the ice floe. In the evening Biagi even intercepted a newscast from Rome's radio station.

At about the same time a banquet sponsored by the newspaper *Aftenposten* at the Royal Yacht Club in Oslo to honor Wilkins and Eielson came to a dramatic end. Great men of the Arctic were assembled there. As they were about to be seated, a message from Spitsbergen came in: Still no news from the *Italia*. The *Città di Milano* was preparing to go north in search of the dirigible. Possible reasons for the silence of the *Italia* were discussed. Was the airship out of fuel and drifting with the wind? Had she had to land because of damage? Was there a crash? Everybody agreed that speed in organizing rescue operations was essential, and all eyes turned to Roald Amundsen, whose voice had the sound of a cracking whip as it cut the silence: "I'll come right away," he said.

A reporter ventured a question. "You must not forget," Amundsen answered, "how enormously difficult the situation is. There is no indication of the position, and because of the ice a ship can search only a very limited area."[13]

"Do you think, sir, that the *Italia* may have crashed?"

"Do not let us discuss a possibility so likely to be fatal. All that can be done, will be done."

Wilkins was asked his opinion. "It is the most difficult time of the year," he said. "The ice is breaking up and you must reckon with lots of foggy weather. I myself am prepared to go at once to the *Italia's* assistance. However, my plane, now at Bergen, has to have runners or skis. That means almost ten days will pass before we can reach Spitsbergen and make a start from there. If we do start, we'll have little chance to land under present conditions, in view of the way the snow is thawing and crevices are appearing in the ice. A search by seaplane would offer the best prospect at this time of the year, but if there is no news to indicate the *Italia's* position, even that would be very much a matter of chance."

Eielson, the other guest of honor, added: "From what I saw in our own flight . . . and in my three years experience as an aviator in these regions, it would be more merciful for the *Italia's* crew to meet a rapid end than be forced to land on the ice at this time of year in regions where the nearest assistance is hundreds of miles away. However, if I am wanted or can be of help, I am ready to look for them."

Pensively, Major Gran volunteered: "The polar equipment of the *Italia* is very complete. I saw to it myself and I should know, but the Italians have no training in making long marches across the ice and their chances are very slight if the airship has come down at a great distance from Spitsbergen."

Captain Sverdrup, remembering an arctic rescue operation in which he had been actively involved, thought that an icebreaker was needed. There was no icebreaker in Norway . . .[14]

In the press, there was widespread confusion. A German newspaper reported authoritatively that the *Italia* had made an emergency landing, and the New York *Times* devoted four columns of its front page to Nobile's expedition, "Italia reported down on the ice and sending appeals for help. Relief ship ready. Amundsen may go." Among the pictures of crew members reported lost were those of the meteorologist Eredia, the tailor Bellochi, and Angioletti, all three actually safe and sound in Spitsbergen.

In New York, Lincoln Ellsworth saw "no cause for alarm," but cabled Amundsen, offering his assistance. Richard Byrd saw "no reason for great concern," and Lieutenant Commander Rosendahl, the senior surviving officer of the *Shenandoah,* expressed doubts that the *Italia* had met with disaster.

On Sunday, May 27, the Norwegian Government issued a statement saying that it has been approached by Mussolini's Government with a request to start rescue operations, and that both Amundsen and Sverdrup had been invited to attend an emergency cabinet meeting. On the same day Norway's Minister of the Navy accepted Amundsen's advice and ordered Commodore Von der Lippe, Chief of the Norwegian Air Force, to ready a seaplane while the steamship *Hobby* was alerted to leave for Tromso on the following day.

In the meantime a routine had been established in Nobile's camp. Viglieri was in charge of food stores and was keeping watch over what was on hand, a total of 143 pounds. Malmgren provided water by hacking chunks of sweet ice and carrying them in a dirty gasoline can to the tent where they would melt. On a salvaged calendar, Trojani had started marking off days; stirring greasy pemmican in dirty brown lukewarm water, Behounek was preparing a soup which Mariano then ceremoniously poured into the bottom part of a thermos bottle, to be passed from mouth to mouth; at spaced intervals small chocolate bars were distributed.

The mood of the men was mute resignation as the radio remained silent. They could eavesdrop on the world, they could intercept newscasts from Rome, thousands of miles away, but they received no answer to their desperate appeals for help from their base ship only some 200 miles away. Instead, the *Città di Milano* kept on sending: "Assume you to be near North Coast of Spitsbergen; have faith; organizing rescue party." Obviously their messages were not being received. Zappi was sure that their transmitter was too weak and Biagi was blaming atmospheric conditions, but Nobile remained confident. "Keep on sending," he repeated. ". . . they will hear us . . ."

At nine o'clock in the evening an eagerly awaited newscast from Rome informed them that the *Città di Milano* was proceeding northward. It stirred up renewed hope that, with lessened distance, the base ship would finally hear Biagi's messages.

Night was approaching; their third on the floe. Their hands were dirty, their bodies smelly and their faces bearded, but their will to survive had increased. Suddenly Nobile's tent shook to an ear-splitting roar as two floes collided with a massive impact; the space of water between them disappeared under crushed and turned-over ice. It was a frightening phenomenon, bringing with it fear akin to that of being in an earthquake.

When the white night came to the floe, it was a long one for Professor Behounek. His thoughts kept on wandering and he could not sleep. Barely a few feet from him, in the center of the tent, leaning against the pole, Mariano and Zappi were sitting and whispering to each other. The Czech professor did not want to eavesdrop—even had he wanted to, he would not have understood their conversation, because he did not speak Italian. But the fragment of one sentence reached his ear. "Facciamo segreto," Zappi was saying. That much he understood—"Let's keep it a secret." Then the whispering became softer and the professor heard nothing else. "Secret," he thought. "What kind of a secret?"[15]

The *Città di Milano* had left Kings Bay for South Gate, there to establish contact with some hunters who might have heard or seen the *Italia*. Summoned by blasts of a siren, one of them came aboard, but had no news of the dirigible. Otherwise there is no record of any steps taken by the Italian Government to set up rescue machinery for the missing men, and the only contribution from Rome was a special mass for the crew of the *Italia*, read by the Pope.

ER : *145* :

In Washington, Secretary of the Navy Wilbur was reported considering
dispatch of the dirigible *Los Angeles* to Nobile's aid, but not before
more information was available and not until the position of survivors,
if there were any, was known.[16] In the meantime Nobile continued making
headlines in the New York *Times,* which proclaimed in large letters on
its front page: "Italia in distress. Say repeated calls for help heard on
Pacific Coast. No word in Spitsbergen." Indeed, said the paper, messages
in Italian, French, English and Russian were heard distinctly and repeatedly by an amateur radio "ham," Charles E. Bialack, President of
Western Sulphur Company in San Francisco: "CQ—the dirigible of General Nobile is in distress, asking for help. She is equipped with shortwave
radio 30-33. Dirigible Italia of General Nobile AS-RAO 3." A similar
message was intercepted by the Radio Corporation of America. A closer
check, however, revealed that "AS" were the call letters used by certain
Iberian radio stations and that "RAO 3" was the identification of a
Mr. Golovstchikov from the Far Eastern University at Vladivostok.

There was much more activity in the Scandinavian countries. The
Swedish branch of the Radio Relay League alerted all radio amateurs
to listen for messages originating with the *Italia,* and in Oslo Norway's
Minister of Defense, Ryst Anderson, convoked an extraordinary meeting
with various arctic pioneer's such as Amundsen, Sverdrup, Isachson, and
Riiser-Larsen. The latter was especially summoned from the flying base
at Horten. A three-stage rescue plan was worked out and handed over
to Italy's representative in Norway for transmission to Rome. According
to this plan, Lieutenant Lützow-Holm was to fly on the following day
a short-range naval plane from Horten to Tromso, where both he and
the plane would be taken aboard the *Hobby* for transshipment to Spitsbergen. Italy was to make two long-range Dornier-Wals available in which
Amundsen and Riiser-Larsen would fly directly to Kings Bay. From a
suitable base in Spitsbergen all three planes were then to start an intensive
aerial search for Nobile and the *Italia.*[17]

On that same Sunday, May 27, Davide Giudici, Berlin correspondent
of Italy's respected daily *Corriere della Sera,* received an unexpected phone
call from his home office in Milan. Eugenio Balzan, the director of the
paper, was on the wire: "There is a big story in Spitsbergen," he said,
"the *Italia.* Nobody here knows anything . . . pack your bags and leave
right away . . ."[18]

Giudici was hardly the right man for such an assignment. He was
an intellectual, deeply engrossed in reporting and analyzing political events,
and had never before covered a sensational accident. In the evening of
the same day he left Berlin, bound for Oslo.

On May 28, the sun broke through the mist again and Nobile's officers
could determine their position once more. It was 80°48′ North, 26°20′

East. The men looked at each other in disbelief—the floe had drift
twenty-eight miles to the southeast in two days. But the determinati
was accurate, because the island of King Charles XII, which they h
never seen before, now became visible on the horizon.

For the men on the floe, reality looked grim: Their position was chan
ing daily, their radio messages had not been heard, and the possibili
of rescue appeared remote. Furthermore, on page 264 of *Arctic Pil*
a navigational guide they had salvaged, it said: ". . . the main directi
of the ice on the coast of Northeast Land is toward the east . .
and "toward the east" meant into the warm waters of Barents Sea. "On
we are in the Barents Sea," Lieutenant Commander Zappi told radiom
Biagi, "we've had it. There will be no more floe."

Outside the tent, hands in his pockets, feet apart, Mariano was waiti
for Malmgren, who was returning with a fresh supply of sweet ice. "Mal
gren," he said, "how do you feel about a march to the mainland?"

Finn Malmgren put his can down and without hesitation answer
with a counter-question: "With those two?"

Mariano nodded. He knew that if there was to be a march, Malmg
had to be in on it, because he was the only one among them w
knew the Arctic.

"No," Malmgren said, "that's impossible. In their state . . . qu
impossible."[19]

Mariano nodded in silence. His eyes, the color of tempered steel, w
cold; his mouth was thin like a line drawn with a hard pencil. This w
a probe only. In his mind an idea was clear. Plant the seed of a thou
and wait. But not too long. Now the outline of land could be seen on t
horizon. It was not there yesterday and may not be there tomorrow.

Later, joined by Zappi, Mariano talked to Nobile. The situation w
hopeless, both officers maintained. They pointed out the drift, the usele
ness of the radio, the limited food. In short, they said, the rescue
all could be brought about only if a group of them undertook a mar
to the mainland, where they might secure help.

Nobile was not convinced. Mariano's suggestion had been in the fo
of a request; confronted with the general's hesitation, both naval offic
became more insistent. They had already made up their minds. Tr
they would have preferred to leave with the consent of their lead
but they were equally determined to meet refusal with stubbc
determination.

Once again each man reacted differently. Panic-stricken, Cecioni we
with tears running down his bearded cheeks, he kept repeating: "\
came together, we must leave together . . ."[20] He would build sle
he said, on which he and the general could be transported; if only
did not have a broken leg, he would take the general on his back a
carry him, but, as it was, he repeated, "We came together and we m

leave together." Cecioni rebelled against the idea of being left behind
on the ice. Blinded by fear, he refused to see the impossibility of his
plan or to consider the makeup of pack ice.

Nobile, not convinced of the hopelessness of their situation and unsure
of Mariano's plan, was anxious to avoid an open break, and stalled
for time. He asked for a definite proposal. Then Malmgren, urged on
by the two naval officers, became spokesman for the group of insurgents:
"The only hope lies in sending a patrol to North Cape, which is near
the 20th meridian and within the area in which the *Città di Milano*
is planning rescue operations," he said. "There it may be possible to
establish contact and to arrange for rescue of those who are left behind."[21]
Malmgren spoke quietly and logically.

Nobile gave in. "Who is to go?" he asked.

"I gladly volunteer." Mariano's answer was crisp and all too prompt.
"And how many are to go?"

Now it was Zappi's turn to speak: "At least four men," he said,
"the three Naval officers and Dr. Malmgren."

Malmgren nodded. Biagi was silent, Viglieri was silent, and so was
Trojani. But Behounek, obviously too fat and too nearsighted for a hazardous march to the mainland, had something to say. His voice was quiet
but determined. "As far as I am concerned," he said, "I shall be glad
to stay with the general. But I must insist that a naval officer who knows
how to determine our changing position and operate the radio remain
with us. In that case Biagi would not have to stay."[21]

"We came together, we must leave together," Cecioni kept repeating.
Nobile was hedging. "There is no immediate danger," he said. "There
is enough food, rescue operations have started." The general postponed
further discussions until the following day.

In the outside world, the New York *Times* proclaimed: "Rush Nobile
rescue plans with airplanes and dogs. Base ship blocked by ice." These
headlines had a solid foundation. Rome had received the Norwegian plan
and the Italian Government had chartered the 350-ton vessel *Braganza*
which was to leave for Spitsbergen. Lieutenant Lützow-Holm had reached
Bergen and was on his way to Tromso, where the *Hobby* was being
loaded. Stopped by ice at Cloven Cliff, the *Città di Milano* was doubling
back to South Gate. In answer to an inquiry from the Norwegian War
Department, Spitsbergen's Governor Bassoe had recommended that dog
teams be sent out from Advent Bay or Green Harbor, in addition to
whatever planes might be used.

Anxiety began to mount in Rome. It was generally conceded that
the *Italia* must have met with disaster; Mussolini gave instructions to
be kept informed of new developments at all times, and Balbo returned
from Spain, where he had been watching General De Pineda's preparations

for a mass flight across the Mediterranean, to take charge of Italian rescue efforts.[22] He read the contract governing the loan of the *Italia* to the Royal Italian Geographic Society and became painfully aware that the dirigible was not insured. "Nobile mi ha fregato," he is reported to have said. "Nobile has pulled a fast one, if he is still alive, he'll pay for it."[23]

Mussolini received a telegram from Wilkins and Eielson saying: "On hearing that the Norwegian Government has placed Captain Riiser-Larsen at your disposal, we realize that all things possible will be done in the most competent manner. If it is considered that the service of our machine or ourselves can be of the least aid to our friend Nobile, please consider us yours to command."[24]

In the United States, Commander Rosendahl had changed his mind and talked pessimistically about the *Italia* and her crew. In Congress a bill introduced the previous day by Representative Burton from Ohio to award Lincoln Ellsworth a gold medal for his part in the first transpolar crossing of the Arctic Ocean was blocked by Representative Fiorello LaGuardia, who demanded that the same award be given to General Nobile.

Everywhere, certain people followed the story of the *Italia* with a high degree of interest. In Rome Marta Trojani bought a copy of every available newspaper. In Leningrad Professor Samoilovich, director of the Arctic Institute,[25] eagerly scanned the morning paper. On none of the four pages was there any news of the *Italia*. Frankly worried, the professor put in a call to Mr. Voronov, Member of the Supreme Soviet in Moscow. Yes, Voronov agreed, perhaps a rescue operation should be considered. Samoilovich was instructed to form a regional committee of experts and to discuss the matter with Italy's consul.

Armed with a valid passport and a ticket for Oslo, the special correspondent, Davide Giudici, arrived in Copenhagen, only to encounter a new difficulty. The Danish airline had canceled its Oslo-bound flight because its planes—all two of them—were needed to provide an honor escort for Wilkins and Eielson, expected to arrive soon in the Danish capital.

3

By May 29, Nobile's floe had moved three more miles to the east. The island of King Charles XII was no longer on the horizon, but two small stretches of land were now visible to the southwest—the islands of Broch and Foyn. As on the four preceding days, the radio failed to bring any word that Biagi's messages had been received. The idea of a march had now split the group into three factions. Four men were opposed, three were committed to it, and two were undecided. Nobile's opposition sprang from confidence in the radio and an eventual rescue. For Behounek and Trojani it was a matter of loyalty, although the Czech admittedly was not fit for so strenuous a march. Big, powerful Cecioni, suddenly reduced to helplessness, was dominated by fear.

The two naval officers and Malmgren felt their determination grow with each passing hour, yet their motives were quite different. Malmgren was sure that the two inexperienced Italians were doomed unless their physical strength could be supplemented by his arctic experience. Mariano and Zappi were only concerned with saving themselves, and were quite willing to abandon the others if that was the price for survival.[26]

Viglieri and Biagi remained undecided and silent. The waiting continued. Each man waited in his own way and with his own thoughts. Nobile waited, preoccupied. Should he continue to oppose the split-up of his group, possibly sentencing to death three able-bodied men who could conceivably save themselves? Cecioni waited, using his physical energy. Cursing and sweating, he spent most of the day hammering aluminum tubing and lumber, salvaged from the broken-up gondola of the *Italia,* into the semblance of a crude sled. Behounek and Trojani waited in a state of resignation. Biagi waited in the hope that he would not have to make a decision at all, while Viglieri was hoping that naval solidarity might force the general to let him go too. The minority of three just waited, hopefully eying the dim outline of the two small islands on the horizon.

Slowly the day passed. May nights are bright in the Arctic. The men were in their tent; their eyes were closed and sleep had come. Cecioni suddenly woke out of a nightmare and grabbed Nobile's arm.

"Don't worry, Cecioni," Nobile said. "You won't be left alone. *Ci penserò io a te* (I will take care of you)."

At 1:30 in the morning the sun broke through a cloudy sky. Zappi blinked, got up, woke Mariano and making their way over the twisted bodies that covered every inch of the floor, the two went outside to determine the floe's position. Within seconds, Zappi's contorted face reappeared in the round door of the tent and his yells aroused everybody: "A bear, a big icebear . . . near the tent. . . ."

Instantly everyone was up. Each grabbed whatever weapon he could find; one man a knife, another a file. Faced with an emergency, Malmgren was a clear-thinking expert. "Let me have the pistol, general," he said. Rushing out of the tent, they dragged the two wounded men out, leaving them huddled at the entrance. Yes, there was a bear. Malmgren was in sure command. "Silence," he said, and started advancing quietly and cautiously, followed by Mariano, Zappi and Trojani. Nobile gripped his dog Titina's nose to prevent her from barking.

The bear did not even see the men. Sniffling, he was playfully pushing a red fire extinguisher with his paw. Malmgren advanced to within twenty feet, crouched behind an ice block, aimed the pistol and shot. The bear roared, looked wildly about and tried to flee, only to fall. There were two more shots, but the beast was already quite dead.

The reward for Malmgren's courage and marksmanship was approximately 400 pounds of fresh bear meat—enough to feed the nine men for several weeks. The two wounded men dragged themselves back into the tent, while the others started skinning the bear. Gone were fatigue and depression. "Now there is no need for a march," Cecioni said, "we have enough food. . . ."

When the bear was dismembered, a hundred pounds of meat were put on Cecioni's sled. For almost an hour, four men pushed and pulled the contraption, to cover a distance of about forty yards. Then the sled bent and cracked. One by one the men returned to the tent, tired, dirty and covered with blood. They were more talkative and their spirits were better. It was still nighttime, and exhausted by the heavy physical work, they fell asleep. There was more room in the tent, too. Covered in the greasy, smelly skin of the bear, Malmgren slept in the open and Mariano remained outside as a sentry. (It turned out that the bear had been hungry. His stomach was empty except for a piece of paper with some English writing, which he had found among the debris and eaten.)

Back in Oslo, a spokesman for the Norwegian Government said that Rome had rejected the Norwegian rescue plan it previously had solicited. Conceding that the *Italia* had crashed, Mussolini's Government was considering organization of its own rescue mission. At this time, Lieutenant Lützow-Holm arrived in Tromso, twenty-three hours after leaving Horten and after having flown hundreds of miles, landing several times to replenish fuel. The plane and her pilot were immediately taken aboard the *Hobby,* the ship weighed anchor and headed for Spitsbergen.

At Bluff Point, in Spitsbergen, students Albertini and Matteoda, sergeant Sandrini and private Pedrotti from the Italian Alpini regiment "Tirano" (crack mountain troops) disembarked from the *Città di Milano*. Led by a hunter named Kramer, the group proceeded overland toward Mossel Bay to search for survivors of the *Italia* and to gather information from the local inhabitants, if any.

In Paris, the famous explorer Charcot was prepared to offer his services but his exploring ship, the *Pourquoi-Pas?,* was in dry dock until June 5.

In Moscow, the Territorial Defense Organization called an extraordinary session of its Aeronautical Committee and recommended the formation of a National Relief Organization. Vice Commissar for War Unshlikht, immediately appointed an advisory committee consisting of four professors: Samoilovich, Wiese, Voroblev and Lavrov.

There were other happenings on May 29. Wilkins and Eielson arrived in Copenhagen, and Giudici won his battle for air transportation to Oslo. After arguments and threats of lawsuits, the German Lufthansa organized a special flight for him alone.

Aboard the *Città di Milano,* radio operator Pedretti heard a faint message which caused him intense excitement. "It's the *Italia* . . . I heard the *Italia* . . ." he yelled. Communications officer Baccarani snatched the earphones, listened himself, turned the dial and shook his head. No, he decided, that was not the *Italia,* it was a message from Madagascar. Nevertheless, this *had* been a message from the *Italia;* Pedretti's sensitive ear had recognized it because of Biagi's familiar touch.

On May 30, an easterly wind had pushed the floe five miles southwest and the island of Foyn was now only seven miles away. Nervous and irritable at further delays, Zappi renewed his attack. Whereas on Tuesday the scarcity of food was an argument in favor of an over the ice march to the mainland, its abundance on Wednesday was twisted into a good reason for leaving the floe. Nobile's appeals for obedience, Cecioni's protests, and Behounek's firm insistence bounced off Zappi's stubbornness like rubber balls. Nothing, he said, could deter him from doing what he considered right. In this time of crisis, Filippo Zappi, a career officer in the Royal Italian Navy, deliberately defied the leader of the expedition whose judgment he no longer trusted.

Nobile resisted, but not with the strength of a commander. Mariano then entered the tent, showing the same insistence and making the same arguments. Nobile gave in.

There was one more skirmish when the general called for Malmgren. "Some of the men," he said, "including myself, feel that either Mariano as senior officer or you because of your experience should remain with us." Malmgren listened. "Those who leave must have a leader," he replied, "a man who knows pack ice. A march like this is difficult with many dangers. There has to be someone who knows them . . . who can anticipate them." His face bore a look of resignation. He remained silent for a moment, then added: "All right. I'll do whatever you want. I'll go or I'll stay, just as you wish, general."[27]

Instead of seizing this opportunity to keep his expedition together, Nobile asked: "Can you make such a march with your injured arm?"

"Yes, sir," Malmgren answered. "There is no fracture, it's just a contusion. I won't be able to carry as much as the others, but I can carry thirty to forty pounds."

Dinner that night featured bear soup, which was greasy and only lukewarm. It was eaten in silence. When Mariano got up to leave the tent, Nobile tried to stop him. "Commander," he said, "I want to talk to you . . . alone . . ." There was no answer as Mariano pretended not to hear. A short time later his voice came through the wall of the tent while he was talking to Zappi. "No," he was saying, "we must leave together . . . we know each other too well . . ." A curious variation of Cecioni's refrain: "We came together, we must leave together . . ."

The general had turned out to be a civilian wearing a gold-braided uniform; a leader who could not assert his authority in an emergency, who could not lead. Unlike Amundsen, who always knew how to make his men agree, both among themselves and with him, Nobile had never mastered the technique of leadership. He gave in and sanctioned an over the ice march to the mainland by a group of three men. Slowly the men filed out to make final preparations, and only Malmgren remained inside the tent with Cecioni and Nobile.

"They don't understand how difficult and dangerous a march on pack ice is," the Swede said. "Only a few years ago a group of Germans perished and they were excellently equipped . . ."

"And us," Nobile asked, "what about us?"

The answer was simple: "The drift will carry you eastward."[28] It was an answer which called for no elaboration and Malmgren remained silent. Then, in a voice which was quiet and resigned, he added: "Both parties will die . . ."

"How?" Nobile persisted.

"Starvation, probably. But death by starvation in this climate is said to be painless." Malmgren's blue eyes met the brown ones of Nobile and neither man had anything else to say.

When Malmgren left, Nobile and Cecioni were silent. Viglieri came back and sat down between the two. Behounek and Trojani entered and remained at the door. Biagi, too, returned and sat down in front of Nobile. His forehead was wrinkled and his eyes were sparkling with anger.

"What's the matter, Biagi?" Nobile asked.[29]

"Nothing."

"Oh, no, it's not 'nothing.' You want to go too, don't you? All right, you can do whatever you want. If you want to go, go. . . ." The general was getting angrier and his voice was growing louder. "Don't worry about me and the others," he went on, "we'll manage. You do exactly what you think is right. To me it makes no difference whether you stay or not."

"I'm fit to march," Biagi managed to say.

"All right, then make up your mind," and turning angrily to the others, the general shouted: "Whoever wants to leave, may do so. Cecioni and I we can remain alone. Everybody can do as he pleases. Just make up your minds, either you stay or you go. . . ." His uninjured hand was trembling in impotent rage as he turned on his back and stared up at the tent ceiling.

Victory by default is hollow, and Biagi, not used to making decisions but trained to accept orders, probably would have preferred a firm stand by the general.

Now it was Viglieri's turn to talk. Looking down, he mumbled: "If he leaves, I want to leave too." Two factions had joined forces; the two who had remained undecided were now willing to join the three who were leaving, and the stage was set for all strong men to leave the floe.

There was more bickering, but in the end it was Malmgren who resolved the impasse. ". . . if they leave," he announced, "I will remain. . . . Biagi represents the only hope you have." He could not leave and still live with himself in the knowledge that he had abandoned two wounded men under completely hopeless conditions, he said. The naval personnel discussed the changed situation among themselves. Zappi was in favor of taking the strong, robust Biagi along, but Mariano was opposed. If there was to be a choice between Malmgren and Biagi, he preferred Malmgren. "You cannot just ask to be taken along," he told the radioman. "You are indispensable here; could you justify it if you left?"

There was the voice of authority, which was all Biagi needed to make up his mind. He turned around, retraced the few paces toward the tent, went in, and, crossing his legs, he sat down again. The expression on his face had changed; determination had given way to embarrassment and a faint smile was playing around his lips.

"Sir," he said, looking straight at Nobile, "I did not know what I was saying. I'm not going. There is nobody here to service the radio . . ."

Stands having been taken, the decision was now made final. The two senior naval officers and Malmgren, the meteorologist, were to go. Carefully, Viglieri checked his list of available supplies. The three were entitled to 121 pounds of food and they got it in the form of pemmican, chocolate, and condensed milk—all items easy to carry, less bulky than bear meat. The clothing was adequate except for the shoes. The men had finnskos, designed to give protection against cold, but these were neither water-resistant nor strong enough for a march over the jagged ice.[30] Only Biagi had leather boots, which he had appropriated from the dead Pomella, and Malmgren made a tempting offer: He was willing to trade his watch and its gold chain for Biagi's boots, but Biagi declined.

Now Malmgren became the man of the hour. His depression was gone and he did not seem to remember the mournful prediction he had made only a few hours earlier. He told Nobile: "We will try to make it as fast as possible. If we make ten miles a day, we can reach Cape North within two weeks. Then we will proceed to Kings Bay. There I will

ask Tromso and Oslo for reports on wind and drifts in this area and
we will be able to determine your position. I myself will return with
Swedish airplanes to look for you. . . ." He then gave Nobile an assortment of advice, most of which the general subsequently followed. Finally
the Swede took Nobile's hand and said: "I want you to believe firmly
that the main body of the expedition will be rescued at the last
minute . . ."

Preparations for departure of the three were completed. Mariano's supplies went into Pomella's rucksack; Zappi took one belonging to Angiolotti,
which somehow had been sent on the flight even though its owner remained
in Spitsbergen. Other supplies were carried in small packages tied to
the men's waists. One by one the men went back into the tent for their
last meal together, and only the two scientists remained outside for a
while.

"I'm sorry,"[31] Malmgren said, "that I have to leave you here. I have
known only one other man able to accept fate as philosophically as
you—Sverdrup.[32] But then again it is quite possible that you will be
saved and that it is we who will die."

"In that case," Behounek asked, "what kind of message do you want
me to take back?" Malmgren remained silent. "How about your mother?"
Behounek insisted. "Do you want me to tell her something?"

Malmgren shook his head. "No, that won't be necessary."[33]

Gloom now settled on Frantisek Behounek of Prague. Not only was
he stranded on an ice floe, but he was among a lot of foreigners, with
some of whom he could communicate only by using sign language.

Mariano asked Nobile for a written report. It was a clever move because
such a document automatically gave the commander's party the status
of a mission. The fact of desertion would be hidden more easily behind
the appearance of self-sacrifice. Seeing through the idea, Nobile coldly
eyed his subordinate and said: "Just report verbally."

In the tent whose silence was as grave as that of a church, the men
wrote what they thought would be their last letters. An old pen, borrowed
from Trojani, was passed from one to the other and its scratching noise
was the only sound. Then each handed his message to either Mariano
or Zappi. Realist Trojani even remembered to slip the 3,000 lire he had
on him into his brief letter.

Turning two notes over to Malmgren, Behounek said: "Please don't
send them until three months from today."

"And if you are rescued, what am I to do with them?" Malmgren
asked. "Why, destroy them, of course."[34]

Their last meal together consisted of sugar and three bars of dehydrated
milk for each man. Then they embraced and shook hands. "See you
tomorrow night," Cecioni said, still somehow believing that the three might

come back and take him along. Once more they looked at each other through a veil of tears. "Don't worry," Mariano said, slapping Viglieri on the back, "I'll be back, looking for you in an airplane."[35]

Once outside the tent again, the three men picked up their rucksacks and their packages. "Who leads?" Mariano asked.

"You, of course, you have my compass." Malmgren answered.[36] Professor Behounek would remember these words. And so would Trojani.

With a last wave of the hand, Lieutenant Commanders Zappi and Mariano and Dr. Finn Malmgren were off on their march, only to stop after a few paces. One of Malmgren's finnskos had come loose and he needed Biagi's help to tie it. How would he manage when Biagi was no longer around to help, Felice Trojani wondered.

The three figures, gradually diminishing, disappeared behind blocks of ice, stumbling and sliding slowly along the vast expanse of virgin white.

Standing on hummocks, Behounek, Viglieri, Trojani, and Biagi followed the progress of their companions, then climbed down and went back to the tent, bringing with them an atmosphere of sadness, mixed with relief. At least the bickering was over.

On the following day the weather was calm, there was no perceptible drift and the island of Foyn remained visible. Daily routine on the floe continued. Behounek and Trojani had been designated as cooks and there was breakfast, consisting of chocolate and dehydrated milk; for lunch and supper there was bear meat, which they tried to cook in different ways to make it more palatable. Nobile ordered Biagi to keep on sending his messages. Again and again Biagi would run from sender to receiver, only to be disappointed each time. Cecioni was now making shoes out of pieces of canvas and spoons out of some aluminum. All but the two wounded men stood guard for two hours at a time, watching for polar bears and also for cracks in the floe. The men talked about the three who had left and watched their progress through field glasses. Actually the tiny figures remained visible for two days, moving west at first, then turning eastward. In two days they had only advanced five miles instead of the twenty they had hoped for. In subdued voices the men left behind talked about those who had disappeared with the dirigible, but mostly they just sat and waited. Trojani, now the chief cook, was a philosopher and the language of philosophers is Latin. *"Ede et bibe,"* he would say, dishing out some food, *"post mortem nulla voluptas, pemmican nulla."**

On this, as on any other day, nine o'clock in the evening was the most important moment for the men on the floe. This was the time when Rome's radio station, *San Paolo,* began its daily newscast. On this

* Eat and drink; after death there is no pleasure and no pemmican."

day they heard that the *Hobby* with Lützow-Holm aboard, was making good progress; that skiers Albertini and Matteoda continued their search for survivors of the *Italia* along the northern coast of Spitsbergen. Although the news was generally disappointing, at least they knew that the world had not forgotten them.

Newspapers around the globe had only little to say about rescue efforts. From Friedrichshafen, Germany, it was reported that the Dornier works had offered one of their most powerful planes to the Norwegian Government, and in Rome a committee of "experts" from the Foreign Office and the Ministries for Navy and Air had met "to coordinate all efforts." What these efforts were was not further spelled out, and the official Italian news agency *Stefani* said only that the search would be directed from "three angles," before losing itself in meaningless generalities.

Although not widely publicized, there were other developments. In Oslo, Italy's Ambassador Senni brought a message to Riiser-Larsen. His Government, he said politely, has rejected the rescue plan submitted by Norway, because Mussolini considered the first step, already taken, to be sufficient.[37] *Il Duce* obviously had not bothered taking into account that this first step, the dispatch of Lützow-Holm, was only a part of a larger, more elaborate plan. The worried Riiser-Larsen hurriedly made an appointment with Prime Minister Morwinkel, because he knew that a lone Lützow-Holm flying in a short-range plane with no radio might very well never come back.

"Stop him," the Prime Minister said. "Tell him not to fly."[37]

Riiser-Larsen shook his head: "I know Lützow-Holm," he answered. "He will fly."

"The Government just cannot risk losing Lützow-Holm and the mechanic," Morwinkel said, and Riiser-Larsen nodded his head. So it was decided that Riiser-Larsen would join Lützow-Holm in Spitsbergen, and that rescue flights would be made with two planes, thus decreasing the chance of a lone pilot disappearing in the unexplored Arctic.

In Moscow, the Nobile Relief Committee had been organized under the chairmanship of Vice Commissar for War, Unshlikht and included in its membership the Chief of the Soviet General Staff Kamenev.

Viewing with concern Italy's apparent lack of initiative, Sweden decided to organize a rescue mission for Nobile's expedition. Captain Tornberg of the Swedish Navy was designated Commander of the mission, and, in a telephone call, Major General Amundsen (no kin to Roald of Norway), Commander-in-Chief of the Swedish Air Force, asked Riisser-Larsen to meet with Tornberg. "Okay," Riiser-Larsen said, "but I am leaving for Spitsbergen and the only chance for such a meeting would be in my car on the way to Bergen."[37] Pilots and mechanics were selected from Sweden's armed services, and the Commandant of the School for Aerial

Marksmanship at Rinkaby asked Lieutenant Einar Pal Lundborg to volunteer for "a special mission," the nature of which was not further clarified at the time.

Correspondent Giudici meanwhile interviewed Fridtjof Nansen. The sad-eyed explorer said that rescue efforts in Spitsbergen should be based on an icebreaker. He considered air reconnaissance essential and thought that England should be asked to supply an airship for such a purpose. He concluded the interview by saying: "Certainly in these regions it is . . . necessary to have particular experience with polar ice fields. You will see that eventually the expedition, or the major part of it, will be saved. But it is necessary to act quickly and energetically."[38]

On June 1, Commander Riiser-Larsen left Horten with his navy plane *Maake* 37 aboard the *Ingefire;* Captain Tornberg, having managed to confer with Riiser-Larsen, returned to Sweden, and Lieutenant Lundborg received orders to proceed to Malmslatt "for certain preparations." The Swedish plan was ready. Two Hansa planes with an 800-mile range each would be flown to Goteborg, there to be taken aboard the ship *Tanja.* The 255, with Lieutenant Christell aboard, was to be piloted by Captain Tornberg; the 257 was to carry Lieutenants Rosensvärd and Jacobsson. The small Fokker-31, to be piloted by Lieutenant Lundborg, would be dismantled and transported by rail. In Goteborg most members of the expedition would board the *Quest,*[39] and then both vessels, the *Tanja* and *Quest,* would proceed to Spitsbergen, there to be joined later by the larger plane *Uppland* which Sergeant Nilsson was to fly directly from Tromso across the Barents Sea.

In New York, Lincoln Ellsworth told reporters that he had cabled Amundsen, "offering to do what he could to help in the search for the *Italia,*" but he denied having offered financial assistance. A dispatch from Rome printed in the New York *Times* said: "Exactly one week since Nobile's last wireless message was received, Premier Mussolini has decided to speed efforts to find the lost explorers." A big seaplane, a Savoia 55, was being readied in Italy, but its pilot-designate Umberto Maddalena was still in Spain with General De Pineda. In a further "effort," the paper reported, Balbo had accepted help offered by the Norwegian Government. This was the help Italy had first solicited and then torpedoed by refusing to accept its own part in the plan.

On June 2, the routine and waiting continued. Buried on page 5 of the New York *Times* there were further reports on developments in rescue efforts: The *Braganza,* chartered by the Italian Government, with a crew of sixteen, had arrived in Kings Bay. There, her food stores had been replenished and a group of fifteen Italians had come aboard. Included in this party were: Captain of Alpini, Gennaro Sora, with three ski troopers; a journalist, Cesco Tomaselli; cameraman Montelli; and a Dr. Guido Cendali (*specialist in tropical diseases!*). Work on the Savoia 55 was expected to be completed by Monday, June 4, but somehow Major Maddalena hadn't planned to return from Spain before Tuesday. In Moscow, the Nobile Relief Committee met to draw up plans. According to the New York *Times,* the Russian icebreaker *Persei* was to search the area between Franz Josef Land and Novaya Zemlya, while another Soviet icebreaker, the *Taimyr* was to be sent to the Barents Sea.

When June 3 dawned, Nobile's men found themselves only four miles northeast of Foyn. By now this little piece of uninhabited land was simply called "the island," and had become the yardstick of the men's mood as well as subject of many questions, spoken and unspoken. "Is the island visible? Where? How far?" Often there was no need for questions, because when Foyn was close, birds appeared on the pack ice, temporarily displacing feelings of hopelessness and despair.

Stripped to the waist, his face overgrown by beard, Biagi stood near the radio, outside the tent. Dipping his hands, black with dirt, into an aluminum can, he took some bear fat and smeared it over his body. The nauseating fishy smell did not bother him. The fat would keep him warm when the temperature dropped later in the day. He started singing a popular Italian tune and Trojani, standing a few paces away, joined in. Behounek went to ask Nobile for permission to use some additional butter to fry the bear meat. "Will you be able to make some more observations with your instruments?" Nobile asked. "Certainly," was the answer, "I have been taking readings for several days already."

Biagi had tried his hand at fishing but with no luck; a polar bear was seen and shot at, but escaped unharmed. A strong drift set in again and "the island" vanished in the fog; with it, hope again vanished. Biagi turned moody and dejected. "This stupid wind," he kept on mumbling, "this stupid wind." Again and again, repeated in English, Italian and French, he sent out the same message: "SOS, SOS, *Italia* on pack ice near Foyn, northeast Spitsbergen, latitude . . . longitude . . . cannot move lacking sleds and having two wounded. Airship crashed elsewhere. Answer via *Ido* 32."* The answer was always silence.

On this day, the *Braganza* left Kings Bay and made her way past Amsterdam Island; the *Hobby,* with Lützow-Holm aboard, was nearing Advent Bay. Riiser-Larsen was on the high seas; the *Quest* was standing by in Tromso; and at Malmslatt, Sweden, Lieutenants Lundborg and Schyberg had made a test flight in the ski-equipped Fokker-31. Dietrichson and Meisterlin now arrived in Berlin to negotiate the purchase of a suitable plane for Amundsen to make flights in search of Nobile.

---

* IDO—call letters of radio station San Paolo, Rome. 32 refers to the wave length, expressed in meters.

In Italy, the start of the Savoia 55 was postponed until June 6. In a short dispatch from Moscow the New York *Times* reported: "A radio amateur at Voznesensk reported tonight that he had heard a thin message Italia-Nobile-SOS-Franz Josef . . . ."

A music-loving farmer and radio amateur named Schmidt in the tiny village of Voznesenye* had actually intercepted, between two concerts, a faint message: ". . . Tengo terra . . . SOS . . . SOS . . . RAO, RAO . . . Foyn . . . Nobile . . ." Nicholas Schmidt duly notified his local Soviet, whose members, after some head-scratching, forwarded a report to Moscow.

Norwegian papers called Italy's attitude insulting to Norway, and the *Times* noted: "Official circles in Norway are at a loss to understand Italy's attitude toward the rescue operation." Italy's contribution to the search for the *Italia* was pretty pathetic as the *Città di Milano* returned to Kings Bay.

On the 4th of June there were no birds on the floe and the drift continued. Conversation among the men was short. They were tense and snapped at each other. With an impassive face, Biagi listened to the radio station of *San Paolo*. Suddenly he grew frenzied with excitement. "Victory," he yelled, "victory . . ." Reverberating in the tent, his shouts roused the others out of apathy, and Biagi felt five pairs of eyes staring at him hopefully and with eager anticipation. "No," he said, shaking his head sadly. His messages had not been heard. He had become aroused because, in a championship soccer game in Amsterdam, Italy defeated Spain, 7 to 1.

The *Braganza* reached Mossel Bay, where hunters came aboard, but the locals had no news of the *Italia*. Accompanied by two of them, Captain Sora and three of his men set out to cross New Friesland on skis, while the *Braganza* continued toward Cape North. The *Hobby* had reached Advent Bay, where she took some dog teams aboard and then went to Kings Bay. The ship had no radio and had to be back in Norway within ten days because of a previous charter.

On June 5, *Maddalena's* departure from Italy was again postponed, and in Moscow Professor Samoilovich sat in on a session of Russia's National Relief Committee which decided that the icebreaker *Malygin* would take an airplane, the JU13, aboard and go northward along the west coast of Novaya Semlya. The *Sedov* was to be readied in Archangel for another, as yet undefined, rescue expedition. An Italian embassy official

---

* The *Times* was in error. Voznesensk is a city in the Ukraine; Voznesenye is located in the district of Archangel.

in Moscow, while acknowledging the good will of the Soviet Government, considered it unlikely that Russia could come to Nobile's assistance.

The *Braganza* entered Hinlopen Strait to explore Lomme Bay; the *Hobby* stopped briefly at South Gate, then dropped anchor at Biscay Hook and Lieutenant Lützow-Holm took off on his first reconnaissance flight. Three hours later he was back, having seen no trace of either the *Italia* or her men.

The Kramer-led group of skiers came aboard the *Hobby* after a fruitless six-day search, while on a siding of Malmslatt airfield, Lundborg's dismantled plane was packed in a railroad car. Swedish Major General Amundsen met with members of the Swedish expedition to wish them good luck.

4

IN the evening of June 6, twelve days after the crash and six days after the splitup of the survivors, Biagi was once more listening to the newscast from Rome, when his face suddenly lit up and his hands began to tremble. "They heard us," he yelled, "they heard us." Listening and writing at the same time, Biagi took down the news they all had been waiting for: "The Soviet Government has notified the Italian Government that . . . ." Snatched from despair, the survivors were suddenly exalted to the peaks. The message, sent by Biagi three days earlier, traveling half way around the earth, had completed a course from the floe near Foyn Island to the Russian village of Voznesenye, to Moscow, to Rome, and then back to the drifting lump of ice.

"Now there is no doubt that the *Città* will hear us," Nobile said.

"Do you think that we will get home?" Trojani asked.

Nobile knew that this message was only a step in a series of events which *might* lead to salvation. "That," he answered, "depends on many things, but let us hope."

At 9:20 in the evening, six dirty, bearded men floating in the Arctic Ocean had a celebration: An extra ration of three grams of milk and five grams of sugar was distributed, and each man toasted Nicholas Schmidt, the farmer, with a carefully measured ounce of alcohol.

Excitement and anticipation did not die easily on the floe. Sleep did not come and the night stretched into another day. The business of living went on. With a pair of rusty scissors, Cecioni cut meat into small pieces so that only a minimum of fuel would be needed to cook it. Biagi kept on sending for a full hour without interruption but everyone on the floe waited with more impatience than ever to hear the nine o'clock news from Rome.

When the hour came, the men heard that a radio amateur, Clyde Amos from Altoona, Pennsylvania, had reported hearing a message from the *Italia,* which, he said, had crashed along the 84th degree northern latitude. Again a cycle was completed, and in utter error as far as facts went. If the American report was accepted as true, the rescue efforts would be directed toward an area off the coast of Greenland, at least three hundred and fifty miles from the actual location of the floe. On the other hand, if the message was disregarded, what guarantee was there that Schmidt's word would be believed?

Elsewhere during this time, Lieutenant Lützow-Holm had taken off on a search flight to Brandy Bay. With gas enough for four hours of flight, he had disappeared into the dense fog and was now long overdue.

While members of the Swedish expedition were already leaving for Spitsbergen, Major Maddalena, in Italy, expressed hope that he might be able to start on June 8.

Riiser-Larsen arrived in fog-smothered Kings Bay and his plane was lowered onto the water; the *Braganza* was stuck in Hinlopen Strait and the *Hobby* was icebound near Moffen Island. Russia's Professor Wiese went to Archangel to board the icebreaker *Malygin,* while Dietrichson and Meisterlin were returning from Berlin to Oslo after fruitless negotiations to get an airplane for Amundsen. The conditions set forth by the Lufthansa proved inacceptable and the Dornier works were in no position to sell a plane because the only one available had already been contracted for by the Italian Government. There was no recent news about the leisurely Major Maddalena and his Savoia 55.

June 8 was a good day for the men on the floe. The wind had stopped and a bright sun hung in the sky. The uncertainty had finally come to an end. Radio Rome broadcast that the *Città di Milano* had heard Biagi quite clearly in the morning. There were smiles and jokes, a mood of optimism and some of the men even used the small, carefully guarded cake of soap to wash their hands for the first time in two weeks.

That evening the first direct radio contact between the floe and the *Città di Milano* was established, and Biagi transmitted the men's position as well as his own serial number to assure that his message was not a hoax.

In Kings Bay, bad weather immobilized Riiser-Larsen. Lützow-Holm, who had been forced down by heavy fog shortly after takeoff fifty-two hours earlier, managed to take off again and flew to explore Framlin Bay and New Friesland. His search was fruitless and one hour later, out of gas, he was forced to make another emergency landing in Mossel Bay. The *Braganza* succeeded in reaching the *Hobby* and a radioman was transferred to the base ship of the Norwegian expedition to operate its newly installed radio.

On the following day there was a steady exchange of messages between

Nobile and the *Città di Milano*. The general asked for shoes, guns, sleds and boats, described the morale of his men, talked about worsening ice conditions, and sent lengthy, exasperating advice on how to conduct rescue operations. There was only a brief account of what had happened; the names of survivors were not given, and Pomella's death was not even mentioned. It appeared that the general was still disguising himself as a great arctic expert and wanted to salvage success out of failure by assuming long-distance command of the rescue operations.

Aboard the *Città di Milano* a nervous Captain Romagna, ill-prepared for his role, felt the weight of responsibility resting upon him, and advised abruptly:

> Use batteries sparingly . . . leave it to us to organize and equip rescue parties. . . . Three Swedish planes are on their way; Captain Riiser-Larsen is aboard the *Hobby* near Moffen Island, which is blocked by ice. Russia is preparing a big icebreaker, and we will try to locate the group of three near North Cape.

There was still no word of Major Maddalena's departure for Spitsbergen.

On June 10 the floe was drifting back toward "the island" again. At a distance of about ten yards from the tent, Behounek suddenly saw the ice splitting and, as he watched, the crack widened to a lead some three yards wide. It became obvious that camp would have to be moved. In the meantime, heavy lines had been painted on the outside walls of the tent with dye from salvaged glass markers to make it more conspicuous. It would soon be referred to all over the world as "The Red Tent."

In the early hours of the day, the Italian contingent of the *Braganza,* which included the reporter Tomaselli, heard for the first time that Nobile's group had been heard from. It had taken Captain Romagna more than a day to notify this ship which he himself considered as having the best chance of reaching the survivors of the *Italia.*

In the Kings Bay area the weather was better, and Commander Riiser-Larsen, with a mechanic aboard, took off in his *Maake 37* plane. Flying over Mossel Bay, he found Lützow-Holm and landed near by. On his return to the *Hobby* he dispatched a message to the Norwegian Ministry of Defense:

> If position given by the *Italia* 80°30′ N—28° E is verified, it is imperative that every effort at rescue be made immediately. Weather conditions prevent my flying north. At my request, the *Braganza* has been recalled to Kings Bay and will act as base ship. Will proceed as far east as possible. Have advised Captain of *Città di Milano* to ask for powerful Soviet icebreaker. Have further requested him to ask airman Maddalena to hasten his departure since our planes are too small to carry needed supplies.

On the *Città di Milano,* strict censorship went into effect. Every message from Nobile was forwarded to Rome and every decision had to await Government sanction. All individual initiative was stifled. A correspondent succeeded in approaching taciturn Captain Romagna. "Are all the crew members alive?" he asked.

"Of course," the captain answered evasively. "I'm quite sure they are together."

"Is this information which you have received from the general?"

"I know it."[40]

At about the same time, Major Umberto Maddalena finally took off in his plane from Sesto Calende in Italy. His intermediate destination was Zurich in Switzerland, but, unable to cross the Alps, the pilot changed course and flew via Marseilles. South of Lyons he was forced down to an emergency landing in the Rhone. It had taken the Italian Government exactly sixteen days to initiate this first move. At a time when sixty-one seaplanes were on an exhibition flight in the Mediterranean, Italy could spare only one aircraft for the rescue mission.

On June 11 Captain Sora and his skiers returned to the *Braganza,* and the ship steamed back to Kings Bay in accordance with Riiser-Larsen's request. An emergency supply of gasoline was delivered to Lützow-Holm, who then returned to the *Hobby.* Thus all the Spitsbergen-based rescue teams were again in Kings Bay harbor: The two small Norwegian planes, Italy's *Città di Milano,* Norway's *Hobby* and the *Braganza.*

By two in the afternoon a telegram, addressed to Professor Samoilovich was sent off in Moscow. The message read:

> By order of the Commissar, preparations to start immediately for departure icebreaker *Krassin* Spitsbergen. Readiness to be accomplished latest morning June thirteenth. Relief Committee, Unshlikht.

The *Krassin** was an English-built icebreaker of 1917 vintage with a maximum displacement of 10,620 tons. For eighteen months the ship had been lying idle in the port of Leningrad, guarded by a bored detachment of twenty-five men. Samoilovich called a meeting of his regional committee, which was attended by members of Leningrad's port authorities. There were several subjects on the hastily drawn agenda. Procurement of a new crew for the *Krassin* had priority as well as getting food sufficient for a six months' trip.

In a reassuring message the *Città di Milano* informed the men on the floe of rescue efforts under way:

> Swedish expedition with three planes and a base ship is on its way to Kings Bay. Moffen Island no longer snowbound and *Hobby*, with two small planes aboard, has left. It is hoped she may advance far enough to the east to enable planes to reach you. Seaplane (S55) piloted

by Maddalena has left Italy. Plane of Major Penzo is to take off shortly. A Russian icebreaker with two planes, one of which is a big three-motored job, sailing today from Archangel. Another icebreaker being readied.

Never before June 1928 had so gigantic a rescue operation been mounted. Before the spiraling drama was over, six nations—Norway, Sweden, Russia, Finland, France, and Italy—mobilized a total of eighteen ships and about fifteen hundred men. There were small ships with crews ranging from fifteen to thirty men: the *Hobby, Quest, Tanja, Braganza, Heimland, Quentin Roosevelt,** *Pourquois-Pas?* and *Michael Sars.* And there were the giants: the *Strasbourg* with 475 men, the *Tordenskjold* with 250, and the *Krassin* with 138.[41] The *Città di Milano* carried, between her crew and the auxiliary personnel, a total of 220 men; there were other icebreakers—*Malvgin, Sedov* and *Peresi.* Also, there was a total of twenty-two planes. Norway sent four, Sweden five, Finland one, and France and Russia two each. In addition there were two teams, with a total of nineteen dogs, scouting the northern coast of Spitsbergen.

On June 12 a strong wind from the west carried Nobile's floe far away from "the island." Radio communication became poor, and once again the men's mood was depressed. The ice was beginning to melt: there were puddles everywhere, some of them knee-deep.

 All the American press was fairly confused, but in the editorial offices of the *Times* confusion grew into fantasy as the paper reported on its front page: "Nobile leads group in quest of land. 3 of crew missing. Separated from main party, he and 3 others carry two injured." The story itself said: "Nobile's attempted landing was a partial failure as only 6 men succeeded in reaching the ice. The airship continued to drift until it had covered 30 kilometers and another group succeeded in escaping onto the ice. After this the balloon [sic] drifted still farther until finally the remainder of the crew jumped free."

The Norwegian press was angry at Italy. Oslo's *Dagbladet* blasted Mussolini:

> If the Italian Government had not . . . nullified the plan . . . pre-
> pared by the Ministry of War and . . . Riiser-Larsen, the relief
> expedition would long ago have had a Dornier-Wal from Friedrichshafen
> at Spitsbergen. Instead of taking the Norwegian Government's advice,
> the Italian Government decided Italy wanted to deal with the situation
> herself. If Rome had listened to the experienced polar explorers and
> ice experts, a great Russian icebreaker would long ago have been at

---

 * A French ship named in honor of Theodore Roosevelt's son, killed in France during World War I.

Spitsbergen. Now it will be sent at Italy's request but in all probability too late.[42]

The same paper quoted Meisterlin, head of the Norwegian Air Transport Company:

It is strange how everything has been delayed if one considers that relief activities could have been organized here long ago and the *Italia's* crew . . . could have been rescued. The responsibility must be placed where it belongs and it is beyond all doubt where that is.[42]

Knowing how inexperienced Nobile and his men were, Amundsen said gloomily, "If they try to reach land, they will not get far."

The fog had stalled rescue operations in Spitsbergen. Arriving from Green Harbor, a motorboat brought two weather-beaten men to Kings Bay: Ludwig Varming and Joseph Van Dongen with his nine dogs. They disembarked and went aboard the *Braganza*.

In Leningrad, Professor Samoilovich received another telegram: ". . . you are appointed chief of the expedition. Previous instructions to proceed Spitsbergen hereby confirmed . . ." Samoilovich was to be chairman of the "Big Three" directorate aboard the *Krassin*. The other two were a political commissar, Paul Oras, and a pilot named Chukhnovsky. At that moment Chukhnovsky knew nothing about all this, since he was laid up in hospital, all prepared for an appendectomy.[43]

The *Krassin* was towed along the Neva to the port of Leningrad, and at eleven o'clock in the evening coaling began, while a new crew was being selected for the icebreaker. Her regular skipper was on another assignment so a Captain Eggi took his place. Eggi's first assistant was young Paul Ponamarev, who one day would command Russia's first atomic icebreaker.

Meanwhile, preparations aboard the *Malygin* were completed and at midnight she left Archangel. Among those aboard were Professor Wiese, leader of the expedition, and two pilots, one of them Michael Babushkin.[44] The *Malygin* was to proceed to Hope Island, then push northward as far as possible so its pilots could take off in search of Nobile's group, drop supplies, and, if feasible, even attempt a direct rescue.

On June 13 "the island" remained invisible, the radio was mute, and the men on the floe were in the throes of hopelessness. They stayed silently in the tent, listening to a howling wind. The floe drifted to the southeast, and at the end of the day the men found themselves farther from the mainland than ever. A few feet from the tent a channel formed and grew rapidly to a width of six yards.

In Spitsbergen, Norwegians Nois and Tandberg disembarked from the *Hobby* with a sled and ten dogs and started on a march from Wahlenberg

Bay to Cape Platen, in an attempt to locate Mariano's party.[45] The *Braganza* replenished her supplies and turned northward again, toward Beverly Sound. Among those aboard were Sora, Varming and Van Dongen. In a pocket of his trousers Van Dongen carried a note written in English, stamped and signed by Captain Romagna-Manoja, skipper of the *Città di Milano*. It read:

> I hereby . . . engage Mr. Varming, Ludwig, and Mr. Van Dongen, Joseph, and their dog teams to send them . . . to the rescue of General Nobile's party, under the same conditions made by the Norwegian Government to Mr. Nois and his dog team for the same purpose.

The conditions were simple, for men and dogs were to be provided with food and shelter; no payment for any services that might be rendered.

Pilots Riiser-Larsen and Lützow-Holm now started together on their first flight toward Nobile's tent. It was to be one of a series of seven, all of them unsuccessful.

Elsewhere the *Krassin's* crew had been assembled, and the ship was being loaded. Walter Bruns, Secretary General of the German Aero-Arctic Society, urged the United States to dispatch its big dirigible, the *Los Angeles* to Nobile's rescue. Secretary of the Navy Wilbur replied: "The *Los Angeles* is filled with helium. Because of this, movements of the airship are so limited that a flight, as you propose it, is not possible. For this reason the Navy Department expresses its deep regret at not being able to participate in the rescue of the Nobile expedition."[46] In a similar manner, Britain too, expressed regret at being unable to send her dirigible R-31 to the Arctic.

Toward evening, Major Maddalena arrived in Vadso, some three days after having left Italy. At every intermediate stop the major stalled until his demands for increased remuneration were met.[47] At about the same time, Major Penzo, the pilot of Italy's second rescue plane, reached Amsterdam.

On June 14 atmospheric conditions again made radio contact with the men on the floe impossible. The night was cold; an ice hummock broke loose and crashed with a thunderous noise into the newly formed lead, not far from the tent. The floe was reduced to a small area of dirty irregular ice, in danger of breaking up at any minute, and Nobile decided to move his camp forty yards.

Fog immobilized the two Norwegian fliers in Spitsbergen and a rough sea thwarted Maddalena's attempt to take off from Vadso. Airman Chukhnovsky's plane was loaded aboard the *Krassin,* and the French Government offered Amundsen a big plane in which a flier named Guil-

baud was to have attempted a transatlantic flight. In London, Wilkins was knighted by King George V and was henceforth to be known as Sir Hubert.[48]

June 15 brought good weather to the floe. The sky was blue, the visibility perfect, and the drift slight. Trojani sighted another bear and Biagi tried to shoot him, but the animal escaped. "I had to shoot from too far away," he apologized. "The bear was about to eat Pomella . . . he had already pushed the ice off his right arm."

"Well," Nobile said, "we'd better bury him. You, Biagi, go and drop him into the water." And while the others remained back in the tent, Biagi covered the body with canvas. "I'm sending him down now," he yelled. There was no answer.[49]

In Spitsbergen both the *Hobby* and the *Braganza* were on their way toward Cape North. Riiser-Larsen attempted a flight, but was forced back by fog. Maddalena tried twice to take off from Vadso and failed both times. Captain Tornberg's two-ship, three-plane expedition was battling strong winds. Swedish Sergeant Nilson flew his *Uppland* to Narvik and Amundsen accepted France's offer, whereupon preparations began to adjust Guilbaud's plane for its new northern mission.

The Italian reporter Giudici had an interview with Amundsen. "There is a sentiment of solidarity," Amundsen said, "which must bind men. . . . Before this sentiment our personal resentments must disappear. Anything that has disturbed my relations with General Nobile has been forgotten. . . . Today I see one thing only. General Nobile and his companions are in danger, and it is necessary to do everything humanly possible to save them . . . it is necessary to act with the greatest promptness." Then, looking at a model of his N-25, Amundsen added, while his eyes assumed a faraway look: ". . . if you only knew how splendid it is up there! That's where I want to die; and I only hope death will come to me chivalrously, that it will overtake me in the fulfillment of a high mission, quickly, without suffering . . ."[50]

At 1:00 A.M. there was a farewell party aboard the *Krassin*. Venerated 82-year-old Professor Karpinski was hoisted up in a basket, and there was Italian Consul General Spano, a representative of the Soviet Foreign Office, as well as friends and relatives. There were toasts and speeches and the Arctic Institute sent a big bouquet of chrysanthemums.

At 3:15 the *Krassin* lifted anchor and set course for Bergen, Norway. It had taken barely 112 hours to man, equip, supply, test, and take out to sea the icebreaker, which carried 134 men, two women, and a plane. Mussolini needed one week to make up his mind, nine more days to prepare a plane, and now, five days out of Italy, Major Maddalena was still in Vadso.

On June 16, at Cape North, the *Hobby* was preparing for her return trip to Norway. Men, planes and supplies of the Norwegian expedition headed by Riiser-Larsen were transferred aboard the *Braganza*. Maddalena took off from Vadso but returned after five flying hours because of unfavorable weather, while Major Penzo landed in Stockholm. The *Uppland* arrived in Narvik, and Germany offered Balbo two planes, which the Italian Undersecretary declined with thanks. At 7:13 A.M. the *Krassin* was in the open sea, its decks a mess. Coal and food were scattered everywhere. Journalists were drafted to help the crew carry supplies downstairs, while the ship got up a speed of ten knots.

At Caudebeque-sur-Seine, in France, under the skillful hands of pilot Guilbaud, the huge Latham 47 slowly rose into the air and set off for Bergen, while at Oslo's railroad station a crowd waited for Amundsen, who was taking the night express to meet Guilbaud. A little girl had a bouquet of flowers. The man with the grizzled face and the knotty hands gently patted the back of her head; some women cried.

"Come back!" someone yelled. "Norway needs you!"

"Our machine is speedy," Amundsen said. He was planning to reach Spitsbergen in one day and to start reconnaissance flights immediately.

At midnight the position of icebreaker *Malygin* was 72°28′ N. 30°50′ E., as she also headed north through open sea at 10 knots.

June 17 was a clear and bright day on the floe. The sky was blue, the sun warm and the vast emptiness of the ice was silent. In the afternoon, however, the silence was broken by a monotonous drone and straining eyes scanned the horizon.

"Airplanes," Biagi yelled suddenly, "airplanes . . ."

Two dots appeared in the distance. Approaching from the south, they seemed to be headed straight for the tent. They soon became clearly visible. There was shouting and excitement. "Start the fire, fire the signals," somebody yelled. But when still at a distance of some two or three miles, the planes turned and disappeared.

Riiser-Larsen and Lützow-Holm had made a four-hour flight in search of the "Red Tent," reported at 80°33′ North, 27°12′ East, some five miles northeast of Foyn Island, but had been unable to find it.

Nobile sent a message to the *Città di Milano:*

Take advantage of favorable weather and have planes return today. Notify us of time of departure so we can be ready to make signals.

But the day ended, the night passed, and no planes returned. The difference between success and failure had been three miles.

The *Braganza* was vainly trying to go north, and Maddalena had made two more abortive attempts to take off; Penzo landed with his *Marina II* in Luleo, Sweden. Tornberg's Swedish Rescue Expedition was now some two hundred miles from Kings Bay, and Norway's Wisting left by boat, to meet Amundsen in Spitsbergen. Sweden's big airplane *Uppland* took off from Narvik, but was forced to land in Tromso. Also in Tromso on that day was a newly arrived Finnish rescue mission, comprising pilots Sarko and Lihr with their plane called *Turku,* as well as Guilbaud's Latham.

On June 18, Swedish Lieutenant Lundborg was standing on the bridge of the *Quest,* which was groping its way through a dense fog. Shortly after midnight he saw pack ice for the first time and the ship slowed down.

Penzo arrived in Tromso. There were now four planes in that northern Norwegian harbor, three of them set for a final hop to Spitsbergen.[51]

The White Eagle of Norway, Roald Amundsen, silent and very serious, climbed into the big silvery-blue Latham. With him were Leif Dietrichson, René Guilbaud, copilot De Cuverville, a mechanic named Gilbert Brazy, and the radioman, Emile Valette. All eyes were on the famous Amundsen as he nodded his head to signal the start. The plane took to the air, circled and swept out over the murky waters, disappearing into the gray skies.

In Spitsbergen the *Braganza* had reached Beverly Sound. Carrying with them food sufficient for thirty-eight days, Sora, Varming, and young Van Dongen left with their team of nine dogs, in search of Mariano's group. Their pace was fast and covering forty-odd miles they reached Cape Wrede in fourteen hours.

Twice, Riiser-Larsen and Lützow-Holm flew toward the "Red Tent" and twice they returned without having found it. Shadows and weird reflections cast on the ice made the identification of a small tent almost impossible, so much the more because available maps were inaccurate and the drift was steadily changing the location of Nobile's floe. Riiser-Larsen knew that a radio was desperately needed, but the two small Norwegian planes had none.

At 7 P.M. the *Quest* was in Kings Bay, anchored alongside the *Città di Milano* and a barge carried Tornberg to a conference with Romagna-Manoja. Nobile's position was said to be six miles northeast of Foyn, but the island was marked incorrectly on the maps which were available, although this was not known.

At 8 P.M. there was a routine message from the Latham's radio operator, Valette.

At 9:30 P.M. the *Quest* lifted anchor and headed north to Virgo Bay.

Maddalena took off from Vadso, but engine trouble forced him to make an emergency landing on Bear Island. Within sight of Hope Island, the *Malygin* reached the perimeter of arctic ice. Steadily pounding the water, the icebreaker *Krassin* was making its way toward Bergen, as an occasional melancholy Russian folksong was heard over the drumming noise of the waves. Everywhere there was coal, in the food, in the clothes . . . and somebody had maliciously mixed ground glass with cabbage.[52] At the dining table an angry Professor Samoilovich saw a new face: that of young Ljubov Andreevna Vorontsova, a stowaway journalist.

June 19: At 2:30 A.M. the silence of Kings Bay was broken by the roar of a huge silvery bird, which came down smoothly on the water, not far from the *Città di Milano*. Major Maddalena at long last had made it. It had taken him eleven days but now he was there. Standing on the plane's fuselage, he said dramatically, "Gas," before boarding a launch which was to carry him to a conference with Romagna-Manoja. There was new excitement among the Italians. Where everybody else had failed, Maddalena would of course succeed!

Once again the Norwegian fliers took off, but they could not find the camp and returned after a three-hour flight.

5:00 A.M. The *Quest* dropped anchor in Virgo Bay.

5:20 A.M. Maddalena, copilot Cagna, and mechanic Rampini were ready for a takeoff in their Savoia 55. The pilot gunned his motors and one hour later he was flying over the *Braganza*.

At five minutes past seven o'clock the men on the floe again heard the distant but distinct drone of motors. They even recognized the *Savoia*. Maddalena was heading in a northeasterly direction. Twice they saw him cruising, coming as close as four miles to the tent, before he disappeared again in the mist at 7:30 A.M. Toward noon he was back in Kings Bay.

Later in the day, a lone Norwegian plane which had both Riiser-Larsen and Lützow-Holm aboard was again sighted by Nobile's men. Again the pilots could not see the tent. Nobile sent lengthy messages with more suggestions and Romagna promised that planes would return on the following day.

Nois, Tandberg and their Italian satellites reached Cape Platen after vainly searching Scoresby Island and the northern coast along Cape Cloven. Their mission was finished and they went aboard the *Braganza* in Beverly Sound, while another all-Italian ski patrol headed by Albertini started out on still another search for Mariano's party.

The *Hobby* was now homeward bound, and the icebreaker *Malygin* was off Hope Island. The *Krassin* was just approaching Bergen, and the Finnish plane *Turku* was enroute to Kings Bay aboard the *Marita*. And then, of course, there was Amundsen's Latham . . . But where was the Latham? Her radio was silent and the six-hundred-mile flight should not have taken more than seven hours . . .

In the afternoon the *Tanja,* with her cargo of aircraft, arrived in Virgo

Bay. The unloading and assembly of both Hansa planes started immediately so that by nine o'clock in the evening lieutenants Rosensvärd
and Jacobsson were ready for their first test flight in the 255.

In Oslo, reporter Giudici ran out of people to interview. He managed
to obtain an invitation to a reception given by Russia's Ambassador,
Mrs. Kollontai, and unexpectedly his request to accompany the *Krassin*
was granted. He was to be the only non-Russian correspondent aboard
the icebreaker.

June 20: At twenty-five minutes past midnight, the silence of Kings
Bay was pierced by the drone of a plane as Penzo arrived in the *Marina II*
and shortly thereafter Sergeant Nilsson's *Uppland* came to a landing,
after a flight of six hours and ten minutes, before proceeding to join
the main body of the Swedish expedition.

At 6 A.M. the *Città di Milano* informed Nobile that Maddalena was
about to take off again in search of him. This time chances for success
were better: Both Nobile and Romagna had accepted advice from the
experienced Riiser-Larsen. Nobile now had mirrrors, improvised out of
tin and aluminum, with which the sun's rays could be reflected at an
approaching plane to attract attention. Maddalena's aircraft was now
equipped with a radio and the ingenious Baccarani worked out a simple
code. Transmitting single letters, Biagi should be able to guide the pilot
toward the "Red Tent," as soon as radio contact between plane and
floe was established.*

At 7 A.M. the floats of the Savoia 55 cut through the icy water.
Leaving a spray behind, the plane gained altitude and disappeared in
a northeasterly direction. On the floe everybody was outside the tent,
waiting. Trojani had a supply of oil-soaked rags which he was to set
afire as soon as Maddalena was within sight. Viglieri was on a hummock
and with prearranged hand signals he was to tell Biagi the plane's course.
On still another hummock stood Professor Behounek, holding one of the
improvised mirrors. Cecioni was sitting at the tent's entrance and next
to him, on the broken-down hand-made sled, was Nobile, frail, intense,
and partly snowblind.

It was 8:20 A.M. There was direct radio contact between the men
in the air and those on the floe. Biagi signaled:

DDDD 70 (Turn seventy degrees to the right!)—The plane turned.

SSSS 90 (Ninety degrees to the left!)—The plane obeyed.

VVVV 6 (Straight ahead for six kilometers!) †

As if pulled by invisible wires, Maddalena was headed straight for the

---

* D—Destra (Right); S—Sinistra (Left); V—Via (straight ahead);
T—Tenda (tent); R—Ritorno (Return); K (drop supplies).
† Approximately 4 miles.

tent. The motors droned louder, the plane grew bigger, its markings were becoming visible to the men on the floe. All of them became excited, with Biagi leaving the radio to joyfully throw his hat into the air. Everybody was waving jubilantly as the plane flew on, past them, and proceeded in a straight line, the noise of its motors gradually dying down. Twelve anxious eyes followed the silvery bird as it turned and glided, apparently trying to retrace its course.

It was simply unbelievable. The pilot had overshot his goal without even seeing either tent or men. Radio contact was now lost and the men watched in helpless frustration as the plane kept on circling aimlessly in the distance. It took thirty minutes before radio contact was re-established and Maddalena was seen heading once more for the tent.

This time Biagi did *not* throw his hat into the air. His fingers kept on sending the series of T's, indicating that the plane was directly overhead and this time the pilot saw them.[53] Packages started sailing down through the air. Maddalena circled the camp eleven times, before leaving again for the base.

There were 650 pounds of supplies—all of which had been improperly packaged and were dropped with inadequate parachutes. Some of the parcels fell into the water and could not be found. Both rifles broke on impact and the radio batteries were useless. There were six pairs of shoes, none of them big enough to fit Viglieri. But there were rubber boats, sleeping bags and some food, including thirty eggs, most of which were broken, and fifty bananas, mostly rotten.

Nobile was fuming. He sent a long politely worded message to Romagna, asking for other batteries, cigarettes, pemmican and handkerchiefs. He was still dispensing advice: Never mind these ski patrols, he seemed to say, let us have more air action; but above all, let Amundsen take over, let Amundsen co-ordinate rescue activities. Nobile finally wanted Amundsen.

Where was Amundsen?

Captain Romagna was a career officer in the Royal Italian Navy, who did not like this interference. There were directives from Rome, there was a chain of command. Who was Nobile, this Air Force general, to tell the Royal Italian Navy how to rescue him? Romagna felt that he was doing the best he could, strictly in accordance with instructions from higher up. In addition he had still other things to worry about: The Albertini group was at Rips Bay and Sora's party was at Cape Platen. The *Braganza* was standing by east of Cape North, and there were coded telegrams from Rome. So what if Maddalena did not take pemmican and salt? And what was wrong with eggs and bananas?

Tornberg's men continued their preparations: The *Quest* went to Murchison Bay in Hinlopen Strait to establish an advance base. At noon the Hansa 257 made her first trial flight.

At 1:50 P.M. a triumphant Umberto Maddalena was back in Kings Bay, greeted with three blasts from a siren of the *Città di Milano,* whose sailors were lining the deck and shouting "Eviva!" Nobile's brother, the meteorologist Amadeo said: "This is the first day of sunshine for me . . ."

The *Marita,* carrying the Finnish expedition, now arrived in Kings Bay. . . . Some four hundred miles from the Red Tent the *Malygin* was icebound and the unloading of Babushkin's plane started. . . . There was the *Persei.* . . . There was icebreaker *Krassin* coming. . . . There was Amundsen's Latham—but where *was* the Latham?

Journalist Odd Arnesen was walking the deck with the captain of the *Città di Milano.*

"What has become of your countryman," Romagna asked nervously. "Why has he not reported to me here?"[54]

"The captain knows that Amundsen is a man who acts according to his own ideas and a man who usually knows what he is doing." Arnesen said.

"Yes, but why has he not come here? I have the latest position reports and other details."

"Possibly Amundsen is of the opinion that speedy aid is essential—he may have made straight for the dirigible group about which we know nothing. You may be sure he knows what he is doing."

"Rescue of the Nobile group is more urgent. The men with the dirigible have a better supply of food and are not in such a precarious position."

"But Amundsen felt just the other way . . ."

Anxiety was beginning to be felt for the White Eagle. For more than two days there had been no word from the Latham, whose fuel supply was sufficient for only 30 flight hours.

At Cape Platen, ambitious little Sora abandoned Varming, now snow-blind. The captain had set out to prove that Italians were as good on skis as anyone. Afraid that Van Dongen might decide to stay with his helpless friend, Sora kept the two men separated until he and the Dutch youth could continue their march toward Broch Island.[55] In the evening they pitched their tent on Rips Island, where they had arrived without having seen a trace of Mariano's party.

At 8:15 P.M. Captain Tornberg's two Hansa planes and the *Uppland* were on an extended reconnaissance flight. They passed within two miles of Nobile's floe and returned to base without having seen a thing.

Throughout Norway, Amundsen's picture was beginning to appear in store windows. Strangers would stop one another and ask: "Any news?" Sorrowfully shaking their heads, each would walk away in silence.

The New York *Times* carried a four-column headline:

"Flier Finds Nobile—Drops Food. Fear For Amundsen Missing Two Days."

June 21: Heavy fog blanketed Spitsbergen and planes were grounded. Only Lützow-Holm was flying. Locating Captain Sora, he dropped a message: "Nobile has received supplies. Ice and water conditions make a march to Foyn Island dangerous." In effect, Sora was told to return, but he chose to disregard the order and kept on going.

Lundborg's Fokker was unloaded and on a fog-shrouded ice ledge, people started assembling the plane. The Albertini patrol came back and went aboard the *Braganza,* having accomplished nothing. Elsewhere, the Russian pilot Babushkin made his first trial flight with the *Malygin's* Junkers-13 plane and the icebreaker *Krassin* reached Bergen. In Leningrad, Nobile, in absentia, was elected second vice-president of the Arctic Congress which was then in session!

Where was Amundsen? Could he have gone on to Advent Bay? Did his radio break down? Had he been forced to make an emergency landing? Without further delay, France dispatched the cruiser *Strasbourg* and ordered its *Quentin Roosevelt* to Spitsbergen. Norway readied the *Tordenskjold* with a crew of 250 and the *Michael Sars*[56] got orders to start a search for the Latham.

June 22: At 9:30 A.M. both Penzo and Maddalena, carrying a total of two tons of supplies, left Kings Bay. At noon they were over Foyn Island. The men on the floe had taken their positions and Biagi established radio contact.

At 12:13 P.M. the planes found the tent without difficulty and a profusion of food rained from the sky. There was meat and milk, marmalade and chocolate, enough to sustain life for twenty days. There were medicines and clothes, cigarettes, letters, and newspapers. Viglieri finally got two pairs of shoes, big enough even for him.

Nobile's men could see the face of Maddalena, and they saw his mechanic Rampini waving. Penzo came down to some ten feet and yelled, "*Arrivederci,*" while a cameraman busily took pictures.

Captain Sora continued his march toward Cape Bruun. The little captain was happy. He saw a small piece of land, marked on his map as being part of the mainland. Actually it was an island. Promptly he named it "Alpini Island." Despite Van Dongen's protests, he wanted to cross the pack ice toward Broch Island.

Where was Amundsen? The motorship *Svalbard* reached Advent Bay—and found no trace of the Latham.

Italian pilot Ravazzoni left for Spitsbergen aboard a Dornier-Wal; the German Transport Ministry offered Captain Romagna still another seaplane. Politely Romagna declined. His reasoning was simple. The more planes there were, the more worry there was and the greater were the chances for misfortune.

Riiser-Larsen requested that the *Braganza* be released to him. His main objective now was an air search for Amundsen; the request was granted.

A telegram from Italy's Ministry for Aviation in Rome:

> Chief of Norwegian Rescue Mission. Maddalena's success could only be achieved because of your generosity and your experience . . .

Reaching the German island of Sylt, Commander Ravazzoni made an emergency landing to repair a defective oil pump. There he received new orders: Instead of proceeding to Spitsbergen, he was to fly to Tromso and remain temporarily on detached duty with the French admiral commanding the *Strasbourg*. His mission: find Amundsen. The *Pourquoi Pas?* was ordered by the French Government to leave for the Arctic as soon as possible.

At 6:30 P.M. three Swedish planes took to the air from Murchison Bay.

At 7:30 P.M. the humming of airplanes was a welcome disruption to the monotony of waiting on the floe five miles from Foyn Island. Guided by smoke signals, the Swedes approached the camp and circled overhead, while five packages, attached to red parachutes, came out of the sky. Only one bottle of Scotch whiskey broke, another landed safely, and all the packages, expertly dropped, were recovered.

Now there was an abundance of cigarettes, oranges, drugs, ammunition and guns, but more important than anything else, there was a message written on the yellowish wrapping paper of one of the packages:

> If you can find a landing field at least 250 m long, suitable for planes equipped with skis, lay the red parachutes out on the leeward side in a way that they will form a T.

The planes disappeared again and flew off in search for Amundsen.

A few days before, Trojani had noticed at a distance of some 250 yards an even floe with no apparent crevices or leads, measuring about 300 by 250 yards.

Silence reclaimed the men huddled together in the tent. Until then, the desire to live had forged them into a unit, dedicated to survival, but now that rescue seemed near, their pent-up emotions started both bickering and recrimination: But for Biagi's laziness, they would all have been saved by now . . . but for Cecioni's injury they could have marched off and reached the mainland . . . but for Trojani, but for Behounek . . .

Depression seized Nobile, who felt that rescue efforts were not being handled properly. There was lack of co-ordination, lack of communication; and nobody seemed to pay any attention to his advice. How he would like to take full charge!

June 23: Lundborg's Fokker, assembled and tested, was ready for flight. A meeting was called aboard the *Quest,* base ship of Sweden's

Italia Rescue Operation: June 24 — July 12
— Drift of tent
—·— Russian Ship to X, where
—·— Russian Flight takes off for search
········ Albertini Dogsled Patrol
········ Sora Dogsled Patrol
—·— Schyberg Flight

rescue mission. "All right," Tornberg said, "here is our plan: Both Hansas and the Fokker will leave at 8 P.M. Rosensvärd and Jacobssen will go with us as far as Hinlopen Strait where they will reconnoiter for a base suitable for both sea and land planes. The rest of us will proceed north. Your mission—" a forefinger was thrust toward Lieutenant Lundborg—"is to land at the Nobile camp. Christell and I will lead. We all meet again in Hinlopen Strait. Any questions?"

A team of ten dogs led by Nois and Tandberg and accompanied by Albertini and Matteoda had set out to explore the northern coast of Spitsbergen from Cape Clover to Cape Leigh Smith. Penzo flew some 500 miles in search of Amundsen, without sighting a trace of the Latham. Fishermen, remote radio stations and amateurs all reported having heard messages which might have come from Amundsen, but none could be confirmed.

For the men on the floe, waiting became physically painful. The sky was blue and the sun seemed to be everywhere, as its rays, reflected by the snow, became blinding. The men's eyes began to hurt and some of them actually became snowblind. Each was left with his own thoughts, but in every man's mind there was the same question. Where is Maddalena? Why did he not come back and land? Why should Swedes succeed where Italians would not even try?

On Saturday, as it happened, Maddalena was idle. He remained idle on Sunday and Monday; in fact, he remained idle for ten days. Captain Romagna's contribution on Saturday: A trip with the *Città di Milano* to Virgo Bay.

5

On the floe, at the appointed hour of 8:55 P.M., there was no message from the base ship. Supper was eaten in silence. Impatience and disappointment were mirrored on the faces of the six bearded survivors. Nobile had established the order in which his men were to leave the floe: Cecioni, the most helpless, must go first. Behounek and Trojani were to follow; Viglieri and Biagi to remain to the last. Both were healthy and strong and only they could determine the position of the floe and maintain radio contact.

Then someone heard a humming noise. The sound soon grew louder. There was no doubt any longer that planes were approaching. Despair and sadness vanished as Viglieri and Biagi rushed out and ran to the landing field. Even the wounded crept from the tent. Outside they saw a beautiful sight: Two planes were approaching, their motors roaring a song of hope.

On a hummock Behounek started waving a red cloth. "Give smoke signals," Nobile yelled. Overhead the planes kept on circling in narrowing circles and minutes passed slowly as tension and expectation mounted. Next to a faint streak of smoke, Lundborg saw a group of men who appeared to him "like a few tiny dots or dark pinheads."

One of the planes came lower and its skis touched the ice, the engine roaring, and then the pilot pulled his craft up in a steep climb. He came back and repeated the maneuver. This time, the plane glided over a longer stretch of the icy surface before climbing back into the sky.

On its third approach the aircraft came down, touched ice, glided on and stopped some fifteen yards from the end of the field. The suspense was over. "Thank God," Nobile said. Big Cecioni cried. Hardly anybody noticed that the Hansa plane, whose vigil was over, veered off and flew on in a westerly direction.

"Three men are coming this way," Behounek shouted, "three. . . ." Wearing a gray sweater, a dirty bandage around one arm, his face covered with an unkempt beard, Umberto Nobile hardly looked like a dashing, handsome young general.

A well-groomed stranger wearing a dark brown uniform appeared with Viglieri and Biagi. "The General," Viglieri said, motioning toward Nobile. Tall, red-cheeked Lieutenant Lundborg saluted smartly and smiled. He had come, he said, to airlift them all, one at a time. Would the general, please hurry up and get ready? Nobile wanted Cecioni to leave first, but the young Swede remained firm. He pointed out that the big man was too heavy, that the plane could not lift both Cecioni and the copilot, that it would take too long to carry him to the landing field, and, finally, that he considered the general's presence aboard the *Città di Milano* desirable for directing future rescue efforts.

Nobile turned to the others and explained in Italian the gist of this conversation. Lundborg was serious and sober-faced; his blue eyes swept over the untidy camp, littered with dirty cans, old newspapers, broken boxes and other rubbish. Farther off, hanging on an aluminum pipe, was some bear meat; on a blanket, tobacco and biscuits were laid out to dry.

"There is no time to waste," Viglieri prodded. "The sooner you go the sooner we can all leave this place." Biagi, hands in his pockets, muttered: "It's better if you go; we'll all feel more secure . . ."

Nobile looked at Cecioni. "Go ahead," the big man said. "Whatever happens, at least there will be somebody to think of our families." There was disappointment in his voice, even resentment.

Nobile's eyes sparkled and he grew more excited. He crawled into the tent to ask fever-stricken Trojani. "Yes," said the sick man, "it's better this way; go!" As Nobile emotionally embraced the serious-looking young man, Trojani felt as if something inside him were being crushed.

At 10:30 in the evening of June 23, General Umberto Nobile set out in a single-motored Fokker plane—to go down in history as "the man who left first." Leaving, he made sure to take with him the logbook of the *Italia* and his dog, dear Titina.[57]

In less than two hours Lundborg deposited his passenger on Russ Island, at the entrance to Hinlopen Strait, where the advance headquarters of the Swedish Rescue Mission was then located.

On the floe the men wasted no time. Lundborg had promised to return the same night and Cecioni had to be taken to the landing field. Assisted by the others, he crawled over the treacherous ice, cursing and dragging his broken right leg. Only Trojani, weak and feverish, stayed behind in the tent.

In Bergen, the icebreaker *Krassin* had a total of 2,789 tons of coal aboard. The Albertini group continued its march toward Cape Leigh Smith; nobody now knew the whereabouts of Van Dongen and Sora. Norway's Government ordered Riiser-Larsen and Lützow-Holm to search for Amundsen; so their *Braganza,* with planes and pilots aboard, was to return to Kings Bay.

Tornberg sent a telegram to the Swedish Minister of Defense: "General Nobile . . . saved. Rescue work continues."

The score: One rescued, five marooned, sixteen missing or dead.[58]

June 24: At twenty-five minutes past midnight, pilot Babushkin's plane took off from an icefield near the *Malygin* and headed for King Charles Land, where a supply depot was to be established which might later serve as an advance base for future flights. At the same time, Viglieri, Behounek, Biagi, and Cecioni, panting and perspiring, arrived at the edge of their makeshift airfield; and, in Hinlopen Strait, Lundborg's Fokker was being refueled. All nonessential equipment was removed. This time Lundborg would fly without a copilot, escorted only by the Hansa 255.

On the floe time was passing slowly. At 3 A.M., conversation among the men had ceased as the sun rose and the air became warmer. Now and then the silence was broken by the thunderlike noise caused by a collapsing iceberg. "They won't come anymore," Behounek said cheerily. "You'll see that they will be satisfied with having saved the general."

Just then Cecioni leaned forward. "Here they are," he said.

"I don't hear anything."

"I can."

Cecioni was right. There were two planes. Viglieri fired a Very flare, and soon Lundborg's plane became clearly visible in the mist as it descended in a steep spiral.

Coming in for a landing, the overconfident Lundborg was too high. His plane touched down in the center of the field, its skis digging into the slushy snow. Its nose went down as the tail rose, leaving the pilot hanging by his straps from an overturned plane.

Lundborg climbed out. His nose was bleeding; otherwise he was unharmed. With outstretched arms he signaled to the Hansa 255. Far from looking like a majestic bird, the overturned Fokker with its broken skis and a propeller damaged beyond repair resembled a helpless turtle stretched out on its back. Lundborg cursed, Biagi sobbed, and Behounek remained silent.

Viglieri was facing his first command decision. Their floe had shrunk, its edges melting away, and the surface was now one big puddle. The camp must be relocated. Leaving Cecioni on a wing of the overturned plane, the others returned to the tent, where Trojani was waiting for them.

Huddled in sleeping bags by an open fire, three men were lying on the shore of Russ Island. Bearded Nobile was awake when he heard the drone of an approaching plane. He woke Christell, who was next to him. The lieutenant rubbed his eyes, got up, looked and listened. "The Fokker must have crashed," he said matter-of-factly.

At 6 A.M. on the floe, a message was dispatched to Nobile, and another one to Anna Lundborg, the pilot's wife. The Swede then entered the tent and went to sleep for the first time in three days. Yearning for escape from fear and helplessness, the others followed. Behounek wedged his bulky frame into a sleeping bag outside the tent and was soon snoring away, lying in a puddle of icy water.

At 11 A.M., through fieldglasses, Lundborg saw "the island" at a distance of some 18 miles. With the temperature rising, the ice continued to melt and the men on the floe knew that no plane could attempt a landing. The only hope was a ship. And the only ship bearing hope was the *Krassin,* which was just off Bergen.

7 P.M.: Nobile arrived in Virgo Bay. Turning to Baccarani, Romagna said: "Here comes trouble . . . you'll see, we will have to defend ourselves yet. . . ."[59]

Nobile conferred with Romagna. "General," the captain said, "the fact that you have been rescued first could be misinterpreted. It would be advisable to make a clarifying statement."

Nobile was stunned. Was he not to assume command? Had Lundborg not rescued him on orders from higher up? Romagna shook his head.

Telegram:

> Undersecretary for Navy Sirianni: Am here to establish command post. The body is weak, but the mind active. Nobile.

Communiqué from the *Città di Milano:*

> During Saturday night the Swedish plane equipped with skis landed boldly near the Nobile group and departed with General Nobile. It transported him to Hinlopen Strait whence another Swedish plane took him to Virgo Bay. There he was placed aboard the *Città di Milano.*

Releasing the communique a few hours later, Italy's official new agency Stefani added: "Reasons for Nobile's return are unknown" and emphasized that future rescue operations would continue to be commanded by Captain Romagna.

Telegram:

> Senior Lieutenant Alfredo Viglieri: You will assume command of Italian contingent. Am certain that despite difficult circumstances you will measure up to this difficult assignment. Signed: Admiral Sirianni, Undersecretary for Navy.

9 P.M.: Relocation of the tent was under way. When Viglieri's men appeared at the site of Lundborg's wrecked Fokker, Cecioni was happy. Lying on a wing of the plane, he was now snowblind. Afraid of polar bears, he had not been able to sleep and somehow no one had bothered to think that he had been left alone without food.

On his way back to the *Malygin,* Babushkin ran into a bank of dense fog and had to make an emergency landing fifty miles from the icebreaker. Blocked by ice near Cape North, the *Braganza* was immobilized. Riiser-Larsen and Lützow-Holm were condemned to inactivity. There was no word from Sora and Van Dongen. Idle in the harbor of Virgo Bay were three ships, the *Quest,* the *Tanja,* and the *Città di Milano,* as well as three planes: the Savoia 55, the *Marina II,* and the *Turku.*

There was a lot of coming and going in Nobile's small cabin aboard the *Città di Milano.* Tornberg and Christell came and advised the purchase of small ski-equipped sports planes in England; Finland's pilot, Sarko, thought that his *Turku,* then being equipped with skis, would be ready for takeoff within a few days, Maddalena doubted the possibility of any more flights. For one thing his plane was too big, he said, and the risk too great. Furthermore, the weather was too unpredictable, but, above all, the engines of his plane had to be changed and he had made no arrangements to get spare motors. Penzo was willing to attempt a landing if a suitable lead could be found near the "Red Tent," but there was none.

Within hours, radio and newspapers had spread the word around the world that a general of Fascist Italy had allowed himself to be rescued first, abandoning his companions, but not forgetting to save his dog.

The icebreaker *Krassin* was at sea. Aboard were 136 men, including a Norwegian scientist named Hoel* and the Italian reporter Giudici, and two women, housekeeper Xenia and journalist Ljubov Andreevna Vorontsonva.

June 25: Dense fog was enveloping Viglieri's group like a damp blanket. Lundborg was thinking of his wife and was revolted by the sight of fishy smelling unsalted bear meat. "Out here," veteran Viglieri said, "you

---

* Samoilovich had invited Prof. Adolf Hoel, Norway's leading authority on Spitsbergen, to join the expedition. The two men knew each other from the time before World War I, when both were in Spitsbergen.

must eat; calories count, not flavor." But Lundborg choked on the meat, could not swallow it, and was given some chocolate with crackers instead. "You don't have to be stingy with fuel," the pilot said, "I have plenty of gasoline in my plane," but, as it happened, through a crack in the tank the gasoline had leaked out.

The day was spent inside the tent wrapped in gloom. There were reassuring messages from Nobile, promising more food drops, and asserting that two planes had been ordered in England while a Finnish aircraft was being equipped with skis in Spitsbergen.

Without wasting time the Swedish Government ordered a Lieutenant Ekman to Malmslatt to take charge of yet another Fokker for transshipment to Spitsbergen, while arrangements were also made for the purchase of a small English *Moth* airplane, as suggested by Captain Tornberg.

At 3 P.M., Babushkin managed to return to the *Malygin*.

The disposition of the rescue forces was now as follows:

Ships: *Città di Milano* idle in Virgo Bay; *Braganza* icebound; *Malygin* icebound; *Tanja* on her way to Kings Bay; *Quest* anchored in Hinlopen Strait; *Krassin* off the coast of Norway.

Planes: In Virgo Bay—the Savoia 55, the *Marina II* and the Finnish *Turku*. In Hinlopen Strait—Hansa planes 255 and 257 as well as the *Uppland*. Near the *Malygin*—Babushkin's Junkers. On the *Braganza,* relieved from further rescue work for Viglieri's group—Riiser-Larsen's Norwegian mission with its planes *Maake* 36 and 37. Aboard the *Krassin*—Pilot Chukhnovsky's still crated Junkers.

Men on skis: Sora and Van Dongen. They had had to abandon one sled; their lead dog had died, and there was no food for the others; Sora had fallen into the water and had been rescued by Van Dongen.

June 26: The *Quentin Roosevelt* arrived in Tromso, while the *Strasbourg* and *Tordenskjold* were still en route. Miss Boyd, a wealthy American who had previously chartered the *Hobby*, offered the ship to the Norwegian Government, which gratefully accepted the offer and ordered the vessel to go in search of Amundsen. Aboard an express train, a *Moth* and a Fokker plane were moving from Malmslatt to Narvik, where they were to be loaded on a coal boat going to Green Harbor, Spitsbergen.

Report from the *Krassin:*

> Bulletin No. 1. According to a newscast just received, Swedish pilot Lundborg aboard a Fokker plane has rescued Nobile. . .[60]

The reaction of the men and women aboard the icebreaker was one of disbelief. Wiring congratulations to Nobile, Professor Samoilovich suggested co-ordination of further rescue efforts. He received no answer. (A second such request made ten hours later was answered three days later.) At the northernmost point of Norway the Norwegian pilot left the icebreaker, and the *Krassin* was on its own.

Report from the floe: The fog had lifted and relocation of the camp was completed, with the tent pitched near Lundborg's overturned plane. Canvas, cut off the Fokker with pocket knives, covered with the bear hide and assorted parachutes formed the floor. Even so, the cold and damp penetrated everything. Biagi saw another bear, but the beast escaped unharmed. Behounek was glad because there would be no more bear meat for a while. Lundborg was sad because he would have loved to have a trophy.

June 27: At 1 A.M. the icebreaker *Krassin* entered open sea. Fishermen approached the ship in their small boats, cupped their hands and shouted: "Save Amundsen . . . Bring back Amundsen!"

Aboard the *Città di Milano* Nobile continued making suggestions: How about joining Tornberg's group in Murchison Bay? How about establishing an advance base in Hinlopen Strait? Captain Romagna listened politely and remained silent. As a matter of fact, Nobile, once a national hero, was being held a virtual prisoner, and interviews with him were ruled out.

June 28: The drift carried Viglieri's group more than twenty miles to the Southeast and, as the fog lifted temporarily, the outline of Cape Leigh Smith appeared on the horizon like a beckoning finger. The *Città di Milano* promised early dispatch of planes. "Come as soon as possible." Viglieri radioed, but thick fog continued to blanket Spitsbergen and no planes took off; Riiser-Larsen and Lützow-Holm were immobilized aboard the *Braganza* and Babushkin was fogbound near the *Malygin*.

With pick and shovel, Lundborg was working to improve the landing field, while the others went back to the old tent site. On their return they had to inflate a rubber boat to cross a wide channel which had formed suddenly. The bulky, nearsighted Behounek was caught in an awkward position with one foot on the ice, the other on the rubber boat. He lost his balance and took an involuntary bath. The evening was cold, the ice firm and the sky clear. A restless and despondent Lundborg wondered why no planes were flying.

The *Krassin's* bulletin No. 3:

Orders for *Krassin* from Moscow—Confirming again that you are to proceed without slowdown to north of Spitsbergen, where you are to initiate work without delay to reach region Foyn for search and rescue crew of *Italia* and also Amundsen. Priority to be given Nobile group where they are wounded. . . . Establish contact with *Città di Milano*. If desired, take Nobile aboard icebreaker. Responsibility for leadership yours.   Nobile Relief Committee.[60]

With men on constant lookout for Amundsen, the *Krassin* reached Bear Island, while steadily increasing fog reduced visibility and cut the ship's speed to six knots.

Samoilovich received a radio message from the *Città di Milano:*

> Imperative to take ten dogs aboard. Shall make arrangements for same . . .

Actually, the Russians wanted no dogs. They did want co-ordination of the rescue efforts, but Romagna still had not answered the two telegrams sent on June 26.

Swedish Lieutenant Ekman and two small planes now arrived in Narvik and were taken aboard the Norwegian vessel *Ingerto.*

June 29: As the fog lifted, Viglieri could barely see the islands of Foyn and Broch to the northwest, but steep black-blue rocks became visible some ten miles away. In some of the men a desire to reach solid land, no matter how desolate, became overwhelming. Now there was only one wounded man who would have to be carried, and instead of a helpless Nobile there was a healthy Lundborg. But Viglieri remained firm in his opposition. He considered an over-ice march a gamble justified only when there was no other hope. As long as the ice held and as long as their food lasted, they would sit it out, he decided.

Radio message from Viglieri to *Città di Milano:*

> Weather improving. Visibility 5–10 miles. Slight wind from NW. . . .
> Come as soon as possible . . .

Through "wonderfully blue waters" the *Krassin* moved at normal speed. The west coast of Spitsbergen was in sight and journalist Vorontsova, now in the good graces of Samoilovich and officially listed as a radio operator, was busy sewing parachutes and teaching Russian to Professor Hoel. There was a radio message from Captain Romagna saying that he was sorry, but the dogs he had offered previously were not available, after all!

From Norway, Ravazzoni made an unsuccessful seven-hour flight in search of Amundsen. Leif Dietrichson now missing eleven days, was promoted to captain in the Norwegian Navy.

At 5 P.M. Nobile received a message from Lundborg:[61]

> Some parts of our field have yesterday and today get very bad stop There is water under the snow and that water will make the ice very, very bad stop That part where the T now is is better but the weather is warm and I don't know how long it can be used stop I will ask you if we dont had better beginn walking to Grosses Insel where your pilots could put down food to us till the icebreaker can save us stop I ask you Sir to think on my question and if not today latest tomorrow

answere stop Perhaps you could help us with information how to walk and so on.

The answer arrived on the floe at 5:55 P.M.:[62]

Four planes are ready to start. Only they wait for visibility a little better. . . . My opinion is that you shall wait there and not walk. Please tell if you think that conditions of the field are still good enough for landing tomorrow morning . . .

Captain Romagna radioed that the Finnish plane, *Turku,* was ready for takeoff and that Italian planes too might come . . . .

At 9:20 P.M., with a mechanic and a radioman aboard his Junkers plane, Babushkin took to the air again.

Captain Sora and Van Dongen had now reached Broch Island. Their dogs had not had food in four days; Van Dongen killed one of them and fed him to the others, and Sora managed to shoot some wild ducks. However, the men's primary mission, to find Mariano's group, had not been accomplished.

June 30: Some radio messages—
5:55 A.M., Viglieri to *Città di Milano:*

Visibility excellent. . . . Weather perfect. No wind.

(Romagna alerted Maddalena and Penzo for takeoff at eleven o'clock in the evening.)
8:45 A.M., *Città di Milano* to *Krassin:*

. . . but you are not coming here. Was waiting for you here, in Virgo Bay.

10:10 A.M., *Krassin* to *Città di Milano:*

. . . have orders to proceed as fast as possible to Leigh-Smith . . .

10:12 A.M., *Città di Milano* to *Krassin:*

General Nobile would like to come aboard to give instructions.

11:25 A.M., *Krassin* to *Città di Milano:*

Welcome General Nobile's intention. *Krassin's* entry into Virgo difficult. Reasons: Great draught of twenty-eight feet, constant fog and loss of time. Do you not find approach *Città di Milano* to us possible?

Answer from Captain Romagna:

. . . impossible . . . .
2 P.M., Romagna to Viglieri:

. . . *Krassin* near Cape North. Hope that she will reach you in one or two days.

Nobile to Viglieri:

> . . . you should see *Krassin* smokestacks within seven to eight days . . .

Italo-Finnish flights to the floe were canceled for the day; Michael Babushkin's J-13 was twelve hours overdue.

The score: 1 rescued, 6 marooned, 19 missing or dead.

July 1: Previously announced plans were changed. The *Turku* was not flying; instead the two Italian planes and the *Uppland* took off. At Cape Leigh Smith, fog forced them back, and at three o'clock in the afternoon they were again moored in Virgo Bay, the pilots having sighted neither Viglieri's men nor the Alessandrini group, carried away with the dirigible.

The icebreaker *Krassin* was now reported some 250 miles from the floe and tent. In Moscow Kamenev, the Red Army's chief of staff, had some unkind words for the Italians at Spitsbergen. According to the New York *Times* he deplored the ". . . chaotic lack of co-ordination and co-operation."

Lieutenant Lundborg was discouraged. As the newcomer to the floe, he was at a distinct disadvantage. The others had had time to get used to beards, dirt, hopelessness and bear meat, but he missed his shaving kit, his pipe. . . . Above all he felt lonely and a stray among strangers, with some of whom he could not even communicate. Lundborg, the soldier of fortune, the adventurer, the all-around athlete, longed for action.

"They are afraid of this ice," he told Behounek; "after what happened to me, they lost their courage." Lundborg kept urging the men to start on a march toward the mainland. He preferred to meet danger with active resistance. Passive acceptance of fate, while waiting for something to happen, was not for him. He found some support in Behounek, but Viglieri still remained opposed.

"All right," Lundborg said, "then I'll go alone."

Even Behounek balked at this: "Lieutenant," he said, "do you see how gray the sky is in the east? That is where you would go, you know."

"Yes. So what?"

"Well, it is gray because open water is reflected on clouds. Look how white the clouds are there—" and he pointed westward—"because there is ice below."

Lundborg clenched his fist and remainded silent.

Covered with a piece of canvas, the Swede and the Czech huddled together and formed an imaginary "Polar Sea Shipwreck Co." Each man on the floe was allotted a number of shares and all were willing to sell theirs at an average of 40–60 per cent below the imaginary par value. Only Behounek was in a speculative mood and occasionally bid as high as 80 per cent of their nominal value. The men talked about soap and clean sheets and spoke wistfully of food in no way related to pemmican or bear meat.

Aboard the *Krassin,* Giudici was watching the ship's progress, as it fought against ice, at times more than eight feet thick.

The ice became too dense and compact. At times, the ship's speed was reduced to one knot an hour. Broken-off hummocks wedged themselves between the ship's hull and a solid lower sheet of thick ice, and the *Krassin* was trapped. Samoilovich decided to change course and bypass the Seven Islands from the north.

The Italian planes were useless. After eighty-two flying hours their motors would have to be changed before further flights could be made, but spare engines, although ordered, were still in transit.

July 2: Crushed by conflicting messages, inactivity and constant danger, apathy took hold of the men on the floe.

Viglieri radioed: "Landing impossible."

Answer from the *Città di Milano:* "Will send supplies. *Krassin* will reach you soon."

Trojani felt better, but now Biagi was sick (the bear meat had gone bad) and Viglieri stayed in the tent most of the time. He was feverish and his limbs ached. Lundborg, lying next to him, pistol under his head, stared morosely at the blue ceiling of the small tent. Behounek, who spent his nights on watch duty, was sleeping. Every night the Czech and the Swede, unable to sleep, got together. "Let's make smoke," Behounek would say. Lundborg was glad to have somebody to talk to.

"I'm surprised" he said, "that you did not lose your mind in all those weeks, when you found yourself drifting in every direction."[63]

The professor had nothing to say. He exhaled some smoke and shrugged his shoulders.

"Who knows where we will wind up?" Lundborg went on. "Open Sea . . . Franz Josef Land . . ."

They talked about Lundborg's career as a stunt pilot. Behounek sensed the man's loneliness, his despair and fear. They talked about Finn Malmgren.

"I saw his mother," Lundborg said. "She is not too concerned about him. He told her once that in the Arctic there is hope for rescue even as late as six months after an accident."

Racked by pains in his joints, Viglieri became silent and irritable. Trojani, however, turned more talkative, reminiscing about Japan, geishas, midget gardens and cherry blossoms.

The *Krassin* advanced at the rate of a few hundred yards an hour. Friable ice, compressed by the ship's weight, stuck to the hull and formed a barrier, many feet high. In twelve hours the ship was stopped cold three times. Seven hundred tons of water were pumped into one set of side tanks, the ship tilted, and leaned over. The ice was crushed, and gave way as a narrow lead formed. The tanks were emptied, the ship righted itself, while water was pumped into tanks on the opposite side. Again there was the crushing weight of the leaning icebreaker and the thunderous grating noise of falling hummocks. The *Krassin* was free again.

"Struggle against ice," Captain Eggi said, "is a question of patience and coal." The *Krassin* turned south. Strong northern winds were pushing ice toward the coast, rendering it too compact to steam against, and progress remained agonizingly slow.

The *Braganza* reached Virgo Bay. Riiser-Larsen, Lützow-Holm, and their planes were transferred to the *Hobby,* which had just arrived from Tromso, with Miss Louise Boyd aboard, and the ship proceeded to Kings Bay.

That day, Sir Hubert Wilkins and Ben Eielson arrived in New York to a traditional welcome.*

Charcot's *Pourquois-Pas?* was ready to leave for Spitsbergen in search of Amundsen. The German Government notified Italy that it was willing to send two ski-equipped planes as well as one of their ace pilots, Ernst Udet, to help rescue the Viglieri group, and the British Air Ministry offered to a group of Norwegians the loan of two light planes for the Amundsen search.[64] Answering an inquiry of Lieutenant Commander Kentworthy, Undersecretary for Aviation, Sir Phillip Sassoon said in the House of Commons:

> His Majesty's Government have invited the Italian Government to call upon the Royal Air Force without hesitation for help.

The Italian Government declined politely. It apparently needed no outside help.

The icebreaker *Malygin,* trapped in the ice and shrouded by fog, was helplessly drifting toward Hope Island, while the depth of the ocean receded from 67 fathoms to 27. When the fog lifted, the captain saw that his ship was a precarious 1½ miles from the rocky coast. With supreme skill he managed to maneuver the ship six miles away from the coast.

At the same time Babushkin and his air crew were three days overdue, while seventy miles from the Viglieri group, the *Krassin* became icebound.

On the floe, extra rations (chocolate and whiskey) were distributed for supper to celebrate the birthday of Mrs. Lundborg and Lieutenant Viglieri. A cold night descended and the melting ice froze again.

Polar explorers returning from Leningrad had unkind words for Nobile.

---

* Among the officials of the welcoming party was a pretty Australian actress, Suzanne Bennett, whom Sir Hubert later married.

"It was not a case of tragedy only," Peter Freuchen said, "but Nobile's expedition was the darkest blot in the annals of arctic expeditions. Nobile, meeting both technical and moral defeat, has discredited entirely arctic expeditions by means of airships."[64]

"But how about his election to the vice-presidency of the Congress?" a reporter asked.

"Oh, that—just a gesture . . . just a gesture . . ."

July 3: Movement of the floe could be felt distinctly. The pack ice was splitting everywhere. Another large hummock broke off and fell with deafening roar into a newly formed channel. Foyn Island was only nine miles away, but a storm was coming up and news received by radio was bad. Swedish planes flying toward the floe had to turn back, taking with them the supplies they had intended dropping, as well as a newspaper announcing Lundborg's promotion to captain.

The *Braganza* had reverted to the command of Captain Romagna and was idle in Kings Bay.

At four o'clock in the afternoon, the *Krassin* was sixty-five miles from the Viglieri group. Meticulous Samoilovich was keeping a detailed record. Between six and seven o'clock in the evening the ship made fifteen forward lurches and backed up sixteen times. Progress: 500 yards. Between four and eight o'clock the *Krassin* had advanced barely one mile at the prohibitive cost of twenty tons of coal.

At 8:30 P.M., within sight of Cape Platen, the *Krassin's* engines were stopped. Fuel had to be conserved and the ship checked, because there had been some unusual and strong vibrations in her hull. At latitude 80°42′ North, longitude 22°57′ East, amid ice more than eight feet thick, covered with almost three feet of snow, the ship started a drift westward, away from her destination. A propeller seemed to be broken.

There was still no word from Amundsen or Babushkin, no trace of Mariano, Zappi and Malmgren, and anxiety was beginning to be felt for Captain Sora's land party.

The score: 1 rescued, 6 marooned, 22 missing or dead.

July 4: The storm became stronger. A mighty wind roared over the white desert, and from a bleak sky, snow fell in fine flakes. Rescue efforts were being made—that much the men on the floe knew. But would rescue come in time or would the floe break up before help could reach them? Should they hope for wind and warmer weather to break up the ice and facilitate the *Krassin's* progress or should they wish for cold so that the Finnish pilot, Sarko, could land?

Few words were spoken on the floe and Cecioni morosely traced the icebreaker's course on a map, not knowing that the ship was stuck, blocked by huge masses of ice, handicapped by a broken propeller, and with available coal supplies running low.

During the night the weather improved. On guard duty, sitting outside the tent, Behounek listened to the wind. He had become an expert in gauging the wind's direction. A wind from the east blew through cracks in the plane causing mournful sounds like those of a harp. Winds from the north shook the tent and everything hanging on the pole rattled. With west winds, the tent walls fluttered like the wings of a dying bird.

This night Behounek heard rattling and fluttering. They must be drifting toward the southeast. Behounek kept on smoking. His mind was a blank and he was lonely.

After midnight a yellow sun crept through a layer of gray clouds, and Behounek went into the tent. Cecioni, studying his map, was stating what he was going to do once safe aboard the *Krassin.* "Mangiare, poi whiskey"* he kept repeating to Lundborg, who lay on his back, staring into emptiness.

"Mangiare, poi whiskey," Cecioni said again, his eyes fixed on a doubtful future.

Behounek said something to Lundborg, but got no answer. Water trickled into the tent and Behounek went out again to fasten some guy ropes. It was hopeless; the pegs would not hold in the loose snow. He inspected the radio—the antenna was still standing. On a wing of Lundborg's plane, Biagi was snoring. Professor Behounek of Prague lit a cigarette and listened once more to the howling wind.

The *Ingerto,* a Norwegian steamer, was approaching Spitsbergen, carrying a new Fokker plane, a De Havilland *Moth,* and a four-man detachment headed by flying instructor Erik Ekman. The *Moth* was mounted on floats and had skis tied to her fuselage. Lieutenant Ekman was planning to lower the plane into the water and take off for Hinlopen as soon as he arrived in Long Year City. Such were his orders.

An unpleasant surprise awaited Ekman. Arriving in a Hansa plane, Lieutenants Jacobsson and Schyberg carried instructions from Tornberg, Chief of the Swedish rescue expedition. Being mounted on floats, the *Moth* was considered a seaplane, and therefore should be flown by Lieutenant Jacobssen of the Navy to Hinlopen Strait. Lieutenant Ekman of the Army was ordered to take command of the base ship *Tanja* instead, and take her and the remaining Fokker plane to Virgo Bay. . . .[65]

Aboard the *Malygin,* joy replaced gloom on the fourth, for Michael Babushkin had found his way back to the ship. At the southern tip of Hope Island, some eighty miles north of the icebreaker, strong head winds had forced him to make an emergency landing, and then fog and ice had kept him and his crew prisoners for five days.

---

* "Eat, then whiskey."

The score: 1 rescued, 6 marooned, 19 missing or dead.

On the same day two Italian soldiers, stationed at Beverly Sound to guard a food depot, saw a man staggering toward them from the southeast. It was Ludwig Varming, who had been left at Cape Platen by Sora two weeks earlier.

The score: 1 rescued, 6 marooned, 18 missing or dead.

Sora and Van Dongen reached Foyn Island. Only six miles distant from Broch, it had taken them five days to cover the distance and of the nine dogs they started with, only four were left. They had seen no trace of Mariano. Exhausted, out of food and carrying no supplies, Sora decided to locate the "Red Tent" instead.

From the deck of the icebound *Krassin,* melancholy Russian folksongs floated into the night. Reports from Berlin had it that a 1,400-ton ship, the *Cattaro,* was being coaled in expectation of leaving for Spitsbergen on the following day with Ernst Udet and three *Flamingo* planes.

July 5: At 8 A.M., Behounek awakened Trojani, who was to prepare breakfast. He went to a nearby puddle for some sweet water and roused Biagi. With this his night watch was finished until next time.

With meticulous care Trojani distributed hot chocolate, which tasted bitter, and a biscuit to each man. "A breakfast such as many ordinary people have," said Lundborg. Behounek had a vision of a middle-class businessman sitting at his breakfast table, glancing at the headlines of his favorite newspaper and wondering what all the fuss was about and why this Viglieri group did not get up and walk a few miles to the mainland.

Indeed, Viglieri found that they were just five miles from the northern coast of Spitsbergen. The shortest distance between two points is not always, however, a straight line.

Now Behounek wanted to sleep. Just then Biagi came in. He had talked with the *Città di Milano* and had good news. The Swedish Rescue Mission had moved its headquarters farther to the east, and the small *Moth* plane was to set out for the tent site.

They had experienced disappointment so often in the past that the news failed to stir any excitement. Nevertheless, everybody except Cecioni went out to inspect the landing field. It looked really hopeless. Everywhere the men sank ankle deep into the watery snow, and only on the eastern border of the floe was there a narrow strip firm enough to support a small plane. Even there, puddles had to be filled in and rugged spots evened out. There was no point in doing it now, because the evening's cold would make the work easier, and the plane was not due until then anyway.

At 11 A.M. There was once again a dense fog. Lundborg and Behounek again proposed a march to the mainland. Viglieri lost his temper and shouted in French: *"Chacun est libre de fair ce qu'il veut. Chacun peut s'en aller, s'il veut."**

"That's not the point," Behounek answered, also in French. "We must make a concerted effort. We need leadership."

"And that's exactly what you have," Viglieri snapped back. "When the time comes and there is no other choice, we will march . . . but only then, when we have nothing to lose."[66]

There was nothing more to be said. Biagi came running. "A plane," he shouted, "a plane," and, gesticulating, he pointed skyward. It was half past four o'clock in the afternoon.

Lundborg rushed out of the tent and shaded his eyes against the painful glare of the sunlight.

"I hope he sees us," he mumbled.

"Shall I fire a signal?" Viglieri asked.

"No, save it; he is still too far away."

The plane headed eastward. Midway between Great Island and Cape Leigh Smith, the pilot changed course.

"Now fire your signal."

A pillar of wavy smoke rose and, correcting its course, the Hansa headed straight for the tent. Lundborg recognized the 255 and could plainly see Rosensvärd and Jacobssen waving to him. They came down, flew low over the long side of the field, dropped supplies and then were gone again. (They were off in search of Alessandrini's group.)

"No cigarettes," Viglieri said.

"But at least there is a bottle of whiskey."

An hour later the *Uppland* appeared, made four passes and dropped more packages. Mechanic Karlsson was seen leaning out of a window and Lundborg signaled with outstretched arms: "Landing possible." Karlsson acknowledged, and then the *Uppland,* too, flew off, in search of Amundsen, as it happened.

"Why are there no Italian planes?" Viglieri asked as if talking to himself.

In his rucksack, which had just been dropped, Lundborg found tobacco, food, his pipe, and his harmonica. There was also a newspaper, a letter addressed to "Captain Lundborg," and, on a piece of paper, a scribbled message:

> Shall try to come with the *Moth* tonight. Schyberg will fly it. Greetings.
> Karlsson.

The prospect of rescue brought on a new mood of exhilaration. Lundborg grew excited and the silence on the floe was broken by the Swede playing *Gubben Noak* (Old Man Noah) on his harmonica.

---

* "Everyone is free to do what he wants. Everyone can go if he wants to."

"Does the Swedish expedition contemplate establishing a base closer to our position so as to be able to save us all?" Viglieri asked.

"I don't think so."

A shadow of disappointment wiped out the smile on the boyish face of Viglieri. His mind was working fast. Without an advance base a small sport plane could not make two flights in one night. As for tomorrow, would weather permit flying tomorrow?

An ugly suspicion came over Lundborg. What if the Italians refused to help him repair the field? What if they wouldn't let him be the one to leave? True, it was agreed that he was to be the next flown out. But promises can be broken.

Lundborg changed his story. There was actually no need for an advance base, he said, because the plane would take off from Cape Bruun within easy flying distance.

But the seed of suspicion, once sown, quickly grew into certainty. Lundborg alone was to be rescued. Viglieri and Trojani knew it and so did Lundborg. For him alone the immediate future was bright with hope.

In the evening they started rebuilding the field. "There is a big deep puddle here," Viglieri said. "Would it not be better to make a runway on another part of the floe?"

Lundborg was angry: "Never mind, if it is too much trouble, I will finish the job myself."

The Swede kept on digging and cursing; everyone but the sick Biagi was helping. Shaking his head, rolling his r's, repeating the few English words he had learned on the floe, Biagi instead angrily mimicked Lundborg, who was now nervous and ill at ease. "Very good, very bad—very good, very bad."

In Berlin, Dr. Eckener announced that his new zeppelin would go on an arctic rescue mission in three weeks, if the men were still alive and still on the floe. The German Ministry of Transportation decided that Udet should have at least one seaplane with him, but none would be obtainable for another day or two.

Both the *Hobby* and the *Braganza* were icebound again and hope of finding either the Alessandrini group or Mariano's party was practically abandoned.

The *Krassin* was still drifting. From its deck the islands of Broch and Charles XII were visible on the horizon, and pilot Chukhnovsky was thinking of making a reconnaissance flight.

6

July 6: It was shortly past midnight. The field on the floe had been repaired as well as possible, and from the top of Lundborg's useless

Fokker, Viglieri's men scanned the horizon. For all but one of them it was the dawn of the forty-third day on the ice.

At one o'clock in the morning they saw the Hansa 257, escorting a small *Moth* plane toward the floe. Twelve eyes remained glued to the tiny plane, while scant attention was paid to the larger Hansa. The landing strip was only about 150 yards long, and the pilot of the *Moth* circled it only once, then he came down and made a perfect landing on the worse part of the floe.

At the controls of the ski-equipped De Haviland *Moth,* which had thus been transformed into a land plane, was Birger Schyberg of the Swedish Army. The engine of the little aircraft kept on turning over and the pilot did not leave his cockpit. Within a minute, Viglieri and Lundborg were at his side and a tense Schyberg urged Lundborg to hurry up. There was no question in anybody's mind that only Lundborg was to leave. Snatching up his camera, and leaving the rest of his belongings behind, the newly made captain climbed into the rear seat of the *Moth* . . . and promised once again to return the same night. The pilot gunned the engine, the plane started gliding, and the *Moth* rose easily and circled, joined the other craft and disappeared in a southerly direction. Its destination was Esmark Island, the new advance base of the Swedish Rescue Mission, only fourteen miles from the "Red Tent." The arctic adventure of Captain Lundborg had come to an end. The rough, superstitious daredevil was saved. He had become a national hero, and for a short time he would remain in the limelight. But to the men on the floe, as well as to others who would not say so publicly, Lundborg the hero had shown that he was quite an ordinary man, who could be both despondent and self-centered.

A radiogram from Moscow meanwhile brought the answer to an earlier inquiry of Professor Samoilovich. Despite damage to the propeller, the icebreaker *Krassin* was to continue rescue efforts until its coal supply was down to 1,100 tons. At this time the coal available was 1,700 tons. Its ordinary daily consumption en route had been somewhat more than 100 tons. The Unshlikht Committee also sanctioned a reconnaissance flight by Chukhnovsky and there ensued great activity on the icebreaker as a scaffolding was built to lower the Junkers onto the ice.

Back on Viglieri's floe, there was the usual watchful waiting. Once again there were five of them, and they tried to figure out how long it would be before they would hear the drone of a plane again. Cape Bruun was less than sixty miles away. With time out for landing and refueling, the plane could be back within two hours. Of course, the men did not know that a round trip to Esmark Island could be made in less than half that time.

Behounek, the skeptic, knew that Schyberg was not coming back.

Trojani, too, knew it and went to sleep. Time passed slowly as the men waited in vain.

At eight o'clock in the morning, Chukhnovsky's plane was lowered from the *Krassin,* and by noon it had been dragged over the uneven ice to a landing field 150 yards from the icebreaker.

In the evening Viglieri received a radio message from Lundborg. He promised to drop food, advised the stranded men to eat more, and urged them not to start on a march. He had seen from the air how broken-up the ice was, he said, and had noticed wide stretches of open water. There was no mention of another aerial rescue effort.

Lieutenant Viglieri rose to the occasion. His answer carried no reproach, no plea for help, no mention of a broken promise. "Congratulations on the occasion of your rescue and thanks for your help . . .."

Viglieri received another radiogram the same day. The sender was Romagna, Italy's chief rescue operations officer. He wanted to know how many men had been rescued!

Born out of impotent rage, came the answer:

> Viglieri, Behounek, Trojani, Cecioni, Biagi request information about *Krassin's* position.[67]

After these messages had been sent, Biagi's radio fell silent.

The score: 1 rescued, 5 marooned, 18 missing or dead.

The icebreaker *Malygin* finally freed itself from the ice, made a new start and advanced at a speed of ten miles an hour. Its position at 8 P.M.: 76° North, 33° East. Sora and Van Dongen were marooned on Foyn Island, where they shot a dog and ate him. Berlin sent an official inquiry to Stockholm: Were the services of Ernst Udet needed or not?

July 7: After a fruitless two-week overland expedition, Albertini's group returned to Beverly Sound. Despite the scrupulous search they claimed to have made, they had managed to miss the exhausted Ludwig Varming, struggling back on his own, as well as the tent in which he had been abandoned. Waiting for the *Braganza* to pick them up, there were now seven men at the food depot in Beverly Sound. Tornberg conferred with Romagna before the *Città di Milano* returned to Kings Bay. Moored in the waters of Kings Bay and completely idle were Maddalena's Savoia 55 and Penzo's *Marina II,* still waiting for new motors.

Abandoning their sled and the remaining dogs, Sora and Van Dongen senselessly pushed eastward, across treacherous ice, beyond Foyn Island. What on earth did the captain expect to accomplish?[68] The Czech Government alerted a prominent pilot for a flight to Spitsbergen. A reply received from the Swedish Government prompted the German ace, Udet, to abandon his plans for a rescue expedition to Spitsbergen. Near the *Krassin,*

Chukhnovsky's plane was assembled and the pilot made a first brief test flight.

A report from the floe: the radio was dead. No messages were being received, no news was coming in. The ice was melting, and new channels formed everywhere and kept on growing. The camp had to be moved to a new location. The men knew that they were pitching their tent for the last time. Theirs was the retreat to a last holding position.

July 8: For Viglieri's men the end was in sight. There was no more hope for planes, as there was now no place for a plane to land. Their only hope lay with the *Krassin,* but the position and progress of the icebreaker were unknown to the men on the floe, since the radio remained inoperative.

Lundborg's plane was cannibalized and one of its wings cut off to serve as foundation for the tent. The guy ropes were tied to the inflated rubber rafts, which in turn had been loaded with food.

The *Braganza* had left Kings Bay on her third trip north. Her mission was to pick up seven men in Beverly Sound; then push on and look for Sora, and, if possible, proceed to the "Red Tent."

At 10:15 A.M. the *Krassin's* airman Chukhnovsky started on another test flight. As he circled, some horrified sailors, looking up saw one of the plane's skis hanging down vertically. A crash seemed inevitable, but as the pilot prepared to land again, the wind miraculously pushed the damaged ski back into place and the big plane came to a smooth landing on rugged ice.

In the meantime the ship's diver Sheliudin and the captain's assistant, Ponamarev, had gone down into the icy waters to examine the *Krassin's* propeller. The damage was more extensive than had been anticipated. One blade of the propeller was missing and a part of the rudder was broken.

July 9: Guard duty on the floe was discontinued. Surrounded by water, the men were cornered and even polar bears did not have to be watched for any longer. If their ice floe split, the men's only hope lay in reaching the rubber rafts.

Talk on the floe centered around the Russians. Behounek, a fellow Slav, was confident. "They may be slow," he said, "but once determined, they are stubborn and do not give up." Now and again, with growing resentment, they talked about Nobile. For days there has been no word from the general. Had he abandoned them? Had he written them off like the Alessandrini group? They had no way of knowing that censor Romagna had ordered deletion of Nobile's name from all messages originating aboard the *Città di Milano.*

The radio was checked. The batteries were good. The receiver was taken apart, but in Cecioni's massive hand a condenser wire snapped. Looking over the big man's shoulders, Trojani gasped. Cecioni was literally holding their lives in his big beefy hands. There were neither spare parts nor tools to speak of. With unbelievable dexterity master mechanic Cecioni soldered the wire, using two coins, some tin scraped off a can, and the heat of a match.

But the receiver stayed dead. They checked the antenna, and then gave up. They all knew that, one way or another, these were their last days on the ice.

With pieces crudely cut out of cardboard, the men played chess and checkers. The chess champion of the floe was Trojani. Behounek, considered something of a professional, was disqualified; Biagi and Cecioni did not know the game. Trojani's only opponent, Viglieri, lost by a small margin.

Their carefully rationed cigarettes were gone, and the food consisted of canned meat, served three times daily, with biscuits. The atmosphere was one of apparent relaxation, as the men gathered in their tent. His arm resting on the silent receiver, Biagi used pidgin Italian to tell Behounek a story, which the Czech did not understand. "Thirteen planes," he said, "seven ships, forty thousand horsepowers, and we are still on the pack!" Biagi's figures were a bit off, but basically he was right.

A strong wind pushed the floe north and the last outline of land was swallowed up in a misty haze.

On the pack ice, only nine miles east of Foyn Island, Captain Sora realized that his self-imposed mission had ended in failure. He decided to retreat. His score: The "Red Tent" not found; Mariano's party not located; Varming abandoned; sleds and the three surviving dogs left behind on Foyn Island.

July 10: The position of the "Red Tent" was 80°29′N, 28°E. In five days the men had moved twenty-five miles without walking. The wind shifted to the west and the ice deteriorated steadily. Trojani bet Biagi a hundred lire that the *Krassin* would arrive—and in time. Shares of the "Polar Shipwreck Co." were being offered at 2 per cent of their nominal value.

At an earlier time the radio silence would have thrown the men into depression, now it deserved no more than a shrug of the shoulders. They had accepted their fate.

At three o'clock, pilot Chukhnovsky, wearing his flying suit, approached Samoilovich: "I think I'll take off, O.K.?" The professor nodded. "Fine," he said. "Good luck." At 4:25 P.M., with copilot Straube, navigator Alexeiev, mechanics Shelagin and Fedotov as well as cameraman Blumshtein aboard, Chukhnovsky was ready.

Sliding heavily over rough ice, the plane's skis dug into snow and

The *Città di Milano* with Chukhnovsky's plane tied up at her stern.

sank into puddles thinly covered with ice. The Junkers gathered speed, rose, circled twice, climbed higher and disappeared in the east, just as fog began to roll in from all sides.

On the *Krassin,* work had stopped to minimize interference with radio reception. In the smoke-filled radio cabin, Commissar Oras leaned over the shoulder of radio operator Yudikhin. Standing near was Professor Samoilovich.

4:42 P.M. "Approaching Charles Island . . ."

5:15 P.M. "Flying over Esmark Island . . ."

5:50 P.M. "Have not found camp . . ."

6:18 P.M. "We are returning . . ."

A dense blanket of fog by now hung over the *Krassin.* On the icefields near by, burning oil and tar belched thick black smoke into the haze, to serve as a beacon for Chukhnovsky.

6:45 P.M. Yudikhin's face twitched, and Samoilovich saw him write two words: "Malmgren group." Questions raced through the mind of

Professor Samoilovich: Where? On ice? On land? Just then the radio became silent. Yudikhin turned the dial to the right, to the left—nothing. Minutes ticked by.

6:56 P.M. Samoilovich to Chukhnovsky: "Where are you? Answer . . ."

An hour passed by. Somewhere, over fog-shrouded mountains and in- visible ice, the Junkers flew on, with its pilot trying desperately to get back to the icebreaker.

Then there was a message: "Cannot find *Krassin* in the fog. Sighted Malmgren group. Searching landing field in Seven Island district."

Excited, Professor Samoilovich stepped out of the cabin, waving a paper with the message hastily scribbled by radio operator Yudikhin.

7:16 P.M. Chukhnovsky: "How is visibility?" Samoilovich: "Very poor."

7:26 P.M. Samoilovich: "Do you read us?" Silence.

9:10 P.M. Samoilovich to Chukhnovsky: "Where are you? Answer . . ."

The clock kept on ticking, but radio operator Yudikhin heard only the crackling noise of static.

9:40 P.M. Samoilovich: "Why no answer?"

10:10 P.M. Samoilovich: "Where are you? What happened?"

Again and again the same questions. The answer only silence.

10:53 P.M. "Where are you? What happened? . . ."

Sweat ran down bearded faces, blank eyes stared into nothingness, and straining ears heard—silence.

11:46 P.M. "Krasny Medved*—our position 80°25′ N. 23°30′ E. at Cape Wrede. Landing gear damaged.

Chukhnovsky was safe. Men in the radio cabin aboard the *Krassin* wiped sweat off their brows and smiled. The sound of the clock no longer bothered anybody.

According to the New York *Times*, the *Braganza* would reach the "Red Tent" by the end of the month. Holding out no hope for either Mariano's party or the Alessandrini group, Tornberg was reported as saying:

> Swedish planes have so materially relieved the . . . wants of the Viglieri group that further relief will be principally moral.

Lundborg was quoted as having said:

> Most of the survivors show signs of mental derangement.

A totally confused correspondent sharing the general pessimism wrote:

---

* *Krasny Medved*—"Red Bear" (name of Chukhnovsky's plane).

Dr. Malmgren is old and one of his companions, Mariano, suffers from heart trouble.

Meanwhile, the *Hobby* continued her search for Amundsen. The plan was to proceed southwest, search an area between Amsterdam Island and Greenland until she met the French-chartered *Heimland,* coming from the opposite direction. The *Braganza* reached Murchison Bay, but all planes in Spitsbergen remained grounded. The *Uppland* received orders to return to Sweden as soon as the weather improved.

On July 11, at 1:10 in the morning, Chukhnovsky sent a detailed report:

> Malmgren is on a small floe of 80°42′ N., 25°45′ E. Two of the men stood waving, a third was lying on the ground. Circled five times. . . . Having food for two weeks, consider it imperative that *Krassin* go to Malmgren's aid soonest, without worrying about us . . .[60]

He had been unable to drop supplies, he said, because the floe was too small. Forced to make an emergency landing in the fog, he had hit a hummock, which damaged the undercarriage and smashed two propellers.

At that moment, the *Krassin* was only about fifteen miles from where the Malmgren group had been sighted. Orders were shouted, and stokers got busy. Belching, fuming, and snorting, the big ship came to life.

Elsewhere, life went on. Aboard the *Quest,* Lundborg wrote his story for Stockholm's *Tidninges.* At a special meeting, the Swedish Government authorized Tornberg to act on his own initiative in a renewed search for Malmgren, and the orders of the *Uppland* to return home were canceled. The *Braganza* arrived in Beverly Sound, took aboard Varming and the Italian contingent of the food depot, and proceeded east. Sora and Van Dongen were now back on Foyn Island, where they shot and ate still another dog. Charcot's *Pourquoi-Pas?* was on her way to join the *Strasbourg* and the *Quentin Roosevelt* in their joint search for Amundsen's Latham plane.

On the floe, life went on too. Within twenty-four hours, the "Red Tent" had drifted six miles east. In the evening, more as·a matter of routine rather than conviction, Biagi put on his earphones. Faint but audible he heard a newscast from Rome. Even this failed to cause any particular excitement among the apathetic group.

Lurching forward and backing up, the *Krassin* slammed on. Between four and six o'clock in the afternoon, the ship advanced only two hundred yards. Snow was falling and visibility was poor.

July 12: Hacking and pounding through six-foot ice, the *Krassin* advanced at two knots an hour and passed Charles XII Island at midnight.

All but the men from the boiler room were on deck. Now and again the piercing shrill wail of the siren went out over the white expanse. The man who first saw Malmgren's party was promised a reward of one hundred rubles.

At 5:20 A.M., Breinkopf, a lookout, his face red with excitement, yelled: "A man, a man, I see him . . ."

The word passed quickly and eyes strained, but for twenty minutes nobody knew whether or not Breinkopf was right.

At length others saw a dark dot in the distance. Could it be a seal? As the *Krassin* approached, two dots became visible. They seemed to be moving—they *were* moving. Those were human forms . . . But who were they? Mariano's group? Men from the Latham? The Sora party?

Sailors crowded the bridge, and for an emotion-packed half hour dozens of eyes remained glued to the two tiny black dots on an immense icefield One man was waving and jumping from hummock to hummock, the other was lying on the ice, only now and then lifting his head.

At 6:40 A.M., when at a distance of a hundred yards from the floe carrying the men, the *Krassin* came to a stop.

A tall man, his skin deeply sunburnt, face covered with a shaggy beard, cupped his hands and yelled: *"Krassin!* Welcome. . . ." A ladder was thrown overboard, Breinkopf, Ivanov and Dr. Srednevsky were first to step on the floe which measured about 24 feet by 30 feet. Ropes were needed, planks, ladders, stretchers. Ivanov, secretary of the *Krassin* expedition, approached the standing man. "Malmgren?" he asked. The man shook his head. "No," he answered. "Commander Zappi . . ."

Others ran to the human form lying in a pool of watery snow. On a neighboring floe, strips of clothes were seen laid out to read: Help— Food—Mariano—Zippi.

From the bridge Giudici yelled in Italian: "How about Malmgren? Where is Malmgren?" In the weeks to come, the same questions would be asked again and again . . . in Swedish, Italian, German, Russian, English. They would be asked with anger and in disbelief. They would be repeated loudly and in print. "How about Malmgren? Where is Malmgren?"

Filippo Zappi, Lieutenant Commander in the Royal Italian Navy, pointed downward, under the ice.

Supported by Ivanov and two sailors, Zappi climbed the rope ladder without great difficulty, as Samoilovich was to remember, and shook hands with the leader of the *Krassin* expedition.

"No food for thirteen days . . ." he said.

". . . and Malmgren, where is Malmgren?" Samoilovich asked.

"That was a man . . ." Zappi replied, hesitating and looking away, "he died a month ago . . ."

Mariano was brought aboard on a stretcher; his gaunt arm reached

weakly for the leg of Professor Samoilovich. His face overgrown with
an unruly beard, his eyes had receded in their sockets and he remained
silent. Lieutenant Commander Adalberto Mariano appeared to be at
death's door.

In the messroom, Zappi let himself fall into a chair. "I would like
some hot coffee," he said. "Some very hot coffee . . . I have not had
a warm drink since May 30th. . . ." There was no coffee aboard the
Krassin, so Zappi got tea instead. "Something to eat, I'm hungry. . . ."
Dr. Srednevsky permitted only tea and a biscuit.

"But why?" Zappi asked. "You save us from starvation and now you
don't want to let us eat . . ."

Commander Zappi smoked greedily. With a steady hand he wrote two
short messages—one to his mother and the other to the Undersecretary
for Navy in Rome. . .

7

After an exchange of congratulatory messages, Samoilovich now sent
this radio message to Nobile: ". . . proceeding to Viglieri stop please
advise position . . ."

At 9:40 A.M., an answer came from Romagna to Samoilovich:

> Contact with Viglieri group possible only at 3:55 P.M. Please accept
> expressions of gratitude . . .

Professor Samoilovich, a short, bespectacled veteran of thirteen arctic
expeditions, kept a meticulous log. He had an exact list made of the
clothes worn by both survivors. Over and above what Mariano had,
Zappi was wearing a fur cap, a hooded jacket, two pairs of pants, two
pair of socks, and finnskos.[70]

Zappi, too, was taken to the sick bay, and both men were given enemas.
The returns seemed to indicate that Zappi had been without food for
about five days, Mariano for considerably longer. No facilities for chemical
analysis existed aboard the *Krassin,* and thus some ugly questions would
never receive a scientific answer.

Correspondent Davide Giudici got an exclusive account from Lieutenant Commander Zappi: "For fourteen days we pushed on," Zappi
said, "covering ground which could not have averaged more than two
miles a day."[71] The steady drift rendered all their efforts useless, and
two weeks after leaving Nobile's group the three men found themselves
farther away from Broch Island than ever. Malmgren was depressed and
grew weaker by the day until he could hardly walk at all. Letting himself
fall, he urged the two Italians to leave him behind and go on. Mariano
and Zappi moved on a hundred yards and rested, hoping that Malmgren
would join them. They waited about twenty-four hours and then saw

Malmgren's compass.

Malmgren's head rise from the shallow trench in which he was lying. "Go, go on, don't waste time," the Swede shouted. On June 16, Mariano and Zappi went on, taking with them all of Malmgren's food.

Scrambling over ice blocks, jumping across canals, they continued moving on the drifting pack ice without advancing. Mariano became snowblind and had to be led by the hand. The two scooped out a trench in the dry snow and lay in it for five or six days.

"On June 20th," Zappi continued," the weather cleared and we could see Broch Island much nearer." By that time Mariano had improved and both men resumed walking. Suddenly they were startled by the drone of a plane flying overhead. They waved frantically, but the plane flew on without noticing them. During the following five days they saw planes repeatedly, without themselves ever being noticed by the pilots. Mariano became snowblind again and twisted his ankle in a fall. A sudden eastward drift caught the floe on which the two were, and Broch Island disappeared in the fog.

"That day," Zappi said, "I considered for the first time the possibility of abandoning Mariano and trying to reach land alone." But seeing how broken up the pack ice was, he dropped the idea. Instead, spreading a blanket out on the snow, the two lay down and allowed themselves to drift. Eventually their floe was carried to a point near Cape Leigh Smith, and Zappi again thought of leaving Mariano, but reluctantly gave up the idea once more. Then their food gave out, and, on June 30, the two ate their last piece of pemmican. Resigned to die, they waited passively for the end as days passed by. On July 10 there was again the drone of a plane, again Zappi frantically waved a rag, and as the plane started circling overhead, the two men on the floe realized to their surprise that they had been spotted. Two days later they heard the shrill blast of a siren and finally the smokestacks of the *Krassin* had appeared.

As if anticipating a question, Zappi paused and exhaled the smoke of a cigarette, then he added: "That Malmgren died is indisputable . . he refused to keep with him even a small amount of food . . ."

Correspondent Giudici, listening attentively, became the recorder of history. Under a coat of flamboyant words, skillfully applied by his pen, were certain realities: What Zappi kept on calling a "mission" had not been a mission but an act of selfish self-preservation, and his "march" had not really been a march but only a passive drift. Zappi's wardrobe included clothes taken from his best friend Mariano, who had been found ill-clad and lying in a puddle with a frost-bitten foot. Zappi's food consumption must have been in excess of 750 grams daily—almost three times as much as was allotted to any of Amundsen's men engaged in heavy physical work on the 88th parallel![72] Zappi and his friend Mariano abandoned Finn Malmgren in desolate loneliness. It does not matter whether Malmgren offered the two Italians his rations or not, or even whether he asked them to leave him.[73] What matters is that Finn Malmgren was left. Zappi had also taken it upon himself, incidentally, to baptize Dr. Malmgren, a Protestant, against his will.

Was Malmgren alive when he was abandoned? Did he ask to be abandoned? Did he offer his food or was it taken away from him?

Omitted from the transcribed account of correspondent Guidici was a statement made by Filippo Zappi, which he repeated with several variations: "Mariano allowed me to eat his liver, as soon as he was dead. . ."[74]

Giudici's carefully edited account is the only one available and it certainly doesn't answer all the questions, but some inescapable observations were made by those aboard the *Krassin,* who looked with ill-concealed disdain on Zappi. He was strong, with no trace of malnutrition, and was wearing clothes belonging to Mariano. Mariano, on the other hand, was emaciated, weak and feverish. With the sole of his right foot frozen and gangrene setting in, he listened, with his eyes closed, but said nothing.

The *Krassin* resumed its course through ten-foot thick ice. The coal consumption in twelve hours was 72 tons. Coal remaining, 1,564 tons of which 1,100 tons were needed for the return voyage.

Highly agitated, Zappi kept talking incessantly in a shrill voice.

"Comrade," the sickbay attendant Shchukin said, "you're disturbing your friend!"

"To you I'm no 'comrade,' to you I'm Mister Zappi . . . mister Filippo Zappi."

At 11 A.M. the icebreaker *Krassin* passed Foyn Island and Captain's assistant Ponamarev saw two men on the shore, waving . . . Sora and Van Dongen!

There was a short conference in Samoilovich's cabin. Should the ship stop or proceed?

Telegram: Samoilovich to Tornberg aboard the *Quest:*

> . . . if they are not picked up before, we will take them aboard on our way back . . . proceeding to Viglieri group . . .

Mariano's temperature was 102 degrees and Dr. Srednevsky considered amputation of the frostbitten leg essential, but Zappi objected. Under the circumstances the doctor declined to assume responsibility.

Equipped with a long-wave radio only, the *Krassin* could not contact the "Red Tent" directly and had to rely on Captain Romagna.

12 o'clock noon: Samoilovich to Romagna:

> Did Viglieri group sight *Krassin?* Contact every thirty minutes advisable . . .

It took the Italian Navy one hour to answer:

> . . . our next contact with tent at 2:55 P.M.

2:45 P.M.: Samoilovich to Romagna:

> We are three miles from Viglieri. Visibility ten miles but cannot see tent. Indicate new position.

There was no answer at all from Captain Romagna-Manoja.

At 4:15 P.M. Viglieri was the first to hear the piercing, whining sound of a ship's siren in the distance. The men dropped everything and piled out of the tent. Even Cecioni, leaning on two oars, went outside. They strained their eyes, fired rifles, and built a fire. Standing on top of Lundborg's Fokker, radioman Biagi scanned the horizon through fieldglasses.

"There, I can see her," he yelled. "There is smoke some fifteen kilometers* away . . . but she seems to be going away rather than coming closer."

The sky was overcast and visibility limited. The forty minutes that followed were easily the longest in the life of any of the men on the floe. Only at five o'clock would Captain Romagna find time to listen to them again.

5 P.M.: Viglieri to Romagna:

> Sighted Krassin 15 kilometers* to southwest . . .

Promptly Romagna gave Samoilovich the following fantastic correction:

> Your objective is 15 kilometers *southwest from you.*

Her siren howling, the big ship turned away.

At 6:15 P.M. Helmsman Legsdin of the *Krassin* saw a thin column of smoke forty-five degrees off the course indicated by Captain Romagna. The ship once more turned about and steamed toward the floe.

At 7 P.M. Viglieri's men could see with their naked eyes the black smoke of the *Krassin*. There was nothing more to be done and they sat down for their last meal on the ice. Biagi had lost his bet and owed Trojani one hundred lire. He paid with a cigarette. Inflation had come to the Arctic.

Everyone on the *Krassin* was jubilant. On a floe, the overturned plane was visible and some black dots could be seen moving in the distance. The silence of the Arctic was broken by the rhythmic rumbling of the *Krassin's* engines and the crunching and grinding of ice as the ship proceeded.

At 8 P.M. the icebreaker was clearly visible from the floe and the five were ready to leave their prison.

At 8:25 P.M. the icebreaker dropped anchor on the west side of the floe, a hundred yards from the "Red Tent."

---

* 9.3 miles.

The *Krassin* reaches the Red Tent.

First to come forward was a tall figure. The man halted some twenty yards from the ship and called out "Viglieri." Following him were Behounek, Trojani, and limping on his oars, Cecioni.

Samoilovich, Captain Eggi, Commissar Oras, and Secretary Ivanov were the first to set foot on the floe. There was handshaking, embracing and kissing as the little cake of ice was overrun by sailors and reporters.

"And Malmgren," Viglieri asked, "how about Malmgren?"

Near the radio, Giudici met Biagi, who wore a heavy beard and the general's cap of Umberto Nobile. He now sent his last message: "Long live Italy! Long live the King! Long live the Duce!"

Cameras snapped as the Russians wandered off to inspect the floe. Biagi showed his mahogany boxes to the *Krassin's* chief radio operator, Eckstein. "And this," he said, pointing to two inflated rafts standing next to the tent whose walls were covered with sun-bleached red stripes, "this is our fleet."

Trojani approached Samoilovich and shook his hand again. His grasp was firm and there was no need for words. Behounek, too, went back to the Russian. "Do you think," he asked, "it would be possible to continue my work aboard the ship?" Samoilovich smiled. "We are scientists too," he answered. "As a matter of fact, if you want, I will help you." There was one more question Behounek had: "Malmgren? What about Malmgren?"

The five survivors of the *Italia* went aboard the *Krassin*. There they got a bath and fresh clothes. Samoilovich, on the other hand, received a formal request from Lieutenant Commander Zappi: Biagi and Cecioni ought not to be lodged in the same cabin as the officer personnel of the *Italia!* The answer was a firm "nyet," and Cecioni was given a cabin all to himself.

From Hinlopen Strait, the *Turku,* with Finnish pilot Lihr at the controls, took off, accompanied by two Swedish aircraft piloted by Tornberg and Jacobsson. Their destination was Foyn Island. The planes flew through dense fog and after ninety minutes they found the Sora party and landed. Only two men and two dogs were left. Sora boarded the *Turku,* while Van Dongen went with Tornberg. The channel on which the planes had landed was narrowing rapidly as ice was closing in. The pilots did not dare delay departure, and the dogs were left behind. One hour later the planes were back at the *Quest;* and the two rescued men were flown to the *Città di Milano* in Kings Bay.

The Italian captain had accomplished nothing. But he would tell it all in a 238-page book, complete with photos, in which his 5'4" likeness appeared not less than twelve times. "I was brought back," he would insist, "not rescued . . ."[75]

On the front page of its Friday edition the New York *Times* carried a four-column headline: "Heroes Of The Arctic Wastes." Also featured was a photograph of Dr. Finn Malmgren, flanked by Mariano and Zappi, handsome in the dress uniform of the Royal Italian Navy. The caption: "His comrades had stayed with his body having been without food for thirteen days when found." An imaginative reporter supplied emotional additions to fact:

> Starving and exhausted but still standing guard over the body of their dead comrade, the two Italians were taken aboard. While all stood at salute, the body was carried aboard the vessel and laid in state. It was a moving scene and many of the hardened men participating were not afraid to show their tearstained faces . . .

Cleaned and shaven, wearing high Russian boots and his general's hat, Biagi strutted on the *Krassin's* deck, humming. Viglieri was allowed a brief visit with his two fellow officers and then the men sat down to a meal. Among shuffling of feet and clattering of dishes there were toasts and brief speeches exchanged between Samoilovich and Viglieri.

The contribution of Mussolini's Italy on this 12th day of July: The *Braganza* headed toward Cape Platen, and new motors were finally installed in the planes of Majors Maddalena and Penzo. But Captain Romagna also received orders from Rome prohibiting use of both Italian planes for any further rescue operations.

The score now was: 11 saved; 2 dead; 12 missing. Airman Chuknovsky and his Russian crew were still marooned.

July 13: News of the rescue spread over the world. But the men of the *Krassin* still had work to do. Lundborg's plane, the "Red Tent" and other relics of the *Italia* were taken aboard the icebreaker, while congratulatory messages were pouring in.

At 7:30 A.M. Samoilovich radioed Nobile. The icebreaker was disabled, he said; its coal supplies dwindling. But nevertheless the *Krassin* would resume search for the Alessandrini group, if Italy would provide planes for air reconnaissance.

At 4:40 P.M. Samoilovich received a pompous radiogram from Premier Mussolini:

> Your work will go down in history . . . In the name of all Italians I thank you and your assistants . . .

Missing, however, was any permission for Maddalena and Penzo to resume flying.

5:30 P.M.: Samoilovich to Nobile:

> Please notify whether planes available. If so, shall wait at camp site.

Viglieri conversed with Samoilovich in French, and Giudici interviewed Trojani in Italian. In Eckstein's radio cabin, Biagi tapped out a personal greeting to Baccarani, aboard the *Città di Milano*. Back came an answer in the Bolognese dialect, intelligible only to Biagi, who was born in Medicina, near Bologna. Its gist: Tell Zappi to shut up and don't talk yourself . . .

In the absence of any Pilsener beer, Professor Behounek drank strong tea and smoked. No longer afraid of dying, Cecioni sat in a soft armchair and smiled. Mariano was getting worse but managed to dictate his first telegram.

Zappi was noisy, and loquacious. In a fit of temper he threw a bowl of cereal at the sickbay orderly Shuchukin, and complained to Samoilovich about the inefficient radio service aboard the *Krassin*. It seems that it had taken the radiomen more than a whole hour to send out Zappi's telegrams, whose number happened to be in excess of official ship messages for the day. An inquiry was received aboard the *Krassin* which was addressed to Zappi: Is further search for the Alessandrini group warranted? Zappi had the answer. Of course not, he wired back, the men are dead and there is no point in wasting time. Zappi was in a hurry to go home.

In Italy, the *Popolo di Roma* said:

> Human solidarity has written another page which kindles in all hearts a sense of infinite gratitude . . .

In Germany the press considered the *Krassin's* feat not only a great human effort but a political victory as well. "The Nobile affair" was expected to cause a rift in the Fascist Party. *Der Abend* gloated:

> Some of the victims of mad fascist ambition have been saved by a Soviet Russian icebreaker.

Die Welt Am Abend said:

> Coward Nobile . . . not only gave incorrect information for the rescue work for the remainder of his crew but told barefaced lies to cover up his criminal undertaking.

The Swedish press demanded a clear statement from Nobile.

July 14: At seven minutes past midnight a radiogram signed "*Città di Milano*" was received aboard *the Krassin*. No planes were available and further search was deemed inadvisible. Delivery of the rescued was expected as soon as possible.

At 2 A.M. a four-man group, led by Albertini, left the *Braganza* and set out to rescue Chukhnovsky.

At 3:25 in the morning the icebreaker lifted anchor. Viglieri stood on its bridge, taking a last look at the familiar floe, empty except for some rubbish.

"Are we going east or west?" Guidici asked Samoilovich.

"To Kings Bay—but we won't be away long. We have to pick up Chukhnovsky, deliver your countrymen and take on water and coal; then we will be back," the Professor said. There was no reproach, nor any expression of judgment.

Both the *Turku* and the *Uppland* were homeward bound aboard a Norwegian freighter. The *Malygin* was ordered to discontinue further rescue efforts and to head for Murmansk. Only the search for Amundsen was to be continued.

Anger mounted in Sweden. The two Italians had abandoned Malmgren when he was still alive, the press argued. Therefore they could only *assume* that he had died; they could not be sure. The Swedish War Department saw the situation more realistically, but considered it a matter of honor that Malmgren's body should be recovered. It ordered Captain Tornberg to continue the search. The possibility of an official inquiry was discussed and some papers demanded an investigation conducted by Norway, from whose territory the *Italia* had taken off. Norway's Prime Minister, J. L. Morwinckel, was interviewed by the *Dagebladet* and pleaded against a too hasty judgment.

In an authoritative dispatch from Moscow, Walter Duranty reported the growing hostility of the Soviet press. From the *Young Communist Pravda:*

> . . . we know the meaning of the word 'comrade.' To Fascist Italy it is evidently alien . . . .

From a sarcastic article in *Evening Moscow,* entitled "A Dog's Life":

> . . . Malmgren died of exposure on June 15. Nobile better, his dog Titina feels fine . . . .

An angry headline was composed for the Sunday edition of the New York *Times,* "Malmgren Left To Die." Nobile could certainly claim few favorable press notices. *Die Rote Fahne,* published by Germany's Communist Party, referred in a long editorial to the "criminally dangerous project of the fascist bandit," and spoke of the "victims of fascist madness." It called Nobile a "criminal," whose expedition was a "militaristic-imperialistic comedy" which resulted in a "sad fiasco."[76]

Slowly, the *Krassin* made its way toward Cape Wrede. Trojani, whose legs were swollen and painful, lay in a bunk above that of Mariano and was tenderly attended by the young woman journalist, Vorontsova.

"Doctor," Mariano said, "I had already given up any hope so, if it is necessary, amputate. I shall still be ahead of the game." But Dr. Srednevsky again declined. Captain Romagna had agreed to send the Italian physician Cendali aboard the *Braganza* to meet the icebreaker.

Dr. Cendali, as mentioned before, happened to be a specialist in tropical diseases.

July 15: Russian sentiment, Walter Duranty wired, was stirred by the Nobile disaster "as it has been stirred by no foreign nonpolitical event in the last seven years." Under the title "Cross and Champagne" famous poet Mayakovsky published a poem:

> The Fascist general who took the cross to the Pole but deserted his comrades, who took champagne to celebrate the Italian victory and left Italians to die. We await Nobile's live word: Why have you fled? Where is Malmgren? Has he died or have they left him alive?

The Swedish press joined in:

> Is it possible that two Italian officers abandoned their companion to a certain death or was Malmgren no longer alive—a much more terrible but a more humane procedure?

The Albertini group reached Chukhnovsky's party . . . in time to share their supper. The Russians had shot a reindeer, but the meat was not particularly tasty and the Italians had forgotten to bring the only thing they had been asked for, salt.

At 8:00 P.M., the *Krassin* dropped anchor a mile from Chukhnovsky's wrecked plane and nine men boarded the icebreaker. There were five Russians, three Italians and one Norwegian. There was talking and dancing to nostalgic balalaika music on the *Krassin* that night while the plane was being dragged over the ice, to be taken aboard.

July 16: Vociferous anti-Italian sentiment persisted in Sweden. Contributions to a memorial fund for Malmgren started pouring in spontaneously and the government was urged to ask Mussolini for an "official explanation." [77]

Italy's controlled press hinted at a possible inquiry of the *Italia* disaster, but reports of Nobile's virtual imprisonment aboard the *Città di Milano* were scornfully dismissed. Noisily supporting Mariano and Zappi, the *Giornale d'Italia* proclaimed: Questioning the conduct and actions of the two Italian officers amounts to "defamation of Italy!"

In Seattle, Mr. Haakon H. Hammer, Amundsen's friend, made sure that a little stunt of his was properly reported by the American press. To celebrate Amundsen's birthday, he drank a toast to an empty chair draped in the colors of Norway.

July 17: With Chukhnovsky's plane aboard, the *Krassin* was on its way back to Kings Bay. In the afternoon, Captain Eggi skillfully maneuvered his ship alongside the icebound *Braganza*, and Dr. Cendali

came aboard the icebreaker. After a brief examination, he concurred
with his Russian colleague: Mariano's leg must be amputated. It was
agreed, however, that the operation be performed aboard the *Città di
Milano,* where better facilities were available.

The New York *Times* printed the first picture of General Nobile taken
aboard the *Città di Milano*. The press kept clamoring for an investigation.
Bitterness was growing throughout Norway, and an angry, threatening
crowd demanded removal of Nobile's picture from the window of Oslo's
Aftenposten.

July 18: Mario Carli and Emilio Settinelli, editors of a small Italian
paper with the imposing title *Impero di Roma,** took exception to stories
about Mariano and Zappi printed in France and challenged the editors
of France's *Le Matin* to a duel. They wrote an open letter:

> Ignoble slanderers . . . false and malicious reports are reflecting on
> the honor of Italy . . . . Hoping to punch your nose as soon as possible,
> we remain . . .[78]

Le Matin ignored the challenge, but circulation of the *Impero di Roma*
soared.

In Sweden people still wondered, "What about Malmgren?" Professor
Behounek also wondered what had happened to the two letters he had
given Malmgren? He was sure that the methodical Swede would not
have forgotten to turn them over to the Italian officers. In that case,
what had happened to the letters?[79]

Aboard the *Krassin,* Trojani started reading a book *The Voyage of
the "Jeannette."* It was the story of De Long's ill-fated arctic expedition.
Crushed by ice, his ship had sunk and thirty-two men were left on a
floe, about five hundred miles off the Siberian coast. Lieutenant George
Washington De Long of the United States Navy lived long enough to
see his men die one by one, before he made a last entry in his diary,
140 days after the *Jeannette* had gone down.[80] Trojani later said:

> Any comment would be profane, but a comparison with facts emerging
> from our expedition came spontaneously and filled my soul with a
> sadness which amounted almost to a state of anxiety.[81]

At 7:30 in the morning of July 19, the *Krassin* steamed into the
waters of Kings Bay, where wildly cheering Italians crowded the deck
of the *Città di Milano*. A motor launch brought Captain Romanga and
within an hour all the survivors of the *Italia* were back on their own
ship. There was coming and going aboard the *Krassin*. Tornberg arrived,
and so did Maddalena, Penzo and Lundborg. There were reporters and
photographers and an overeager Italian cameraman managed to fall into

---

* Roman Empire.

:he water. While some sailors pulled him out by the seat of his pants, a fast-thinking American was filming the scene.

Everybody scribbled something for the guest book of Professor Samoilo-⁄ich. Trojani wrote:

> My deep, sincere gratitude, Professor Samoilovich, for giving me back to my family. I admire your courage, I admire your selflessness and the skill with which the *Krassin* has performed its humanitarian work.[82]

Mussolini ordered the *Italia* survivors to return home and prohibited interviews. In Moscow, Kamenev said:

> We intend to continue rescue work all the more energetically because it appears that we will be alone.

In Germany, Professor Bruns, prominent member of Aeroarctica, an international society for aerial exploration of the Arctic, thought it was 'quite incorrect to abandon further search on the basis of such vague nformation."

The ship carrying Sergeant Nilsson, the *Uppland*, and the *Turku* arrived n Narvik, and the remainder of the Swedish rescue mission was recalled. Dslo decided that difficulties in international law made it impossible for Norway to start an inquiry unless requested to do so by Italy, and a report from Stockholm had it that Mussolini's Government was planning :o investigate the Nobile disaster.

The drama was over. The survivors were aboard the *Città di Milano* ind Lundborg's Fokker and relics of the *Italia* were taken off the *Krassin*. Now was the time for courtesy visits.

Samoilovich was authorized to take Nobile aboard the *Krassin*, but Mussolini's veto could not be overridden. Nobile remained a virtual prisoner on the *Città di Milano,* and at an official reception given by Captain Romagna for the Russians, he was conspicuous by his absence.

Before Mariano underwent amputation of his gangrenous foot, he asked :o be recommended for Italy's coveted Gold Medal of Honor, but Nobile declined to accommodate him. He did not feel that Mariano's actions had been above and beyond the call of duty.[83]

Leaving behind the Italian planes and their crews, and Captain Sora and some of his soldiers, the *Città di Milano* departed for Narvik on July 22. A day later Mussolini made a speech in which he rejected as "absurd and offensive" the suggestion of a non-Italian investigation of the dirigible disaster. He told his council of ministers:

> Before pronouncing definite judgment, we must wait until the anti-human, anti-Italian wave which has dashed against the participants in this unfortunate enterprise subsides.

He did promise, however, that there would be an investigation, "a disinterested, dispassionate and normal one."[84]

On that same day a sleeper was chartered which was to take survivo
of the *Italia* home from Narvik, and the Soviet Relief Committee receive
an official request from the Italian Government to take up a searc
for the Alessandrini group. But by then it was obvious that the *Krass*
would have to be repaired and refueled before it could venture bac
into pack ice.

There was a general exodus from Spitsbergen. Leaving Chukhnovsk
his plane, and its crew in Kings Bay, the *Krassin* steamed for Stavange
the *Quest*, with the Swedish fliers aboard, went to Tromso, and th
Malygin was already anchored off Archangel. Only the Norwegian ar
French vessels continued their search for Amundsen and his companior

At 7:30 A.M. of a dreary Friday the *Città di Milano* arrived in Narvi
There were no officials to greet her, no bands, no flags, and only
small group of sullen men with expressionless faces lined the pier.[84] Whe
the ship was in position to throw her lines, there were no hands
grab them. Nobody moved to assist the *Città di Milano* in dockin
and Captain Romagna had to send some sailors to secure the ship.

Mariano was taken to a hospital for convalescence, and the oth
survivors of the *Italia* walked silently across a gangway leading direct
from their ship to the special train which was to take them home. The
were under explicit orders not to talk to outsiders nor to leave the
car. On the same train, but in a compartment of their own, were Tornbe
and Lundborg.

The train pulled out, accompanied by a few scattered hisses and fc
lowed by the glare of a silent crowd. Norway was still stunned, st
all too conscious that Roald Amundsen was almost certainly no more.

All through Sweden, Nobile's party was met with silence and occasion
signs of hostility. Now and then, when the train stopped, someone wou
break out of a group of onlookers and start banging an angry fist again
the closed windows and shouting just one word: "Malmgren!"[85]

At Krylbo, the ways of rescued and rescuers parted. Tornberg ar
Lundborg proceeded for Stockholm, to be greeted by an enthusiastic crov
and official representatives, while the Italian party went on to Copenhage
Zappi, too, went to Stockholm. Accompanied by the Italian Consul Ge
eral, he visited Mrs. Malmgren and repeated to her the story which I
then was well known to everybody. At the conclusion of the vis
Malmgren's brother-in-law, Dr. Fagerstein, issued a statement to the pre
in which he said:

> Captain Zappi is a perfect gentlemen whose story gives a clear id
> of what really happened.[86]

Viglieri brought a Swedish paper carrying an article in which Mariar
and Zappi were openly accused of cannibalism. Nobile had it translate

and his face reddened with rage. "Madness" he yelled; "it is madness, a foolish idea born of a wicked imagination."

"Why are you being kept a prisoner?" A journalist asked.

"Prisoner, I am no prisoner . . . Where did that stupid idea come from?"[87]

After one day in Copenhagen, the Italian party proceeded, in a special car of the regular southbound train, through Germany. At Warnemünde, Professor Behounek got off and went on to Prague. There, in front of the Wilson Railroad Station, he was received by an enthusiastic crowd, headed by representatives of the Czech Government, city officials, and members of the Italian embassy, who presented his fiancée, Ludmilla Felixowa, with a big bouquet of roses, bound in Italy's green, white and red colors.

The reception accorded the Nobile group on its way through Germany was at first cool, and, in Munich, police had to break up a hostile demonstration,[87] but farther south, people waiting at railroad stations became friendlier.

In the early hours of July 31, Nobile and his men reached the Italian border. In Bressanone they were met by officers from Alpine regiments, and in Bolzano, Nobile was embraced by local leaders of the Fascist Party. Despite the early hour, the crowds grew bigger and so did the enthusiasm. There were flowers and more flowers. In Verona, ways parted once more as Viglieri went off to his little home town of Borghetto Santo Spirito, and the main party headed south.

In Rome, an exuberant crowd estimated at 100,000 people gathered for a spontaneous demonstration as the train pulled into the station at the end of an oppressively hot day. There was Rome's governor, a personal representative of Mussolini, and all the press, who devoted tons of newsprint to Nobile.

But unlike his earlier triumph, Umberto Nobile has not returned as a victor but as the vanquished. Soon, the spontaneous national enthusiasm, rooted in sensationalism as well as sympathy for the underdog, would die, and soon a one-time hero would be remembered only as "the man who left first."[88]

Unlike the previous *Norge* flight, the venture of the *Italia* was not followed by official receptions, high-sounding speeches, promotions and honors. The only medal awarded the rescued was the one given to Guiseppe Biagi at the Radio World Fair in New York's Madison Square Garden.[89]

Italy's Government was to be more generous with foreigners. Both Sjef Van Dongen and Professor Hoel were given decorations, and Mrs. Anna Malmgren was voted a pension for life.

The search for Amundsen continued. There was still the *Heimland*, the *Hobby*, the *Braganza*. Oscar Wisting was aboard the *Veslekari*,

Malmgren with his mother in 1928.

Professor Hoel went with Admiral Herr, whose cruiser *Strasbourg* had already searched an area of some 30,000 square miles. Denmark's ship *Gustave Adlu* joined the combined effort.

Toward the end of August the *Città di Milano* returned to Kings Bay. She had aboard two small planes, but they were never used for arctic rescue flights. Major Maddalena considered further search useless and left for Italy.

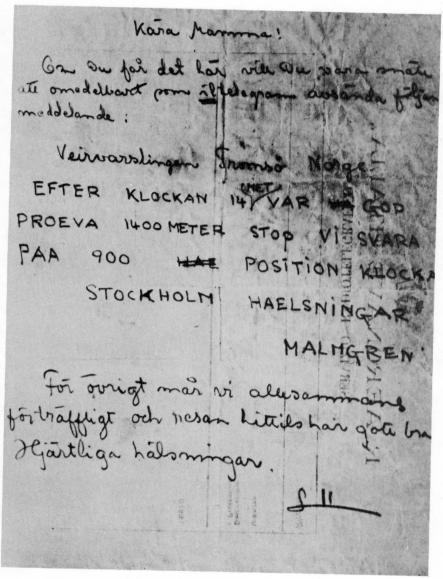

Malmgren's message, dropped from the *Italia* over Stockholm.

On August 31, repaired, refueled and with its water supplies replenished, the *Krassin* again headed northward and approached Bear Island once more.[90] At 7:45 in the evening of that day Captain Haeig, of the fishing boat *Brood*, was passing off the Fugloe Islands, not far from Tromso when he saw what appeared to be an oil barrel bobbing in the water. When taken aboard, the object, gray-blue and some seven feet long, closely resembled the float of a seaplane.

That same night, the *Brood* was back in Tromso and the French consul, Thils, identified the float. Crew members of the *Durance* and *Michael Sars* examined it and they too recognized it. There was no longer any doubt. Welded to the bottom was the copper plate which had been used to patch up a small hole in one of the Latham's floats. There was no doubt about the fate of Amundsen and those with him. On September 6, both the French and Norwegian Governments decided to call off the search.

Questions lived on. When did the Latham crash? Where and why? But they were blotted out by the facts, which brought mourning to Norway and sadness to the rest of the world.

On September 29 Major Penzo was flying his *Marina II* back to Italy. The plane hit a high-tension wire and crashed into the Rhone, carrying to their deaths Penzo, copilot Croscio, and Sergeant Della Gatta.

The final score of the *Italia* disaster: 8 rescued, 17 dead.[91]

V. MILESTONES
1929-1935

1

WITH the flights of Amundsen and Wilkins, large-scale exploration of the north polar regions was virtually completed. The top of the world had turned out to be just a landless frozen sea. It seemed as if a gigantic fist had smashed into the summit of the earth, causing all land to disappear, only to create a protrusion at the bottom of the globe as the Antarctic Continent, a huge ice-covered territory, almost half the size of North America and twice as large as Europe. Now men of action and courage turned to the challenge presented by this virtually unknown part of the earth. Among those who set their sights on exploration of Antarctica were some of the men who had pioneered in the north polar regions: Wilkins and Eielson, Byrd, Ellsworth and Riiser-Larsen, as well as Bernt Balchen, whose name would become firmly associated with historic feats both at the top and the bottom of the world.*

In the Arctic emphasis shifted more and more from exploration to exploitation. In the western hemisphere, a year-long aerial survey of Hudson Strait was completed, and the knowledge thus gained of ice and weather conditions in that area was invaluable for the development of sea and air traffic.[1]

In the Arctic of the eastern hemisphere, natural wealth was exploited more systematically then ever before. There was wealth, which Michigan-born Olaf Swenson had come to appreciate ever since he made his first trip from Nome, Alaska, to Anadyr, Siberia, in 1905. He was then twenty-two and part of a group of adventurous prospectors who had accepted a sub-concession on arctic territory as big as the states of Washington and Oregon combined, from the North-Eastern Siberian Company, an enterprise with vast trading and mining interests.[2]

The ship Swenson was traveling on struck a reef and had to be beached. The supplies aboard were ruined by water. Swenson, enterprising and resourceful, bought up all the sacks of useless saltwater-drenched flour, tobacco leaves, and pressed tea-sweepings. Dried and repacked, these goods were to lay the foundation for his trading empire in Siberia. Dealing cunningly with primitive natives, Swenson collected valuable furs and outdid competitors by bringing a new scheme to Siberia's fur trading business. Where other traders had to give five cases of tea, he got identical skins for only four cases of tea plus a "free gift" and everybody was happy. The childlike natives were happy with a cheap knife, a shiny pot or a useless pan and Swenson was happy with a rebate of twenty per cent, less the few pennies he had invested in the "free gift." He found trading

---

* See Appendix 1.

in Siberia most lucrative, as he kept on amassing valuable furs and selling them at a handsome profit on the world market. Eventually he established trading posts, stopped dealing directly with the natives whose language he did not know, and middlemen began collecting goods for him from a large sector of northern Siberia.

In time Olaf Swenson became an important trader, with at least four large trading posts, and his activities materially influenced the economy of Siberia's Chukchi Peninsula. Then came political upheaval, followed by civil war and, reminiscing, Olaf Swenson said: "We ran smack into the Russian Revolution." Swenson's goods, valued at more than a million dollars, were put "under arrest" by the Soviet Government, which demanded payment of taxes. Grudgingly he settled his tax obligations and sold one parcel of Siberian furs to the new government for what he considered the low price of $161,000. (A month or so later he bought the same parcel back for $191,000 and still realized a very handsome profit when he sold it at an auction in the United States.)

By 1928 he had negotiated a contract which allowed him to purchase Siberian goods on terms approved by the Soviet Fur Trust and had made two successful trips to Siberia aboard his schooner *Nanuk*. In August 1929 he was again on a trading trip to the Soviet Arctic, this time aboard another of his ships, the *Elisif*. Only eleven miles off Cape North,[3] where a valuable cargo was waiting to be taken on, the *Elisif* became hopelessly icebound. Leaving his disabled ship behind, Swenson set out for Seattle to outfit the *Nanuk* for another voyage to Siberia. Successively using dogs, reindeers and horses, he made a four months, 4,500-mile trip across the desolate, snow-covered, wind-swept country to reach Irkutsk, from which he went on to Seattle by boat and train.

The following year, the *Nanuk* crossed Bering Strait and the eastern sector of the Northern Sea Route to complete the job which the hopelessly damaged and beached *Elisif* had left undone. At the estuary of the Kolyma River trader Swenson picked up a cargo whose market value exceeded one million dollars.

Heading homeward across an ice-covered waterway the ship's progress slowed steadily, and, at Cape North, the *Nanuk* was gripped by ice. Carrying fifteen passengers, her holds crammed with cargo, she, too, became icebound. Across the Cape, about five miles away, the *Stavropol,* veteran of many an arctic voyage, was also immobilized. In addition to her crew, the Russian ship had some thirty passengers aboard, and her skipper, Captain Milovzorov, was sick with purulent pleurisy.

Jammed in a solid mass of ice, both ships needed help. Both were in danger of being crushed or carried away with the drift. Help could come only on the wings of planes. Swenson negotiated with Alaska Airways in Fairbanks. The price agreed on—$4.00 for a pound of furs and $750 for each passenger airlifted—added up to some $50,000. It was a sum which looked good to Ben C. Eielson, the new executive vice president and general manager of the young company.

With permission from the Soviet Government to overfly the Chukchi Peninsula, two planes reached the *Nanuk* in October. A Hamilton carrying Eielson and his mechanic Borland arrived after an uneventful 500-mile flight from Fairbanks, and a pilot, Dorbandt, came from Nome in a Stinson.[4] The two planes airlifted six passengers and 1,300 pounds of furs. It was estimated that six trips would be required to complete the job. For a new company it was a well-paying proposition. About $9,700 for two round trips totaling only two thousand miles.

The next flight was scheduled for November 9. At that time preparations were also in progress to take the men, women and children off the *Stavropol.* The Russian plan called for an icebreaker, the *Litke,* to transport two Junkers planes from Vladivostok to Providesniya Bay, on Chukchi Peninsula. From there the Soviet aircraft were to proceed to Cape North. Chief of the *Litke's* air section was Mavriki Slepnev, pilot of plane No. 177. In charge of plane No. 182 was Victor Galyshev, decorated with the Order of the Red Banner for his exploits during Russia's civil war. The operation was to be completed before onset of the long polar night, November 27, but on its way to Providesniya Bay, the icebreaker had to stop at a Japanese port to take on supplies. It arrived there on November 9, already one week behind schedule.

On that day the weather in Alaska was bad. The sky was overcast and north of Fairbanks a storm was raging. Eielson knew very well that it was no weather for flying. Yet, impulsively taking up a taunt flung at him by Dorbandt, Eielson took to the air in his radio-less Hamilton plane together with Borland. Following him was Dorbandt in the Stinson. A wall of wind-driven snow forced Dorbandt back, but fighting his way across stormy Bering Strait, Eielson flew to Russia's mainland, and setting a course for Cape North, reached an area west of Kolyuchin Bay. There some hunters heard the drone of a plane, passing overhead, hidden in low-lying cloud.

Its supplies replenished, the *Litke* left Japan for Providesniya Bay on November 11. That day disquieting news had come by radio from the *Nanuk:* Eielson and Borland had neither arrived at Cape North nor returned to Fairbanks. The Hamilton was two days overdue.

What had happened? Was there an emergency landing? Were the men making their way to the Siberian coast on foot? Or were they already safe in the hut of a hunter? No one knew the answer. Time dragged on, no word came from Eielson and nowhere was there the drone of a Hamilton flying to meet Olaf Swenson's icebound *Nanuk* and her nine anxious passengers.

In Fairbanks, anxiety grew into fear and pilot Joe Crosson took off for Cape North to start a search for the missing plane. So did pilots Gillam and Young.

On November 23 Mavriki Slepnev's detachment arrived in Provideniya Bay aboard the *Litke*. On rowboats nailed together with boards, a crew working around the clock unloaded the dismantled planes, seven months' food supply for 25 people, and barrels containing 183 gallons of gasoline. When the planes were assembled and tested, a sudden blizzard reduced visibility and made flying impossible. The deadline passed and the darkness of polar night descended over Provideniya Bay. All attempts to reach Cape North had to be postponed. Leaving planes and their crews on the inhospitable shore, the *Litke* returned to Vladivostok.

At Cape North, the darkness limited search activities of Crosson, Gillam, and Young. There was still no word from Eielson and Borland.

On January 25, Joe Crosson was flying along the Siberian coast when he saw a long dark object glinting in the weak sun. It was the wing of a plane, protruding through the snow like the lifeless arm of a corpse. Crosson's search was over, but instead of an answer, there were more questions. Did the plane crash, or had Eielson made an emergency landing? Was the snow hiding Eielson's and Borland's bodies, or were the two men safe somewhere?

On that day, January 25, the polar night was retreating, and the days were beginning to lengthen. Commander Slepnev was belatedly getting ready for his flight to the marooned *Stavropol*. Somehow, he had managed to locate natives and enough dogs to form fifteen sled teams, which could take food and gasoline to Kolyuchin Bay. There, a base was to be established for projected flights of the famous arctic pilot, Boris Chukhnovsky and an unknown named Michael Gromov.

On January 27, the heavy planes of Slepnev and Galychev landed near the *Stavropol*. Soon the two Russians met Crosson, Gillam, and Young. Borrowing fuel from the Russians, Joe Crosson returned to the site of the Hamilton wreck, together with Slepnev.

While Olaf Swenson and ailing Captain Milovzorov left by air for Teller and Galyshev was airlifting more of the *Stavropol's* passengers to Lavrentiya Bay, a ground party was organized to conduct a systematic search of the crash area. Among those forming this group were some sailors from the *Stavropol*, Commander Slepnev and his mechanic Farikh. One hundred feet beyond the plane's fuselage they found the Hamilton's motor, and scattered in the snow were guns, ammunition, and twisted pieces of metal. On February 18, Eielson's snow-covered body was found a few hundred feet from his wrecked plane. Borland's body was recovered a short time later.

The place of their death was some ninety miles southeast of the fur-loaded schooner *Nanuk*. The hands of Eielson's watch had stopped at sixteen minutes past one o'clock.[5] A few days later the bodies of the two men were flown to Cape North in Slepnev's mourning-draped USSR-177.

On March 4, 1930, three planes arrived in Teller, Alaska. They were the Russian Junkers carrying Slepnev and Farikh, especially invited by the State Department, Harold Gillam's Stearman, and a Fairchild piloted by Ed Young, with Crosson as passenger, and carrying the canvas-covered bodies of Ben Eielson and Earl Borland. Left behind in Siberia were Crosson's disabled Waco, another aircraft with a broken undercarriage, and the smashed Hamilton.

While Slepnev's party returned via California and Japan to the Soviet Union, a train carried the remains of Ben Eielson back to Hatton, North Dakota. Another train brought to North Dakota a single-engined Fokker, the unlucky *Alaskan*. As a sign of gratitude and respect, Sir Hubert Wilkins had thoughtfully arranged for the aircraft to be taken from a warehouse in Seattle to a museum room in Bismarck. There it would remain, as a symbol of fearless determination, a monument to the memory of Eielson, first man ever to pilot a plane both in the Arctic and the Antarctic.

2

For a few ambitious men, further study of the Arctic remained a challenge which would end only with the establishment of a safe Northern Air Route—an air bridge between the Old World and the New, across the barren lands and ice-covered waters above the Arctic Circle.

Scott, Lindbergh, and the others who had crossed the Atlantic had shown that the two continents could be linked by air. The next step was to establish a commercial route which was both safe and economically profitable. For planes available in the Twenties, the 4,000-mile stretch separating Europe from America was too much. It had to be broken up into smaller segments to provide refueling facilities. Lindbergh himself said:

> A commercial airline must eventually pay its cost of operation from the revenue received. . . . Therefore, it is desirable from an economic standpoint not to have refueling bases too far apart. Every additional mile which must be flown without refueling means that more fuel and less payload are carried.[6]

Such bases could conceivably be established on Greenland, a huge territory of some 825,000 square miles. On a map it looks like a giant airfield rising out of the Atlantic Ocean. But Greenland is an island and most of it lies north of the Arctic Circle. Four fifths of its terrain is buried under a slow-moving glacier, second in size only to that hiding the

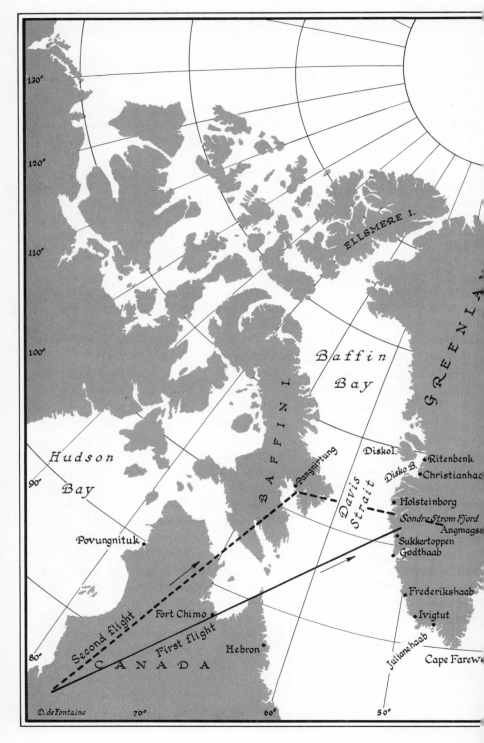

130°
120°
110°
100°
90°
80°

70°   60°   50°

Hudson
Bay

ELLSMERE I.

Baffin
Bay

Baffin I.

Davis Strait

GREENLAND

Diskol.
Disko B.
• Ritenbenk
• Christianhac
• Holsteinborg
Sondre Strom Fjord
Angmagss
• Sukkertoppen
Godthaab
• Frederikshaab
• Ivigtut
Julianehaab
Cape Farew

Pangnirtung

Povungnituk •

Fort Chimo •

Hebron •

Second flight
First flight

C A N A D A

D. de Fontaine

SPITSBERGEN

ARCTIC OCEAN

50°

40°

Greenland Sea

SWEDEN

30°

75°

70°

20°

Eskimonaes • Clavering I.

Ella I.

Scoresby Sd.

65°

NORWAY

Rangerdlugssauk

Denmark Str.

Seydis Fjord

Akureyri • Eskifjordur

Lake Fjord

ICELAND

Reykjavik

Vik

Trangisvaant

60°

List

10°

Cramer's Flights

55°

GREAT BRITAIN

Londonderry

30°

20°

10°

0°

Antarctic Continent. As the icecap moves across the underlying rough land, it becomes gashed, and crevasses of varying depth form, most of which remain hidden under treacherous snow bridges. Greenland is a cold, desertlike territory, which has defied man for centuries. Partially explored by Nordensköld, it was crossed for the first time by Nansen, and Peary spent many years there before his final assault on the North Pole.

The first planes ever to land in Greenland were those of Lowell H. Smith and Erik H. Nelson, two pilots of the United States Army Air Service, who came down in Fredericksdal, on that island's southern tip,[7] during the homeward stretch of their historic 195-day flight around the world in the year 1924.[8] Four days later, Bert Hassell and Parker Cramer took off on a flight to Stockholm. Starting out from Rockford, Illinois, they planned to make an intermediate landing at Sondre Strom Fjord, on the west coast of Greenland, where a scientific observatory had been established by the University of Michigan. Five miles out of Rockford the plane crashed. After it had been repaired, Hassell and Cramer took off again and reached Cochrane, Ontario. Four days later they started out for the primitive airstrip prepared for them in Greenland. They crossed Davis Strait, but high winds carried them off course. Their gasoline was running low and they had to make an emergency landing on the icecap, about seventy miles from Sondre Strom Fjord. For two weeks they wandered over the ice, until the smoke of a fire they had lit was seen by members of the Michigan University expedition, who had all but given up hope for the two men.[9]

The following year, Parker Cramer set out again, trying for the second time to pioneer a Northern Air Route, but again he met with failure. Under the sponsorship of the Chicago *Tribune* he left Chicago with pilot Robert H. Gast and aviation editor Robert Wood aboard a Sikorsky amphibian. They reached Hudson Strait in northern Canada, but a storm drove heavy ice into the cove at Port Burwell where the plane was moored and the Sikorsky was crushed in the ice. The anchor ropes broke and the plane sank.[10]

Then a Spanish pilot named Franco tried to cross the Atlantic, but he failed and had to make an emergency landing in the ocean. Swedish Captain Ahrenberg made it from Stockholm to the west coast of Greenland but was unable to cross Davis Strait to the North American Continent.[11]

In 1930, Wolfgang von Gronau made his first meticulously prepared flight, sponsored by the German Government, to survey a practical arctic air route.[12] In his Dornier-Wal (Amundsen's battered N-25), which had been equipped with a new BMW motor, he flew from the island of Sylt by way of the Faeroes and Reykjavik to Ivigtut in southern Greenland. There he helped himself to gasoline that had been left behind by Ahrenberg, before flying to Halifax, Nova Scotia. He ended his flight in New York, where a tumultuous welcome awaited him. It had taken von Gronau and his three-man crew eight days to complete the 4,670-mile crossing and their actual flying time was forty-seven hours.

Other men knew that what was needed was not a headline stunt, nor another spectacular First, but a thorough scientific approach, one which would lay the foundation for regular flight patterns.

Led by young Cambridge-trained Gino Watkins, the British Arctic Air Route Expedition sailed in July 1930 aboard the *Quest*, Shackleton's old ship, which had also carried Wilkins, and later had been used in rescue operations for Nobile and his men. The expedition consisted of fourteen men (average age 25.1 years) and its manifold objectives were all geared toward gaining knowledge essential to the establishment of a transarctic intercontinental flight route. Plans had been made for the geographic exploration of Greenland and for establishing of a meteorological station on the icecap, in which a year-round study of local climatic conditions could be made.[13]

The expedition was privately financed and the contribution of the British Government was limited to the loan of two R.A.F. pilots (N. H. D'Aeth and W. C. Hampton) as well as the granting of a 15 per cent discount on the purchase of two De Havilland *Moth* planes, equipped with special tanks.

Watkins chose Lake Fjord for his base—a bay forty miles west of Angmagssalik, a small Danish settlement, on Greenland's east coast, consisting of some four tin-roofed wooden buildings.

In August, two men were planted in an igloo-type dome-shaped tent on the icecap, approximately 127 miles from the base and at an altitude of some 8,600 feet. They recorded meteorological observations and passed the rest of the time in reading. For six weeks they remained there, totally isolated, while other members of the expedition explored the east coast of Greenland north of the base.

The two-man observation party on the icecap was relieved early in October, but the group which was then to take over was held up by blizzards and arrived three weeks later, with provisions greatly depleted. Rather than abandon the station completely, it was decided to leave only one man, August Courtauld, behind.

Driven by powerful winds, heavy snow soon covered the meteorological station. Lonely August Courtauld was unable to clear the snow away, and his tent became completely buried, except for a battered British flag which remained forlornly sticking out of the huge mound of ice.

A relief party started out from the base near Angmagssalik on March 1, but was turned back by blizzards. It went out again and returned after forty days without having found a trace of Courtauld's buried station.

Another relief party, headed by the youthful Gino Watkins himself, set out in search of the icecap site on April 21, after sending a radiogram to London:

> . . . there is always the possibility that Courtauld is not alive . . . in which case station is probably completely covered.

On the following day Watkins's radio operator, Lemon, received a message from London:

> Great anxiety felt about Courtauld . . .

Lemon replied:

> Watkins does not consider situation precarious.

He added that everything possible was being done and discouraged the dispatch of a relief expedition.

On April 28 London advised that the Swedish Pilot Ahrenberg was being sent with a large plane to help locate Courtauld and that an ice-breaker would be leaving a week later.

Sensing a good story, the British press started publishing imaginary interviews with Courtauld's family. Eager journalists went into verbal contortions, liberally sprinkling their dramatic long-distance accounts with expressions like "icy wastes" and "frozen wilderness." Elaborating on a dispatch from an Icelandic journalist who in turn was quoting a radio message allegedly sent by Courtauld, one paper shouted:

> Absolutely no provisions!

No editor seems to have checked and noticed that Courtauld had no radio equipment at the meteorological station! But newspapers were selling well and the headlines became bolder:

> Snow hunt for rich young explorer.

One daily became even more dramatic as it proclaimed:

> New Arctic drama. A further disastrous development. Four English explorers are now lost in Greenland.[14]

A certain Professor Alexander Johannesson announced his plan for a rescue operation. He would come aboard the patrol boat *Odinn,* bringing with him a hydroplane, and would start a search from the air.[15] In the meantime Captain Ahrenberg's plane had become fogbound in Bergen and his rescue flight was delayed. The confused radioman, Lemon, asked that any arriving plane bring some sugar and jam.

On May 1 Lemon asked London:

> Who is Professor Johannesson and who told him to come?

And the New York *Times* carried a story headed:

> Riiser-Larsen contemplates rescue of Briton Courtauld, marooned off Greenland.

On that day Captain Ahrenberg arrived in Reykjavik.

One day later, Johannesson had his plane lowered into the water and took to the air with gasoline of the wrong type and a defective oil pump. After four minutes his aircraft came down, to be dismantled and taken aboard the *Odinn* again for return to Iceland, together with the promised jam and sugar. At about the same time, a radio message from London advised Watkins's expedition that nothing was known of Professor Johannesson and that his help had been neither solicited nor authorized.

Ahrenberg took off from Reykjavik, but was forced back by fog. Watkins's own pilot, D'Aeth, started out in the *Moth* and flew sixty-five miles inland, when he, too, had to retreat because of heavy fog.

On May 3 Ahrenberg brought his ice-coated aircraft safely down in Angmagssalik after a five-hour flight through low-hanging clouds, and the plane's floats were exchanged for skis.

A day later, Watkins's party was only one and a half miles from the snow-hidden tent, where the unsuspecting Courtauld was living in cold and darkness, trying to smoke crushed tea and burning ski-wax, which produced little light but a great deal of soot.

On the following day, Watkins saw the tattered remains of the Union Jack sticking out of a mountain of snow. Racing toward it, the men saw no sign of life and no tunnel leading into a tent. Their shouts pierced the silence. They yelled again—and heard an answering voice coming from underneath the ice. Anxiety and fear vanished. Courtauld was alive! The rescue mission had not been a failure.

On May 6 Ahrenberg set out on his first search mission. He failed to find a sledging party or icecap station and returned to the base downhearted. On his second flight, the following day, Ahrenberg saw some dark spots against a white blanket of snow. Changing course and coming closer, he could distinguish men and dogs. He counted; not trusting himself, he counted again. There were four men. Three members of Watkins's sledging party and Courtauld, released after five months of icy entombment.

Within a few minutes Lemon received a radio message from Captain Ahrenberg. Throwing his earphones off, Lemon yelled: "August's O.K." For fellow explorer Martin Lindsay, dejectedly sitting on a pile of dirty linen in the radio room, time stopped. When the repeated words penetrated consciousness, "even the dust swimming in a sunbeam seemed to stand still," he remembered.[16] Courtauld would soon be back at the base, apologizing for any inconvenience he had caused by allowing himself to be buried for five months.

Toward the end of June, the final stage of the expedition was at
hand. Six men went home, and the other eight, divided into three groups,
either crossed the icecap into southwest Greenland or explored the east
coast, before rounding Greenland's southern tip and then proceeding northward along the shore. After that all of them returned to England.[17]

During the course of this expedition seventy-four flights, totaling eighty-
six hours and five minutes flying time, had been made; a stretch of
Greenland's east coast had been photographed from the air, and several
new islands as well as a mountain had been discovered.[18]

Soon, Watkins set out to organize a new venture, conceived as "the
logical outcome of the British Arctic Air Route Expedition."[19] Conceding
that more work was needed in Greenland, he said: ". . . it is quite clear
that some day this route will be used . . . ." But Watkins did not live
to see his prediction come true. Not long afterward he was drowned
in an overturned kayak.

The distinguished Director of Britain's Royal Geographic Society later
said:

> The expedition's most important contribution was probably their very
> careful survey of the eastern coastal strip [of Greenland].[20]

The expedition had failed to scout an air route across Greenland to
Winnipeg as had originally been planned.[21] Nevertheless, ground and air
observations of climatic conditions at the east coast of Greenland over
a whole year, combined with results obtained during long sled journeys
to Cape Farewell and across the icecap, were the first steps toward laying
the foundation of all arctic air routes.

On July 31, 1931, Parker Cramer was set once more to pioneer a
transarctic air route from the American continent to Europe. The flight
was sponsored by the Transamerican Airlines Corporation, which hoped
to inaugurate a transatlantic airmail route, via Greenland and Iceland.
With Oliver Paquette, as radio operator, Cramer took off in his Bellanca
seaplane from Wakeham Bay on Canada's Hudson Strait and landed
at Pangnirtung, on the east coast of Baffin Island. Four days later he
arrived in Angmagssalik after a five-hour flight. Cramer and Paquette
were the first men ever to have flown across the icecap. They reached
Reykjavik in Iceland, but on their way to the Faeroe Islands they had
to make an emergency landing in rough sea.

On August 14, 1931, the Chicago *Daily Tribune* carried a story on
its third page: "Lindbergh's Plan to Circle Globe on Vacation Trip."
The subcaption read: "Ship Sights Body in Sea; May Be Cramer's." A
dispatch wired from Haugesund, Norway, said:

> A body believed to be that of Parker D. Cramer or his compan-
> ion . . . was sighted floating in the North Sea . . . about twenty miles

northwest of the Shetland Islands by the . . . trawler *Soejint* . . . . The weather was too violent for the crew to make any investigation of the body, which apparently was dressed in aviator's clothing and was floating upright, supported by a life preserver . . .

On the same page, the *Tribune* carried another story:

> Captain Wolfgang von Gronau, German aviator, landed at Scoresby Sound at . . . 4:59 Chicago time today from Reykjavik . . .

After the successful transarctic flight of the previous year, Amundsen's old N-25 had been turned over to a museum, and von Gronau given a new Dornier flying boat. On August 8, 1931, he took off from List with the same crew and after intermediate stops in Trangisvaag and Reykjavik he reached Scoresby Sound on August 13. There, he started on a flight across the icecap two days later.[22] With enough gasoline for ten hours, he was flying at an altitude of 9,850 feet and discovered a new mountain whose peaks were too high for his plane.[23] Skirting it in a westerly direction, the pilot thought that he had a clearance of 600 feet, but actually his radio aerial was already trailing along the snow. He felt "like a fly in a bathtub," the horizon being higher than the plane, an immense white surface stretching in every direction. In a 9 hour 55 minute flight covering 1,037 miles at an average speed of 103 miles an hour von Gronau and his crew reached Sukkertoppen, a settlement of 600 people on Greeland's west coast. From there, they proceeded via Godthaab, Povungnituk, Port Harrison, and Long Lake to Chicago.[24]

By that time Pan American Airways had purchased the assets of Transamerican Air Lines including rights it had acquired for the transarctic intercontinental flight route which Cramer had set out to investigate. Vilhjalmur Stefansson was Pan American's adviser and Charles Lindbergh was assigned to make an aerial survey of Greenland, to establish whether there were sites suitable for intermediate landings. When Lindbergh and his wife took off from Flushing Bay on July 9, 1933, in a red-winged, single-engined plane which was eventually christened *Tingmissartoq* (Eskimo for, "The one who flies like a big bird"), they were accompanied by the best wishes of Stefansson, who had closed a farewell letter by saying:

> . . . my chief concern, till you are back safe and successful, will be your safety rather than your success.[25]

The Lindberghs flew via South Pond and North Haven, Maine; Halifax, Nova Scotia; St. John's, Newfoundland, and arrived in Cartwright, Labrador, just one day after the city had witnessed the arrival of the twenty-four

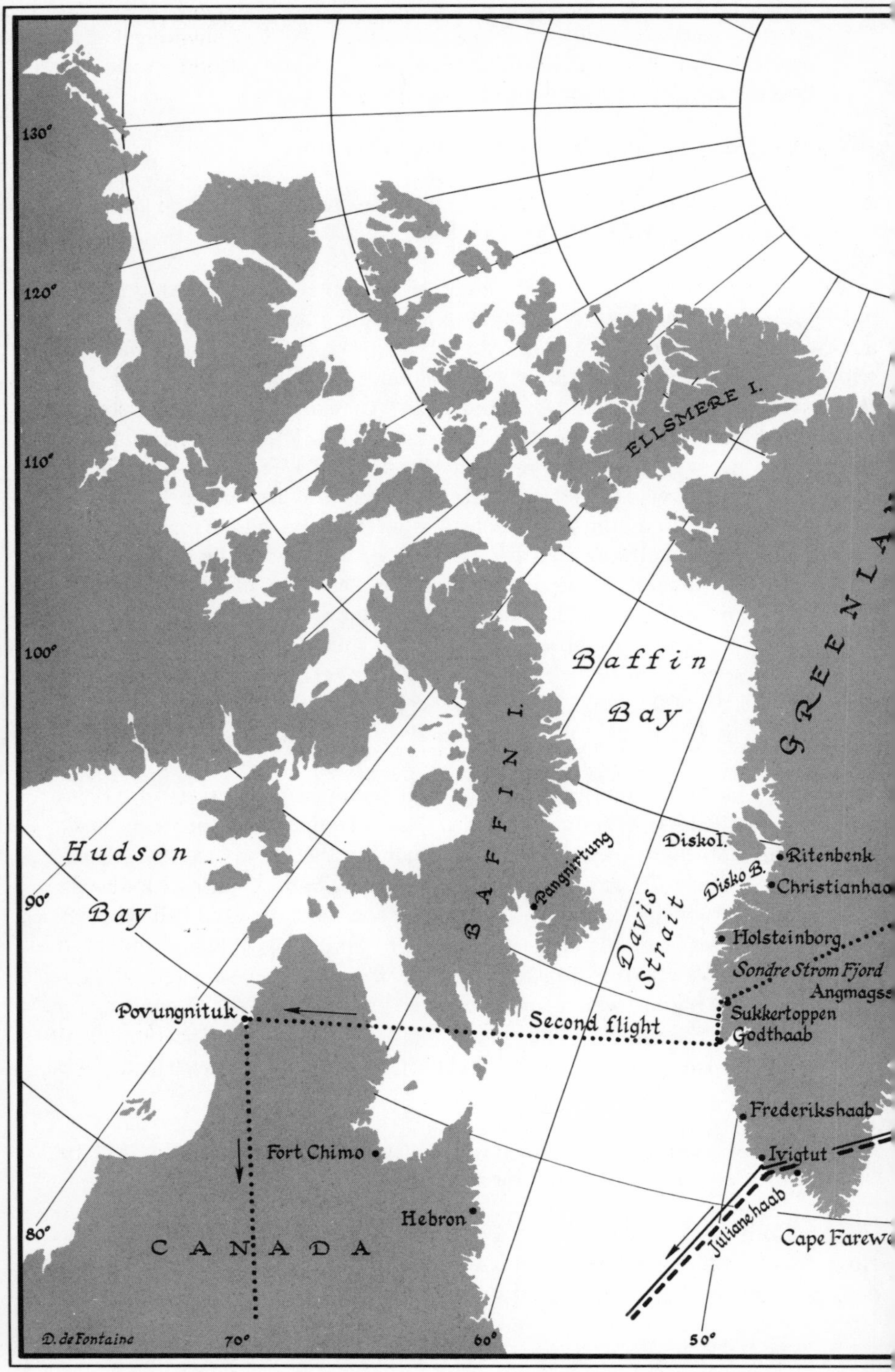

130°
120°
110°
100°
90°
80°
70°
60°
50°
ELLSMERE I.
GREENLA
Baffin Bay
BAFFIN I.
Hudson Bay
Davis Strait
Pangnirtung
Disko I.
Disko B.
Ritenbenk
Christianhaa
Holsteinborg
Sondre Strom Fjord
Angmagss
Sukkertoppen
Godthaab
Povungnituk
Second flight
Frederikshaab
Fort Chimo
Ivigtut
Julianehaab
Hebron
Cape Farewe
CANADA
D. de Fontaine

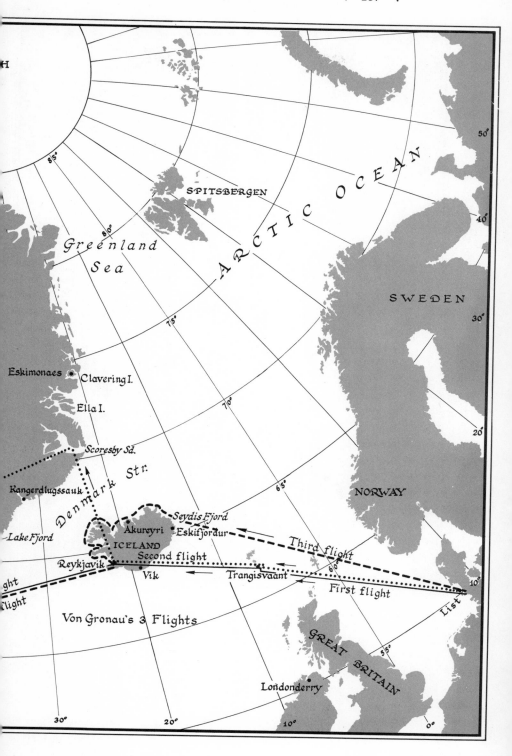

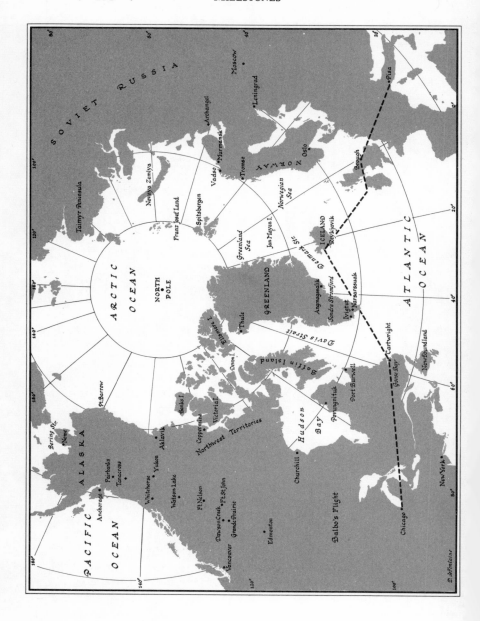

plane fleet of Italo Balbo, which had made an impressive mass flight from Italy to the United States via a transarctic air route.[26]

From Cartwright, the Lindberghs flew on to Godthaab, a small settlement located in a valley surrounded by rocky hills.[27] They flew north along Greenland's western coast—passing over the site at Sondre Strom Fjord where the expedition of the University of Michigan continued its work under the leadership of William H. Hobbs—and went as far north as Ritenbenk. They flew across Davis Strait to Baffin Island and then crossed the icecap from Christanshaab to Ella Island, on the east coast of Greenland, which at the time was serving as an airplane base for the expedition of Dr. Lauge Koch.[28] To Anne Lindbergh the icecap looked "dirty and streaked, as though raked by snow plows" and "with no horizon distinguishable, the whole world looked like a gigantic white bowl." Colonel Lindbergh passed a note to his wife: "Every five minutes we save a day's walk." The trans-Greenland flight took six hours. They flew on to Eskimonaes on Clavering Island, where Koch's expedition had another base, before turning south and flying along Greenland's east coast, making their way over glaciers and pack ice and discovering new mountain ranges, some as high as 12,300 feet.

After the Lindberghs reached Angmagssalik, they cut across the icecap once more, flying a westerly direction and landing at Godthaab. From there they winged their way south, over Greenland's tip, and also north, to Angmagssalik and Lake Fjord, which a few years earlier had served as the base for Watkins's British Air Route expedition, before continuing across Denmark Strait to Iceland.

It had been an extensive aerial survey, and since the aircraft used was a hydroplane, all landings had been made on water. The report on possible landing sites which Lindbergh submitted to Pan American Airways, however, was cautious[29] and contributed to delaying the establishment of regular commercial flights from America to Europe by way of Greenland.[30] Citing rough terrain and frequent unfavorable weather conditions, Lindbergh was under the impression, that Greenland was not a territory suitable for the establishment of intermediate landing sites. The plan of a commercial transarctic route was therefore abandoned, pending development of bigger aircraft with greater fuel capacity.

Nevertheless the route was flown once more, in 1934, by a headstrong British pilot named John Grierson. His flight was distinguished by a number of accidents, his inability to find Angmagssalik, and an emergency landing. It took Grierson 390 days from the time he first took off from Brough, England, in his *Moth* called "Rouge et Noir" until he finally landed at Ottowa in another plane, the "Robert Bruce."[31]

It would be several years before the necessities of war would made the establishment of a northern air route of paramount importance and then Greenland would be called America's "aircraft carrier."[32]

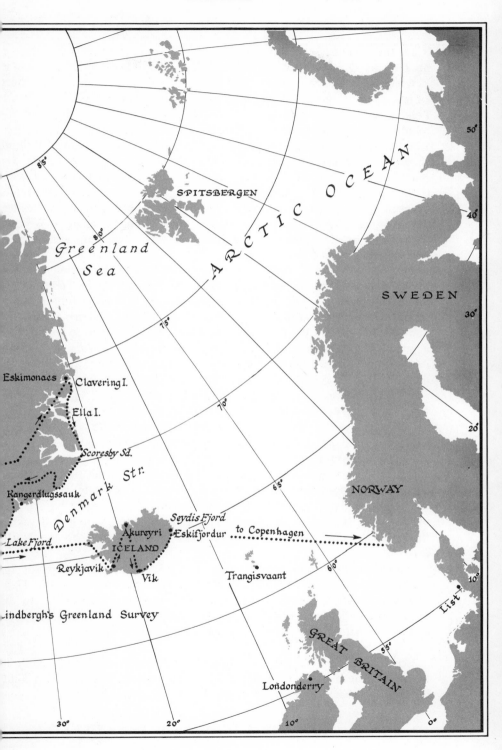

SPITSBERGEN

ARCTIC OCEAN

Greenland
Sea

SWEDEN

Eskimonaes • Clavering I.

Ella I.

Scoresby Sd.

Denmark Str.

Kangerdlugssauk

NORWAY

Seydis Fjord

Akureyri • Eskifjordur   to Copenhagen

Lake Fjord   ICELAND

Reykjavik

Vik   Trangisvaant

List

Lindbergh's Greenland Survey

GREAT BRITAIN

Londonderry

3

In the summer of 1930, when Gino Watkins was just starting on his Greenland expedition, Sir Hubert Wilkins and his pretty wife, Suzanne Bennett, an ex-actress, were visiting Lincoln Ellsworth at his Lenzburg castle in Switzerland. Wilkins was thinking of a new project—a North Pole expedition by submarine. The idea had been in the back of his mind ever since Stefansson had first brought it up seventeen years earlier. It fitted nearly into the framework of weather research, which Wilkins so ardently advocated. Ellsworth could see merit in the project, but was not overly enthusiastic. He was the fresh air type and did not want to be cooped up in a submarine. Further, he had resolved that should he ever again participate in an expedition, it would only be as leader. However, he agreed to serve as technical adviser, but it was up to Wilkins, he said, to procure personnel, equipment, financial backing and actually make the underwater trip.

At that time the United States was committed to destroying and dismantling many ships in accordance with the London Naval Treaty. After much hedging and prolonged negotiations, the Shipping Board finally agreed to turn over an obsolete and badly run-down submarine, formerly known as *0-12* for the sum of one dollar. Wilkins knew it would take a great deal of money and work to adapt the ship to its new mission. Also, there was a clause in the contract requiring that the submarine be scuttled after the expedition, so that it could never be used again.

With the vision of an obsolete *0-12* transformed into a modern underwater laboratory, Wilkins turned the submarine over to the firm of Lake and Danenhower in Philadelphia. Both these men were well known in naval circles. Simon Lake was a pioneer inventor in the submarine field and Sloan Danenhower, an Annapolis graduate, was an experienced submariner. The contract which Wilkins signed gave them the right to decide what modifications and equipment were necessary for safe operation of the vessel. Wilkins hoped to have the undersea boat ready by the end of the year as well as to have had six months for testing and taking the sub to a base from which he could start on the trip to the North Pole.[33]

Backed by important organizations, such as Washington's Carnegie Institution, Cleveland's Museum of Natural History, and Norway's Geophysical Institute, Wilkins assembled his group of scientists, to be headed by world renowned Professor Harold Sverdrup, Amundsen's friend and the former chief of meteorologist Finn Malmgren.

On July 31, 1930, Britain's dirigible R-100 arrived triumphantly in Montreal after a flight of 78 hours 52 minutes from Cardington, England, but on October 5 her sister ship, the R-101, crashed on a hill near

Beauvais in France.[34] As in war so also in the field of commercial aviation, the dirigible was giving place to the airplane. But Aeroarctic, the International Society for Aerial Exploration of the Arctic, had drawn up plans for a northern flight of Dr. Eckener's Graf Zeppelin.[35] And so, a two-pronged attack on the Arctic was under preparation.

Visualizing the publicity potential of a dramatic exchange of mail in the Arctic, between Wilkins, underwater, and Eckener in the air, publisher William Randolph Hearst lent financial support to both undertakings. Yet, despite all this backing, Wilkins had spent more than a quarter of a million dollars of his own money before the submarine expedition was over.

In March 1931, more than two months after the original deadline for completion of work, Wilkins' submarine was ready. But the vessel turned over to him by experts Lake and Danenhower was not what Wilkins had wanted it to be. It had some impractical and untested devices, thought up by Simon Lake, such as drills attached to the superstructure for making holes in ice, a hydraulic guide arm to help the submarine glide along the undersurface of pack ice, and there was both a jackknifing periscope and a hydraulically cushioned bowsprit.

Everything seemed to go wrong. On her way to New York the engine failed and the submarine had to be ingnominiously towed down Delaware Bay. As she entered the Hudson River a man fell overboard and drowned.

At the Brooklyn Navy Yard, where refitting and a complete overhaul was to get under way, Lady Wilkins christened the reconditioned *0-12* with cracked ice,[36] poured over the bow from a silver bucket, and the submarine was henceforth known as the *Nautilus*. Among the eight-hundred-odd spectators present at the ceremony were airshipman Dr. Hugo Eckener and Jean Jules Verne, grandson of the novelist who had so vividly and imaginatively forecast the undersea voyage of a scientific party, in Captain Nemo's wonderful ship of the same name.[37]

On June 4, the *Nautilus* finally set out from Provincetown, Massachusetts, to cross the North Atlantic. Her destination was Spitsbergen.

The *Nautilus* was 175 feet long, and weighed 560 tons. She was built so as to be able to travel 7,000 miles without refueling. Her huge Exide batteries could supply sufficient electricity to allow submerged travel for 125 miles before recharging was necessary. The hull was strong enough to withstand the pressure at two hundred feet down, and she had an air capacity believed to be adequate for one hundred man-days. The submarine was commanded by Sloan Danenhower, whose father had been a survivor of de Long's ill-fated *Jeannette,* and Sir Hubert Wilkins was leader of the expedition. As chief scientist, Dr. Harold Sverdrup would board the *Nautilus* at Bergen.

Ten days later and one thousand miles out at sea, Captain Danenhower was forced to send a distress signal and to ask for help. One of the submarine's two engines was out of commission, sparks were flying from broken wires, and through a defective valve, water was contaminating the fuel. The *Nautilus* lay, helplessly wallowing, in a rough sea. The battleship U.S.S. *Wyoming* answered the call and, assisted by the tug *Morsecock*, pulled Wilkins's inert and sadly disabled sub to a drydock in Davenport, some 850 miles away. Repairs took three weeks and as a result the *Nautilus* did not make Bergen until August 1. By that time the season was too far advanced. The ambitious plan to cross the Polar Sea from Spitsbergen to Bering Strait by way of the Pole had to be scrapped, and the best that could be expected was a trial run under arctic conditions as preparation for a renewed effort to be made the following year.

In July of 1931 Nobile arrived in Leningrad. He had accepted an invitation to join an expedition aboard the icebreaker *Malygin*—as a passenger, although for publicity purposes he shrewdly let it be known as a search effort for the six men who had vanished with the dirigible *Italia* three years earlier.[38] At the Arctic Institute he met Professor Samoilovich and hydrologist Wiese, who had once gone to his rescue.

As Nobile went on to Archangel, Samoilovich was on his way to Friedrichshafen, to join Eckener aboard the Graf Zeppelin. Within two weeks Samoilovich and Nobile would meet again—off Hooker Island above the Arctic Circle.

Wilkins was far behind schedule, and time was being lost. The arctic rendezvous between dirigible and submarine, desirable through it might be for publicity, was not essential from a scientific point of view and was abandoned. So, on July 24, the Graf Zeppelin took off. Gone were the customary luxuries—double-decker bunks had been substituted for the usual beds, lightweight seats had taken the place of the heavy mahogany chairs, and instead of china the pantry held aluminum plates.[39] Aboard the dirigible were more than six hundred pounds of mail, and nine thousand pounds of food, including four tons of pemmican. In addition to a crew of 31, headed by Eckener, there was a 15-man scientific group under Samoilovich. This group included Lincoln Ellsworth, styled "Arctic Navigation Expert" and authorized "to communicate by radio to the American Geographical Society geographical discoveries made."[40]

The Zeppelin's route led over Berlin, banner-bedecked Leningrad, Archangel, and across the White Sea, toward Franz Josef Land. At Hooker Island, site of the world's northernmost weather station, under the Russian scientist Ivanov former secretary of the *Krassin* relief expedition, a sentimental meeting took place.

As the dirigible was anchored with canvas dip buckets on the waters of the island's Tikhaya Bay, a small boat left the icebreaker *Malygin*, at anchor in the bay, and headed for the Graf Zeppelin. In the stern of the boat, standing next to Russian explorer Ivan Papanin, was a frail civilian, Umberto Nobile, still handsome, with his hair turning gray at the temples. Lincoln Ellsworth, symbol of success and perseverance, shook hands with the living symbol of failure.

Ellsworth said later:

> I had to look twice to recognize him, . . . he had aged visibly. . . . The *Italia* disaster had made a different man of him.[41]

More than fifty thousand pieces of mail bearing special commemorative stamps were exchanged between the icebreaker and the dirigible. It was a substitute stunt, not rating much publicity. Then the canvas dip bags were emptied again, the sea anchor was pulled up, and the *Graf Zeppelin* rose, heading north to begin its scientific mission. Below, the figure of Nobile became smaller. Ellsworth commented:

> As he stood unsteadily in the stern of the boat waving good-bye . . . the scene held a touch of pathos . . .[41]

Turning east, the Zeppelin headed for her next objective, icelocked Severnaya Zemlya. With a special instrument loaned by the Carnegie Institute, the earth's magnetic field would be measured, and with photogrammatic equipment, a geographic survey was to be made. Using his ingenious device—a balloon-borne payload of scientific instruments for the measurement of atmospheric pressure, humidity and temperature—Professor Moltshanov, of Samoilovich's staff, recorded meteorological data transmitted back by a small battery-powered radio. Before the fog descended, an important geographic discovery was made. Severnaya Zemlya, marked on maps as being one island, was actually composed of two land masses separated by a narrow channel.[42]

From an altitude of 3,000 feet Franz Josef Land was mapped while cameras methodically completed an aerial survey of the main islands. Ellsworth noted: "The dark ground was patched with colors that suggested mosses and lichens, ice rivers glinted in deep gorges cutting through. I had never seen anything more beautiful."[43] Included in the survey was Rudolf Island, northernmost land of the archipelago—only some 500 miles from the North Pole—and northernmost point of the flight. Why, with winds favorable and weather clear, did he not make for the Pole? reporters later asked Eckener. The answer was stereotyped and unrevealing: "I had my reason."

The reason was actually insurance. Premiums for flights north of the 85th parallel were prohibitive and the cautious Eckener, unlike an adventurous Nobile, did not want to risk an uninsured ship and the lives of those aboard.[44]

Turning south, the Graf Zeppelin flew over Vilkitski Strait and the Taimyr Peninsula, where thousands of wild reindeer were frightened into flight by the drone of the airborne monster. Past Dikson Island, Eckener cut across to Novaya Zemlya to complete a massive program of air-mapping. Then he set course for Archangel, Leningrad and back to Berlin.

At 4 A.M. on July 31 the Graf Zeppelin was again firmly moored to her mast in Friedrichshafen. A voyage of 8,142 miles had been completed in 136 hours. Ellsworth said:

> It seemed like a dream. . . . The sight of arctic ice had fired me with a zeal for exploration such as had not burned within me since my first meeting with Amundsen.[45]

A day later, August 1, 1931, Wilkins's strange-looking submarine arrived in Bergen. More repairs were needed, and now there were more delays. Finally, the *Nautilus* left for the North Pole. It was late in the season and only on August 19 could Professor Sverdrup say: ". . . the northern coast of Spitsbergen disappeared on the southern horizon."[46]

Three days later Captain Danenhower gave orders to submerge but—nothing happened! The *Nautilus* did not respond to the controls. Looking at the stern of his underseaboat, the puzzled Danenhower saw the last thing he had expected: the submarine had no diving rudders! The skipper found himself in charge of a submarine which had been sabotaged by members of its own crew. Apparently, the crewmen had no intention to go under the ice in the highly undependable *Nautilus*.

Scientific work aboard the *Nautilus* still continued. Sverdrup kept sounding the depths, bringing up water samples and recording temperatures at various levels of the Arctic Sea. There were violent storms and fog, but moving north, pursued by the edge of advancing pack ice, the *Nautilus* reached latitude 82° a hundred miles north of Spitsbergen.

On August 31, merely depending on thrust and inclination of her bow, the crippled *Nautilus* started a dive as Danenhower gave the command: "Flood the main ballast!" Crunching and screeching of ice broke the normal silence inside the hull, as the submarine slid down. Her bow hit the ice, and the scraping of a protruding drill reverberated like the rumble of an earthquake. Her propeller thrashing wildly like the tail of a wounded fish, the *Nautilus* stalled. Through glass ports in the conning tower Wilkins took some remarkable pictures of the anatomy of pack ice. The underbelly of a floe is a rough surface with peaks and valleys like an inverted snow-covered mountain.

Danenhower backed his ship out and tried again. For five days the *Nautilus* slid under floes of various sizes and shapes, to the accompaniment of angry crunching and grating of ice. Her diving gear gone, her drill frozen fast in its bearings, the edges of her propellers now bent and saw-toothed, the *Nautilus* could do no more. The first submarine venture to the Arctic was over. Surfacing again, Wilkins broke five days of radio silence.

Back in Spitsbergen's Advent Bay, the scientific complement disembarked and Wilkins took the *Nautilus* on her last voyage. Her hull dented, paint scraped off, the submarine did not look at all like a proud, victorious ship but she had made history. At Bergen, in accordance with the original contract, she was scuttled in a fjord more than 600 feet deep. The city which had seen Nansen's *Fram* depart, Amundsen leave to go on his last flight, which had welcomed the *Krassin* (and which one day would see the U. S. nuclear submarine *Skate*), witnessed the death plunge of the *Nautilus*.

Wilkins had failed to reach the Pole by submarine and, compared with expectations, the scientific results actually obtained were small, but he was more than ever certain that someday, someone would succeed where he had failed.

4

By midsummer of 1933, Riiser-Larsen was in Norway again, after his third expedition to the Antarctic, which had ended in total failure.* The tables of organization were filled and the flying arm of the Norwegian Navy had no command commensurate with his rank. Burdened with an 80,000-kroner debt,† he had to take an extended leave of absence without pay and began traveling, selling radio sets to shipowners.

Recognizing new developments and the need for faster transportation, a shipping magnate, Rudolf Olsen, telephoned Riiser-Larsen and asked: "Is it true that you have no job?"

"Yes," Riiser-Larsen said, "that's true."

"Come to my office at eleven o'clock tomorrow. I have something that may interest you."

Next day, Riiser-Larsen called on Olsen. The businessman wasted no words. Olsen wanted to form a Norwegian Air Line and he wanted Riiser-Larsen to organize it. Taught caution over the years, Riiser-Larsen thought fast. "Yes," he said. "I am very much interested . . . if the firm is prepared to lose five million kroner, before getting into the black. . . ."

Olsen had the right answer: "Yes, we are willing to risk that much," he said. "We consider this a big national task. . . ." There was one more obstacle to a new beginning for Riiser-Larsen. Norway's Labor Party was likely to assume power soon. If so, would the new government nationalize an airline? In a meeting with the Labor Party's leader, Oscar

---

* See Appendix 1.
† Approximately $18,000 at the current rate of exchange.

Torp, Riiser-Larsen discussed such a possibility. "This matter has been taken up by the Executive Committee," Mr. Torp said, "and we feel that civil aviation is better left to private enterprise." So the stumbling block was not there after all.

"All right, Riiser, start in the morning and go ahead," said Olsen.

Thus Riiser-Larsen was a founding father for *Det Norske Luftfartselskap* (DNL), Norway's future airline. Soon he wrote to Bernt Balchen, offering him a job with the new company.

Exploration of the Soviet Arctic continued, as did exploitation of its natural resources. Both were hampered, however, by the lack of an adequate transportation system along which raw materials from northern Siberia could be exported, and machinery as well as building materials necessary for the development of Russia's Arctic regions could be shipped from the interior of the country. There were those who proposed establishment of an extensive railway network linking ports of the Atlantic, Arctic, and Pacific Oceans, but this project appeared to be less sound economically than development of the already existing waterway along the northern coast of Siberia.[47]

Such a plan had not originated with the Soviet Government. Long before the Russian Revolution, ships had traveled along both ends of Siberia's 3,000-mile coast, and this route, then known as the Northeast Passage, had already been traversed from the Atlantic to the Pacific by Nordenskjöld in the *Vega,* by Amundsen's *Maud* and two other ships. During the initial period of Soviet rule, however, progressively longer stretches of this waterway had been made navigable. To make the route completely useful and economically profitable, all of it had to be opened to navigation and it had to be made possible for ships to move all the way along it during one navigational season.[48]

In 1932, Professor Otto Yulevich Schmidt,[49] Director of Leningrad's Arctic Institute, submitted a memorandum to the Soviet Government:

> Despite the importance it has for Siberia's economic life, the problem of linking the central portion of Eastern Siberia . . . and Siberia's northern seas with the most important ports of the USSR (Murmansk, Archangel in the West and Vladivostok in the East) . . . still remains unsolved. Exploitation of natural resources in the North is based on cheap transportation of things which constitute basic necessities. . . . Until such a route is found and mastered, there can be no talk of extensive utilization of the natural productive capacity of the North, not any more than of an adequate expansion of the population in this territory. . . .[50]

The year 1932 was the second International Polar Year and the Soviet Union had pledged participation. Stalin's Government authorized seven

expeditions to various parts of the Soviet Arctic and the co-operation
of ninety-two weather stations, thirty-three of which had just been established.[51] In addition, the sum of one million rubles was appropriated,*
for a through voyage along the Northeast Passage (now being referred
to as the Northern Sea Route) which had been projected by Otto Schmidt.†
The voyage, which was to extend from Archangel to Vladivostok, was
to be a scientific expedition, led by Schmidt himself. It was to be made
with a twenty-three-year-old English-built icebreaker named *Sibiriakov,*
considered satisfactory for this purpose. It was realized, however, that
the number of weather stations functioning in the easternmost sector
of arctic Siberia was too limited. Meteorological and ice forecasts which
the ship needed might thus be inadequate. Captain Voronin was designated
skipper of the *Sibiriakov* and Professor Wiese was placed in charge of
the scientific work to be carried on. Among the scientists was young
Peter Shirshov, and responsibility for radio operation was given to Ernest
Krenkel. The procurement of food, supplies, and equipment was entrusted
to Ivan Kopusov, a deputy Director of the Arctic Institute.

On July 28, 1932, the *Sibiriakov* left Archangel, heading east. Moving
through Matochkin Shar,‡ over which pilot Chukhnovsky had once
pioneered reconnaissance flights, the ship entered the ice-free waters of
the Kara Sea and reached Dikson Island.

It had been planned originally to have a plane suitable for reconnaissance flights aboard the ship, but the aircraft selected was haunted
by engine troubles and arrived in Archangel too late. Following Schmidt's
instructions, the pilot flew on to Dikson Island where he was supposed
to catch up with the icebreaker. The plane never got there. Fuel ran
low, the pilot turned back toward Archangel, engine trouble developed
again and the plane crashed into the sea.[52]

At Dikson Island, the *Sibiriakov* had a rendezvous with the *Rusanov,*
a vessel which had aboard another expedition headed by Professor
Samoilovich, the veteran of the north. Joining forces, both ships proceeded
to Sverdrup Island, uninhabited and unexplored. Then the *Sibiriakov* kept
on going eastward.

Now the icebreaker ran into really heavy ice.[53] Explosives were set
off and deftly maneuvering his vessel through waters thick with floating
ice-floes, Captain Voronin reached the estuary of the Lena River on
August 26, with one blade of the ship's propeller broken. A week later,

* At that time the ruble was worth approximately 30 cents. However,
complexities inherent in the Soviet economic system, make it impossible to
determine the equivalent value of 1 million rubles.

† For convenience this German spelling of the name is retained, rather
than the Russian version, Shmidt.

‡ Matochkin Shar is a 60-mile-long strait separating the northern and
southern islands of Novaya Zemlya. It joins the Barents Sea with the Kara Sea.

the *Sibiriakov* was at the Kolyma delta, where it met a seven-ship west-bound convoy from the Far East escorted by another icebreaker, the *Litke*. Progress in the development of the Northern Sea route was evident, as eleven ships gathered at the Kolyma estuary.

Farther east, however, navigation became more difficult. Ice was heavier, and there were only three functioning weather stations—on Wrangel Island, at North Cape, and in Uelen, a tiny settlement on the extreme tip of Chukchi Peninsula. Further, navigational aids previously erected on the mainland had been torn down by superstitious natives, who were convinced that they scared away seal and walrus.

Traveling within sight of the Siberian coast, sorely missing aerial reconnaissance, fighting its way through unusually compact ice fields, disaster struck the battered icebreaker within less than two hundred miles from Bering Strait. The remaining blades of the propeller broke and the ship became powerless. Immediate repairs were essential. Spare parts were available, but there was no diver aboard. In an unprecedented maneuver repairs were effected amidst drifting ice. Based on calculations made by Schmidt, a mathematician, the ship's bow was lowered by shifting cargo, including 400 tons of coal, thus raising the rudder, carefully avoiding the critical point at which the ship might capsize. This labor took six days. On September 16, repairs were completed and the icebreaker once more set off under its own power.

Two days later, the *Sibiriakov* was again ramming ice. The ship's shaft broke and the rudder vanished at the bottom of the Arctic Ocean. Repairs were impossible and the *Sibiriakov* drifted at the mercy of currents, winds and ice.

Help was requested from a nearby trawler, the *Ussurnetz,* and valiantly the little ship tried to reach the crippled icebreaker. Originally at a distance from which her light signals were clearly visible aboard the *Sibiriakov* at night, adverse currents carried the *Ussurnetz* back into the Bering Strait and she was unable to reach the disabled icebreaker.

At first the impotent *Sibiriakov* was carried southeast, but then the drift reversed itself, the ice started moving backward, and even the anchor could not prevent the ship from being dragged along. On September 27 a favorable wind sprang up. By sewing together odd pieces of canvas, the *Sibiriakov's* crew improvised sails and the once powerful icebreaker was transformed into a strange-looking sailing vessel, somewhat reminiscent of the *Flying Dutchman*. Limping, moving slowly and passively, yet moving, the *Sibiriakov* advanced toward its goal. On October 1, sixty-six days after leaving its berth in Archangel, the ship reached the ice-free waters of the Bering Strait, where it was finally taken in tow by the *Ussurnetz.*

A remarkable feat had been accomplished, and an important mission completed. Otto Youlevitch Schmidt had succeeded where Sir Hugh

Willoughby, Willem Barents, and Henry Hudson had failed. For the first time in history the whole length of the Northern Sea Route had been attained in one season. Where it had taken Nordenskiöld two seasons to pass, and Amundsen's *Maud* had had to winter twice, the 1,384-ton Russian ship, crippled but victorious, had made the passage in sixty-one days, blazing the trail for a new route with a potentially great economic and strategic importance.

After repairs in Japan, the icebreaker returned to Murmansk by a long southern route, while Professor Schmidt and members of his expedition headed for a heroes' welcome in Moscow aboard a Trans-Siberian Railroad train.

Even more than the mere passage itself, success lay buried in the cold figures which scientists aboard the *Sibiriakov* had meticulously recorded in their notebooks. These formed the foundation for what Commissar Molotov would someday demand and get: "Establishment of the Northern Sea Route as a normally functioning waterway."[54]

A few months later, Germany's emergence as a potential enemy caused Russia to revise her second five-year plan. Industrialization was to be speeded and the transport system enlarged. Coal and iron mined in the Donets Basin were no longer considered safe from invasion, in terms of long-range planning. Now emphasis was to be placed on exploitation of areas more remote from potential attack, the Urals and Siberia.[55] A key point in the development of these Arctic regions was a working Northern Sea Route over which ships could pass safely between the European and Asiatic parts of Russia without entering hostile waters. A new government department was created: Glavsevmorput, Chief Administration of the Northern Sea Route.[56] It was a huge organization with a business monopoly responsible directly to the central government, and whose mission was:

> . . . conclusively developing the Northern Sea Route from the White Sea to Bering Strait, of equipping it, keeping it in good order and securing the shipping along it.[57]

Its jurisdiction extended over an area of more than 2 million square miles and its responsibility covered transportation, as well as development of economic enterprises concerned with coal, salt and minerals, fish, seal and reindeer. It was responsible for education, health and cultural development in the vast territory as well as for exploration, exploitation of natural resources, and expansion of local production.

Within four years the working force of this giant organization would mushroom to 32,352 people. It controlled all radio stations and meteorological posts in the Soviet Arctic and incorporated within its structure Leningrad's Arctic Institute as well as a fleet of ten icebreakers and an Aviation Training School.[58]

Professor Schmidt, eminent mathematician, explorer, and member of

the Academy of Sciences, was made head of Glavsevmorput. In the first
year of his administration, thirteen different expeditions were dispatched,
a three-freighter convoy escorted by the icebreaker *Krassin* made the first
trip from Archangel to the Lena River, nine freighters reached the Kolyma
from the East, and some thirty vessels sailed to the rivers of Kara
Sea. The total freight turnover along the Northern Sea Route reached
136,000 metric tons, more than a thirteenfold increase over the 10,000
tons carried on the same waterway in 1920.[59]

On June 25, 1933, the Russian newspaper *Pravda* carried a short
dispatch from its Leningrad correspondent:

> A new Soviet icebreaker, *Chelyuskin,* built in Copenhagen by order
> of Glavsevmorput, has arrived today in the port of Leningrad. Its water
> displacement: 7,400 tons; strength: 2,400 horsepower; speed: up to
> 12½ knots an hour. Last year's historic trip of the *Sibiriakov* from
> Archangel to Vladivostok will be repeated this year by the *Chelyuskin.*
> Chief of the expedition aboard the *Chelyuskin* is Professor O. Y.
> Schmidt.

This new ship actually was not a true icebreaker. It was rather a
coal-burning freighter with a strengthened hull, which embodied in its design some other special features. Much weaker and less powerful than
a true icebreaker, the *Chelyuskin* instead had greater range, because it
could carry, in addition to freight, a large amount of coal. The plan called
for the ship to attempt a through voyage unescorted, but should impassable
ice be encountered, the icebreaker *Krassin* was to leave the ships it was
convoying to the Lena delta and come to the assistance of the *Chelyuskin.*[60]

The voyage had many purposes. A new group of men and women
was to be taken to Wrangel Island, there to relieve a wintering party
which had remained isolated for several years because ice conditions had
made earlier relief impossible. The *Chelyuskin* was to transport building
materials needed for enlargement of the weather station on the island
and was to carry a scientific group to explore sections of the waterway
still inadequately known, to determine what parts could be navigated
without the assistance of an icebreaker and to find where joint operations
were needed.

Assistant expedition commander Kopusov, deputy director of the Arctic
Institute in charge of supply and administration, had a big job on his
hands. Within three and a half months he had to equip a new ship, and
provide it with essentials of life for more than 100 people. In an underdeveloped country, poor in consumer goods, he had to literally "find"
thousands of items, ranging from sewing needles to 300 yards of a special
cable needed for measurements of metal stress! Procurement of enough
food for eighteen months was the biggest headache. Finally, some three
hundred tons of perishables had been obtained. (Fresh meat was to be

Rendezvous of the *Chelyuskin* (left) and the *Krassin*.

supplied in the form of twenty-six live cows and four piglets.) Anticipating the possibility of an enforced winter on ice, sleeping bags were especially ordered and warm clothes collected. In the end, the freight, composed of some 1,500 different items, amounted to approximately 800 tons, including building materials, gasoline, oil, explosives, and scientific instruments. In addition there was 3,500 tons of coal.

Captain Voronin and part of his crew were transferred from the *Sibiriakov,* other sailors were recruited in Leningrad and Murmansk and a scientific party was provided by the Arctic Institute. There were reporters, photographers, and an aviation section consisting of the arctic pilot Babushkin, one mechanic, and a small amphibian plane.

The *Chelyuskin* left Leningrad on July 12, 1933, and at 4:30 in the morning of August 10, the fully loaded ship steamed out of Murmansk with 112 people aboard, including ten women and a year-old infant. At the first contact with ice in the Kara Sea the freighter's bow was damaged. The ship's ice-resistant qualities were obviously inadequate.

Three weeks later, on August 31, there was a terse entry in the log of the *Chelyuskin:*

> 5:30 A.M. a female child born to the Vassilievs, latitude 75° 46.5' North, longitude 91° 06' West.

The girl was named Karina, in honor of the Kara Sea, whose depth at the place of birth, according to the logbook, was 170 feet. The ice

got heavier. Babushkin, with Captain Voronin as observer, made reconnaissance flights in the small two-seater and reported on free lanes through
which the ship threaded her way eastward. At the halfway mark of the
trip, passing through Vilkitski Strait, between Severnaya Zemlya and the
Taimyr Peninsula, the Chief Administrator of the Northern Sea Route
had reason to be proud. In the once forbidding waters surrounding Cape
Chelyuskin he saw the welcome sight of four icebreakers. Eleven ships
had rounded the cape in the short navigational season of 1933 as against
only nine to have done so in all previous history.[61]

September, heralding the end of summer, found the *Chelyuskin* near
the mountainous shores of the Chukchi Peninsula. Massive and stern,
the mountains glistened silvery under a heavy cover of fresh snow. Soon,
the ice-covered waters off the Peninsula were swept by savage blizzards,
the remaining clear lanes froze over, and the ocean turned into a
monotonous field of gray set off with bizarre hummocks and irregular
ridges. Gripped by heavy floes, the *Chelyuskin* became powerless in the
midst of pack ice.

From the air Babushkin saw two wide strips of ice moving northward,
but beyond, some fifteen miles ahead, the water was clear. Captain
Voronin attempted a breakthrough, but a strong northwest wind blew
the floes shoreward and heavy snow started falling. Impotently, the
Chelyuskin kept on ramming the thick ice. The freighter quivered and
shook, its body whined and the bow cracked, but only small pieces of
ice broke off, to fall back against the hull, their impact reverberating
inside the ship with the rumbling of thunder.

Slowly the ship drifted eastward, accompanied by the howling of violent
winds, which, vibrating the rigging, turned into mournful melodies. "I had
already worked eight years in Arctic regions," pilot Babushkin said later,
"but never once had I seen such chaotic ice. It was all broken up and
tumbled. It was difficult to go on foot over the floes, and as for thinking
to take off from that surface, it was out of the question. It was not even
possible to clear a field, because it was bound to be smashed immediately—
the ice was in constant motion. All that could be done was to wait for
whatever was to come."[62]

Life on the ship died down, as no rhythmic knocking of engines disrupted the monotonous drift; bored helmsmen had nothing to do and
the stokers had only to keep a small fire going.

Climbing over the railing, men scrambled onto the ice hummocks, occasionally breaking through recently frozen leads. They dug holes in the
ice, filled them with ammonal and exploded it. To the rumbling noise
of explosives the floes shuddered, but only small breaks appeared in
the ice, which soon froze over again, and no lanes of clear water formed.
The *Chelyuskin* was stuck in the vicious grip of the frozen sea.

In the night of September 22, a powerful wind began to push the ship straight toward Kolyuchin Island. From the bridge Captain Voronin saw stationary ice to the starboard, and more moving in from the port. Experienced, he knew that the *Chelyuskin,* as if caught in a vise, was being crushed by moving ice. Although creaking and groaning, the hull held, and some thirty hours later the ship, welded into a mass of motionless ice, lay still, about five miles from Kolyuchin Island.

Long dreary days followed, filled with impatience and boredom for the men and women aboard the *Chelyuskin.* Going aground had barely been prevented, but the navigation season was coming to an end, and the passengers and crew of the ship might have to spend the winter in the desolate loneliness of the Arctic Ocean. To save supplies, Schmidt wanted to evacuate part of his expedition, but neither of the two nearby icebreakers could come to the *Chelyuskin's* assistance. Power on the *Krassin* was reduced 50 per cent because of a broken-down engine and the *Litke* was busy freeing the icebound ships of a Kolyma-bound convoy.

No planes were available in the eastern sector of the Soviet Arctic. Levanevsky's craft was no longer airworthy. After having provided reconnaissance for the Kolyma-bound ships, it had flown a stranded world flier named Mattern from Anadyr to Alaska, and four other planes on the Chukchi Peninsula, in charge of pilots Lyapidevsky and Kukhanov, were either not suitable for arctic flying or were in various states of disrepair.

On the sparsely populated Siberian coast Schmidt could locate only four dog teams. He used them to evacuate eight men from the *Chelyuskin,* choosing a sick stoker, a physician to accompany him, and six other men whom he had previously promised to release if the expedition threatened to become prolonged. This party had to travel about 20 miles across shore ice and more than 200 miles on the mainland to reach the nearest settlement, Uelen, site of a newly established weather station on the east coast of Chukchi Peninsula. The icebreaker *Litke* was to pick them up there. Among those who left was a motion picture photographer, Mark Troianovski, the young son of Russia's ambassador to the United States.

On October 4 the wind changed direction and started coming from the southwest. Fissures appeared in the ice. Where man-made explosions had failed, the wind succeeded. The floes, laced with water-filled channels, started moving away from Kolyuchin Island. The ship came to life again, steam was built up and more explosive charges were set off. As men frenziedly kept digging, hacking and smashing ice, the ship lurched forward and started moving again under its own power, while the panting crew from the floe hastily clambered back aboard. The *Chelyuskin,* now carrying 105 people, entered a lane of clear water and once again began moving toward Bering Strait, some 168 miles away.

There was more ice, more fog, more impotent ramming of floes, until a wounded, helpless *Chelyuskin,* again solidly frozen in and at the mercy of invisible currents and unpredictable winds, started drifting aimlessly back and forth near Cape Serdtse Kamen. Three weeks later, a reverse drift carried the ship in a southeasterly direction, and on November 3, the *Chelyuskin* finally entered Bering Strait, after rounding the coast of Chukchi Peninsula.

Another through voyage was over. The scientific program of the expedition had been completed. But the *Chelyuskin* did not enter Bering Strait under its own power. Dragged and pushed, the ship was a helpless prisoner of ice. Met by a powerful current coming from the Pacific Ocean, the drift reversed itself again and the *Chelyuskin* started to angle northward, toward the central Polar Basin and an unpredictable fate.

Help could come only from the icebreaker *Litke.* Partially damaged, its coal supply limited, the morale of the crew lowered by continuous work in the Arctic, the icebreaker reluctantly answered the call for help. Weakly, the *Litke* started ramming ice, but progress was slow. After five days, still some forty miles from the *Chelyuskin,* the icebreaker's captain, acknowledging defeat, requested permission to withdraw.

On that same day, November 17, Lyapidevsky prepared for a takeoff from Provideniya Bay in a reconditioned plane, to evacuate members of the helpless freighter. While taxiing on uneven ice, the plane's undercarriage collapsed and the aircraft was immobilized. Around that very time the *Chelyuskin*'s own pilot, Babushkin, was set to take off on a reconnaissance flight from a runway some 200 yards long, painfully cleared by hand on an icefield near the freighter. The throttle was opened, the plane started gliding, rose, bounced back, and its runners smashed, the only available aircraft, the "eyes of the ship," lay broken on the ice.

On that day of bad luck, aboard the ice-locked *Chelyuskin* an extraordinary meeting of the ship's twelve-man executive committee was held in Schmidt's austere cabin. One subject only was on the agenda: Was the *Litke* to be sent back?

"Captain Voronin," Schmidt asked, "what do you think?"

"Hard to say," the captain said, shrugging his shoulders, *"Litke* doesn't even tell us how much coal it has left." His words carried an ill-concealed sound of disdain and disapproval. Reluctant to insist on help from an impotent icebreaker, torn by impatience and unwillingness to abandon his own ship to destruction, the captain hedged.

Ivan Kopusov, deputy director of the Arctic Institute, interrupted impatiently: "Let her go!" he said. Baievsky, the assistant expedition leader, agreed and so did Babushkin. Others joined in. Schmidt, the leader, stroking his beard, kept on glancing from one man to the other. He had the last word. "The unanimous decision of those present," he finally said, "apparently favors letting *Litke* go." There was silence. "Then let's let her go!"

Schmidt had sentenced the *Chelyuskin* to death. An icebound ship, rudder broken, deprived of air reconnaissance, and unable to obtain assistance, was abandoned to her fate in the inaccessible Chukchi Sea. So were the 105 people aboard.

Gripped by the ice, the ship was now drifting hopelessly, helplessly and aimlessly. Except for a short hour and a half of twilight daily, the *Chelyuskin* was enveloped in the eerie darkness of polar night lit only by a cold moon.

Routine work continued. The last cow was slaughtered. To prevent boredom from becoming paralyzing, classes were started in arithmetic, grammar and history. In the evenings Schmidt, editor of the Soviet encyclopedia, lectured, by the weak light of paraffin lamps lazily swinging from rafters, on Freud, Marx, and something called "Dialectical Materialism." Sometimes the creaking body of the tortured ship was swept by melancholy tunes of guitars, balalaikas and mandolins.

As December imperceptibly faded into January and January gave way to February, the *Chelyuskin* kept drifting relentlessly.

5

On Tuesday, February 13, 1934, somewhere in the Chukchi Sea, the temperature was 22° below zero and a powerful wind was driving blinding gusts of snow. On the bridge of the *Chelyuskin,* Voronin and Schmidt anxiously listened to every sound coming from the shifting, grating ice as they stared silently into the blizzard. Behind a dense curtain of falling snow a thick ice sheet collapsed, as if crumpled by a gigantic invisible hand. Huge blocks of ice broke loose, and drifted menacingly toward the ship. Helpless, the fragile ship groaned. Glistening snowflakes on her tortured hull looked like tears as the moving ice-ridge crept on.

At 1:20 P.M., as the drumbeat of pounding ice merged with the whine of tortured steel, Voronin knew that his ship was doomed. Schmidt also knew. In quiet, measured words he ordered the emergency supplies, which had been stored on deck in anticipation of catastrophe, to be lowered onto the ice.

The creaking grew into grinding and snapping as the ship's frame bent. Metal plates bulged, bursting along their seams, and heavy rivets started popping out like corks of champagne bottles. The *Chelyuskin* quivered, and then the port side of the ship split wide open. The ugly gaping hole, over a hundred feet long, resembled a vast, thin-lipped mouth contorted in the agony of death.

Hold Number Two was open under the waterline, engine rooms were flooded with ice and water, and, with a hissing sound, steam started escaping through broken pipes.

Helmsman Markov had just completed an entry in the logbook when he saw a sailor running along the railing. "The port side is ripped," the man yelled. Markov did not know that his entry—"at 1:20 P.M. the drift has stopped"—was to be the last one in the log of the *Chelyuskin.*

The deck was teeming with bundled-up men and women. Their screams and curses were carried away by the wind as they jostled their way to predetermined stations and began lowering planks onto the ice. Cases of food, barrels of oil, coal sacks—all were thrown overside, to mingle on the ice with loose bricks, bundles of clothes, furs, and the still warm carcasses of three piglets.

The swirling, gurgling water rose to almost five feet in hold Number Two and poured into the steam-filled engine room. The dynamo went out of commission along with the water pumps. Seeing the destruction, chief mechanic Matusevich quickly led his men to the deck, through a ship now plunged into total darkness.

The death certificate was already signed, only the exact moment of death remained to be filled in, as the *Chelyuskin* slowly settled by the bow.

Back in his cabin, Khmuznikov, a hydrographer, methodically gathered his instruments, notebooks, charts and tables. Wading to his bunk through knee-deep water, helmsman Markov grabbed his diary, and the third volume of Sholokov's *Quiet Flows the Don.* Standing on the ice, his feet wide apart, braced against a fierce wind, photographer Shafran tried to set up his heavy tripod and camera to film the slow death of the *Chelyuskin.*

With her bow under water, the ship's deck was now awash. Over the howling of wind and the grating of ice, the command went out: "All onto the ice! Everybody leave the ship!" As men and women hastily slid down the slippery planks, the shouts were repeated: Everybody leave the ship! All out onto ice! Leave the ship!"

As Voronin and Schmidt, without looking back, went down an ice-covered plank, the stern of the ship rose. A piece of lumber tore loose, slid down, and struck the captain in the back, knocking him to the ice.

Boris Mogilevich, the quartermaster, ran to the railing, swung one leg over and stopped for a fraction of a second to look back at the rising stern of his dying ship. A wildly tumbling barrel rolled toward him. In the maelstrom of cascading boxes and lumber, merging with the hissing of escaping steam, no one heard the sickening thump of a barrel crashing into the back of Boris Mogilevich.

The stern rose higher, the bridge collapsed and the ship slid down, her rudder high in the air, while the funnel vomited sticky soot. Shafran, his gloveless hands numb with cold, filmed the final seconds of the

Chelyuskin, as the ship disappeared in the cold waters, carrying down the lifeless body of Boris Mogilevich.

This happened in the Chukchi Sea, at latitude 68° 16′ North and longitude 172° 51′ West. Left on a drifting floe were 102 grim, weather-beaten men and women with two children, including Karina Vasilieva who had spent all her life—23 weeks and 5 days—in the Arctic.[63] There were no screaming headlines, there was no world-wide anxiety as there was at the time of Nobile's disaster.

On the following day radioman Ernest Krenkel, a veteran of the arctic flight of the Graf Zeppelin, established contact with the new wireless station in Uelen, on Siberia's mainland, operated by a woman, Ludmilla Shrader. At 4:24 P.M. on February 14 the first message went out from what was to become known as "Camp Schmidt":

> Emergency—Governmental . . . Kuibyshev, Soviet of People's Commissars, Moscow. . . . On February 13th, at 3:30 P.M. the Chelyuskin was crushed by ice and sank. . . . Within two hours everything was over. . . .[64]

V. Molotov, then Chairman of the Council of People's Commissars of the Soviet Union, immediately established a commission "for the organization of relief to members of the expedition of O. Y. Schmidt and members of the crew of the sunken ship *Chelyuskin.*"[65] The five-man group, headed by V. V. Kuibyshev, included S. S. Kamenev and I. S. Unshlikht, who had also been so active in the rescue of Nobile and his men less than six years previously.

Stranded on a cake of drifting ice some 90 miles from shore, the 102 adults awaiting rescue discussed their chances for survival. Some favored an over-ice march to the coast, others expected dog teams from the mainland to bring relief.

Schmidt, as a mathematician, did not take long to figure out that neither of these proposals was possible. Innumerable hummocks and open lanes blocked any direct route to the mainland. Detours caused by these obstacles might extend a march to some 720 miles for which more than four weeks would be needed. Such an over-ice march, at temperatures ranging around 40° below zero, was clearly impossible for a party which included women and children. Schmidt also knew that not enough dogs, sleds, food and guides could possibly be found along a coast so sparsely populated and so lacking in roads and communications. He saw in air evacuation the only chance for quick rescue and until planes could arrive, his function was to maintain morale and discipline in the camp.

Upon ice drifting in the Chukchi Sea a primitive village rose; tents went up; scientific work was resumed, and community life continued. Within a forty-two-day period Schmidt gave thirty-three lectures, on subjects ranging from Scandinavian mythology to the history of South

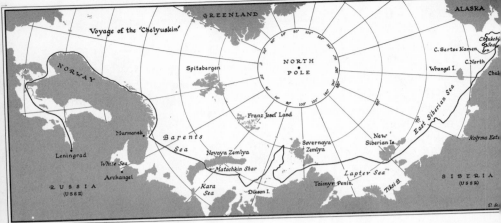

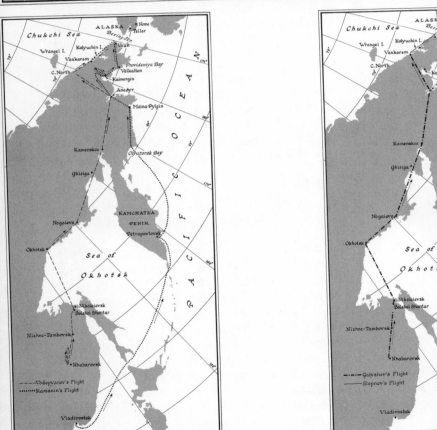

The voyage of the *Chelyuskin*. "X" in Chukchi Sea marks spot where the vessel went down and where the survivors awaited rescue. (This area is shown greatly enlarged in the maps of the rescue operation that follow.)

America, from Freud's concept of psychoanalysis to socialism, fascism, and the theory of evolution. Huddled in tents whose windows were improvised out of bottles cemented into crude frames, men and women read in an old copy of *National Geographic Magazine* about penguins in Antarctica and recited Heine's poems in German. The third volume of *Quiet Flows the Don* passed from hand to hand, as did tattered copies of Longfellow's *Hiawatha* and Zola's *Nana*. Above all, men and women of the *Chelyuskin* loved to recite from memory the poems of Pushkin.

In Moscow, the special commission created for the rescue of the marooned burst into tremendous activity. All polar stations were instructed to listen without interruption for Schmidt's messages and to transmit them to Moscow on an emergency basis. All stations in the northeastern sector were to broadcast data on weather and ice four times a day. A special three-man subcommittee, headed by the chief of Uelen's weather station, was charged with mobilizing food, gasoline and any locally available means of rescue.

Ships were alerted, oil, gasoline, food, equipment and supplies were requisitioned, and the speed-up of repairs on the icebreakers *Krassin* and *Litke* was ordered. In widely separated parts of the Soviet Union, pilots received special orders to proceed without delay to Vladivostok, taking with them mechanics, planes and spare parts. Pilots Lipp, Gorelov, Sviatogorov, Farikh, Tishkov, and Pindshikov left for Vladivostok.[66]

Within days a gigantic bureaucratic machine was created, solely devoted to the rescue of 104 people. In a country recently ravaged by a famine that had claimed thousands of lives, a national purpose shaped around the rescue of a group of faceless men and women who became known as the Chelyuskinites. Kuibyshev's office was swamped with letters from volunteers, offering their help. Among those who wrote, was Mavriki Slepnev, who suggested that a plane be sent via Alaska to rescue Schmidt's party.

On a crude bulletin board, the first issue of Camp Schmidt's community paper appeared. Written in longhand, it was defiantly called "We Won't Give Up" and carried a challenging message: "The *Chelyuskin* is dead— long live the *Chelyuskin!* Long live the work of the chelyuskinites."[67]

In a small tent crowded with eleven men, Michael Markov, a helmsman, wrote in his diary:

> February 17th: Went to see the hummock at the spot where the *Chelyuskin* went down. It is the first time I have seen such monstrous floes. Climbed up on top of them—about 25 feet high. It is difficult to describe the blinding picture of the Arctic and the might of its spaces. At my feet were huge lumps of snow . . . The transparent green mass of the blocks of ice is shot through with veins of marble-white compressed snow. . . . Here and there split floes have come to the

surface, their thickness being twice my size. . . . Babushkin and a few assistants are out clearing a landing strip and erecting a tent there. . . . We must be ready to receive planes . . .[68]

In Moscow, rescue operations were planned by land, sea and air. While the subcommittee in Uelen was charged with assembling as many dog teams as possible, pilot Lyapidevsky, in charge of the only airworthy plane on Chukchi Peninsula, was ordered to "take all measures for rescue of expedition and equipment of the *Chelyuskin.*"
Michael Markov kept up his diary:

> February 18th: . . . A clear day. . . . Everybody expects a plane. . . . The aircraft which has arrived in Uelen from Lavrentiya Bay should fly out to us. Visibility good. Our women and children are getting ready for the flight. In the afternoon Uelen told us that the plane is not leaving—engine trouble.

> February 19th: . . . Again no luck with the plane. It left Uelen, passed Onman and set course for us. Fifteen miles off shore it ran into a blizzard. . . . The pilot returned to Uelen . . .[68]

Kuibyshev's committee was planning a four-pronged air approach to Camp Schmidt: (*a*) Lyapidevsky was to continue his efforts from Uelen. (*b*) The Soviet Far Eastern Army was to send planes and personnel to Vladivostok for shipment to Kamchatka aboard the steamer *Smolensk.* From Kamchatka the planes were to be flown to Camp Schmidt. (*c*) A squadron of civilian planes, to be assembled in Khabarovsk, was to fly north along a route never before attempted in wintertime, via Nikolaievsk, Okhotsk, Ghiziga, and Anadyr to Camp Schmidt. (*d*) A fourth air group was to approach the drifting camp from Nome, Alaska.
From Markov's diary:

> February 21st: The plane set out to fly to us at 8:55. The group scheduled to leave had just started for the airfield, when a phenomenon resembling an earthquake occurred. The floe cracked. The crack passed through the whole camp, cutting the kitchen tent in two. The ice-covered wall collapsed. The crack passed close to the food depot; supplies had to be lugged to another spot. Twice we had to move the aerial. . . . The crack widened to three meters [117 inches]. At 11:20 the plane should have been here, but there is no plane. Yet, the day is unusually clear . . .

On the same day, Ivan Kranklin, commanding an air squadron of the Soviet Far Eastern Army, received orders to select and equip a detachment which was to fly to Camp Schmidt from Kamchatka. He appointed a hardheaded twenty-five-year-old pilot named Nikolai Kamanin as the leader of this group. The son of a shoemaker, Kamanin had logged 1,200 flying hours, but had never flown in the Arctic. Traveling by rail,

Kamanin's fifteen men and three dismantled planes, reached Vladivostok the following day, there to await shipment to Kamchatka.

Old-time pilot Vasili Molokov left for Vladivostok. Ivan Doronin and Boris Galyshev entrained for Khabarovsk, in eastern Siberia, taking with them mechanics and dismantled planes. Pilots Sigismund Levanevsky and Mavriki Slepnev, togèther with artic expert Ushakov,[69] were alerted to go via Berlin, London and New York to Alaska, where American planes would be bought for them.

Omitted from the list of pilots selected by Kuibyshev was a certain Michael Vodopyanov, a young man with vast flying experience. He was slated for the rescue of some fishermen who, together with a herd of horses, were just then adrift on a broken-off floe in the Caspian Sea. Feeling slighted, Vodopyanov protested to *Pravda*. His plane, he said, was well equipped for the Arctic and he himself was well qualified to take part in the rescue of the Chelyuskinites. Kuibyshev read the protest and ordered Vodopyanov and his plane on a nine-day train trip to Khabarovsk.

By the end of February, little more than a week after the *Chelyuskin* had gone down, sixteen planes were mobilized in Vladivostok alone, thirteen pilots had been assembled, each of them accompanied by his mechanics. Inevitably there was confusion. Planes were put on slow-moving trains and some pilots reported to wrong places, but gradually order emerged from chaos, as both planes and pilots arrived at Khabarovsk or Vladivostok, the designated points for departure.

Kamanin's detachment, code-named "Blue," had grown to seven planes by the time it was loaded aboard the *Smolensk*. Two planes and their crews were on the *Stalingrad* and two others on the *Soviet*. In Khabarovsk three aircraft were being readied for a long flight northward across the immense, snow-covered and sparsely populated country.

On March 1, the liner *Olympia* arrived in New York. Among its passengers were members of the Soviet rescue party that was to proceed across the United States to Fairbanks, Alaska, whence the men were to reach Camp Schmidt in American planes.

In Camp Schmidt, meanwhile, men and women of the *Chelyuskin,* working in three shifts, built landing strips. Their tools were few and inadequate and the work was backbreaking. Tons of snow and ice had to be moved under the constant threat of new cracks and breaks in the floe. Working in fog and snow, they hopefully waited to hear the welcome drone of the plane from Uelen.

Time and again, Ludmilla Shrader, Uelen's radio operator, sent encouraging messages to Camp Schmidt. There was activity on Uelen's improvised airfield. Lyapidevsky's plane was often started, but time and again either fog blanketed the peninsula, making flying impossible, or the engines of Lyapidevsky's plane refused to start in freezing weather.

On March 5, the sky over Camp Schmidt was clear, there was no wind although the temperature hovered somewhere around 40° below zero. Once more Ludmilla Shrader reported that Lyapidevsky's plane was being prepared for a takeoff. Used to false alarms and disappoint- ments, the Chelyuskinites did not raise their hopes again. After all, they knew that plane engines could not be expected to work at such low temperatures.

Then an excited shout went up: "All women to the airfield! The plane left half an hour ago! All those who are to go to the airfield, get ready!" Buoyed on wings of hope, the repeated shouts reverberated through the busy camp. "We did not have to be told twice," scientist Anna Sushkin later recalled. "There was not much to pack. All our things were already at the airfield."

Soon ten women and two children were making their way across the floe to the landing field. In the escorting party was Arkadi Shafran, anxious to snap a picture of the first plane to land at Camp Schmidt.

"On that sunny day the whole wild beauty of the primeval chaos surrounding us looked especially brilliant," remembered Anna Sushkin. "Floes were piled up fantastically, some hummocks looked like petrified monsters, and all of them were shot through with live, unexpectedly chang- ing colors. It seemed as if we were wading through piles of precious stones. . . . Without wanting to, we were caught up in this big silence and went on without talking. There was the desire to saturate oneself to carry away at least a minute particle of this undescribable beauty."[70]

As these Chelyuskinites neared the landing site, a humming noise grew louder, to become a roar, and, quite clearly outlined, a place became visible. To Anna Sushkin it looked like a grasshopper dancing in a blue sky. Circling the camp, the plane, piloted by Anatol Lyapidevsky, came lower and lower, finally landing beyond a deep canal that split the floe and behind a high ridge of ice, which hid the landing site from Shafran's camera.

A raft was dragged over the ice and lowered into the canal. Waving laughing Chelyuskinites soon surrounded the plane, whose propellers kept on turning. Women, shapeless in their thick furs, were pushed and pulled inside the aircraft which was quivering like an impatient horse. Then, in no time at all it seemed, the ten women and two children, huddled in the seat-less open cabin, heard the roar of the engines grow louder. Numbed by a cold, propeller-made wind, they felt themselves lifted up as the plane rose. Two hours and twenty minutes later they were in Uelen, on the mainland. Left in Camp Schmidt were ninety-two men.

That night ice split under a barrack housing some forty Chelyuskinites. The crack widened to a yard. Hastily the wooden structure was sawed in half and dawn found the two parts of a mutilated makeshift house some fifty yards apart. Literally on the brink of disaster, one Chelyuskinite a scientist named Peter Shirshov took time out to record in his diary:

At a temperature of 24° below zero it is quite possible to wash hands, face, ears and neck with lukewarm water. When the temperature drops to 38° below, it takes an effort to wash the neck and so a rather noticeable line appears near the ears, between neck and face after shaving."[71]

Lyapidevsky was anxious to fly again, but the weather turned bad and storms continued buffeting Uelen through March 13th, foiling the pilot's hopes to repeat what had become known as "the flight of March fifth."

To shorten the flight distance, the center of rescue operations was shifted from Uelen to Vankarem, a native settlement of ten huts and one wooden building, located farther west. There an airfield was cleared. From Cape North and Provideniya Bay, gasoline was brought, and the tiny village, unmarked on maps, soon became known to millions of people.

On March 14, Shirshov wrote that the weather was cold, but clear. Lyapidevsky had left Uelen in the morning, Shirshov noted, but by 3 P.M. the plane was "neither in Uelen nor in Vankarem."

Shirshov did not know it, but Lyapidevsky's plane was in trouble. While flying over treacherous Kolyuchin Bay with six men and a heavy cargo of gasoline, one engine had gone dead. "I spotted a small level patch," Lyapidevsky later reported," and without giving it much thought, I shut the other engine off and came down. . . . The overloaded plane touched ice, slid onto a hummock, gently settled down and slowly the right wing drooped, dragging along the ice. We jumped out. The right mainstay of the undercarriage was bent and the frame was damaged under the radiator. . . . The shaft of the left engine was broken."[72]

The plane's navigator cracked a limp joke: "Well," he said, "we are making progress; now we have a Camp Lyapidevsky!" Without a radio, the pilot had no way of communicating with his own base.

Lyapidevsky and some of his men made their way to Kolyuchin Island. There they passed the night in a native hut before setting out on sleds for Vankarem in the midst of a violent snowstorm. The blizzard knocked down Vankarem's radio antenna, and for three days the station remained silent. No news of Lyapidevsky could reach Moscow or Camp Schmidt, and newspapers in the United States carried headlines like: "Loss of Russian Polar Hero Lyapidevsky. Crashes among floes during second flight."

6

The rescue machinery set up in Moscow moved into high gear: Kamanin's seven-plane Blue Detachment was on its way to Kamchatka aboard the *Smolensk;* two other vessels, carrying two planes each, steamed northword, and, in Khabarovsk, Boris Galyshev was appointed commander of a three-plane squadron. Still planeless, Levanevsky and Slepnev were on their way to Alaska.

By the beginning of March, the first phase of a gigantic effort to rescue the marooned men of the *Chelyuskin* had been completed. Two small Russian-built dirigibles were put on a train for Vladivostok, and the hastily repaired *Krassin,* manned by a crew of 46 and provisioned for nine months, left Leningrad for Camp Schmidt via the Suez Canal. The estimated duration of the roundabout trip was 48 days. The ice-breaker's mission was to pluck off the Chelyuskinites should the floe break up into small fragments on which no planes could land.[73]

In Fairbanks, Alaska, two nine-passenger planes were purchased by the Soviet Government from Pacific Alaska Airways. After being checked by Joe Crosson, they were turned over to Levanevsky and Slepnev, the Soviet pilots, who had crossed the continent by train.

On March 17, five planes of the Blue Detachment, unloaded from the *Smolensk,* were being assembled in Olyutorsk Bay on Kamchatka Peninsula, and Commander Kamanin had to make a decision. Farikh, one of his pilots, was grumbling and objecting to the proposed flight route. Emphasizing his arctic experience, Farikh wanted to fly individually. Team work had to prevail, Kamanin decided, and there was no time for individual heroics. Farikh's attitude therefore rendered him unsuited to be part of a team and he was dropped. Itching to go, the team nevertheless had to sit around idly for three days because storm and fog made flying impossible.

That same day four planes took off from wind-swept Khabarovsk, where temperatures hovered below zero. The leader of this team was arctic pilot Galyshev. Four years earlier he, Commander Slepnev, and the then mechanic Farikh had flown to the rescue of Captain Milovzorov's *Stavropol,* icebound off Cape North, not far from Olaf Swenson's disabled *Nanuk.* In Galyshev's group were Ivan Doronin and Michael Vodopyanov. A commercial aircraft was to escort the three to Nikolaievsk. Later, over a route never before flown in wintertime, spanning wide expanses where landmarks were blotted out by snow, Galyshev, Doronin and Vodopyanov were to continue northeastward unescorted, toward Camp Schmidt.

After less than an hour's flight, a misty haze condensed into thick clouds. Snow started falling, wiping out visibility and hiding the Amur River, along which the planes were flying toward Nikolaievsk.

"I could not see the other planes," Doronin said later. "Sometimes the leading machine would appear for a second, then to be immediately lost again. . . . I could see that the leader was flying quite low, right above the snow and scrub. The other two had disappeared entirely from my sight."[74] Doronin was justifiably worried. Any minute might bring a collision with one of the planes flying nearby.

Vodopyanov was worried too. Bringing up the rear, he knew that his plane, the fastest of the group, might at any minute run into one of the others. "Suddenly," he said later, "one of the planes ahead appeared out of the clouds." Instinctively pulling back on the stick, he narrowly avoided a mid-air crash. With the throttle wide open, his plane climbed, roaring to an altitude of 8,200 feet, where the sky suddenly turned clear. Below was a sea of black clouds. What should he do? Should he take a compass course for Nikolaievsk or return to his point of departure? The reckless impulse died down, and choosing a temporary defeat, Vodopyanov turned back to Khabarovsk. After some six hours of flight, Galyshev and Doronin, led by the commercial plane, arrived in Nikolaievsk, just ahead of an oncoming blizzard.

From Shirshov's diary for March 17:

> A gray morning. Blizzard continues. Snowdrifts everywhere. . . . Everybody is scared at the thought of the pilots. Where are they? How are they?

On March 18, Vodopyanov took off once more from Khabarovsk, but was forced to land at Nizhne-Tambovsk, only 280 miles away. The same blizzard which held Galyshev and Doronin prisoners at Nikolaievsk prevented him from flying on. When he took to the air again two days later, he made it only to Bolshoi Shantar, where a defective fuel pump forced him to make an emergency landing.

On March 20 Galyshev and Doronin reached Okhotsk after a total flying time of nine hours and ten minutes, during which they had steadily fought fog and snow. About two hours later, Vodopyanov, his fuel pump having been repaired, flew in, and once more the Galyshev team was complete. The goal, Camp Schmidt, was still far away, however, both in time and space. Taking off from Okhotsk on the same day, Galyshev's men were caught in the fringe of a typhoon racing over Japan. Although tossed about like flimsy kites, the planes managed to reach Nagaievo and to land on a frozen bay being swept by seventy-mile-an-hour winds. For four days fierce gusts battered the anchored aircraft, while the blizzard dumped tons of snow. Afterward it took another precious day to dig out the planes.

Also on March 20, five identical planes of Detachment Blue—heavily loaded with gasoline, spare parts, and a six-week supply of food—finally took to the air from frozen Olyutorsk Bay. In the lead was squadron commander Nikolai Kamanin. Following him was Vasili Molokov, a crack pilot and former flying instructor (among his pupils had been Ivan Doronin and Boris Galyshev). The three other planes were in the hands of pilots Demirov, Bastanzhiev, and Pivenshtein. Only Kamanin had a navigator, and only his plane was equipped with a radio. Flying at 8,300 feet over the sharp peaks of snow-covered mountains while using a map which had not been revised for thirty-eight years, the fifteen men—five pilots, nine mechanics, and a navigator—fought steady head winds and constantly stared into the face of disaster. It took them six hours to fly 500 miles to Maina Pylgin, a small fish cannery post closed for the winter and left in charge of a five-man housekeeping detail.

In Maina Pylgin, Kamanin's squad carefully prepared for its next hop. At takeoff time one engine of Bastanzhiev's plane refused to start in the cold. Leaving plane and men behind, Kamanin, his detachment reduced to four aircraft, took off. Ahead of them towered the massive fog-shrouded Anadyr range.

Buffeted by a new storm and flying through dense layers of cloud, Kamanin's planes could not stay in formation. Emerging from a clammy fog bank, the commander saw only two planes following him. One was missing—Demirov. What had happened to him?

Minutes passed slowly, to the monotonous drone of engines enveloped in opaque cloud over invisible mountain peaks. Only Kamanin, Molokov and Pivenshtein reached Anadyr that day. Anadyr was a small village of some fifty houses buried in deep snow. There, the impatient Kamanin and his eight men were held up for five days by a howling snow-driving storm (in which five of Anadyr's inhabitants, incidentally, simply disappeared).

The storm had put Kamanin's radio out of commission and no word reached Moscow about the flight from Maina Pylgin. Commission chairman Kuibyshev had no news about the fate of the fliers, and Kamanin had no word from Demirov, lost somewhere in the white wilderness with neither radio nor navigator. (Demirov had managed to set his plane down near a river, there to remain stranded for six days.)

On March 26, the two passenger planes purchased from Pacific Alaska Airways and repainted red, took off from Fairbanks, in Alaska. At the controls were the two Russian pilots. Both men had been in the United States before on mercy missions. Thirty-two-year-old Sigismund Levanevsky had brought James Mattern from Anadyr to Alaska a few months earlier, and Mavriki Slepnev had escorted the bodies of Ben Eielson and Earl Borland home. Their current mission was to proceed to Nome, then to Vankarem and Camp Schmidt, where the 92 Chelyuskinites were still waiting for rescue.

On that same day of March 26, Bastanzhiev was still in Maina Pylgin; Demirov was lost, and the rest of Kamanin's squad was stranded in blizzard-struck Anadyr. But in Nagaievo the weather cleared and Galyshev's group took to the air. Fog forced two of the planes back and only Vodopyanov in his better equipped military aircraft reached Gizhiga, where he circled hesitantly over an improvised snow strip 3,200 feet long but only 560 feet wide. In the middle of the strip, Vodopyanov, speechless with anger, saw a wind-direction indicating letter T, crudely cut out of black canvas and held down by big heavy beams to prevent its being blown away. These beams, of course, blocked most of the runway. The pilot circled the strip three times, then took a chance and landed without running into any of the wooden beams. By the time Galyshev and Doronin arrived, the field was cleared and the runway widened. Galyshev's three planes, trailing those of Kamanin, were 530 miles closer to Camp Schmidt. Then, again, there were two more days of enforced idleness while waiting for yet another snowstorm to pass.

From Shirshov's diary:

> March 27: Warm, humid wind. It is quite warm: $-1°.8$ Fog, a slight storm. Yesterday clearing of the new airstrip was finished. It is about 1,000 feet long. Its width is somewhat narrow but all in all the field is not bad. If it only does not break up! Today we work in two shifts on the old field—one has been completely destroyed by a new pressure ridge. Information from the mainland gives us food for thought today: According to the newspaper *Czech Word* we are "the symbol of rehabilitation of contemporaneous civilization!" There is little space left in this notebook, have to watch it because there is going to be a long wait on the ice yet.[75]

On March 28, Kamanin's three remaining planes set out from Anadyr. A little later, only a little more than 150 miles out, they ran into a vicious storm and had to turn back. Retracing their flight, they landed at the small village of Kainergin, on the Chukchi Peninsula, where some fifteen frightened fur-clad natives scattered at the first sight of these roaring monsters which could drop out of the sky through a blinding snowstorm.

On this day, Demirov, his plane dug out of a mountain of snow, took off from the frozen Opukha River and made his way back to the cannery at Maina Pylgin. Later, he and Bastanzhiev took off five times, hoping to catch up with Kamanin. But five times they had to turn back because fog, snow and wind were blocking their way like a solid wall.

Also on March 28, Slepnev and Levanevsky, their planes ready, waited for favorable weather reports in Nome, while Galyshev's three-plane group was circling, in poor visibility, over a landing field at Kamenskoie, which was ice-caked and covered with drifts as high as five feet. One of Doronin's gas-starved engines coughed and he was first to attempt a landing. Touching the frozen surface of the improvised airfield, his plane bounced, bucked up and came down hard with a broken undercarriage. With two planes still circling a field on which landing was impossible, Doronin, emerging unharmed, barely looked at his disabled craft. Gathering some mechanics and curious bystanders, he arranged them to form a living cross in the snow—a sign prohibiting landing. Seeing the sign, Galyshev and Vodopyanov flew on, and farther off brought their planes down safely on an unprepared stretch of ice.

It took a day to repair the struts of Doronin's plane. Then another blizzard all but buried the aircraft under mountains of fresh snow. Not until a week later, on April 4, eighteen days after leaving Khabarovsk, did Galyshev's men arrive in Anadyr, trailing Kamanin's group by more than a week.

On March 29 weather reports reaching Nome were favorable. The air was crisp and the sky clear. The red-painted plane of Sigismund Levanevsky taxied, answered the throttle and set off for Uelen. With Levanevsky was Georgi Ushakov, official representative of Kuibyshev's Special Rescue Commission. Also aboard was Claude Armistead, a mechanic from Fairbanks and a former U.S. marine. Staying behind in Nome, distrustful of the weather reports, was Commander Slepnev.

The red plane moved westward, flying over the mountains of Alaska and the frozen waters of the Bering Strait. Visibility shrank and snow started falling, but Levanevsky kept to his course. The east coast of the Chukchi Peninsula came into view and then Uelen became visible below. Some fifteen flying minutes past Uelen a bank of cloud barred Levanevsky's way like a huge wall of darkness. Plunging into this mass of humid opacity, the pilot climbed to an altitude of 5,000 feet and emerged from the fog only to find himself surrounded by yet other banks of slowly rolling clouds full of heavy, sticky snow. "It turned so dark in the little pilot's cabin, it was like night," Levanevsky said. He climbed higher. The plane shook, windows froze over, wings became ice-coated, and the needle of the altimeter moved sluggishly as the engines strained to lift the ice-covered plane higher. One motor coughed and died. Instantly the helpless plane, now transformed into a glistening cake of ice gliding through the air, started losing altitude.

With a powerful blow Levanevsky smashed the window of his cabin to see better and a mighty rush of icy air hit him, cutting off his breath. He tried vainly to peer through a solid wall of falling snow. Then he saw ice coming up toward him. Ugly ridges stretched out to him for a grim embrace. There was a jolt, and the loud crunching of ice blended with the groaning of steel as the plane hit the ground and catapulted forward like an unwanted toy thrown by a mischievous child.

Ushakov and Armistead braced themselves and escaped injury. Levanevsky was thrown violently forward and lost consciousness. Later as he felt himself being pulled out of the cabin he instinctively brought a hand up to his throbbing face. When he looked at his hand, it was bloody.

His head bandaged with strips torn from Ushakov's trousers, a feverish Levanevsky spent a trying night, tossing in semiconscious delirium on the floor of a nearby hut reeking with the stench of walrus meat. Suspended from the ceiling, a crude container filled with burning seal oil swung lazily back and forth overhead.

Levanevsky survived and was taken to Vankarem on a sled.

At the same time, pilots Bastanzhiev and Demirov made their sixth attempt to reach Camp Schmidt. Leaving Maina Pylgin, they threaded their way through heavy fog hanging over the snow-covered mountains. Flying blind, with neither radio nor navigator, they became lost and within twelve miles of fog-shrouded Anadyr, both planes crashed, that of Demirov catching fire and burning eerily in the snow. The pilots and crews survived. Frozen and starved, the six men stumbled through waist-deep snow until they found their way to Anadyr three days later.

7

In Moscow, forty-four days after the sinking of the *Chelyuskin,* Commission chairman Kuibyshev had reason to be worried. Of the four planes already on Chukchi Peninsula, three were useless, and the fourth, Lyapidevsky's, was disabled in Kolyuchin Bay. The four craft aboard the steamers *Soviet* and *Stalingrad* had not yet been unloaded. Levanevsky had crashed and there was no word from Kamanin. Only Galyshev's group of three was still intact in Kamenskoie and, finally, there was pilot Slepnev, still waiting for better weather in Nome.

That day, Commander Kamanin and his eight were stranded in a deserted Chukchi hut. Built of wood and whale ribs, the hut was covered with torn strips of canvas through which the snow drifted over the nine men huddled in their sleeping bags. Suffocating under the blanket of snow, they crawled out and vainly tried to brace themselves against the violent wind. Locking arms, they formed a human chain which searched blindly through the all-obliterating wall of falling snow for the nearest inhabited hut, actually only a few yards away. For Kamanin and his men the days dragged on slowly in Kainergin, as they waited for the weather to clear. Two days passed, then three, while snow fell and the wind kept on blowing.

On the last day of March, Commander Mavriki Slepnev, carrying with him an American mechanic, Bill Lavory, twice tried to fly from Nome across the Bering Strait to the eastern shores of Siberia. Twice dense fog turned him back and he finally landed in Teller.

Snow stopped falling in the small settlement of Kainergin on April 1. Hastily Kamanin's planes were dug out and the men took off. At an altitude of some 5,500 feet they flew over mountains whose height was marked on their antiquated maps as being 4,500 feet. But there was simply no getting through the milky fog. Barely thirty-seven miles from Vankarem, their next to last goal, with gasoline dwindling, winds and thick black clouds forced Kamanin and his men back to Kainergin. There the commander changed his flight plan. The direct way being barred, he decided to take a roundabout route, following the shoreline of Chukchi Peninsula, aiming for Provideniya Bay, then Uelen and finally Vankarem.

By April 2, Babushkin's amphibian two-seater had been repaired and tested at Camp Schmidt. The pilot was anxious to fly to Vankarem. Hesitantly, Schmidt consented. Not unlike Babushkin, he, too, had some doubts as to whether the little plane, affectionately called "the flea," (or more rudely, "the flying coffin") could make it to the mainland. Towards noon Babushkin, with mechanic Valavin as a passenger, took off for Vankarem, where he landed an hour and fifteen minutes later. He was now ready to assume his duties as newly appointed Commandant of Vankarem's primitive airport. Babushkin had an airfield and stores of gasoline but what was needed were planes. Left in Camp Schmidt were 90 men.

Slepnev made his third attempt to reach the Chukchi Peninsula on the same day. Leaving Teller, he easily crossed the Bering Strait, and soon Ludmilla Shrader could joyfully tap out the news: An American plane with Commander Mavriki Slepnev at the controls had just landed in Uelen.

Galyshev's detachment was still stranded in Anadyr, but from Kainergin, Kamanin's planes were flying toward Provideniya Bay. Through the dense fog, Commander Kamanin saw Pivenshtein's hand signals: Fuel for only fifteen more minutes of flight. On a frozen river near a village called Valkalten all three planes came down for a landing and Kamanin smashed the shock absorber of his plane's undercarriage. So near victory now, he could not accept defeat. Exercising the prerogative of command, he took Pivenshtein's plane, pooled supplies and gasoline with Molokov and waited in tantalizing inactivity for the end of yet another snow storm.

From Shirshov's diary:

> Landing strip number three (finished yesterday) has split at its western end, but planes can still land. Airstrip number one, damaged a few days ago, is ruined. Clearing of a new strip (number 4) has begun.[75]

Like pieces on a chessboard the rescue planes were advancing purposefully toward their point of attack on April 4. Galyshev, Doronin, and Vodopyanov, far behind Kamanin, finally arrived in Anadyr. There, a few days later, they met planeless pilots Demirov and Bastanzhiev and their crews, staggering from exhaustion, hunger and exposure, but alive. The remnants of Kamanin's original five-plane squadron—two aircraft and six men—arrived in Provideniya Bay. Now Slepnev, Kamanin and Molokov were only two short laps from their goal.

The balance sheet read: Two aircraft crashed and destroyed near Anadyr; one plane damaged in Kolyuchin Bay; Levanevsky's American machine useless; pilot Pivenshtein waiting in Valkalten for gasoline and spare parts. Chairman Kuibyshev nevertheless could breathe easier. No lives had been lost and three planes were actually only a short distance from Camp Schmidt.

In Vankarem, a sleepless Babushkin, now airfield commander, was worriedly watching the sky. His joy over the arrival of planes in Uelen was dampened by a message just received from Camp Schmidt: "Airstrip . . . is broken up. Withhold flights to camp until further notice." Babushkin well knew the power of ice, and he knew well what backbreaking work of reconstruction was facing the ninety Chelyuskinites. However, thirty-six hours later Camp Schmidt radioed that after steady work through a day and a night the field, though smaller, was patched up and again usable.

On Saturday, April 7, 1934, just arrived from Uelen, the three planes of Slepnev, Kamanin, and Molokov were being checked and refueled on Vankarem's improvised airfield under Babushkin's watchful eyes. Then, with a visibility of some five miles and at least some kind of landing strip ready to receive them at Camp Schmidt, Kamanin and Molokov took off. Ten minutes later Slepnev, too, went up, carrying in his plane Georgi Ushakov and eight noisy Chukchi dogs. Kamanin and Molokov soon returned, somewhat dejected. They had been completely unable to find any camp!

A group of anxious men assembled near the landing strip on Camp Schmidt, their eyes scanning the gray sky.

The men on the floe saw a moving speck in the overcast sky, which grew bigger as it approached and which brought with it the reassuring sound of an airplane. It was Slepnev. He circled the camp three times and then came down for a landing. The plane touched the ice, glided on and finally stopped, awkwardly leaning to the left, resting on a broken undercarriage.

There was laughter and back-slapping. Joyfully tossed up, caps sailed through the air as unrestrained men ran toward the plane, screaming and yelling. Help and rescue were no longer wishes and dreams, but reality. What if the undercarriage was damaged? Were there no mechanics among them, were there no steel rods somewhere?

That same day, toward four o'clock in the afternoon, on their second attempt, Kamanin, guided by navigator Shelyganov and followed by a lone Molokov, also reached Camp Schmidt. Shortly thereafter the population of the floe was reduced by three men. (Kamanin airlifted two, Molokov three, but temporarily stranded in Camp Schmidt were pilot Slepnev and arctic expert Ushakov, conspicuous in his Alaska-made reindeer overalls.)

There was no sleep in Camp Schmidt during the night of April 8, as a heavy storm lashed the floe. Ice was breaking, new drifts were forming, and the runway was cut by a deep canal which endangered Slepnev's disabled aircraft. In Vankarem there was no sleep for Babushkin, as he anxiously watched the weather and impatiently kept on waiting for radio messages from Schmidt.

Sunday was another day of frustration. The cooling system in Kaminin's plane froze and the aircraft was temporarily out of commission. Flying without a navigator, Molokov missed the camp and had to return without passengers. Slepnev's plane still had not been repaired, and the flying detachment of Commander Galyshev was still stranded in Anadyr.

On April 10, conditions were better. Molokov, the man of few words, slim, with hair graying at the temples, winged his way over to Camp Schmidt three times, rescuing a total of fourteen men with a plane which had space for only three people. On each trip he carried two additional passengers in empty parachute containers strapped to the wings of his small aircraft. Slepnev flew, so did Kamanin. By the end of the day only sixty-three men and eight dogs were left on the floe.

But Ushakov was worried: Back on the floe strong-willed Schmidt, huddled in a sleeping bag, was lying ill on the floor of the radio tent. Schmidt, who had had tuberculosis, was dozing most of the time. His temperature, already past 103°, was still climbing.

The following day Schmidt received this message from Moscow:

> Emergency—Governmental. . . . In view of your illness the Government Commission instructs you to turn command of your expedition over to your assistant Bobrov. . . . You will be flown out to Alaska in accordance with instructions issued by Ushakov. Warmest greetings.[76]

In the early hours of April 12, Schmidt, bowing to reason and orders, reluctantly turned leadership and authority over to Bobrov and became just another sick Chelyuskinite in need of immediate evacuation.

As April 12 dawned in Anadyr, Galyshev's squad was preparing for takeoff, but the commander's plane would not start; a fuel pump had to be repaired. Vodopyanov was restless, and refusing to wait any longer, he decided to take off on a solo flight. Leaving Anadyr, he flew northward, winging his way over high mountains, crossing snow-covered valleys and frozen rivers, and, mistaking it for Vankarem, landed safely at Cape North, not far from the spot where death had claimed Eielson and Borland.

Looking sadly at his disabled airplane, Galyshev turned to Doronin: "You'd better be going," he said. "You are needed there. We'll manage here." With extra supplies, taken from Galyshev's plane (including a heavy welding unit needed to repair Lyapidevsky's plane in Kolyuchin Bay), Doronin raced his overloaded craft over the bumpy icefield of Anadyr and lifted into the air. He landed in Vankarem the same day.

Now there were four usable planes in Vankarem—those of Slepnev, Kamanin, Molokov, and Doronin. And soon Vodopyanov would arrive from nearby Cape North.

It was still April 12 when a fever-stricken, cough-racked Otto Schmidt left the icefloe aboard the plane of Mavriki Slepnev as the 76th Chelyuskinite to be evacuated.

When Schmidt left, there was little doubt that rescue efforts would be completed within one or two days. In fact, the following day Kamanin airlifted thirteen more Chelyuskinites in three flights, carrying in his three-seater as many as five passengers at a time. Shuttling twice, Vodopyanov brought out eight, and Doronin, his plane damaged on landing, limped to the mainland in a hastily repaired aircraft, carrying two more men.

In Vankarem joy was somewhat dampened by the thought that six men were still left in Camp Schmidt. Captain Voronin, skipper of the ill-fated freighter, acting expedition commander Bobrov, radio operators Krenkel and Ivanov, bosun Zagorski, and Pogossov, the mechanic who was nominal commandant of Camp Schmidt's lonely and deserted airfield. Once again it was a long sleepless night for Michael Babushkin in Vankarem.

In the watchtower of Camp Schmidt, Captain Voronin joined Alexei Bobrov. Later Bobrov would remember:

> For a long time, heads bent backward, we watched the clouds sweep by and tried to figure out what kind of weather tomorrow would bring. The groaning of ice could clearly be heard below. Small clouds appeared from the south and the wind died down. By the end of our stay in camp every one of us had become a meteorologist and was trying to forecast the weather. I turned to Voronin: "Well, Vladimir Ivanovich," I asked, "what kind of weather can we expect tomorrow?" The answer I got was profound: "Come tomorrow and we will see." But from this answer and the grim expression on the captain's face I could deduce that nothing good was to be expected."

Slowly night passed in the once busy camp, now immersed in utter majestic loneliness. There was no light anywhere, no smoke curled out of improvised smokestacks protruding from wind-battered tents. There was only the whimpering of dogs, which merged with the sounds of wind and those made by creaking, breaking ice.

In the morning, a hazy mist covered the horizon. Vodopyanov took off from Vankarem, and six men, nervously pacing their floe, once more anxiously scanned the gray sky for the sight of an approaching plane. "The minutes dragged on and seemed very long," Bobrov would recall.

Indeed, the minutes dragged into hours as Bobrov, Voronin and the others vainly spent half a day in anxious waiting. No plane arrived in Camp Schmidt that morning. Vodopyanov had taken off, but losing his bearings over a maze of newly formed canals and pools in the disintegrating ice, he returned to Vankarem without having found the floe with the six men. Later in the day, however, using last stores of locally available gasoline, the three-plane team of Vodopyanov, Kamanin, and Molokov landed in Camp Schmidt, guided by a huge beacon of black smoke rising out of a heap of battered and abandoned suitcases, discarded blankets and a barrel of paraffin, set afire on the floe by Voronin and his men.

Sleds drawn by the eight dogs carried salvageable equipment to the airstrip. Voronin, a meticulous seaman, carefully nailed up his hut (forgetting his cap inside) and tore from a lifebelt a piece of fabric bearing the name *Chelyuskin.* Bobrov took down the pennant of the Northern Sea Route Administration, and Krenkel tapped out one last message: "Nothing more to transmit; closing down station." He followed up with the call letters of the *Chelyuskin,* transmitting them slowly, three times, with the consciousness of a man who was making history. Then he took the aerial down and made the last entry in his log: "Transmitter disconnected at 2:08 A.M., Moscow time, April 13, 1934." The ears and the voice of Camp Schmidt were no more.

One by one the planes took off from the now abandoned camp. One by one they circled and set course for Vankarem. There some sixty anxious Chelyuskinites and twenty natives crowded the airstrip and climbed to the roof of the wooden trading station, watching a cloud-covered sky, while a steadily falling barometer signaled the approach of a new blizzard. Somebody saw a dark smudge in the gray sky. Then there were two moving dots, then three of them. They kept on growing and coming closer. Pent-up emotions erupted into joyful happiness and laughing men and women were not ashamed to cry. One by one the planes landed, one by one the last six Chelyuskinites stepped onto Siberia's mainland.

"This is real solid land," Vodopyanov said jokingly to his passenger Krenkel, "no more drifting south or north. . . . You had tears in your eyes when I circled the camp for the last time. Were you that sorry to leave?"[78]

"Hell, no! You brought tears to my eyes when you made Ivanov step on my foot," a beaming Krenkel said, stooping down to touch earth below the snow. "Dear Mother Earth," he mumbled. Somebody laughed. "Here you're still on the sea; the shore is a hundred yards farther in."

"Then let me get there, its been almost a year since I've felt solid land."

The *Chelyuskin* saga was over. With determined unity, men and women had lived up to their defiant slogan "We Won't Give Up," carried as the masthead of their little camp paper; proudly they would now change this motto in the last edition to read: "We Didn't Give Up." An epic fight of gallant men against time, space and nature had come to an end. In a total of twenty-five flights, 104 people had been airlifted from a drifting floe. Molokov and Kamanin had successfully flown out nine times each, bringing a total of 73 men; in three flights Vodopyanov had rescued 10; Lyapidevsky, Slepnev and Doronin, each with one flight to his credit, had taken off 19 Chelyuskinites, and Babushkin had brought to Vankarem his plane and the mechanic Valavin.

On the following day, April 14, 1934, a message originating in Moscow was intercepted by radio stations throughout the Soviet Union. Signed by Stalin and other high Government officials, it was addressed to the seven pilots who had just completed the first mass airlift in history. It announced that they were the first recipients of a new title, just created for acts of valor: "Hero of the Soviet Union." (Exactly twenty-seven years later, on April 14, 1961, the 11,175th "Hero of the Soviet Union" would be acclaimed in Moscow's Red Square. His name: Yuri Gagarin, the world's first cosmonaut.)

By plane and sled the Chelyuskinites were taken across Chukchi Peninsula. Eventually the rescued and rescuers boarded the *Smolensk* in Providniya Bay and set out on a triumphant return trip to Moscow. Somewhere along the way a photograph of Russia's most famous airmen of the day was taken. There they stand, against the background of a board inscribed in big white letters "Glory to the Heroes of the Soviet Union." Dapper, tie-wearing Sigismund Levanevsky; slim mustached Mavriki Slepnev with a white cap; Vasili Molokov in a grayish shirt open at the neck and a double-breasted suit with a button missing. There is big Michael Vodopyanov in an ill-fitting jacket whose sleeves are too short, and a smiling bushy-haired Anatol Lyapidevsky. Standing at attention, ill at ease it seems, is Ivan Doronin, looking for all the world

The first seven men to receive the title "Hero of the Soviet Union."

like an oversized shy schoolboy. In the middle of the group, his high-booted legs crossed nonchalantly, is Nikolai Kamanin.

The voyage of the *Chelyuskin* had not been entirely in vain. Engineers had studied the battered freighter with instruments and those three hundred yards of special wire procured with so much effort by Ivan Kopusov. Now they knew what parts of a freighter are exposed to greatest stress and got an idea of how ice-going ships should be redesigned. Scientists had gathered valuable data, and the airlift had planted the seed of a thought in the mind of Otto Yulevich Schmidt. Like Amundsen and Wilkins before him, he also considered the North Pole a weather kitchen. Seas composing the Northern Sea Route are only bays of the Arctic Ocean, and atmospheric conditions prevailing around the North Pole determine ice and weather along these waters. Weather prognostication was essential to shipping along the Northern Sea Route, but reliable forecasts had to be based on meteorological data gathered in polar regions. Since no land exists near the North Pole, it was not possible to obtain such data from fixed land-based stations. But wasn't it possible to establish an observation post on ice? Why couldn't planes take a group of scientists and their instruments to a preselected floe near the Pole? Such a party could establish a drifting station and transmit the meteorological data essential for long-range weather and ice forecasts.

Schmidt was not the originator of such an idea. Fridtjof Nansen had conceived it, and Storker Storkerson had already translated it into reality on a limited scale. The Soviet Union had proposed the establishment of a drifting polar weather station as a project for the International Polar Year 1932, but at that time it was rejected as too expensive.[79] Now, backed by his own experience and in the light of rapidly advancing technology, Schmidt could reconsider such a project.

Later in the year, with the memory of tumultuous receptions accorded members of the *Chelyuskin* still fresh, a repaired icebreaker *Litke* entered the Chukchi Sea. Sixty-nine days later, the ship was moored in Murmansk, after a successful east–west crossing of the Northern Sea Route. With this voyage the period of probing and stumbling was definitely at an end.

Within limitations imposed by lack of adequate long-range ice and weather forecasts, traffic on the Northern Sea Route increased. In 1935, seven ships made complete through voyages and the waterway carried 17,175 metric tons of goods as imports to Siberia.[80] There was a lively exchange of locally produced raw materials; nomadic tribes started settling around newly established weather stations and trading posts; isolated villages grew into towns as roads were built and exploitation of local resources increased. Schools and hospitals were established, bringing once primitive tribes the benefits of science and civilization.

Schmidt, the chief of Glavsevmorput, knew, however, that before the

Northern Sea Route could become a truly important and dependable waterway, there was a need for much more knowledge of polar weather conditions, their fluctuations, and seasonal changes. Laws governing the drift of ice had to be determined because of their direct bearing on navigation along the Northern Sea Route; terrestrial magnetism had to be better understood to facilitate high-latitude flying. Once this was done, transpolar flights between Europe and America could become reality and the earth, no longer a cylinder, would become truly—and permanently—a sphere.

The idea of a drifting polar weather station was past the stage of mere talk. Experienced pilots were available, technology had advanced sufficiently, and an all-out scientific assault on the North Pole was now within the realm of a practical possibility.*

---

* See Appendix 5.

VI. TRANSFORMATION
1936-1963

1

THE seat of the Northern Sea Route administration is in an old sprawling building in Moscow's Rasin Street. There, in a stuffy room choked with heavy old-fashioned furniture, was the office of the Chief Administrator, Otto Yulevich Schmidt. Approaching the heavy oaken door leading into the studio, Michael Vodopyanov knew that he has been called for a good reason.

"So, you have been dreaming of a flight to the North Pole?" Schmidt asked, smiling.[1]

"Yes, indeed," Vodopyanov said. "My ambition is to fly to the Pole . . ."

Letting his long fingers run through a graying beard, Schmidt went on: "You are ambitious and that is exactly why I asked you to come here. Your dream may soon come true. The Government has directed us to begin organization of a scientific station on a drifting icefloe in the North Pole area. We will have to fly men, cargo, and scientific equipment to the Pole. . . . I want you to draft a plan for the flight."

Vodopyanov was caught up by inner excitement as he saw himself at the threshold to new achievement. The Revolution had done well by big Michael Vodopyanov. Thwarting his ambition to become a shepherd, it had made him a pilot instead and a Hero of the Soviet Union as well.

"Thank you, Otto Yulevitch," he said, rising, "you will have the draft."

Before long, Vodopyanov was back in Schmidt's stuffy office, carrying a manuscript entitled *A Pilot's Dream.*

"But that's a whole book," a surprised Schmidt said. Shifting from one foot to the other, the pilot answered uneasily: "I don't know how to write official reports, but you will find everything there . . ."

Within a month Vodopyanov was called again to the office of Otto Schmidt. "The Government has approved the plan," Schmidt said. "I have read your manuscript, Mikhail Vasilevich, and I like it. Go ahead with your plans. First of all fly to Franz Josef Land and choose a base nearer the Pole. The flight will no doubt give you a lot of experience."

Michael Vodopyanov would be the first man to fly a plane from the continent to the archipelago of Franz Josef Land. There, on Rudolf Land, northernmost Russian territory—from whence Cagni had taken off in his unsuccessful quest for the Pole, and where lay the remains of unsuccessful explorer Georgi Sedov—he would find a base suitable for an aerial expedition to the North Pole.[2]

At the Gorbunov factory four powerful airplanes were ordered which embodied in their design innovations proposed by a mechanic named Bassein and a parachute brake suggested by Vodopyanov. The Frunze works built twenty engines; the Institute for Public Nutrition prepared five tons of special concentrated, vitamin-enriched food. There were specially designed clothes and special lightweight tents with double walls and inflatable rubber floor. A powerful radio set was built under the personal supervision of Ernest Krenkel; scientific instruments were selected with meticulous care; special sledges were obtained; and guns, ammunition, oil and gasoline procured in adequate amounts.

Foreseeing the possibility of illness or disaster, the four men selected to man the proposed polar station took instruction in subjects not of their competence. Eugene Feodorov, 27-year-old geophysicist, learned how to be a radiooperator, Ivan Papanin studied astronomy and meteorology, and Peter Shirshov, a hydrobiologist, took a one year course in medicine and surgery.

In August 1936 the icebreaker *Russanov,* loaded with fuel, equipment, building material, spare parts, instruments, food, a tractor and caterpillar trucks, and carrying an expedition headed by Ivan Papanin set out for Franz Josef Land. Soon, in Teplitz Bay on gloomy, ice-covered Rudolf Island, a whole new village sprang up under Papanin's watchful eyes. There were warehouses, garages, a radio station, even a "splendid bathhouse." Twenty-four people were left to winter on the island, while the *Russanov* returned home.

On February 13, 1937, three years after the *Chelyuskin* had disappeared beneath the ice, and one year after submission of his initial proposal for a drifting polar station, Otto Schmidt obtained final sanction of a simple but daring plan at a Kremlin conference with the highest ranking members of the Soviet Government.

Schmidt's plan: As soon as local weather turned favorable on Rudolf Island, a reconnaissance flight was to be made as far north as the 85th or 86th parallel, to report on weather and ice encountered. Once favorable conditions were reported along the route, four special planes were to take off on their final mission, a landing at the Pole. Leaving a fully equipped and provisioned scientific party at the Pole, the planes and all other members of the expedition were then to return to the mainland.

Organization of the first Government-sponsored aerial North Pole expedition was soon completed. Leader-designate was Otto Schmidt, his deputy was Mark Shevelev, chief of the Polar Aviation Department. Vodopyanov was appointed chief of the Air Section.

The expedition numbered forty-five men. Included were pilots Babushkin, Molokov and Alexeiev as well as ace navigator-pilot Ivan Spirin, who usually was in charge of the spectacular May Day air-parades over Moscow. In all, there were ten pilots, five navigators, thirteen mechanics, three engineers, three radio operators, and a meteorologist. Also part of this history-making group were two journalists—*Izvestia's* E. Vilensky and *Pravda's* Lazar Brontman—as well as Mark Troianovski, the movie cameraman, who had prematurely disembarked from the *Chelyuskin,* thus missing a chance to film the dramatic sinking of the freighter.

On March 22, five orange-painted planes took off from Moscow's airfield, which was muddy in the wake of the first stirrings of a premature spring.[3] They were on the first lap of a northward trip of some 2,700 miles. They flew over water and land, intermittently covered by fog and clouds, while being buffeted by winds of cyclonic strength. Four of the aircraft were big, heavy four-engine planes. In the cockpit of the flagship USSR N-170 were Chief Vodopyanov and copilot Babushkin.

The USSR N-166, the fifth aircraft, was a twin-engined scout plane in charge of pilot Peter Golovin.

After some twenty hours of flight, in twenty-nine days filled with waiting, boredom, excitement, expectation, and anticipation, men and planes finally reached, in four laps, Teplitz Bay on desolate Rudolf Island. There to greet them was a wintering party of twenty-four men and a very dead bear. Frozen stiff, a red band around her waist, the bear was holding in her paws salt and a loaf of bread—traditional symbols of welcome—and a key inscribed "Key to the Pole."

Schmidt's expedition was now approximately 600 miles from the top of the world. The engines were overhauled and tested, skis were substituted for landing wheels, thirty-five drums of gasoline were hauled over the ice to each plane. After three days of hard work, preparations for the polar flight were completed, but wind and low-lying clouds caused further delay. Vodopyanov remembered Nansen's saying: "Patience is the greatest polar virtue."

Two light planes for short-range reconnaissance and weather observation flights arrived from Tikhaya Bay.* Schmidt's expedition now had seven planes on Rudolf Island. To reduce the total weight of each plane to a safe 25 tons, the upholstered seats were thrown out; tools, spare parts, and personal belongings had to be left behind; even gasoline supplies had to be reduced.[4]

The waiting went on. Finally, at six o'clock on the morning of May 5, Golovin's orange-colored twin-engine plane was ready for takeoff. A six weeks' supply of food was aboard and the tanks held some 830 gallons of gasoline.

Golovin, conscious of a historic mission, took Vodopyanov aside.

"If I reach the 88th degree and see that I have enough gas for a flight to the Pole and back," he asked, "what should I do?"[5]

There was a moment's hesitation before Vodopyanov answered: "If your gas lasts and the chief does not order you back, make straight for the Pole."

---

* Tikhaya Bay is on Franz Josef Land. These planes had been brought in by ship.

"And suppose I land there?"

"That's your business."

"What would you do if you were me?" Golovin insisted.

"Frankly," Vodopyanov answered, "if the ice on the Pole is good, I'd land without hesitation . . . and report the weather. But, remember, this conversation has never taken place and I know nothing about it."

Golovin nodded. The weather looked good and he had enough fuel for thirteen hours of flight.

A tractor pulled the plane to the airstrip. Soon the propellers of the twin-engined plane started turning and its motors began roaring. Gliding down an icy hill, rapidly gathering momentum, the USSR N-166 rose into the air at 11:23 A.M., May 5, 1937.

The engines of the four big planes were started, while Golovin sent laconic reports at thirty-minute intervals: "83°. Clear. Visibility good. Going ahead." . . . "Crossing 85°. Clear. Visibility good. Steering by sun compass and radio beacon. Ice rough but there are smooth surfaces for landing. Going ahead." "Approaching 86°. Cirrus clouds on my left. Engines working smoothly. Calm. Everybody in excellent spirits." "88°. Facing a blanket of clouds. Decided to climb above them to see their extent and nature . . ."[5]

Pilot Golovin has reached the latitude at which Amundsen, Riiser-Larsen, Ellsworth, and three others had come down to begin a twenty-five-day fight for survival almost twelve years before. Peter Golovin, at age twenty-eight, was less than ninety miles from the North Pole "Flying over a thick cloud bank, 7,000 feet high. Sixty to sixty-five miles from the Pole. Going ahead . . ."

"Ahead?" somebody asked. "He won't have enough gas, shouldn't we order him back?"

Vodopyanov, pencil in hand, had followed the flight on his map; he had calculated Golovin's gasoline consumption and was ready with an answer: "He has enough. Golovin has a head on his shoulders, and it's too late to order him back. Just try to get him to turn back with only sixty miles between him and the Pole. Personally, I wouldn't do it."

Schmidt nodded. "It would be almost impossible to make him come back now," he said, and, smiling, he added: "I wouldn't turn back, either I don't like knocking at a door without going in."

Entering the radio cabin, the meteorologist Dzerdzeyevsky had a serious look on his face. "Weather is getting worse," he said. "A high bank of clouds is moving in from the west, low-flying clouds may follow. . . Hard to say whether the island here will remain open . . ."[5]

Anxiety, mixed with disappointment, gripped Schmidt and Vodopyanov Should Golovin be recalled? Would he reach the Pole and then be unab to find his way back? The instructions they now radioed to Golovi were vague: "Take maximum height stop. See what ahead and return Rudolf . . ."[6]

Moments after sending the message, the radio operator was receiving Golovin's answer: "Flying over the North Pole, proud to have reached the top of the world in our orange bird. . . . Unfortunately Pole is obscured. . . . Impossible to break through. . . . Returning. . . . Not worried about weather on Rudolf. . . . Gasoline more than sufficient . . ."[7]

It was twenty-three minutes past four o'clock on the afternoon of May 5, 1937. A twin-engined Soviet plane with five men aboard was flying over the North Pole.

As an exhibition of courage, skill and ambition, Golovin's flight was a success, but the primary mission of the USSR N-166—to reconnoiter the way for the flight of a squadron to the Pole—was a failure. Rudolf Island and the ocean beyond were covered by a rolling sea of gray clouds, spewing penetrating mist and milky fog. The group flight to the North Pole was canceled.

The signal from Golovin's plane grew fainter. The pilot was approaching Rudolf Island, but, unable to find a break in the cloud cover, he lost his way. Hoping to spot the N-166 and to lead Golovin down to the airfield, Vodopyanov went up in the short-range U-2 plane; he circled the edge of a huge cloudbank for some twenty minutes and then returned. Later Mazuruk went up, but he could not find Golovin either.

Six hours had passed since the first Soviet plane had circled the Pole. Golovin's radioman reported: "Keeping under clouds . . . cannot see Rudolf. Running out of gas . . . broken ice and canals below . . ."[7]

At 10:45 P.M., flying low over open water, Golovin saw a bonfire and brought the N-166 in from the west. Gently he set the plane down, but it glided on the icy surface and raced on. Two mechanics jumped out of the moving plane and, grabbing the undercarriage, broke the forward momentum of the aircraft. They brought the plane to a halt at the very edge of a steep cliff leading into the sea.

Soon the smiling Golovin, taking a deep puff on a cigarette, was surrounded by fellow members of the expedition. "I did get nervous when we drifted off course," he conceded. "It was touch and go—we even had to pump the last bit of gas with a handpump. Only when the plane came to a stop, did I feel tired . . ."

On Rudolf Island fog and blizzards kept chasing each other, and Schmidt's planes remained buried in deep snow. The expedition leader changed his original plan. Weather conditions at the North Pole being so changeable, he did not think it wise to have all four planes take off at the same time. Instead, Vodopyanov's flagship USSR N-170, carrying an advance party, was to fly ahead and land near the North Pole, from whence it could relay weather information to Rudolf Island by radio. When suitable flying conditions developed in the polar area, the remaining planes would take off and bring additional supplies and equipment. The advance party of thirteen men was to include Schmidt, the pilots Vodopyanov and Babushkin, the navigator Spirin, Papanin's four-man scientific group, and motion-picture photographer Troianovski.

There was more waiting and more studying of weather charts. Then one of the light planes, while on a reconnaissance flight, was caught in a snowstorm and forced to make an emergency landing on a floe. Golovin then flew in search of the missing plane and also had to come down on the ice.

By May 15 Schmidt's group has been on Rudolf Island for almost a month. Gasoline stores were dwindling, two planes and six men were marooned on drifting floes, and the main body of the expedition was still some six hundred miles from the Pole. Four days later, on May 19, everything looked brighter again: Both missing planes returned undamaged, and the meteorologist predicted good flying weather for the following day.

On May 20 reconnaissance flights confirmed the meteorologist's prediction and Vodopyanov's USSR N-170 was dug out and made flight-ready, Journalist Brontman noted:

> Ice had to be . . . scraped out of innumerable grooves with steel scrapers, it was a devil of a job and terribly boring.[8]

The following day thirteen men piled into the orange-colored four-engine plane on Rudolf Island. Vodopyanov opened the throttle and propellers whirled; the USSR N-170 moved down an ice-covered hill, gathered speed and became airborne. The pilot circled, soared higher, and disappeared in a northerly direction, while members of the expedition who were left behind gathered around in the radio hut, tensely waiting for Vodopyanov's messages.

Flying over gaping pack ice, the plane crossed the 83rd degree of latitude toward 6 A.M., an hour later, at an altitude of 4,500 feet, Vodopyanov saw masses of rolling fog below, while dark clouds were closing in from above. "We decided to go ahead, and to turn back only if both layers merged and icing set in," he would remember.[9] Just then Bassein, a mechanic, noticed steam escaping from one of the engines. Approaching Schmidt, he whispered: "Within an hour, maybe less, the engine will be out of commission. There's a broken line and antifreeze is escaping. We'll have to make an emergency landing."

"You'd better tell the pilot," Schmidt said.

Bassein told Vodopyanov and received the answer he had anticipated. "We'll go ahead on three engines," Vodopyanov said. Locating the leak in a radiator, Bassein and his men started plugging it with damp rags. Then, pulling the rags out, they squeezed the precious antifreeze into a pail and poured it back into the leaky radiator, all the while working with bare hands at a temperature of 23° below.

The free lane between the two layers of clouds became narrower; then they merged. "Pretty bad, isn't it?" Babushkin shouted over the roar of the engines. Vodopyanov nodded.

They flew on blindly, past the 86th degree, the 87th. At the 88th parallel, less than a hundred miles from the Pole, the cloud curtain opened suddenly and Vodopyanov's plane was bathed in sunshine.

Spirin looked up from his navigator's table. "In twenty minutes we'll be at the Pole," he said. Vodopyanov started looking for a hole in the clouds below him, wondering whether the fog could possibly extend all the way down to the surface of the invisible pack ice. "The twenty minutes dragged on endlessly," he said later.[10]

Then, impassively and matter-of-factly, Spirin announced: "We are over the Pole." To make certain, the pilot flew on, over the top of the world. At 11:12 A.M. the radio operator in Teplitz Bay received a coded message from the flagship: "No. 34-1 . . ."[11] The message was incomplete; Vodopyanov's radio then remained silent, and anxious land-based operators went vainly through the range of their receiving sets. For hours insistent radio-borne questions remained unanswered. But all that had happened was that the transmitter of the USSR N-170 had gone out of commission.

Turning the plane, Vodopyanov throttled down, and from an altitude of 5,500 feet his heavy plane plunged into a sea of gray clouds. Slowly the altimeter needle dipped. 3,000 feet . . . 2,700 . . . 2,400 . . . 2,100. Through a hole in the clouds, ice appeared for a fleeting second and was swallowed up again in all-enveloping fog. At 1,800 feet the pilot finally broke through the opaque barrier. "Boundless sparkling icefields were seamed with blue lanes of open water," Vodopyanov would remember, "and the vast ocean looked as if it had been paved with slabs . . . resembling irregular geometrical figures drawn by the unsteady hand of a child."[12]

Gliding down, the pilot spotted a smooth stretch of ice, some seven hundred yards long. Circling, coming lower, Vodopyanov eased the engines and brought the plane down to within three feet of the ice. Then the skis of the USSR N-170 touched the virgin snow. Vodopyanov shut off the engines, Babushkin pulled the parachute ripcord, the plane slid on for about 250 yards and then came to a standstill.

It was 11:35 A.M. of May 21, 1937, nine years, almost to the day, after the crash of the *Italia* on pack ice.

While gloom reigned at the fog-shrouded base on Rudolf Island, where the other members of Schmidt's party remained in the grip of choking inactivity, there was animated activity on the floe near the North Pole. Men were busy securing the plane, pitching a tent, erecting an aerial, and uncrating Krenkel's powerful radio. While the batteries, which had gone dead in the cold, were being recharged, Chelyuskinite radioman Sima Ivanov, frustrated in the moment of triumph by a defective transformer, kept tinkering with his weak transmitter. "I've been listening to Rudolf," he said. "They are calling incessantly."

"Don't listen," Vodopyanov suggested, "and you won't worry . . ."[13]

Suspense, fear and anxiety in the radio hut on Rudolf Island were suddenly erased toward 10 P.M. by the loud cry of a tired radio operator, suddenly wide awake and leaning over his set, yelling: "They've landed, they've landed, the devils . . ."[14]

Recorded with numb fingers in the radio log on Rudolf Island, was the first message transmitted by Ernest Krenkel: "88 Kolia,"* followed by 26 reassuring words. A few minutes later, carefully phrased in official language by meticulous Professor Schmidt, radio message No. 1 from the North Pole was received. The following day the first weather report was broadcast from what was to become known as NP-1.†

On May 25 Schmidt radioed to cloud-covered Rudolf Island, swept by a 50-mile-an-hour wind: "Marvelous weather, sun, cloudless sky, recommend you fly."[15] Again an altitude flight was made to check the thickness of local clouds, again a plane went on long-range reconnaissance. A moderate cloud cover was found within a 200-mile belt abound Rudolf Island; beyond there were clear, sun-bathed skies.

By ten o'clock in the evening all planes on Rudolf Island were ready. First to take off, at the controls of the USSR N-171, was Vasili Molokov. With him, in a plane choked with equipment, food and supplies, were nine men. Following him was the USSR N-172, in charge of Alexeiev, and bringing up the rear in the USSR N-169 was Ilia Mazuruk, who had already flown more than 44,000 miles in the Soviet Arctic, carrying mail and passengers.

Some seven hours later, guided by Krenkel's radio, Molokov landed at the drifting weather station, on a runway which had been prepared under Babushkin's supervision. Alexeiev, unable to find Schmidt's camp and anxious to conserve fuel, came down on a floe some four miles from the Pole, Mazuruk landed thirty miles away.

On May 27, after a twenty-three minute flight, Alexeiev's plane landed at the polar station, whose population thus increased to twenty-nine men. Alexeiev brought in food, rubber containers holding 260 gallons of gasoline, and a big black tent inscribed: "USSR drifting station of the Northern Sea Route Administration." Among the new arrivals was *Izvestia's* correspondent Vilensky, who said later:

---

* Unofficial code for "love and kisses."
† NP-1 stands for (North Pole 1). The Russians called it SP-1 (*Severny Polus*-1).

. . . to some extent we were disappointed. The icefloe did not betray in any way its respectable geographical standing . . .[16]

Pravda's Lazar Brontman added:

We lost all consciousness of time. It was light all through twenty-four hours. Whatever the time, the sun was always at the same height, there was neither east nor west or north. Everywhere, in all directions, on all sides, there was only south . . .[17]

The camp was transformed into a settlement. In the middle of the floe stood the newly erected tent for Papanin's wintering party. Called the "Government House," it was furnished with "real beds, a real table and real chairs." An electric bulb was suspended from the ceiling, its current supplied by a windmill and dynamo.

A routine was established, scientific work got under way. Only the supplies aboard Mazuruk's plane were still missing. On June 5 flying conditions in the polar region improved. Mazuruk took to the air, and, guided by instructions transmitted by Krenkel, the USSR N-169 came down on Schmidt's flag-marked floe. First to leave the confines of the overloaded plane was Papanin's four-legged friend, "Vesioly (Jolly)" who barked gaily as he ran toward his master, obviously enjoying his newly found freedom. For Mazuruk and his men, ten days of enforced confinement on a rugged floe had come to an end. Those had been days filled with the physical labor of leveling sixty-eight hummocks while waiting for favorable flying conditions.

At last, Papanin's assortment of instruments and his stores of supplies were complete. The total cargo brought to the drifting floe approximated 10 tons, and included a portable typewriter as well as a rubber stamp. Now the stage was set for the supporting party to return to the mainland, leaving Papanin and his men on the floe to record and report weather conditions in the polar basin and to conduct other scientific studies.

In the morning of June 6, Schmidt, standing on a sled in the middle of what was called the floe's "Red Square," made a high-flown speech. Then Papanin made a speech, Soviet Russia's Red Flag was hoisted on a staff, and three volleys from guns and pistols were fired into the air. After the "International," sung by thirty-five voices, had died down, Schmidt concluded the ceremony: "I hereby declare the North Pole drifting station open," he said.[18]

Soon sixteen propellers were whirling, and the roar of sixteen motors shattered the arctic silence, as one by one the men climbed into the planes. As the planes took to the air, four courageous men and a barking dog were left on the floe: Ivan Papanin, aged forty, a man with great arctic experience; Chelyuskinites Ernest Krenkel and Peter Shirshov; and twenty-seven-year-old geophysicist Eugene Feodorov, specializing in the study of terrestrial magnetism.

Running low on gas, Alexeiev made an intermediate landing near the 83rd parallel, while the other planes flew on to Rudolf Island. Two days later, Golovin landed near Alexeiev's N-172 and delivered more fuel. On June 9, Schmidt could report to Moscow that all the expedition's planes were back on Rudolf Island.

While three planes and a six-man detachiment headed by Mazuruk were left in Teplitz Bay, ready should Papanin's group need help, the main body of Schmidt's expedition took off for Moscow. Among the high-ranking members of the Soviet Government who gathered at the airport to greet Schmidt and his men was a pudgy man with a wart on his nose: Nikita Sergeievich Khrushchev, a little known member of the Communist Party's Central Committee. There were the usual festivities, speeches and banquets. Medals were passed out, and cash awards, and eight men were given the title "Hero of the Soviet Union."

2

WHILE Schmidt and his party were on their way to Moscow, a three-man team of Soviet aviators set out on another spectacular achievement. Valery Chkalov, Georgi Baidukov, and Alexander Belyakov were ready to pioneer a transpolar air route between Russia and the United States. Such a route would not exceed 6,000 miles; whereas by way of the Pacific, Moscow is separated from San Francisco by some 9,300 miles and the distance across the Atlantic is approximately 7,500. Their single-engined plane ANT-25 had already successfully made a 5,821-mile non-stop flight from Moscow to Nikolaievsk, for which each of the three men had received the title "Hero of the Soviet Union."[19]

At 1:04 o'clock in the morning of June 18, 1937, Chkalov, Baidukov, and Belyakov took to the air from Moscow's Shelkovo Airfield.[20] They passed over Kolyma Peninsula, flying between two layers of clouds; then they flew blind, eyes glued to their instruments, through solid walls of fog, holding their course for Rudolf Island. Icing set in; the plane quivered and shook. Baidukov opened the throttle and climbed higher. At 8,500 feet he broke through into sunshine which soon wiped off the ice from the windowpanes and the body of the redwinged monoplane.

As if determined to bar their progress, new clouds gathered; the plane climbed higher. In the rarefied atmosphere at 13,000 feet breathing became difficult; more ice formed, coating the wings; at the 76th parallel their altitude exceeded 16,400 feet. Guided by weather reports sent out by Papanin, the ANT-25 held to her northerly course. At 4:15 A.M. on June 19 Chkalov crossed the North Pole, invisible beneath a thick carpet of clouds.

Beyond the geographic Pole there was an area called "Pole of Relative Inaccessibility"—the region most difficult to reach. On June 19 it was

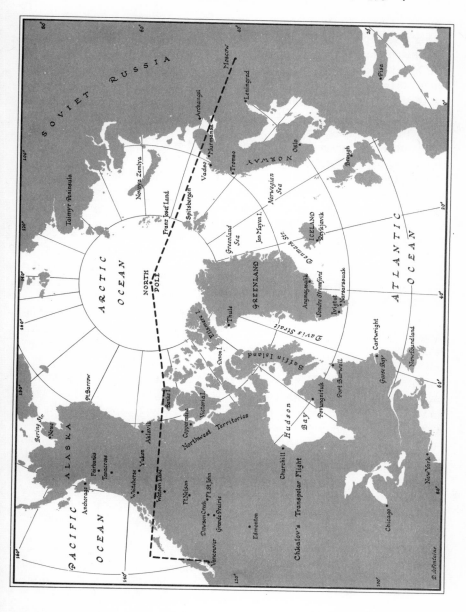

reached. Chkalov's was the first plane to span this ice-covered space. Fighting an approaching storm, the men climbed to 18,700 feet—maximum height the plane could achieve—yet clouds, whipped up by gusty winds, still hovered above them. They dodged, trying to skirt the storm, but caught firmly in the midst of humid grayness, they could find no escape. On they flew, blindly. Humidity condensed to ice. Reaching the thickness of a third of an inch, porcelainlike ice covered the plane. For three hours the squirming, shaking ice-sheathed plane fought the fury of the hostile elements before it emerged in view of Banks Island, once explored on foot by wiry Vilhjalmur Stefansson.

At 4:15 P.M. Canada's Pearce Point was rounded and, turning away from the Mackenzie River to avoid a new storm, the plane flew on at 15,500 feet. The portable oxygen supply was all but exhausted, water was escaping from the motor, the spare tank was frozen . . .

The Rocky Mountains were left behind, now Chkalov was flying over the Pacific Ocean. The oxygen gave out—fatigue, nausea gripped the men, and blood started spurting from Chkalov's nose. Night passed to the monotonous roar of a single engine and then came day, the day of fulfillment.

At 4:20 P.M. Greenwich time on June 20, 1937, Chkalov's redwinged plane rolled to a stop at Borax Airfield near Vancouver, Washington. It had stayed in the air for 63 hours and 16 minutes to cover 5,670 miles.[21] A historic flight was over.

Not unlike Lindbergh's spectacular transatlantic crossing, Chkalov's intercontinental flight—another testimonial to man's courage and endurance, and to the advance of technology—was but a trailblazing stunt. No commercial transpolar flights between Russia and America could possibly be planned for light single-engined planes. Successful pioneering flights by big planes, capable of carrying freight and passengers, were needed before the new route could be exploited commercially.

On July 12, 1937, Michael Gromov, a veteran of many long-distance flights, took off from Moscow in the RD 25-1, an especially modified monoplane. With him was a crew of two.[22]

At 2:07 in the morning of the following day the plane flew near Papanin's station and approximately one hour later it crossed the North Pole. Past the region of "relative inaccessibility," Gromov's men saw Prince Patrick Island. They flew over Canada, the Rocky Mountains, and reached the Pacific Ocean near Seattle. Continuing southward, past San Francisco and Los Angeles, they landed near San Jacinto, California. Lasting 62 hours and 17 minutes, their flight covered a distance of 6,305 miles.[23] Gromov and his men air-linked the Soviet Union and the United States via the transpolar route, breaking by approximately 648 miles the record for long-distance flights, held by Rossi and Codos for almost four years.

With this flight the stage was set for the next milestone in polar aviation: A transarctic intercontinental crossing by a multiengine plane able to carry passengers. Plans were already drawn up and a crew was standing by. The flight commander was Sigismund Levanevsky. He had never felt that his part in the rescue of the Chelyuskinites called for the award of "Hero of the Soviet Union." He felt the need for reassertion, and the idea of a pioneering flight from Moscow to Los Angeles was uppermost in his mind. In 1935 he had set out on such a flight, only to be stopped by a broken oil line some 900 miles out of Moscow. A year later he had made an 11,800-mile flight from Los Angeles to Moscow by way of Seattle, Fairbanks, and Nome, across Bering Strait, the Chukchi Peninsula, and Siberia.[24]

Exactly a month after Gromov's takeoff, on August 12, 1937, Levanevsky's N-209, a powerful four-engine aircraft, capable of carrying cargo and passengers, took to the air. In addition to Levanevsky there was a hand-picked five-man crew aboard. For the first 2,000 miles everything went according to plan. At 1:40 P.M there was a message from Levanevsky's N-209:

> Passing over the North Pole. Had a hard time getting through. . . . Altitude 20,000 feet. . . . Windshield iced. Headwinds in spots. Sixty miles an hour.[25]

After that, radio contact became spotty. When the plane was some 300 miles on the Alaskan side of the Polar Ocean, a dispatch came through:

> Message No. 19. Motor 34. Flying against 100-kilometer wind, losing altitude from 6,000 to 4,300 meters . . .[26]*

There followed a jumble of signals, interpreted by only one of the listening stations: "48-3400." Then there was silence.

Decoded, "motor 34" meant "engine trouble," and "48-3400" stood for "we are going to land in. . . ." The message, hauntingly incomplete and inconclusive, had a heavy tail of silence. Nothing more was ever heard from the N-209 and only questions remained. "Going to land in. . . ." Did that mean "in a minute"? Did it mean "in an hour"? Did it mean "in water," or "in Fairbanks"?

The plane's estimated time of arrival in Fairbanks came and passed. With every succeeding minute hope for the safety of Levanevsky and his men lessened. Soon it was drowned in certainty: Somewhere, somehow, disaster had struck the N-209 and crew.

---

* 100 kilometers = 62.1 miles. 4,300 meters = 14,100 feet.

An emergency meeting was called in the Kremlin. Present were high-ranking Government leaders and arctic experts. A decision was reached. Rescue operations were to be started immediately. Resources were to be marshaled in both the Eastern and Western Hemispheres. Otto Schmidt was placed in charge of all rescue efforts originating in the Soviet Union.

From the Soviet Embassy in Washington chargé d'affaires Constantine Oumansky placed a call to the Explorers Club in New York.[27] (Schmidt was one of its honorary members, filling the vacancy created by the death of General Adolphus Greely, and Levanevsky had been elected to life membership.) It was only natural that the club, with its resources and the pooled knowledge of its members, should be asked for advice and assistance by the Soviet Embassy, which had been charged by Moscow with initiating rescue operations from the American continent.

The rescue plan evolved in Moscow envisioned two Russian search parties: There was to be a western section, based on Rudolf Island (with an auxiliary base on Papanin's icefloe). Leader designate of this party was Shevelev, whose pilots were to be Vodopyanov, Molokov, and Alexeiev. There was to be an eastern section with headquarters on the *Krassin*. Provisioned with coal and gasoline, the icebreaker was to take on three planes and their crews at Cape Schmidt, make for Point Barrow and head as far north as ice would permit. (Ordered to take his seaplane USSR N-2 from Nogaevo Bay, via Uelen, to the *Krassin,* Pilot Zhadkov covered a distance of some 2,400 miles and reached Point Barrow within three days.) Pilots Golovin and Gratsiansky were to establish an additional base for rescue operations on Dikson Island.[28]

On August 14, barely two days after interception of Levanevsky's last message, co-operation was obtained from the Governments of the United States and Canada for an intensive air search to be based on the Western Hemisphere.[29] The Explorers Club, acting as a co-ordinating agency, suggested organization of an American rescue party in command of Sir Hubert Wilkins. The Soviet Embassy adopted the suggestion. Wilkins accepted the assignment, and his former associates in antarctic exploration—Hollick-Kenyon and Cheesman—were engaged as pilots. The Soviet Embassy bought the *Guba,* a Consolidated PBY twin-engined flying boat with a flying radius of 4,000 miles, selected by Wilkins. It was the only suitable aircraft immediately available. The Canadian and Russian Governments established an unprecedented weather information service in Fairbanks, and New York's Amtorg Corporation sent a co-ordinator to Alaska to take care of all details pertaining to necessary equipment and supplies.

On the assumption that Levanevsky might have landed—or crashed—on uninhabited Alaskan territory, the Soviet Government chartered a small plane from Canada's McKenzie Air Service. Its pilot, Robert Randall, flew along the Mackenzie River; then, turning westward toward Point

Barrow, he searched a 500-mile-long strip of Alaska's north coast for signs of the missing N-209. Wherever he saw people, he landed, hoping to gather some useful information. (His task was somewhat difficult. Eskimos like to tell strangers only things that may please them; so Randall had to avoid direct questions. Only in casual gossip about weather, ships, and planes could he hope to get a worthwhile clue).

Randall had little luck. Only from a group of natives on Barter Island did he pick up what sounded like a worthwhile clue. There, on August 13, some men had been butchering reindeer, when they heard what might have been the drone of a plane. Flying inland, Randall searched for the wreckage of a plane along the Brooks mountain range, but saw nothing. On September 1 this phase of the search was discontinued.

News of Randall's clue reached Joe Crosson in Fairbanks, and he set out on several search flights over Alaska's mountains. Other fliers did likewise. None of them found a trace of Levanevsky or his plane.

On August 21, eight days after Levanevsky's disappearance, the refitted *Guba* was on the north coast of Canada. Aboard was a five-man crew headed by Sir Hubert Wilkins.[30] A day later, with sufficient gasoline for 3,500 miles, the plane took off on the first search flight, which lasted 13½ hours.

Wilkins's sphere of search, as specified by the Soviet Government, was to extend between longitudes 90° and 153°, as far north as the famous 88th parallel. The *Guba* flew over cloud-hidden Melville and Banks islands. In the rarefied atmosphere at 10,000 feet, gasoline poured to the rim of spare drums expanded and overflowed. The two-inch-deep puddle of gasoline covered the cabin's floor. Again Wilkins was lucky—there was no explosion. But it took him two hours to soak up the gasoline with rags; eventually, the gasoline evaporated.

Over a 130-mile stretch on a northwesterly course from Prince Patrick Island only scattered patches of broken-up ice were visible. Everything else was bathed in fog. All night the *Guba* flew; every half hour the radioman called Levanevsky and for thirty minutes of each hour he listened. He listened in vain.

On the following day, making a 15-hour flight, the *Guba* went north as far as the 82nd parallel without sighting a trace of the N-209 or her men.

On August 25 three Soviet planes left Moscow and flew to Rudolf Island, which had been designated as the western base of Russian rescue operations. Mounted on wheels, the heavy planes could not take off from snow-covered Rudolf Island. Somehow only one pair of skis was available to be substituted for wheels, and only on October 6 was Vodopyanov able to take off in his lone N-170, to make an unsuccessful search flight for Levanevsky.

Wilkins's base was at Coppermine, in the Coronation Gulf, approximately 1,000 miles from where Levanevsky's last message had originated. To avoid useless shuttling under unfavorable weather conditions, a combined United States-Soviet meteorological service was established, to prepare 36-hour forecasts. Most valuable information received by this service was that coming from Papanin's drifting station.

On the third flight Wilkins had to make two intermediate landings on ice. The fog erased visibility, forcing a premature return to Coppermine. The distance covered in the first three flights exceeded 5,000 miles, but more than half of this had been blotted out by fog. The *Guba* burned gasoline at the rate of 75 gallons an hour and the fuel supply at Coppermine was disappearing rapidly. Wilkins decided to transfer his base to Aklavik, some 600 miles farther to the west.

On September 7 the *Guba* made her fourth search flight, zigzagging between 82nd and 85th degrees north and longitudes 135 and 150 degrees west, an area where the N-209 was most likely to have gone down. The flight lasted 20 hours and 40 minutes. There were no signs of Levanevsky.

On the fifth flight, September 17, Wilkins reached the 86th parallel before clouds and icing forced a return to the base. Thick weather prevented landing at Aklavik and the *Guba* came down on a lake some thirty miles to the east.

With this flight the first phase of Wilkins's effort was over. Winter was coming to the Arctic. Freeze-up, rendering a pontoon-equipped plane useless, was likely to set in any day. In five flights, spanning more than 13,000 miles of the Arctic Ocean, no trace of Levanevsky's plane had been found. During many hours of intent listening, the radio had brought no message from the lost fliers. His search for the six Soviet airmen temporarily halted, Wilkins and his five-man party of Australians, Canadians and one American returned to New York.

The Soviet Embassy in Washington, anxious to have Wilkins continue the search, bought another plane, fitted with skis. Smaller than the *Guba* and carrying only two men on long flights, it had a long cruising radius. In November Wilkins was back in the Arctic, to continue the search by the light of a midday moon. November passed, so did December, but weather in the Arctic was too bad for flying.

On January 16, Wilkins made his first moonlight flight. It took him only to the 78th parallel, where heavy clouds forced him back. Then time-consuming repairs on one of the plane's engines and unfavorable weather conditions forced postponement of flying until March. Two search flights leading over the mountains of northern Alaska and covering a distance of 3,100 miles convinced Wilkins that the Russians had not crashed there.

On March 10, Wilkins's group made an 11 hour 20 minute flight to the 82nd parallel. Four days later, under exceptionally good conditions of visibility, his plane completed a 3,300-mile round trip to the 88th parallel, which lasted 19½ hours. On neither flight was a trace of Levanevsky or his men sighted. Two more search sorties were planned, but Soviet Ambassador Troianovski informed Wilkins of his Government's decision to discontinue further efforts from the coasts of Alaska and Canada. Wilkins's rescue mission had been a failure. Yet, once more, failure had carried within it the germ of success: In 248 hours and 35 minutes of flight over some 34,000 miles of territory north of the Arctic Circle, Wilkins had demonstrated the adequacy of standard aircraft for arctic flying. He had actually explored an estimated 170,000 square miles of the Arctic Ocean, flying in summer and in winter, in the light of day as well as by moonlight—something that had never been done before.

Whatever their deeds and achievements in life, Levanevsky and the men who died with him possibly contributed more to the advancement of humanity than they could have done with success. They brought to life, even though for only a fleeting second of eternity, the spark of compassion and love for fellow men which transcends jealousies and glory-seeking ambitions. In death Sigismund Levanevsky succeeded where he had failed in life. He linked two great countries in the warm glow of brotherly love and international good will.[31]

Meanwhile, Papanin's party was still on their floe, which kept drifting relentlessly southward, moving faster than had been anticipated. By December 7, 1937, they had manned their station for 200 days and found themselves near Greenland. The men had sounded the depth of the Arctic Ocean 12 times, they had obtained water samples from 24 different locations and had made scientific observations with monotonous regularity. The Papaninites, all four of them elected, in absentia, to the Supreme Soviet of the U.S.S.R., celebrated New Year's Day of 1938 in the vicinity of the 80th parallel.

On January 26, a blizzard struck the floe. Papanin's tent was drifted over, its door blocked shut by a solid wall of frozen snow. With pick and shovel Feodorov dug a hole to go outside. When he broke through, a whirling cloud rushed into the tent, as if blown by a giant monster hiding behind a heavy curtain of falling snow. The tent filled with penetrating cold and dampness, as Feodorov went out to read his instruments. For five more days and nights the blizzard raged.

During the night of February 1, Shirshov and Feodorov were sleeping restlessly. At the table, in the middle of the tent, Papanin and Krenkel were playing a game of chess. The men found it hard to concentrate.

Now and again the tent shook, its frame creaked to the echo of dull, muffled thuds coming from outside, while a lone light bulb, suspended from the ceiling, kept on swaying.

"Listen," Papanin said. "They are getting closer! Shall we wake them?" Just then the ice trembled. "Petya! Zhenya!" Papanin yelled, jumping up without waiting for Krenkel's answer. "Get up . . . the ice may be cracking!"

When a new tremor came, Papanin's black queen fell over and rolled across the chessboard.

"Hear the crunching? We'd better go and look," Papanin said.

"Probably the roof settling under the snow," one of the men said.

"What snow? The whole tent is shaking, the walls may cave in any minute!"

Through a small hole Shirshov crawled out to have a look at what was going on outside. Close to the food depot he saw a newly formed crack in the ice.

"Shall we move the depot now?" Feodorov asked.

Papanin shook his head. "No," he said, "let's wait till morning. We've had cracks like this before; we'll just watch it. . . ."

Two hours later Shirshov saw that the crack had widened considerably. The men rushed outside, following the weak light of a lantern which was losing itself in the moist blanket of falling snow. With powerful blows of his fists, husky Papanin smashed the roof of the depot tent, crawled inside and started throwing out bags with clothes, boots, boxes of cartridges. Loaded on sleds, food and supplies were hauled away from the zone of immediate danger.

Feodorov noted in his diary:

> I saw another canal cutting us off from the east, under the howling blizzard our reliable ice field which had seemed to be so firm was slowly breaking up.[32]

There followed days of intense physical effort, with nerves keyed up and ears straining for new rumbles, each of which might be the ominous sound of a splitting floe. During this storm, radio contact was lost with the hydrographic ship *Murmanets,* which was patrolling along the edge of the floe.

In Moscow the men detailed to keep a long-range watch on Papanin's camp were worried. They knew what weather conditions were prevailing at the camp site, but, with radio contact broken, they did not know if the men on the floe were alive or not. Their decision came swiftly. According to plan, station "North Pole 1" was to be evacuated in March. Now, however, caught in a faster drift and relentlessly battered by storms, the floe was obviously breaking up. There was no point in hesitating. Resolute measures for evacuation of the Papaninites—if, indeed, they were still alive—were necessary. The icebreaker *Taimyr* was dispatched to Greenland, the icebreaker *Murman* was being readied, and orders went out to speed repairs on the icebreaker *Yermak*. *Murmanets*, the ship nearest to Papanin's camp, was directed to proceed on a rescue mission.

On February 3 the arctic storm died down and the sun broke weakly through a layer of clouds over Papanin's floe. Krenkel managed to restore radio contact with the outside, and the men could survey the new situation. Their ice floe, once big enough for four heavy planes to land on, was now reduced to a floating cake of ice some fifty yards long and thirty yards wide which was being tossed about mercilessly by an angry ocean. However, there was no panic on Papanin's floe. The men sat down and slowly sipped some hot tea, while listening to a radio account of plans being made for their evacuation.

Hope for rescue rested with the ships, but for ships to find and get through to a small drifting floe, air reconnaissance was needed. The *Taimyr* carried small planes, in charge of pilot Gennady Vlasov. The air detachment to go with *Murman* consisted of a ski-equipped P-5 (pilot: Ivan Spirin) and an amphibian SH-2 (pilot: Ivan Cherevichny). But it would take time for ships and planes to reach the waters of Greenland.

The *Murmanets,* suddenly and unexpectedly ordered to assume the role of a rescue ship, valiantly tried to bring help. She rammed obstructing ice barriers; stopped by heavy ice she retreated, and then hurled herself forward again.

From an ice floe near Greenland four bearded men hopefully waiting for rescue sent reassuring messages to their families. Ernest Krenkel wired his wife:

It so happens, Natasha, that I will come home sooner than you and I expected.[33]

Peter Shirshov, the anxious father of a newborn baby, said somewhat romantically:

The leads of open water make us glad, we are closer to meeting again.[33]

Although the sun was weak, the ice kept on melting. Sloshing through puddles, the men were wet, and shivered from cold as they loaded supplies, instruments, and equipment onto sleds.

On February 6 the four were awakened by a thunderous rumble. Neighboring hummocks were in motion. Closing in, they threatened to crush in a vicious grip what was left of "North Pole Station 1." Iceblocks tumbled onto the floe and, creeping on, pushed food and equipment ahead of them, like bulldozers burying everything in snow. When the movement of ice subsided, a new blizzard struck. Surveying the remaining stock of food, Papanin estimated that it might last for three months, provided, of course, that the inflated rafts in which the food was stored were not swallowed up by new canals, carried away, or smashed by ice.

On February 7, fully equipped, the *Murman* set out to sea, while members of a rescue party, headed by Schmidt, still waited impatiently for repairs on the icebreaker *Yermak* to be completed. The *Murmanets* was stopped by impassable ice some forty miles from Papanin's floe.

Once more the hostile elements unleashed their full fury against the four men and their floe. A violent snowfall limited visibility to three feet, a powerful wind kept knocking the men to the ice and tore their tents to shreds. By evening, with the storm spent, the men could see the bleak coast of Greenland outlined on the horizon by a pale moon. That night and those to follow, the Papaninites spent in a hastily built igloo.

The *Murmanets,* covered by a thick layer of ice, remained helpless. Firmly held by huge floes, the ship shuddered, her concrete deck cracked and her body broke. Emergency stores were assembled, the crew was alerted to prepare to abandon ship. Six days later the ship wrenched loose from the choking ice. Following an open lane, the *Murmanets* headed toward the shore of Greenland, only to become icebound again. In ten days she impotently drifted with the ice for a distance of 500 miles.

On February 8, the *Taimyr* was caught by a violent storm in the Sea of Norway. The ship, a maker of history in a distant prerevolutionary past, was old, weak and tired. Mountainous waves were breaking over her deck, threatening to wash overboard cargo and planes. Barrels filled with gasoline tore loose and started rolling on a deadly course like billard balls. But the storm passed and the ship entered the waters of the Western Hemisphere where she rode out the hurricane. She froze in and started on a slow drift into dangerously shallow waters. Her captain finally resorted to a desperate maneuver, reversed course, and so saved his ship.

On February 10, the ancient battered *Taimyr* established radio contact with Papanin's group. Krenkel tapped out:

> . . . ice is freezing into a solid mass. No place for airplane to land. . . .
> Often, when visibility is good, we see clearly the shores of Greenland.[34]

On February 12 the *Taimyr* entered an area of large floes and at night the glare of her searchlights was faintly visible in Papanin's camp. Rescue was only twenty-five miles away. The icebreaker *Murman* was also coming closer; Schmidt's expedition aboard the *Yermak* was headed northward, and a Soviet submarine was near the Greenwich meridian. Four surface vessels and a submarine were thus closing in along a semi-circle on what was left of "North Pole 1."

When the *Murman* and the *Taimyr* reached the edge of pack ice, air reconnaissance was needed to find an open passage. Taking off from an ice field, pilot Cherevichny flew out and returned after forty-five minutes without having sighted Papanin's camp. He refueled his plane and took off again.

Taimyr's pilot Vlasos also went up. Clouds gathered, visibility shrank, and a storm approached. Not daring to attempt a landing on the small floe near the *Taimyr,* Vlasos stayed in the air. After some two hours, he headed for the *Murman* and landed near by. He, too, had missed Papanin's camp.

Cherevichny was missing; he had not returned from his second flight. Fog was closing in around the *Murman.* Time was running out and no one heard the sound of Cherevichny's SH-2. The men on the *Murman* did not know it, but there was no need for concern. Unable to find his way back, the pilot had flown on and landed safely on an ice floe near Greenland.

On the following day the weather was better, yet there was still no sign of Cherevichny. Vlasov went in search of the missing SH-2. He set out and returned; he took off again and came back.

On his third flight Vlasov unexpectedly sighted Papanin's small ice floe and landed on it. There was an emotional meeting at the site of station "North Pole 1" off Greenland. Vlasov's success was a successful failure: Setting out to find Cherevichny, he had found Papanin instead. However, the pilot *had* seen an open channel through which ships could approach the camp from the west.

On February 17, two days after Cherevichny's disappearance, perseverance paid off for Vlasov. Methodically searching an area marked off into squares, he saw a small black speck on the ice. Recognizing the missing plane, he landed near by and soon returned to the *Murman,* bringing with him Cherevichny.

On February 18, guided by Vlasov from the air, the *Murman* and the *Taimyr,* were proceeding slowly toward station "North Pole 1," and came within sight of the camp. One day later the arctic silence was pierced by joyous hooting of whistles as the two ships, festively decorated with flags, dropped their anchors less than half a mile from Papanin's ice floe. One more arctic venture had come to an end. Men from both ships descended onto the ice, to be met by four brave pioneers who had spent 274 days on an ice floe drifting in the Polar Ocean.

Krenkel's radio dots and dashes submitted to the world a last report:

> We are infinitely happy that the work entrusted to us has been completed. . . . After covering more than 2,500 kilometers [1,552 miles] during 274 days of drift, we are this hour leaving this icefloe at latitude 70° 54′ North and longitude 19° 48′ West. . . . Papanin, Krenkel, Shirshov, Feodorov, North Pole Station, February 19, 3:55 P.M.[35]

There remained but the removal of equipment from the floe. Then the two ships started on their homebound journey, carrying aboard four men who had made good.

Congratulatory messages received aboard the vessels from Moscow were signed by fourteen leaders of the Soviet Union, including Nikita Sergejevich Krushchev. A little less than a month later, on March 15, the icebreaker *Yermak,* to which Papanin's group had been transferred, was moored in the harbor of Leningrad.

3

THE year 1937, which had brought Otto Schmidt many honors and an undisputed place in history as the organizer of the world's first drifting weather station near the North Pole, was a disastrous one for navigation along the Northern Sea Route. Sixty-six ships entered arctic waters of the Soviet Union, seven of them scheduled to complete through voyages in one season. There was a shortage of barges, tugs and cranes; coal in ports of call was of poor quality and in short supply; departure of some ships was delayed as long as 25 days; the duty icebreaker *Litke* did not leave Archangel until late in July; the *Krassin,* used in the search for Levanevsky, was not available for escort through most of the season, and for the same reason Glavsevmorput's air fleet was reduced to two short-range planes which could make only limited reconnaissance flights.[36]

These organizational deficiencies combined with unusually difficult ice conditions to disrupt navigation along the Northern Sea Route. As the end of the season approached, 26 ships were helplessly icebound. Among them were all but one of the eight serviceable icebreakers which Glavsevmorput had at its disposal. The only exception was the small thirty-nine-year-old *Yermak.*

When the ice loosened up somewhat, the *Krassin* freed itself and managed to liberate four other vessels. The *Yermak* extricated 17 ships, but three icebreakers could neither be reached nor could they free themselves.

In February of 1938, three big orange-colored planes, veterans of a historic North Pole flight, took off from Moscow again. Their destination was Tiksi Bay. Their route led over Siberia and their mission was to bring relief to the ill-clothed and poorly equipped men and women trapped on the icebound ships.

Near the ships, landing fields were cleared, but some of them broke up even before the planes arrived. On April 3, the aircraft landed on the unsatisfactory surface of one of these fields. The undercarriage of the leading plane was damaged and only twenty-two people could be airlifted that day.[37]

Then an advance base was established at Ostrov Kostenlny, some 600 miles closer to the three stranded ships. While one plane was detailed to ferry gasoline from Tiksi to the new base, the other two were preparing for another mass airlift. On April 18, eighty-three people were taken off the ships, and eight days later only the three eleven-man crews were left with their vessels. Barely four years after the spectacular aerial rescue of 102 Chelyuskinites, a total of 184 men and women were airlifted from the Arctic without fanfare or publicity. The planes brought in some four tons of badly needed supplies as well as some totally useless items such as spare parts for tractors and instruments for the study of soil samples.[38]

Late in August the icebreaker *Yermak* rammed its way through the ice and reached the stranded ships near the 84th parallel, less than 500 miles from the North Pole. No other ship had gone that far north under its own power. Two more icebreakers were liberated before the *Yermak* lost a propeller and had to beat a hasty retreat. The icebreaker *Sedov* had a broken rudder and was left in the midst of pack ice.

In the afternoon of August 30 the insignificant-looking *Sedov* found itself drifting alone in the white wilderness of the Arctic.[39] Aboard the ship was a reorganized fifteen-man crew, headed by hard-driving, twenty-seven-year-old Captain Badigin. Emergency stores were laid out on the ice, a laboratory was set up, and the men of the abandoned ship accepted the inevitability of passing another winter away from civilization. Two weeks later the *Sedov* received a terse message from newly commissioned icebreaker *Stalin:*

Get your engine ready, await instructions to raise steam.[40]

Captain Badigin had his doubts. He felt that one icebreaker would not be able to rescue his crippled ship; he thought that two of them would be needed. On September 17 the *Stalin* radioed:

. . . received Schmidt's permission to approach *Sedov* with two icebreakers . . .[40]

Hope and expectancy mounted among the men aboard the *Sedov,* as both the *Stalin* and the *Litke* were cutting their way through the ice. However, some 60 miles from the impotent ship the *Stalin* ran into steadily worsening ice conditions, gave up and turned back. So did the *Litke.*

Thus, on September 24, the *Sedov* was definitely left to its own fate at latitude 83°55′ North. Captain Badigin said later:

With every passing day, winds carried us farther into unexplored latitudes.[40]

Two days later some floes supporting the icebreaker shifted, ice unevenly caked to the bottom of the ship pulled the vessel to one side and it assumed a list of 18 degrees. Through a damaged outlet valve, now lying below ice level, water started pouring in and within an hour the list increased to a critical 30 degrees. At any moment freight might break loose and increase the list even more; at any moment the ship bearing the name of courageous explorer Georgi Sedov could break up and sink, leaving fifteen ill-equipped men in a hopeless situation.

In total darkness the engine was fired, pumps were started, cement was poured to seal off the valve. After eight hours of hard work the weary, cold and drenched crew had saved the ship.

Slowly continuing its drift north of the 84th parallel, the *Sedov* entered a region of the globe which was hardly known. Hydrologist Buinitsky was making astronomic observations, measuring gravity and magnetism, the crew kept on sounding the ocean and recording meteorological data.

From a radio message of Captain Badigin.

> Darling, don't worry, the ice is quite quiet now. We are preparing ourselves for the polar night. . . . Suggest you read Nansen's book about the drift of the *Fram*. To a certain extent it will give you an idea of our life.[41]

The drift lasted for 812 days and covered some 3,800 miles, carrying the improvised expedition aboard the little icebreaker to within 230 miles of the North Pole and crossing several times the path taken by Nansen's *Fram* forty-four years earlier. Depth soundings made during the drift confirmed the existence of a submarine ridge on the floor of the Arctic Ocean between Greenland and Spitsbergen and a wealth of scientific data was collected by the group of fifteen men who had been neither trained in advance nor selected for such a special mission.

Only in January 1940 would the powerful icebreaker *Stalin* finally approach the drifting *Sedov*. Recoaled, the ship would then proceed under its own power to Murmansk.

These disastrous operations along the Northern Sea Route in 1937 which resulted in the long immobilization of twenty-six ships, the loss of one freighter, and the drift of the *Sedov* led to purges within the Glavsevmorput. Men who only a few years earlier had been honored and proclaimed benefactors of the Soviet people were accused of incompetence, treason, and sabotage; department heads were branded enemies of the people and purged. Workers were dismissed or liquidated.[42] The structure of Glavsemorput was changed radically and its activities were restricted to conducting traffic along the Northern Sea Route. Schmidt remained Glavsevmorput's chief, but stocky Ivan Papanin became his senior deputy. Among those purged was Professor Samoilovich, head of Leningrad's Arctic Institute. Apparently accused of having devoted too much time to geology, stooped, walrus-mustached geologist Samoilovich was tried as an alleged enemy of the People—and acquitted. But under prevailing conditions of savage persecution he developed pneumonia and died, officially unmourned.[43]

(Another man died violently in 1938. Returning from Franz Josef Land, a four-engined plane crashed near Archangel. Among the dead was passenger Michael Babushkin, veteran arctic pilot.)

During the following year, while the *Sedov* continued its drift and war clouds were gathering heavily over Europe, Glavsevmorput's fleet was reinforced by two powerful Russian-built icebreakers. The total freight turnover along the Northern Sea Route reached 503,000 metric tons, and goods exported from the Siberian Arctic along this waterway amounted to 373,800 tons.[44]

The new icebreaker, *I. Stalin,* made history by accomplishing the double traverse in one navigational season and 1939 was called "the first year of normal exploitation." Molotov's earlier demand "to turn the Northern Sea Route into a normally working waterway, securing a regular link with the Far East," was fulfilled; Stalin's plan "to incorporate the wealth of the North into the socialist economy" had become reality.

And wealth there was: timber and furs for export; tin for domestic use; and for local needs there was coal and salt, so essential for preservation of fish.

Papanin became Glavsevmorput's chief, and at the Eighteenth Congress of the Communist Party he said:

> Tsushima will never be repeated. And, if need be, our naval squadrons will pass along the Northern Sea Route, [they] will pass along it in order to annihilate the enemy on his own territory, on his land and in his waters . . .[45]

Past its infancy, the commercial waterway originally developed for economic reasons was assuming strategic significance.

Take a map of the Arctic. Mark on it the most northerly points reached by ships and draw a circular line uniting them all. There, within a ring, lies the area of the Arctic most difficult to reach. It is the area of inaccessibility. In its center, some four hundred miles from the geographic North Pole and a few degrees east of the meridian of Bering Strait, lies the Pole of Inaccessibility, the spot theoretically most difficult to attain. It is without permanent geographic significance. As if reeling under the impact of man's progressive penetration, it shifts, being the center of an area which is only relatively difficult to reach. It was Stefansson who has first called it the Pole of Relative Inaccessibility.

Wilkins and Eielson reached it, Chkalov's single-engined plane flew over it, as did that of Michael Gromov. In December 1940 pilot Cherevichny, the same one who some two years earlier had failed to locate Papanin's station, set out to completely remove it. Twice, in August 1939 and again eleven months later, he and navigator Akkuratov had flown over it. Theirs had been long sorties (one lasting more than twenty-two hours) which were sandwiched in between routine ice reconnaissance flights along the Northern Sea Route. Now they proposed a revolutionary new technique for an expedition to the least known arctic region.

Their aircraft, Arctic veteran USSR N-169 (which navigator Akkuratov had directed toward the North Pole at the time when Papanin's drifting station was being established) was to become a flying laboratory. The ski-equipped plane, provided with all essentials, including a kitchen, was to take a ten-man group to the Pole of Relative Inaccessibility.[46]

In March 1941 the USSR N-169 flew along the whole length of the Northern Sea Route, passing over stretches which had never before been seen from the air in winter. The plane crossed Novaya Zemlya, Franz Josef Land, Severnaya Zemlya, and the Novosiberian Islands. Landing on Wrangel Island, Cherevichny planned to fly on into the Region of Relative Inaccessibility and land on a suitable floe, where his group would make scientific observations. On April 2, the flying laboratory took off from Wrangel Island. About seven hours later and some 1,000 miles farther north, at 81° northern latitude and 180° longitude, Cherevichny made a successful landing on a floe six feet thick, approximately one mile long. There, in five action-filled days, hydrologists sounded the depth of the ocean with special lightweight equipment; through a tent-covered hole ripped into the ice, they lowered bottles to obtain water from different levels of the sea below; they measured temperatures and studied the chemical composition of different samples. The group of scientists made magnetic, astronomic, and gravimetric observations, and then men, instruments and equipment were again taken aboard the plane and the party returned to Wrangel Island.

On April 13 a second leap was made for another four-day round of scientific studies. This one was to a point some 180 miles south of the previous landing. Nine days later, the laboratory was set up on a third floe in the Region of Relative Inaccessibility. When the party returned to Wrangle Island on April 28, the projected scientific work was completed and a new method in arctic research had been successfully inaugurated.

On May 11 Cherevichny brought the USSR N-169 to a safe landing in Moscow. The 68-day expedition, during which the plane had flown more than 16,000 miles, was over. Among the data gathered was valuable information on the speed and direction of arctic water currents. Scientists had evolved an entirely new conception of the anatomy of the Arctic Ocean.

The revolution in Arctic research which Nansen had started with the drift of his frozen-in *Fram* had been supplanted by a new method. Cheaper, faster, and easier, it allowed for much greater freedom in the choice of areas to be studied.

The next step was to have been a landing of several flying laboratories in different spots of the Arctic at the same time. But in 1941 the war which had broken out in Europe engulfed Russia and arctic research came to an abrupt halt.

In June of 1939, frail, gray-haired engineer Nobile, a self-styled "victim of Fascism," left Italy. Previously he had spent several years in Russia, trying to set up a dirigible construction program, but had succeeded only in building another replica of the *Italia* and had lost both the respect and support of his loyal assistant Trojani.[47] Returning to Italy, Nobile appealed to Pope Pius XI, who obtained for him an appointment at the engineering faculty of Lewis Holy Name School of Aeronautics in Chicago. Mussolini's Government classified the assignment as a "foreign mission," thus enabling Nobile to retain his professorship at the University of Naples and to continue receiving a salary for lectures he would never deliver.[48]

At dawn on September 1, German troops invaded Poland, on September 3 France and Britain declared war on Germany. On the following day DNL's general manager Riiser-Larsen was mobilized and donned again the uniform of a commander in the Norwegian Navy. "How long do you think you'll be wearing this?" Somebody asked. Riiser-Larsen had a ready answer: "Seven years," he said.[49] (Riiser-Larsen firmly believed that his life ran in seven-year cycles. In this instance, he was to be right.)

On September 8, President Roosevelt proclaimed a state of limited national emergency throughout the United States. Exactly one week later, Colonel Lindbergh, an active member of the National Advisory Council on Aeronautics, said in a speech in Des Moines that the Atlantic and Pacific Oceans constituted sufficiently formidable barriers to any invasion.[50]

On September 27, Warsaw surrendered and former Lieutenant Jan Nagursky, first man ever to fly in the Arctic, looked sadly at what remained of the city in which he had lived for so many years.

In the United States once more a proposal had been made to purchase Greenland because of its strategic location.[51] A Major J. K. Lacey was sent to make an aerial survey of the island, but even before his report could be fully evaluated, official Washington, still under the spell of Lindbergh's negative opinion, decided that the ice-covered and frequently fog-bound territory did not provide suitable sites for establishment of bases for the United States' armed forces.

At about this time Germany acquired some of the stock of the Icelandic Aviation Company, obviously for the purpose of assuming control of the Iceland–Greenland air route and eventually establishing an advanced base on which weather stations as well as facilities for submarines and military aircraft could be built.

On April 9, 1940, German troops invaded Denmark and Norway. Denmark capitulated, thereby forfeiting also her sovereignty over Greenland. Oslo put up a fight. From the roof of a building Commanders Riiser-Larsen and Lützow-Holm watched as German bombers landed at nearby Fornebu Airport. On April 26 the New York *Times* carried a short story headlined: "Riiser-Larsen reported killed defending civilian Oslo airport." Very much alive, Riiser-Larsen was encouraging reports of his death, while he kept watching, observing, and gathering information on the strength of German forces in Norway, their equipment, and their techniques. On the very day the *Times* printed the report of his death, he left Oslo for Sweden. Traveling by way of Moscow, Bucharest, Budapest, Milan, and Paris, he reached London. There it took him three days to pass on to the British the firsthand intelligence he had gathered. Soon he would be designated Commander-in-Chief of a Free Norwegian Air Force.

In the same month British troops occupied Iceland, thus forestalling a possible German invasion of that territory. On June 7 fighting in Norway stopped. But even before all fighting had come to an end, Goering's *Luftwaffe* established in the overrun country a base for its weather reconnaissance service. Using planes of the Heinkel III and Junkers 88 type, which had a radius of some 1,900 miles, the *Luftwaffe* would soon be using these bases for weather reconnaissance flights to the Fareoes and Iceland.[52]

Conquest of the two Scandinavian countries gave Germany control over their arctic territories: Greenland, Spitsbergen and rocky Jan Mayen Island. Located along the shortest air route from America to England, these sparsely populated land masses had, indeed, great strategic importance. They provided sites for the establishment of all-important weather stations and could be used as bases from which shipping lanes extending from the Western Hemisphere to Britain and northern Russia could be threatened effectively.

On June 10, Mussolini announced Italy's entry into the war. Nobile heard the speech at the Lockport airfield in Illinois. He did not choose to become a rallying force for opposition against Fascism among the millions of Italians scattered throughout the United States and the world. Instead, he returned to Italy and offered his services to Mussolini.

On June 14, German troops entered Paris, and eight days later an armistice was signed between France and Germany. Firmly entrenched, imbued with the myth of invincibility, German troops formed an unbroken ring from the Arctic to Bordeaux, from the English Channel to the Bug River.

Among those who chose to remain in German-occupied territory was mild-mannered, soft-spoken Adolf Hoel, Norway's foremost authority on Spitsbergen. He was dissatisfied. He should have been made a full professor a long time ago, he felt. He also disagreed with King Haakon's Greenland policy. He maintained that Norway should not have renounced her claims against Denmark for some territorial rights in Greenland. Soon Hoel was promoted to full professor and appointed rector of the Oslo university.[53]

Other men and other countries were determined to keep on fighting. On Toronto's City Island, a training camp for Free Norway's pilots was established. Nostalgically called "Little Norway," it was commanded by Riiser-Larsen, who was no longer wearing decorations bestowed upon him by Italy after the successful transpolar flight of the *Norge*. With him was one-legged Commander Finn Lützow-Holm,[54] who had participated in the searches for Nobile and for Amundsen and had later gone with Riiser-Larsen to explore the Antarctic.*

As summer came and passed into fall, the *Luftwaffe* was carrying on devastating air attacks against England, and German long-range planes were sighted over Greenland.

On his own initiative, William H. Hobbs, an eminent geologist who had headed the Michigan University expedition to Greenland, went to Washington to argue vociferously with the authorities about the importance of that territory for the security of the United States.[55] America's frontier could be pushed northward, he kept insisting, if air bases were established in Greenland, both to deny use of that territory to German forces and to forge links in a lifeline extending from America, "the arsenal of democracy," to beleaguered Britain. Eventually Hobbs's arguments would override the negative attitude of Washington officials, who based themselves on the critical report submitted by Lindbergh following his 1933 aerial survey of Greenland.

In September, Germany moved in on the Arctic. A meteorologist named Holzapfel was sent aboard the *Sachsen* to the sea lying between Iceland and southeastern Greenland, to gather and transmit essential weather data to the German High Command.[56] "Operation Holzapfel" lasted successfully for 76 days; then, in the spring, the ship returned to Denmark Strait, to study ice conditions, mine fields, and the flight routine of Allied aircraft. The *Sachsen* kept sending reports for 86 days, without ever being detected. She provided the information which was essential for the spectacular dash of the German battleship *Bismarck* across waters controlled by the British.

Soon the *Fridtjof Nansen*, a small sloop which had escaped German-

---

* See Appendix 1.

occupied Oslo and was now fighting for Norway's Government-in-Exile, intercepted two vessels loaded with essential supplies, which had been sent out by the Germans to reinforce their weather stations functioning in Greenland. To deny the enemy this weather information originating in Greenland, the *Fridtjof Nansen* steamed to the east coast of that island and destroyed three of the meteorological posts functioning there. A new weather station, manned by personnel loyal to the Allies, was established in Eskimonaes. The *Fridtjof Nansen* then proceeded to evacuate a small party from Jan Mayen Island, which had been sending valuable meteorological information to Germany via Tromso.

England needed weather information just as badly as Germany and mere elimination of these meteorological outposts was not sufficient. Soon both countries made plans to reactivate the weather service on Jan Mayen Island. In November, a German trawler was intercepted in Denmark Strait while on her way to that island. The vessel was beached, but weather and ice conditions combined to prevent the British from landing their own party and re-establishing a weather station on Jan Mayen. Only in March 1941 would a twelve-man group of Norwegians arrive from Iceland, to land on the 140-square-mile rocky territory, which by then had been given the mysterious designation "Island X." Although spotted by German planes, strafed and bombed, the Norwegians stayed. In May the party was increased to thirty, and by July 1941 the island was firmly controlled by a garrison which had been further reinforced and provided with essential equipment as well as antiaircraft defenses.

4

ON October 16, 1940, men throughout the United States registered for the draft and somehow the war seemed to be much nearer. In February 1941, Germany mounted an air attack on Iceland, emphasizing its strategic importance. With Iceland as a base, Germany could play havoc with convoys headed for England and could even become a menace to the North American continent. On April 9, 1941, Danish career diplomat Henrik de Kauffman concluded on his own responsibility, in defiance of German occupation authorities in Denmark, an agreement with Secretary of State Cordell Hull whereby the United States was permitted to establish and defend military bases in Greenland.

Eske Brun, Greenland's governor, undertook to secure his island for the Allies. He ordered evacuation of the eastern coast north of Scoresby Sound (a task which proved not too difficult because that region was inhabited only by twenty-six men and one woman). He also organized scouting patrols and saw to it that weather stations serving the Allied war effort kept on functioning.

An American survey party dispatched to Greenland found a site suitable for an airfield at Sondre Strom Fjord, where Professor Hobbs had had his headquarters, and another one at Narsarssuak, so called by natives because it means "great, flat place." A United States task force was sent there, a weather station was established, barracks for the men, warehouses, hangars, and machine shops were erected. Docking facilities were created, a runway was cleared, and Narsarssuak was code-named Bluie West 1. In time Bluie West 1 would become the principal link in a northern air route leading from the United States to Labrador, Greenland, Iceland and England.

German long-range weather reconnaissance planes were sighted over eastern Greenland, some of them even venturing as far as Narsarssuak. In a fireside chat of May 27, 1941, President Roosevelt said:

> The battle of the Atlantic now extends from the icy waters of the North Pole to the frozen continent of the Antarctic. Throughout this huge area there have been sinkings of merchant ships in alarming and increasing numbers. . . . There have been sinkings even of ships carrying neutral flags. There have been sinkings . . . between the Azores and the islands off the American coast; and between Greenland and Iceland. Great numbers of these sinkings have been actually within the waters of the Western Hemisphere. . . . Most of the supplies for Britain go by a northerly route, which comes close to Greenland and the nearby island of Iceland. . . . Nazi occupation of Iceland or bases in Greenland would bring the war close to our continental shores; because they are stepping stones to Labrador, Newfoundland, Nova Scotia, and the northern United States . . .

On June 22, 1941, German troops invaded Russia. While outnumbered, ill-equipped Soviet forces were being annihilated, the whole nation was being mobilized. Among those called into service was arctic pilot Michael Vodopyanov, who was given the rank of colonel. He set out to organize an air division and on the night of August 10 he led a group of planes on a thirteen-hour round-trip flight to bomb Berlin.[57]

On July 7 American marines landed in Iceland to reinforce British troops already there; in August President Roosevelt met with Winston Churchill and signed, aboard the battleship *Prince of Wales,* the Atlantic Charter, a joint declaration of principles.

In August 1941, while Britain was staggering under devastating German air assaults and while stubbornly resisting Russian forces were reeling under the overwhelming might of German tanks, war came to Spitsbergen. It was a silent war, not heralded by blazing headlines; if reported at all, its story was contained in short accounts, which were printed after great delays. Yet, it was a war fought by men who had to be strong, courageous and resourceful, men of stamina who could fight the enemy as well as the weather and who could withstand the oppressive loneliness of monotonous lifeless icy deserts.

The vast arctic regions could well have been called a "Third Front," an independent theater of war. There, too, operations were directed toward possession and denial to the enemy, although there was no question of occupying extensive barren territories that even lacked roads. Instead, the aim was to establish bases for obtaining weather information, vital to navigation and aerial warfare; to secure sites on which airfields could be erected, so that shipping lanes would be protected, and routes created or maintained, along which war material and military personnel could be transported by air and by sea. All this had to be done, while at the same time operations had to be mounted to deny to the enemy the use of arctic regions for the same purposes.

At seven o'clock in the morning of August 25 the *Empress of Canada*, escorted by two cruisers and three destroyers, steamed into the waters of Green Harbor on Spitsbergen, to initiate "Operation Gauntlet." A Canadian task force, reinforced by a Norwegian platoon, landed to evacuate 2,000-odd Russian miners from Barentsberg and a Norwegian colony from Longyear City. While Operation Gauntlet was under way, fake meteorological reports continued to be transmitted to Tromso for the German command. Only after September 3, when the mines had been set afire and Spitsbergen was once again uninhabited but for a lone Norwegian trapper who had managed to hide, did the Germans realize that they had lost effective control of that arctic archipelago.

As a countermove, Germany's senior meteorologist in Norway, Dr. Weickmann, a man who had been aboard the *Graf Zeppelin* during its arctic flight, organized "Operation Banso." A ten-man party was landed in Spitsbergen for the purpose of establishing and maintaining a meteorological service on that forsaken island. In a series of daring flights, needed supplies were brought in, and in November a four-man wintering party was left to provide the German military with a regular Spitsbergen-based meteorological service.

But Operation Gauntlet, the evacuation of civilians, had been only the first step in a British plan to secure Spitsbergen militarily and to deny its use to the enemy. Early in 1942 a Norwegian task force headed by Colonel Einar Sverdrup, who had previously been director of mines in Spitsbergen, was organized in Iceland. On April 2 a lone British pilot took off from Sullom Voe in Iceland to conduct an air reconnaissance of Spitsbergen in his *Catalina* J-240. Twenty-seven hours later, he returned, after a 2,700-mile flight, without having noticed the presence of Germans in Spitsbergen. On May 2, another reconnaissance flight was made. Aboard the plane were 200 pounds of food and two observers who were to be left behind in Spitsbergen, to await the arrival of Colonel Sverdrup's task force. Fog and ice made a landing impossible. Seeing German soldiers on the ground, the pilot headed back for Iceland with this vitally important intelligence. But before Colonel Sverdrup could be notified, his task force of approximately 100 men had already set out to sea aboard two arctic veterans, the *Selis* and the *Isbjörn*.⁵⁸

Both ships entered the area of an atmospheric disturbance which made radio contact impossible. When they arrived in Barentsberg, on May 12, still unaware that a radio-equipped German outpost was on Spitsbergen, the task force was attacked from the air. Both ships were sunk. Colonel Sverdrup and thirteen other men were killed, and the rest found themselves on a desolate piece of land without a radio, food, or arms. They remained, exposed to attacks from German planes which kept visiting the island with maddening regularity at seven o'clock in the morning and at six in the evening. Only on May 26 was the group spotted from the air by a British pilot. Three days later food and medical supplies were dropped to the waving and happily cheering men. An eyewitness said later, "Perhaps the best of all was the sight of a most respectable colonel . . . sitting on a coal heap, oblivious to all else, as he devoured each spoonful of apricot jam and coal dust out of a four-pound tin which had burst open on impact."⁵⁹

In July Operation Banso was discontinued and the German party was airlifted from Longyear City, where they left behind a robot weather station. Then a six-ship convoy brought reinforcements to the Norwegians. Under cover of fog, and unknown to the Germans, heavy equipment and guns were brought ashore to secure Spitsbergen for the Allies.

On October 15, however, German equipment was once more being unloaded from vessels in Spitsbergen's small Signehamna Bay, which had been the site of a weather station erected by Count Zeppelin in 1910. Two weeks later, a six-man party was again transmitting weather data to Germany from Signehamna. It kept on doing so for nine months, before being evacuated by a U-boat. In September 1943, Germany mounted "Operation Zitronella," as the battleships *Scharnhorst* and *Tirpitz,* accompanied by ten destroyers, steamed into the waters of Spitsbergen and bombarded the island. A month later, another group of Germans, brought by submarine, re-established meteorological service at Spitsbergen. This weather station was maintained until June 1944, when the Germans were frightened off by a Norwegian patrol. They retreated to a previously set up emergency camp and were eventually taken out by U-boat.

Following a series of German submarine and surface attacks on U. S. ships in the waters off Greenland, President Roosevelt said on September 11, 1941: "The time has come when the Americas themselves must now be defended. . . . Attacks in our own waters, or in waters which could be used for further and greater attacks on us, will inevitably weaken American ability to repel Hitlerism." The President ordered American warships to shoot on sight, adding: "When you see a rattlesnake poised to strike, you do not wait until he has struck before you crush him."

Within twenty-four hours, the Coast Guard vessel *Northland*,[60] patrolling the eastern coast of Greenland, sighted the *Busko,* a ship flying the Norwegian flag and suspiciously loaded with excessive radio equipment. A patrol from the *Northland* found on the nearby coast a German installation transmitting weather data to Germany.

Clearly Greenland was a potential springboard for German aggression against the Western Hemisphere. As one of the first steps toward protecting American interests in the Arctic, Task Force Eight, made up of some 1,500 hand-picked volunteers, left Brooklyn under sealed orders aboard the *Munargo* on September 20. The secretly formed unit was commanded by Bernt Balchen, only recently commissioned a captain in the U. S. Army Air Force. He had managed to procure some 50,000 tons of supplies, ranging from scarce building materials to antiaircraft ammunition, sled dogs, and airplanes. Destination of the task force was Sondre Strom Fjord, where a base, auxiliary to the one at Narsarssuak, was to be established and which was to become known under the code name Bluie West Eight.[61]

A few days later, a ship loaded with building materials and supplies docked in Labrador's Goose Bay, where an airfield was to be constructed.[62] A northern air route was beginning to take shape. From industrial centers in the United States, the route was to lead to Goose Bay, from there to Narsarssuak, Iceland, and England, with alternate landing sites on both coasts of Greenland—Sondre Strom Fjord in the west and an Angmagssalik in the east.

Another approach route to Greenland was established with airfields located at The Pas, Churchill, Southampton Island, Fort Chimo and Frobisher Bay on Baffin Island. However, the flight radius of fighter planes was increased by the installation of extra gasoline tanks and this interior route was never used for ferrying purposes. The facilities were maintained only to provide weather services essential for the main route, which led over Goose Bay and Greenland.

In London Hjalmar Riiser-Larsen, now an admiral, had appealed on the BBC for freedom-loving Norwegians to come forward and fight once more for their country. They had arrived, 2,400 of them, all eager volunteers. They were young and many of them had come in small leaky rowboats across waters patrolled by German planes and infested with submarines. Some did not make it and were caught by the Germans. Among those caught was Ole Arntzen, the only son of Norwegian patriot Finn Lützow-Holm, commander of Norway's Iceland-based air squadron 330. He thought of turning himself in to the Germans, in exchange for the life of his son. "How can you?" Riiser-Larsen said. "You can't trust them; they will just shoot both of you."[63] Commander Lützow-Holm remained at his post. Before the war was over, his squadron would fly 7,473 hours in support of the Allied war effort. It would escort 379 convoys, detect 15 submarines, attack 9 and damage 7 of them.[64]

At the same time, Soviet forces were being mauled and forced to retreat. Fighting stubbornly, they grudgingly traded space for time, while armament factories were relocated to Siberia, where they resumed production. New natural resources in the Arctic were tapped. Contact with the Allies was maintained via Archangel, Vladivostok, and Iran, and the United States undertook to supply the Soviets with more than 1 billion dollars' worth of goods in 1942.

The war extended into the Soviet Arctic. Part of Germany's plan for the conquest of Russia was isolation of the country's central region through the disruption of communications and the strangling of supply lanes. Conquest of Murmansk and Archangel meant mastery of the Soviet North and elimination of the Northern Sea Route as a significant supply lane. Deprived of home bases, the Northern fleet would fall into German hands, its loss bringing with it disorganization and the collapse of the Siberian economy.[65]

Soviet peoples of the North rose to the challenge. Icebreakers and freighters were armed, coal continued to be mined in Sangar, and salt, so important for the preservation of fish, continued to reach far-off fisheries.

German troops reached the suburbs of Murmansk. Their artillery was sinking freighters in the port and the city was exposed to heavy air bombardment. But work continued in the drydocks; Murmansk held, and the Germans abandoned their plan to take by assault from land Russia's only northern year-around ice-free port.

In Archangel, within easy reach of German bombers, a new harbor rose to handle war material arriving from England and the United States. On top of ice, a railroad was built which linked the port with the main railway, and soon rickety locomotives began pulling flat-top cars loaded with trucks, food, fuel, and industrial equipment.

German attempts to blockade the Northern Sea Route continued. Armed or not, Russian vessels, some of them carrying women and children, were attacked by German submarines. Approaches to Novaya Zemlya were mined and U-boats lay in wait for approaching convoys. But protected from the air, and escorted along the Northern Sea Route by units of the Soviet Navy, freighters and icebreakers kept on sailing along this waterway. A total of 452,393 tons of American lend-lease goods passed through this supply lane.[66] These essential supplies arrived from San Francisco and Seattle in the shortest possible time aboard Russian-manned vessels, some of which were Liberty ships and thus themselves lend-lease goods.* (Glavsevmorput's wartime boss was Ivan Papanin and among his men, who were guarding the Northern Sea Route from the air, were veteran arctic pilots Chukhnovsky and Cherevichny.)

Then came Pearl Harbor. Soon afterward the possibility loomed of a Japanese attack on the Aleutians and an enemy landing in Alaska. Suddenly Alaska became the focal point in countermoves being planned in the event of a Japanese attack on the American mainland. Underdeveloped and almost without roads, Alaska, without aircraft and the auxiliary facilities needed to keep planes in the air, was wide open to invasion. The light planes of small, privately owned airlines, operated from isolated, inadequate airfields, had barely begun to service wide Alaskan and Canadian territories. What was needed was another reliable northern air route, along which troops and supplies could be flown to Alaska. A northwestern air route, which could assume an importance parallel to that of the northeastern air bridge being built by way of Labrador and Greenland, was essential. Planes, which Russia needed so badly, could then be ferried along this airway, rather than being shipped aboard slow Atlantic convoys exposed to the dangers of submarine attacks.

Throughout Alaska and Canada weather stations were established, and construction of airports was begun. Along 1,700 miles of wilderness a service road was built, leaping into existence at an average daily stretch of some 8 miles, heading north from Dawson Creek and south from Fairbanks.[67]

Out of the inevitable initial confusion created by inaccurate maps, inadequate radio service, and inexperienced personnel, gradually order emerged, both on the Alaska route as well as on the air way across Greenland. On March 14, 1942, the first England-bound bomber landed on the 6,000-foot airstrip which Balchen's men had built on Bluie West Eight.†

In May 1942, Axis forces were stretched over a wide territory. In the Far East, Singapore had fallen, so had Java and the Philippines. In the Atlantic, German submarines were sinking more than half a million tons of shipping a month. General Rommel was preparing his offensive toward the Nile and *Der Fuehrer* was getting ready for a formidable new drive in Russia. For the Allies it was one of the darkest periods of the war.

---

* Nevertheless, the Northern Sea Route was *not* the most important supply lane. Lend-lease goods arrived in greater amounts by way of Murmansk and Iran.

† Bluie West Eight has remained not only an alternate landing site but also an important base for rescue operations on the icecap.

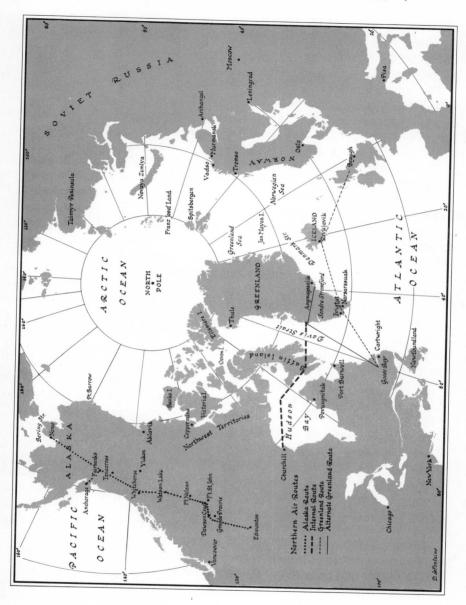

About this time, Nobile left the United States and returned to Italy. His request for active duty with the armed forces remained unanswered, and, officially still on the faculty of the University of Naples, he went to Spain on another "mission."*

That month, General Dwight D. Eisenhower, on a trip to England, flew the Northern Air Route. Later he called it "a significant factor in the final defeat of the European Axis," adding, that "without that route, built in spite of difficulty, discouragement, and even skepticism as to its usability, we could scarcely have maintained the forces we put into Europe."[68]

The actual route and the airfields along it were built by the American Air Force, but its foundation was laid by air pioneers of the Arctic and by others who had explored it on foot, slowly and painfully. All of them had contributed bits of knowledge and experience. Their isolated achievements may have been insignificant and only a testimonial to individual courage and ambition. But the sum total of their efforts made possible the building of a transarctic air link, along which the New World could bring help to the Old.

On June 26, 1942, "Operation Bolero" was started in Goose Bay. That was the code name for the ferrying of American planes to Britain. More and more planes flew out of Goose Bay, coming down for intermediate landings at newly established staging areas in Narsarssuak or Sondre Strom Fjord, before crossing icecapped Greenland and flying on to bolster the defenses of battle-scarred England. Many of them were to form the United States Eighth Air Force. Not all planes came through. Fighting turbulent winds over uncharted mountains, some crashed and others had to make dangerous emergency landings.[69] But by the end of the year, 882 planes, some 700 of them belonging to the Eighth Air Force, had successfully crossed Greenland on their way to Britain. Only 38 aircraft were lost, an accident rate of 5.2 per cent, just about half of what had been anticipated.[70]

On June 26, the very day that Operation Bolero got under way, "Operation Alsib" was spelled out in an order issued by the U. S. Air Transport Command. This involved the delivery to Russia of almost 8,000 planes along the Alaska Air Route, stretching from Edmonton, Canada, to Ladd Field in Fairbanks, Alaska.[71] Airfields for intermediate landings were pro-

---

* Not long after Mussolini was deposed and Allied troops landed in Italy in 1943, Nobile returned from Spain and promptly allowed himself to become involved in a journalistic hoax. The U. S. Army Newspaper *Stars and Stripes* published a story, complete with a photograph, which was headlined: "Explorer Nobile Thanks Savior 16 Years Later in Rome Meeting." Anyone who might have expected to see a picture of the Russian Schmidt, would have been shocked. Referring to an American lieutenant named Merril Beam, the paper said it was he "who first heard the distress signal from General Nobile's party . . . "

vided in Grande Prairie, Fort St. John, Fort Nelson, Watson Lake, and Whitehorse. From Ladd Field one air corridor led to Anchorage, key for the defense of southern Alaska and the Aleutian Islands; another, passing by way of Nome and the Bering Strait, was to become part of Russia's wartime lifeline originating in the United States. On September 29, 1942, the first group of twelve American-built bombers, in charge of a Soviet lieutenant colonel, took off from Ladd Field, to be flown to Russia. Operation Alsib, negotiated in Washington between American officials and a Russian party headed by General Michael Gromov, the transpolar flier, had begun. Chief pilot of the ferry route between Alaska and Siberia was Hero of the Soviet Union Ilya Mazuruk, a veteran arctic pilot.

In August 1942, war came to the heart of the Soviet Arctic, as Germany mounted "Operation Wonderland."[72] Diverted from its raiding mission in the Atlantic, the German battleship *Admiral Scheer,* supported by submarines and planes, entered the Kara Sea to intercept a nine-ship convoy passing through the Sea of Laptev. The *Admiral Scheer* was unable to get to the convoy, but some 180 miles off Mys Chelyuskin the raider met the *Sibiriakov,* and in an uneven battle the old icebreaker was sunk with all but sixteen of the 104 people aboard. Lacking adequate information on ice conditions in the Laptev Sea, the battleship then approached Dikson Island with its important meteorological station. A vicious preliminary bombardment was met with counter-fire from shore, and, damaged by three direct hits, the *Admiral Scheer* retreated, hidden behind a screen of fog and smoke. Among members of the scientific party on Dikson involved in this episode was an unknown hydrographer named Michael Somov.

Meteorological conditions prevailing in Greenland have a direct bearing on weather in a great part of the European continent.[73] Accurate weather forecasts were essential for staging air raids against England. In August 1942, an insignificant-looking German vessel called *Hermann* made its way to the eastern coast of Greenland. A seventeen-man party commanded by a Lieutenant Ritter disembarked on Sabine Island and established a meteorological station which was to function, undetected, for almost six months, transmitting local weather data in coded radio messages to Berlin regularly twice a day.[74]

On a day in March 1943, Marius Jensen, a member of Governor Eske Brun's Greenland patrol, was scouting the uninhabited northern sector of that island's eastern coast. In Germania Harbor, on Sabine Island, he saw smoke curling out of what should have been the abandoned hut of a trapper. Inside the cabin, Jensen and his two Eskimo scouts found half-empty coffee mugs and some swastika-adorned German uniforms. Jensen's patrol carefully retreated, only to be caught off guard during the night by Lieutenant Ritter's men, who had just destroyed the Free Danish outpost at Eskimonaes. Jensen was captured, but managed to disarm Ritter and march him off to Scoresby Sound as his prisoner.

Bernt Balchen, now a lieutenant colonel, was given orders to destroy the German outpost at Eskimonaes. There had been undue delay in issuing the order and when Balchen did arrive at Eskimonaes with two Liberator bombers, the Germans had already abandoned their base, to be evacuated to their homeland by air a short time later.

In all, the German Navy dispatched thirteen parties and the *Luftwaffe* three to bring war to the Arctic. Robot sea weather stations were established off Iceland, Greenland, and Labrador. Others, weighing approximately one ton each, were brought in by air to Spitsbergen, Bear Island, Jan Mayen, and Novaya Zemlya. The Germans tried to establish a weather station on ice drifting between Spitsbergen and Greenland, and their attempt at maintaining a meteorological outpost on Franz Josef Land failed only because the occupying fifteen-man group came down with trichinosis and had to be evacuated.[75]

5

AND then it was Monday, the Monday *after* the war. The last mass graves had been closed; the rubble of destroyed cities had been piled up neatly, and the slate of history was once more clean. But victory, the aftermath of a long road lined with broken bones, blank minds, and shattered homes, had a deceptively impassive face, which somehow remained devoid of meaning.

All over the world, men resumed activities geared to individual ambitions. Sir Hubert Wilkins continued designing and testing arctic equipment for the Quartermaster General. Admiral Byrd returned to the Antarctic as the technical leader of "Operation Highjump."[76] In Italy, Nobile managed to get back the commission he had resigned voluntarily some sixteen years earlier and emerged a major general, with pay due him retroactively to March 1929. Fascism, which had carried him to the summit of adulation, was dead, and the general said: ". . . cynicism, lie, intrigue . . . crime . . . were weapons of the regime."[77] Conceding that he ". . . should have protested against all this publicly while outside Italy," he admitted having made instead what he called "little compromises and adaptations to circumstances." The next step in his attempt at rehabilitation was the submission of a "confidential" memorandum to Italy's High Commissioner for Sanctions against Fascism, accusing General Valle of wartime profiteering and malfeasance while Undersecretary for Aviation.[78] Some three years and 116 witnesses later, a court of law found these accusations to be utterly without foundation and absolved Valle in accordance with the request of the public prosecutor.[79]

Next, the man who had once gloated at Mussolini's destroying a "corrupt and corruptive parliament"[80] proceeded to get himself elected to the legislative chamber of a newly reborn democratic Italy . . . on the ticket of the Communist Party. There he would soon deplore in a speech that there were too many generals in the Italian Air Force.[81]

On October 2, 1945, a month after Japan's surrender, the assault on the North Pole was resumed. On that day, a Soviet pilot named Titlov took his overloaded twin-engined plane N-331 into the air. After a flight of 4 hours and 31 minutes, he reached the Pole, circled, and then turned back to complete a 2,700-mile trip in 15½ hours.[82] Starting with Byrd, this was the sixteenth time that the polar air space had been invaded by an airplane. Titlov's flight was made during the polar night and aboard his plane was Michael Somov, a scientist who would soon be heading Soviet expeditions both to the Arctic and the Antarctic.

The United States also had been awakened to the importance of the arctic regions, not only as a source for meteorological data essential for weather prognostication but also as a field of activity in case of war. General Carl A. Spaatz observed that the United States was exposed to a possible air attack coming by way of the Arctic; General Henry H. Arnold, who had been so greatly responsible for the establishment of northern air routes during World War II, thought that the North Pole would become the "strategic center," should another conflict engulf the world, and General Curtis LeMay said: "Our frontier now lies across the Arctic wastes of the polar regions."[83]

Taking off from Ladd Field in Alaska, an American observation plane flew toward the North Pole on July 21, 1946, to gather information on atmospheric conditions prevailing at the top of the world. In the spring of the following year, a weather reconnaissance squadron began making regularly scheduled flights to collect systematic meteorological data so essential for forecasting purposes. These flights, called "ptarmigan" after a bird widely represented in the Arctic, were flown along a route of some 2,750 nautical miles, and in time became boringly standardized routine missions. More than 3,000 such flights were made in the course of the following three years, during which time the scope was extended to include radar observation and other vigilance and research assignments.

During a routine mission across the polar basin on August 14, 1946, crew members of a plane belonging to the 46th Strategic Photo Reconnaissance Squadron noticed on their radarscope an unusual target, measuring some 200 square miles. At first believed to be land, it was eventually recognized as being an ice island—a fragment broken off the shelf hugging the northern coast of Ellsmere Island—which had floated out to sea and was continuing an imperceptible drift, surrounded by pack ice, born out of the interaction of water and winds. This formation was given the cryptic designation T-1 (the *T* standing for "target."). Much thicker and more durable than pack ice, ice islands have a distinguishing yellowish hue and their snow-covered ridged surface gives a deceptively smooth appearance. Such ice islands had been described by early polar explorers, and it may well be that the Crocker Land which Peary had claimed seeing was such a piece of floating shelf ice.[84] T-1 was subsequently tracked for more than three years, while it kept to its meandering path, covering a distance of some 1,400 miles at an average daily speed of 1.2 miles.

But the interest of the United States was not limited to ice-covered arctic waters.[85] It extended to Greenland, that natural "aircraft carrier," whose surface was covered by a huge glacier some 673,000 square miles in area. On a clear day in July 1947, an American named Donald A. Shaw made an important discovery. Shaw, a man with vast arctic experience, had trained sled dogs and drivers for Byrd's antarctic expeditions and had spent nearly five uninterrupted years in Greenland during the war. On that July day he was flying over Greenland's interior when he spotted a stretch of the wartime Bluie West Eight base. The ice looked firm and appeared to be free of crevasses. It seemed to have potential as a landing site for wheeled planes.[86]

Greenland's icecap is bordered by a 30- to 40-mile belt of rough, heavily fissured ice-encrusted terrain, which permits crossing on foot or in vehicles in only a few places. If the ice seen by Shaw was adequate to serve as a natural airfield, men and equipment could be brought in by air, to establish a base, enabling scientists to fan out from there on exploratory trips. It was to take much planning and time before Shaw would finally get a chance to go to the site he had discovered.

Meticulously prepared, Shaw's expedition, code-named "Mint Julep," landed in the southwest portion of the icecap in May 1953. In addition to Lieutenant Colonel Shaw, there were eleven scientists and a supporting air detachment of twenty-four men. By September, Project Mint Julep was completed and recognized as an unqualified success. In addition to having gathered valuable scientific data in different fields, Shaw's party had established the existence of an area of some 100 square miles where the ice was as permanent as the icecap itself and on which planes could land safely. This finding constituted a major breakthrough for research in Greenland and provided a potential landing site of strategic importance requiring only a minimum of maintenance, in an area where favorable meteorological conditions seem to prevail.

In the year 1948 Soviet scientists returned to the Arctic, supported by dozens of planes, many of which had been transformed into flying laboratories.[87] Eight independent air-supported "high latitude" expeditions

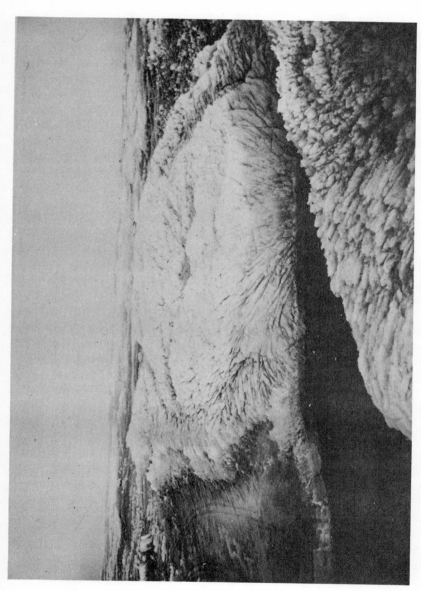

An exhumed channel on Fletcher's Ice Island, T-3.   *U. S. Geological Survey.*

were organized. Equipped with newly designed portable equipment, scientific teams were taken by air to preselected ice floes, where they set about collecting various information from different parts of the Arctic Ocean. Such data blended into a solid body of knowledge which gave a better understanding of the dynamics of arctic phenomena, as expressed in the speed and direction of waters, the thickness of ice, terrestrial magnetism, and other scientifically essential information. This undertaking was highlighted by the discovery of the Lomonosov Ridge, which rises from the bottom of the Arctic Ocean.

Impressive as this effort was, it was to be dwarfed by future Soviet activity along the same lines. The following year thirty-three stations were established for varying periods of time. In 1954 the number rose to 103, and in 1956 a total of 208 scientific outposts were set up on floes or islands drifting in the Arctic Ocean.[8]

Other men returned to the Arctic. There was Colonel Balchen. For him the final stretch of the war had been filled with excitement, adventure, and a sense of satisfaction. He had commanded "Operation Sonnie," to bring out of internment in Sweden several thousand young men who were potential soldiers for the cause of the Allies. He had taken on "Operation Ve Do It," designed to deliver by air weapons, food, supplies and medicines to underground fighters hidden in Norway's mountains. Recalled to duty, he was given command of the Tenth Rescue Squadron, based in Alaska. On constant alert, his crews averaged some three rescues a week. Within two years they emerged as well-trained teams, experienced in polar navigation and veterans of landings on pack ice. When, in 1949, Balchen flew a routine mission to Thule in Greenland by way of the North Pole, he became the first man in history to have piloted a plane over both the top and bottom of the world.

On April 1, 1950, the scientific component of a new Soviet drifting station was delivered by air to a preselected site on a floe, some ten feet thick and covering an area of approximately 11 square miles.[88] Michael Somov led the expedition, which was allotted some 60 tons of equipment and supplies. The station, which became known as "North Pole 2," was established at 76° 02' N., 166° 30' W., some 300 miles northeast of Wrangel Island. In addition to Somov, there were twelve other scientists and a four-man support party which included a physician. The group had especially designed equipment which allowed them to live and work in relative comfort. Dark, round-domed tents each housed two or three men, and had electricity. Some were even equipped with telephones. A resourceful mechanic invented a driftometer, and a special pump designed to bring water to the surface of the floe, where it could be allowed to freeze, thus transforming the uneven surface into a smooth runway.

With the coming of summer, fissures appeared in the floe at unpredictable spots and at unpredictable times; ice melted, creating new problems by bringing physical discomfort to the men, loosening mountings of instruments and radio masts, and transforming the airfield into a lake. Twice the tents had to be moved, and water had to be drained from the surface of the floe by drilling holes into the ice.

The original plan had called for a five-month drift. But in August the proposal was made to extend the lifespan of the station until the following April. More supplies were needed. Commander-designate of the aerial relief expedition was arctic veteran Michael Vodopyanov. His equipment consisted of two twin-engined planes and a four-motor aircraft playfully called the "Arctic Truck."[89] The first two planes came to a landing in the midst of polar night on a short runway, illuminated with kerosene torches improvised out of discarded cans. Among the supplies brought in was a snow vehicle which was to facilitate over-ice transportation of equipment.[90] But the landing strip was too short for the "Arctic Truck" to come down. Several tons of supplies were thrown from the plane onto the floe without parachutes and with varying degrees of success. Of the two planes that had landed, one was irreparably damaged on takeoff and had to be left behind.

Winter brought more discomfort and danger. The floe broke up and was greatly reduced in size; men and equipment had to be relocated to a new site. On April 2, 1951, the objective—a full year of on-the-spot observation—was accomplished, and nine days later the station was evacuated by a detachment of planes in charge of pilot Mazuruk. Somov's men returned to the mainland with a wealth of information.

Some three years later a pilot sighted the abandoned floe again, while flying a routine reconnaissance mission. There were the sun-bleached tents, discarded boxes, and an abandoned plane—all standing on individual ice pedestals several feet high. This curious phenomenon was to be seen in the future again and again. While new ice keeps on forming at the bottom of floes, the upper surface melts under the caressing warmth of the sun, except in spots shielded by solid objects, which thus remain standing on steadily growing ice pedestals that assume the appearance of strange-looking mushrooms.

At the time when Somov's station had already been in operation several months, U. S. airmen aboard "ptarmigan" flights were on the lookout for new ice islands. One such formation was identified on July 21, 1950, and was named T-2; a third island, to become known as T-3, was discovered ten days later by radar aboard a B-29 weather plane.[91]

Living quarters on T-3. The structures stand on ice pedestals about eight feet high at the end of the second melt season. *U. S. Geological Survey.*

The first American effort at establishing a drifting station was made in February 1951, when an eight-man group of Balchen's Tenth Rescue Squadron landed on a floe in the Beaufort Sea, some 115 miles north of Barter Island.[92] The party was headed by Captain Mike Brinegar, but the venture was to be of short duration. On March 10, a violent storm came up. To the accompaniment of thunderlike rumbling, the floe broke up, pressure ridges formed, the ice shook, and the prefabricated huts which had been erected to serve as living quarters were demolished. While wind-blown snow fell from murky skies, spray whipped up from the sea formed a milky wall which reduced visibility to only a few feet. An appeal for help went out. Soon a plane arrived and made a hazardous landing. The lifespan of the first American drifting station had been barely three weeks and aerial reconnaissance made a few days later failed to reveal any trace of the camp, which presumably had broken up completely.

In the spring of 1951 secrecy-veiled "Operation Blue Jay" began.[93] Preliminary surveys had been completed, plans had been drawn up, and contracts awarded. Leading a convoy of some 120 ships, loaded with men and construction materials, the icebreaker *Adak* was making its way toward Thule, in the northern sector of Greenland's west coast, where Balchen had suggested the erection of an airbase in 1942.[94] Now, in the wake of the Korean War part of Greenland was being transformed radically. An area once symbolized by harpoons, seal-blubber lamps, and turf huts became a place of concrete runways, steam-heated barracks, barber shops, and bowling alleys. In years to come the Thule base was to evolve into the most important link in the BMEWS [Ballistic Missile Early Warning System], a radar-equipped protective defense line stretching from Clear in Alaska to Fylingdales in England. Barely one year later, on March 19, 1952, four planes took off from Thule Air Base in accordance with carefully made plans for Project Icicle, whose objective was a landing on ice island T-3, then some 103 miles from the North Pole.[95]

At the controls of the ski-equipped C-47, belonging to the 10th Rescue Squadron, was Captain Lew Erhart, a Balchen-trained veteran of many pack-ice landings. His copilot was General William Old, commander of the Alaska-based air force. In addition to an extra 400-gallon gasoline tank and 1,200 pounds of assorted equipment, the overloaded plane was carrying six other people—a navigator, an engineer, a *Life* photographer, and a three-man landing party.

The C-47 headed for a spot between Greenland and Ellsmere Island, where Erhart had established a six-drum gasoline cache two days earlier. The depot was located, the plane came down, the gasoline was taken aboard, and then Erhart proceeded for ice island T-3 and an aerial rendezvous with three four-engined C-54 planes, each carrying 6,000 pounds of equipment, which had taken off from Thule Air Base on the same day.

Some ten hours after leaving Greenland, Erhart was flying over T-3. He made repeated passes, letting the skis of his plane drag along the snow-covered ice island in search of a suitable landing site, while the three big planes kept on circling overhead at different altitudes. Deceptively smooth-looking, the island was covered by a thick layer of snow which was hiding a rough underlying ice surface.

"We are going in! Hold on to your teeth!" Erhart shouted, as the plane sank lower. Once more the skis hit ice, and the C-47 ploughed on, stirring up a cloud of snow. A biting wind was lashing the island, and the men found themselves in snow up to their knees on an inhospitable piece of ice with ridges as high as ten feet. The temperature was estimated at around 60° below zero. Icicles swiftly forming on their faces, the men moved about, trying to find a landing site suitable for an equipment-laden C-54.

Surveying the situation, General Old thought that no man could live on "this thing" and was about to call the long-planned and carefully prepared operation off. But young Lieutenant Colonel Fletcher, leader of the three-man landing party, was respectfully insistent, and it was decided to leave his three-man group on the ice island, temporarily postponing a definite decision as to whether Project Icicle was to be carried on in accordance with plan or not.

While the C-47 was being unloaded, the first C-54 lined up for a dropping run. Soon gasoline, equipment and food sufficient for 40 days started sailing through the air in a zone which the men had marked on the ice with red flags made out of cloth covered with luminous paint.

After 4 hours and 20 minutes on the ice, the C-47 had been unloaded and was readied for a takeoff. JATO (for Jet-Assisted Take Off) bottles, which previously had been covered with electrically heated blankets, were put into place to give added takeoff thrust. The engines were started and the plane began moving, at first "wobbling like a goose," then rising into the air and heading for Thule, accompanied by two of the C-54s which had continued circling T-3.

Left behind on the wind-swept cake of ice were Lieutenant Colonel Joseph Fletcher, Captain Mike Brinegar, veteran of America's first ill-fated drifting station of the previous year, and Dr. Kaare Rodahl, a physician and an expectant father, who felt "as isolated as anyone can be."

They put up a double-walled tent, collected their equipment, washed some frozen sausages down with hot chocolate, and then settled for a restless night during which the island kept reverberating with roars and thuds like pistol shots, caused by the collision of their island with surrounding pack ice.

During the following days, Fletcher's men vainly kept on exploring T-3 for a site on which a big C-54 could land to bring in additional equipment. Then came a blinding blizzard which raged for a whole day. Only on March 24 did Dr. Rodahl learn from a radio message originating aboard a North Pole-bound ptarmigan plane flying over T-3 that he had become a father two days earlier. (This event was duly celebrated with some whisky which had to be thawed and a cake which the men cut with a saw.)

Throughout this initial period Fletcher's party did not know whether military authorities in the States would sanction the establishment of a semipermanent station on T-3 or whether they would order evacuation of the ice island. Only on March 29 would they finally receive a radio message from a "ptarmigan" flight that two other planes were about to bring additional men and equipment to T-3.

Then Erhart landed once more with his C-47, bringing Captain Green and Dr. Crary, radio equipment, a power plant, a small meteorological station, and Fletcher's dog Tundra. At the same time more supplies and equipment were parachuted from a C-54, which kept on circling cautiously overhead.

When both planes started on their way back to Thule, four men were left on T-3: Fletcher, Brinegan, Green and Crary. They proceeded to erect more permanent quarters, and on April 2 the first meteorological report went out from what had been officially designated "Fletcher's Ice Island." Within a week more landings were made, more equipment was delivered, including a snow-going vehicle called a weasel. The United States had its first drifting station, established on a kidney-shaped piece of thick, durable ice, measuring some five by nine miles. Although men would be rotated, the initial period of occupation of this valuable piece of arctic real estate was to be more than two years, during which time important meteorological and oceanographic studies were to be carried on and the value of ice islands for strategic reasons as well as for purposes of search and research would be more fully realized.[96]

In the meantime, plans were being made to open a commercial passenger route linking Europe and the United States along the shortest distance by way of the Arctic. Hopes of the early pioneers were finally to be realized and the man who was to transform them into reality was Norway's Hjalmar Riiser-Larsen. Soon after the war he retired from the armed forces to become general manager of SAS, an airline formed by the merger of the three Scandinavian companies, which until then had operated independently. On November 19, 1952, a DC-6B, purchased by SAS, manned by a crew of eleven and carrying twenty-two passengers, took off from California. Less than 24 hours later, the plane landed in Copenhagen, after a trailblazing intercontinental flight.[97] Among those aboard were Danish Ambassador Henrik de Kauffman, whose independent efforts during World War II had so greatly contributed toward securing Greenland for the Allies, Colonel Balchen, and retired Major General Riiser-Larsen.[98] Soon SAS would apply to the Civil Aeronautic Board for permission to inaugurate a regularly scheduled transarctic passenger service from Denmark to California. The first such flight would take place on November 15, 1954, and waiting to welcome it in Los Angeles would be arctic pioneer Bernt Balchen.

While preparations were under way in the spring of 1954 to evacuate Fletcher's Ice Island, extensive work was going on in the Soviet Union, preliminary to an ambitious new expedition to the Arctic. On April 8, North Pole 4 was established, which was to function for more than three years, and on April 9, North Pole 3 was inaugurated, destined to remain

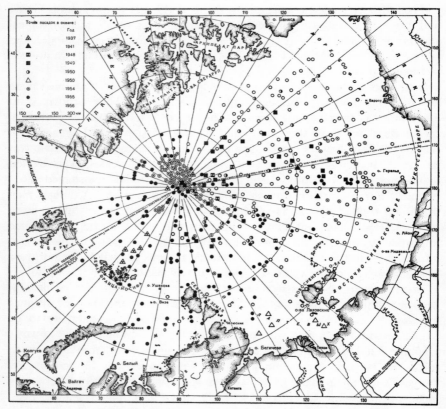

Soviet map showing the proliferation of Soviet drifting stations in the Arctic Ocean between the years 1937 and 1956.

manned for one year. From then on, the Soviet Union was to maintain at all times and for a period of more than ten years at least two ice stations, drifting simultaneously in the Arctic Ocean.*

As the cold war continued and both the United States as well as the Soviet Union test-fired hydrogen bombs, it was decided in Washington that additional safeguards were needed against a possible air attack across arctic regions. Project 572 was conceived, which envisioned the erection of a chain of radar stations across Canada to form an electronic wall, designed to give early warning of an attack on the American continent coming from the north. Men and equipment needed to build these radar outposts had to be taken by air to outlying isolated areas, where such installations were to be erected.

Since there were no landing strips at the selected sites, it was necessary to have aircraft carrying heavy equipment come down on natural ice surfaces. But no adequate information was available as to what thickness and strength ice would have to have to permit landings and takeoffs of heavily loaded C-124 planes.[99]

The problem was turned over to Lieutenant Colonel Shaw. Accompanied by a scientist, Andrew Assur, he flew in a light ski-equipped C-47 to frozen Cambridge Bay. Drilling holes into the icy surface, the men found the ice to be sixty-five inches thick, about two inches less than what had been scientifically predicted as safe. On March 9, 1955, a C-124 landed on the ice, while Shaw was standing at the surveyor's level, measuring how much the ice was bending under the weight of the stationary plane. It was assumed that a three-inch bend was the maximum that ice could be exposed to before it crumbled. The instrument showed a bend of one inch . . . one inch and a half . . . two inches, as seconds ticked by slowly. At 2.16 inches, well within the predicted safety margin, further deformation of the ice stopped, and Lieutenant Colonel Shaw could report to the Pentagon that sea ice 65 inches thick can support the 168,000-pound weight of a stationary plane.

During the following ten weeks, fully loaded C-124s made 932 landings on 28 different locations along a 2,500-mile stretch of wilderness, without a single accident. The DEW [Distant Early Warning] Line, today stretching from the Aleutians, across Alaska, Canada, and the Greenland icecap, came into existence to supplement two other installations—the Pine Tree system, linking Canadian Defense Commands with those of the United States, and the mid-Canada radar line, established roughly along the 55th parallel.

On February 26, 1957, Riiser-Larsen was aboard the SAS plane called *Viking Hjalmar* which made the first transarctic flight from Copenhagen to Tokyo, missing only by minutes a carefully planned historic

---

* See Appendices 6 and 8.

rendezvous with a sister ship flying in the opposite direction. On March 7, T-3 was reoccupied for another series of scientific observations. Code-named "Bravo," this operation was to last for more than three years. At a later time one of the station's rotating commanders was to be Donald A. Shaw. On June 8, another American drifting station was established on a floe within the framework of the International Geophysical Year. Called station Alpha, it was to function for some seventeen months, during which it would traverse a total distance of 1,580 miles.*

In September the atomic submarine *Nautilus* reached latitude 87°, highest yet attained by any ship of the sea. On December 5 the world's first atomic icebreaker was launched in Leningrad, to be placed under the command of Pavel Ponamarev (who had once been assistant to Captain Eggi, when the *Krassin* set out to rescue survivors of the dirigible *Italia*). But, in addition to these peaceful achievements, a disquieting note was sounded by Russia's announcement that she had successfully fired an intercontinental ballistic missile.

In the following year, while both the United States and the Soviet Union had scientific parties working on ice drifting in the Arctic, more spectacular feats were recorded: The *Nautilus* crossed the North Pole on August 3 and another atomic submarine, the *Skate,* did likewise nine days later.

In March 1959 the *Skate* was once again at the North Pole. Breaking through the ice, it surfaced, and in a touching ceremony the ashes of Sir Hubert Wilkins were dispersed to the wind, in accordance with the wish expressed by the man who had done so much to erase blank spots at both the top and the bottom of the globe. During the same year the Soviet station NP-6, which had functioned on an ice island, was abandoned after a drift of 1,246 days, and so was NP-7, while NP-8 was set up, and station Charlie was inaugurated from the American side.

Two other events took place in the same year, both geared to preserving the peace. Representatives of twelve nations, including the United States, the Soviet Union and Norway, signed a treaty designating the Antarctic a scientific preserve for thirty years during which military and economic considerations would be disregarded so that men of good will could carry on exploratory work in peace, without interference from military and business interests. At the other end of the world construction of BMEWS was under way, to help safeguard the American continent against a surprise intercontinental-missile attack across the arctic airspace.

The year 1960 saw other spectacular firsts. In February the *Sargo* traveled to and around the North Pole submerged, emphasizing the part a missile-carrying atomic submarine could play in a future war, and, on April 1, Tiros I was launched, the first satellite to be placed in orbit

---

* See Appendix 7.

for the purpose of transmitting meteorological data back to earth. In August the submarine *Dragon* traversed the northwest passage along which Amundsen had sailed slowly and painfully. Then Arlis I, another American drifting station, was established, and Tiros II was placed into orbit. But these and other achievements were overshadowed when less than five months later, on April 4, 1961, the world heard that a man named Yuri Gagarin had orbited the earth in a space capsule.

As crowds jamming Moscow's Red Square went wild, joyfully celebrating a new hero and his achievement, another man remained discreetly in the background: General Kamanin, one of the original seven "Heroes of the Soviet Union" and a dominant figure in Russia's space program, who was Gagarin's mentor.

All that followed was anticlimactic. Arlis II was established in May 1961 and Tiros III was launched in July, followed by Tiros IV less than eight months later. Then came February 20, 1962, when John Glenn became the first American to orbit the earth. The establishment of more drifting stations was lost on people too sophisticated to hail an achievement which in a not too distant yesterday would have been spectacular. Even when an American B-58 bomber flew across the top of the world from Tokyo to London at almost twice the speed of sound, covering the 8,028-mile distance in somewhat more than eight hours, the feat caused only a ripple of excitement which was soon forgotten.[100]

Times have changed since that day in July of 1900 when Count Zeppelin's first dirigible remained aloft for seventeen minutes. The face of the earth has changed and so have the cold, desolate and inhospitable arctic regions. In Siberia small native huts have been replaced by two-story buildings. There are hospitals, schools, roads, factories, and airports. Scurvey, dreaded by arctic travelers not so long ago, is for all practical purposes now unknown. Similar changes have taken place in Greenland, which is no longer merely a colony, but an integral part of Denmark. Instead of turf huts permeated with the smell of seal oil, the countryside is dotted with neat wooden buildings, clustered around churches and schools. There are now adequate facilities for storage and processing of fish, and modern canneries are in operation at several locations. There is virtually no illiteracy in Greenland, and, instead of trading posts for fishing and hunting gear, there are stores selling books, carpets, radios and the countless other items demanded by a rapidly growing economy and an increasingly affluent society.[101]

Whatever importance Greenland may have had during World War II has been greatly increased, because the Thule Air Base with its BMEWS has become the advance rampart of American defense and a monument to American engineering genius. The same genius which in a different place and at an earlier time dug the Panama Canal out of tropical swamps

On Ice Island T-3 a rodman prepares for a survey of the island. *U. S. Geological Survey.*

overcame the challenge of permafrost to erect a modern fortress on an ice-covered desert.

Within severe time limitations imposed by seasonally frozen waters, ships hauled in supplies, and, during brief summer periods, elaborate structures were erected. Everything had to be brought in from the United States, and new engineering procedures had to be developed to combat the ubiquitous permafrost. All structures had to be built on foundation mats unsusceptible to frost. Complex steps had to be taken to prevent the permafrost from melting and causing the ground to buckle under the installations. This problem was ingeniously solved by providing air spaces between foundation and superstructure or by installing refrigeration coils into the ground to maintain steady temperatures. Modern three-story barracks arose, complete with water and sewage systems, placed above ground, heavily insulated, and heated electrically to prevent freezing.[102]

But despite its elaborate construction, Thule, with its Nike missiles, is capable of providing the Continental Air Defense Command in Colorado with but a fifteen-minute advance warning of an impending attack. Too short a period to avert holocaust, death and destruction, but long enough for retaliatory measures to be put into effect. The certainty and the devastating finality of retaliation may well act as a deterrent to any aggressive action coming across the polar airspace.

Arctic pioneers of the twentieth century laid the foundation for northern routes, which eventually were built up to become vital lifelines.

Now the world once again is standing at a threshold. Only half a century ago the globe was covered with large patches bearing the word "unexplored." Now the earth has become too small and man is looking for new conquests, to be made in outer space and on other planets. There will be new heroes and new exploits; men of many races, who at this moment may still be in their infancy, will set out to make faltering steps toward new conquests. They will blunder and some may fail; new myths will be created, and history will be rewritten to suit the occasion. But if they succeed in laying a foundation for co-operation among peoples; if their efforts bear the seed of coexistence and the perpetuation of peace without fear; then, indeed, their efforts will not have been in vain, and the sacrifices they will have made, the hardships they will have withstood, and the dangers they will have faced—all will have had a justification.

MEN OF THE ARCTIC
A GALLERY

Professor O. Schmidt (above). V. Chkalov (opposite page, top left).
M. Gromov (opposite page, top right). B. Balchen (opposite page, bottom).

F. Trojani (opposite page, top). L. Ellsworth (opposite page, bottom left).
V. Stefansson (opposite page, bottom right). Andrée (directly below). Self-
portrait of Nansen (bottom of page).

R. Amundsen (above). H. Riiser-Larsen (opposite page, top). G. Biagi
(opposite page, bottom left). U. Nobile (opposite page, bottom right).

Sir Hubert Wilkins,
portrait by Lady Wilkins,
(left).
A. Viglieri (below).

EPILOGUE

The Arctic is being exploited everywhere, and Alaska, which not so long ago had only primitive transportation, is now served by twelve domestic air lines. Man has satisfied another of his driving ambitions. He has stood at the North Pole, traveled across it submerged, and flown over it innumerable times. What once was a supreme challenge is now a routine chore; at least six airlines maintain regular transarctic flights that link Europe with America and the Far East.

November 15, 1964, was the tenth anniversary of commercial traffic along the Aerial Northwest Passage. In ten years, SAS, the pioneering carrier, has flown 5,500 flights between Los Angeles and Copenhagen, carrying 235,000 passengers and more than 5,500 tons of freight and mail, while covering a total distance of 32 million miles.* Special equipment and improved radio communication now enable SAS DC-8 jetliners to complete a run in 13 hours and 10 minutes—less than half the time required for the first such flight in 1954.

And what of the men who first blazed the arctic skylanes? Death has come to most of them. Andrée's party perished on White Island, where the remains of the men and a remarkably well preserved record of their expedition was found thirty-three years later. Amundsen vanished in the pursuit of a gallant mission. Cramer lost his life, while almost in sight of fulfillment. Others died of natural causes: Nansen (1930), Ellsworth (1951), Byrd (1957), Wilkins (1958), and Stefansson (1962).

In the early 1960s, only three of Amundsen's Norwegian teammates were still alive: Retired Commander Gottwalt; Odd Dahl, president of the Norwegian Space Research Committee, who once made abortive attempts at arctic flights in Amundsen's "Oriole," and the aerial pioneer of both the top and bottom of the world, Hjalmar Riiser-Larsen, one of the few men who can boast to have been an admiral, a general and the manager of a major airline. Dietrichson disappeared together with Amundsen; Omdal, hired by a Mrs. Grayson to fly her across the Atlantic, vanished with plane and passengers in December, 1927; Feucht emigrated to Argentina and has not been heard from. Wisting and Horgen died of natural causes; Ramm lived only long enough to return to Norway after spending most of World War II in German concentration camps.

Von Gronau, a Nazi general, was wartime military attaché in Japan. Lieutenant Colonel Hassel was Commanding Officer of the U. S. Army Air Corps Base at Goose Bay; D'Aeth fought in the R.A.F., retired as an air vice marshal and later became a parish priest.

Of the seven original Heroes of the Soviet Union, Levanevsky disappeared without trace in the Arctic; Doronin and Molokov died of natural causes, the latter having served as chief of Soviet civil aviation during the war and until 1950, when the post went to Baidukov, co-pilot on the first transpolar flight from Russia to the United States. General Kamanin led an air corps during the war and later assumed an important role in the Soviet space program. Both Vodopyanov and Lyapidevsky finished the war as generals;

---

* By January 1, 1965, SAS had also flown 63,331 passengers in both directions between Copenhagen and Tokyo by way of the Arctic.

one returned to arctic aviation, the other continued his military career. Slepnev, a colonel, retired to become national director for the production of educational aids in Moscow.

Schmidt died of tuberculosis, and Shirshov died of cancer. Feodorov became a prominent scientist; Papanin became director of the Soviet Oceanographic Institute. Chkalov was killed in an airplane crash in 1938. Gromov, a high-ranking general during the war, later headed the test flight service of the Soviet aircraft industry.

In the United States, both Colonels Balchen and Fletcher retired from the Air Force to go into private industry. General Lindbergh remained a technical advisor to Pan American World Airways; he eventually became a director of the company.

Only few of those who had gone in search of the *Italia* were still alive: Among them were, in addition to General Riiser-Larsen, Major Christell, Commodore Rosenvärd, and Holland's respected Senator J. Van Dongen. Captain Lundborg, Sergeant Nilsson, and Major General Schyberg were killed in plane crashes, while Colonel Tornberg, Major General Jacobsson, and Commander Lützow-Holm died of disease. Both Finnish pilots died—Lihr, a commercial pilot, while making an emergency landing, and Sarko, a general, of a heart condition. Italy's Maddalena perished in an aerial plane explosion, and his former co-pilot, General Cagna, was killed during World War II, as was Balbo, who was accidentally shot down by Italian antiaircraft.

Not many of those who were aboard the *Krassin* in 1928 were still alive. Vorontsova was still active as a writer in Moscow; Hoel was retired in Oslo and Giudici in Bergamo. Oras and Samoilovich were purge victims in the late 1930s, and many others perished in the siege of Leningrad during World War II. Eggi, who died of natural causes, never again was prominent, but his former assistant, Ponamarev, became captain of the *Krassin* and eventually assumed command of Russia's first nuclear-powered icebreaker. After returning from wartime service, Colonel Chukhnovsky became a consultant for Soviet antarctic aviation.

Of those who stood at the fringe of the *Italia* disaster, Albertini managed to become a prosperous engineer in Milan; Captain Baccarani and General Valle, both retired, lived in Rome. Romagna-Manoia, Sora, and Tomaselli died of natural causes.

The only arctic team still intact was that of the *Italia* survivors. Behounek was professor of nuclear physics in Prague; Biagi a gasoline station attendant in Rome, and Cecioni a wealthy landowner. After serving some twelve years as a *prefetto* (Provincial Governor), Mariano, an admiral, went into the shipping business. Nobile retired from public and academic life. Trojani spent the war in Italy, then emigrated to Brazil and later returned to publish his book of reminiscences, which finally brought him success and recognition. Viglieri continued his naval career, was awarded Italy's highest military decoration, the Order of Savoy, retired an admiral and became a director of Monaco's International Hydrographic Institute. Zappi was a consular official. Of these eight, Cecioni was first to die, followed a few months later by Zappi.

Whatever their individual contributions, these and many other men laid the foundation for wartime aerial lifelines and for commercial aviation in the Arctic. Their story, gathered from books long out of print, from sources not readily available, was supplemented by reports buried in newspapers brittle with age, and rounded out with verbal accounts from some of them. All this book aims to do is to place into historic perspective many achievements which the tide of time has swept into the pool of things forgotten.

APPENDICES

APPENDIX 1

TARGET: ANTARCTIC

Many pilots and explorers who pioneered in the skies of the arctic also were trail blazers in antarctic skies. Although this book has been confined to arctic aerial history, mention should be made of the antarctic careers of these arctic pioneers. They are briefly recorded in this outline of pioneering flights in Antarctica.

After his successful arctic flight in 1928, Sir Hubert Wilkins planned an expedition to the Antarctic, backed by the American Geographic Society and others. At the same time, Commander Richard E. Byrd was also preparing an Antarctic expedition, costing approximately $800,000, and backed by Edsel Ford, the National Geographic Society, the New York *Times* and the North American Newspaper Alliance.

In September, 1928, Sir Hubert left New York with his fellow pioneer Ben Eielson and the latter's friend, Joe Crosson. The men had the Lockheed-Vega plane of arctic fame, now renamed "Los Angeles," and a sister ship, a newer model called "San Francisco." On November 16, 1928, Wilkins and Eielson, in a short flight flew the first plane to go aloft over the Antarctic continent. On December 20, 1928, they made a 1,300-mile round-trip flight over Graham Land.

In an article written for a national magazine, Sir Hubert spelled out the scope of his pioneering work. Man's very existence, he said, depends upon basic commodities like wheat, wool and meat. The production of these items—and therefore the availability of food and clothes—is greatly influenced by weather, which, in turn, depends on meteorological conditions prevailing at the Poles. Weather observation posts in polar regions are essential, he argued. To set up such stations, the geography of both the top and the bottom of the world must be better known. "Even when that geographical work is done," he said, "there will still be a great deal more to do in the way of detailed exploration." He hoped that the work he and Eielson had done would make it possible "to set up permanent meteorological stations both in the Arctic and Antarctic." Observations made at such posts, correlated with data obtained elsewhere, would make it possible to forecast the weather. "If we can do that," he concluded, "we can enable the primary producers to produce the necessities required in the right quantities at the right time and so eliminate famines, fluctuation in prices and other troubles of mankind."

In August, 1928, Byrd's expedition left Dunedin, New Zealand, with Bernt Balchen in charge of the aviation section, for the Bay of Whales. The party remained in constant contact with a New York radio station. Charted by Sir Ernest Henry Shackleton, the Bay of Whales had seen Roald Amundsen launch his quest of the South Pole. There, at a small inlet, to be named Ver-sur-Mer, Commander Byrd established his base, which he called Little America. On November 28, 1929, Byrd, Balchen, and two other men made their famous flight from Little America to the South Pole and back.

In February of the following year, Little America was closed down, and, outracing another oncoming antarctic winter, Byrd's party sailed home. Leaving the expedition's main body in New Zealand, the leader himself went ahead and returned to the United States, where he had already been promoted to Admiral by Act of Congress.

History had been made in the Antarctic, but the work was not finished; it had only begun. Admiral Byrd would be back, Sir Hubert Wilkins would return and so would Bernt Balchen. And still others, among them Hjalmar Riiser-Larsen and Lincoln Ellsworth, would go South.

In fact, while Byrd was preparing for his polar flight, the second Hearst-Wilkins Antarctic Expedition arrived at Deception Island. Missing this time were Eielson and Crosson, who had accepted jobs with Alaska Airways. In their stead Wilkins had with him as pilots Parker D. Cramer and Al Cheesman, both experienced in cold-weather flying. Cheesman and Wilkins could only make three short exploratory flights. Then the expedition moved south, aboard an auxiliary vessel, loaned Wilkins by the British Colonial Office.

As the year 1929 closed, three groups of men poised for an assault on the Antarctic: the second Hearst-Wilkins Expedition, the party of Australia's Sir Douglas Mawson on the *Discovery,* the old ship of Robert Falcon Scott, and men aboard a 285-ton whaler called *Norvegia.* This vessel, especially outfitted and transformed by explorer-sponsor Lars Christensen into a combination of whaling ship and floating research laboratory, carried Hjalmar Riiser-Larsen, Finn Lützow-Holm and two seaplanes. On December 7, 1929, Riiser-Larsen and Lützow-Holm made a three and one-half-hour mapping flight. On December 22 they flew again, landing on territory claimed by Australia.

There was a friendly meeting aboard the *Discovery* between Riiser-Larsen and the gray-haired Mawson. In an atmosphere of friendship and co-operation, an agreement was reached whereby the Australians would explore the Antarctic to the east of the 45th degree eastern longitude, leaving the Norwegians to work west of this longitude. Eventually, this would be the definitive demarkation line separating Norway's antarctic claims from those of Australia.

Before the flying season was over, Riiser-Larsen took to the air twice more to map a vast stretch of antarctic coast, to the west of Enderby Land. There he named a deep indentation of the Weddell Sea "Cape Norvegia."

By January, Wilkins and Cheesman had made some short flights in the Antarctic and mapped Charcot Land as well as several other islands. On February 1st, they took off from the fringe of the continental shelf-ice, south of Peter Island. Barely passing the coast of Antarctica, they were caught in a storm and had to turn back. The local flying season was over and the Hearst-Wilkins expedition left for Montevideo. Both planes were sold to the Argentine Government and Wilkins's party returned to the United States.

Riiser-Larsen continued aerial exploration of Antarctica. He discovered and charted Princess Martha Coast in 1930 and Princess Ragnhild Coast a year later. By the time he returned to Norway, Riiser-Larsen had flown over approximately one-fifth of the Antarctic continent.

Early in 1933, Riiser-Larsen was again in the Antarctic, heading a carefully prepared and boldly conceived expedition. His plan called for a sled journey from the eastern end of Queen Maud Land, along the coast, all the way to the Weddell Sea and Hope Bay on Graham Land—a distance roughly equivalent to that between New York and Alaska! Following the principle established by Vilhjalmur Stefansson in the Arctic, Riiser-Larsen anticipated living off the land. Seal meat was to feed both men and dogs and blubber was to be used for fuel.

On March 5, his three-man 58-dog party disembarked on sea ice from specially designed aluminum boats. The men pitched their tent and headed inland to establish a winter camp on the continental shelf. During the night a fierce storm broke up the ice, scattering dogs and supplies and causing everything and everybody to float away on small floes. Managing to climb atop an iceberg, the men survived and were rescued by a whaler which had intercepted their radio appeals for help. Riiser-Larsen's last Antarctic expedition, ending in utter failure and disaster, was over, and he returned to Norway.

At about the same time both Byrd and Ellsworth were in the midst of preparations for new and independent expeditions to the Antarctic.

In the fall of 1933, a specially rebuilt Norwegian sealer, named the *Wyatt Earp*, in honor of the famous frontier marshal, by order of Lincoln Ellsworth, was approaching Dunedin, New Zealand. Aboard were Wilkins, Balchen, and a plane named "Polar Star." The *Wyatt Earp* headed for Antarctica's Ross Sea, to a small inlet of the Bay of Whales. It was approximately twelve miles from Little America, a once busy camp now covered by an immense blanket of snow.

Ellsworth wanted to make a transcontinental flight from the Ross Sea to the Weddell Sea and back. The $37,000 plane was almost totally destroyed by an antarctic gale before she ever flew, and the *Wyatt Earp* set off on the return trip to Dunedin. There the ship was damaged while being docked and was left behind for repairs. Ellsworth, Wilkins, Balchen, and the ruined "Polar Star" proceeded to the United States.

In 1934, the *Wyatt Earp* was again in the Antarctic. Once more the repaired "Polar Star" was assembled and checked. Plans for the season had been revised. Instead of a transcontinental round-trip, the plane would make a crossing from Deception Island to the Bay of Whales.

On December 18, after many delays, Balchen and Ellsworth made a two and one-half-hour test flight. The barometer was steady and Ellsworth felt good. He expected to wing his way over Antarctica the following day and wired an advance story to both the New York *Times* and the North American Newspaper Alliance. The story was to be released after receipt of a prearranged confirming "flash" from the *Wyatt Earp*. But when the new day dawned, a storm raged widely over the Weddell Sea. By January 3 of the new year, Ellsworth was ready to accept defeat by weather. His second antarctic expedition was another failure, and the plane had only made a single two-and-a-half-hour flight. There remained only taking the plane, unused oil, and gasoline aboard the *Wyatt Earp* and heading the small ship homeward.

Undaunted, Ellsworth set out to organize a third expedition to Antarctica. He hired two pilots, and after a leisurely trip to South America aboard the *Graf Zeppelin* he joined his staff on the *Wyatt Earp*, which then left Montevideo in October, carrying fourteen men and the "Polar Star."

After many frustrations and upsets, mostly due to bad weather, Ellsworth and his pilot flew over enough of Antarctica to claim for the United States some 350,000 square miles of the frozen continent. There was no doubt this time— the third expedition had been an absolute success.

APPENDIX 2

EVOLUTION OF ARCTIC AVIATION

1897   July 11–14. S. Andrée. First arctic flight. Free balloon took off from Dane Island, Spitsbergen, came down on ice at 82° 56′ N. lat., 20° 52′ E. long.

1907   September 2. W. Wellman. First attempt at an arctic flight in a dirigible. Crashed three hours after takeoff from Dane Island.

1909   August 15. W. Wellman. Second attempt at an arctic flight in a dirigible. Crashed shortly after takeoff from Dane Island.

1914   August 7–31. J. Nagursky. First arctic flights in a plane. Five local flights from Krestovaya Guba, Novaya Zemlya.

1920   July 15–October 20. St. Clair Street, C. C. Nutt, C. H. Crumrine, R. C. Kirkpatrick. New York–Nome and back. First flight into the Arctic of the Western Hemisphere. Organized by U. S. Army Air Service.

1923   May. O. Omdal. Unsuccessful test flight for Amundsen's projected transarctic flight.

June. O. Dahl. Unsuccessful reconnaissance flight in support of the *Maud* expedition.

July 6–8. H. H. Hammer, expedition leader; A. Neuman, pilot. First photographic flights in the Arctic. Takeoff point: Green Harbor, Spitsbergen.

1924   August 2–31. L. H. Smith and E. H. Nelson. First flight from Europe to America by way of the Arctic. Part of the Round the World Flight, organized by the U. S. Army Air Service.

1925   May 21–June 15. Amundsen-Ellsworth Expedition. H. Riiser-Larsen and L. Dietrichson, pilots. Takeoff in Kings Bay, Spitsbergen, landing at 87° 44′ N. lat., 10° 30′ W. long. and return to Bennevingsfjord, Spitsbergen.

August 8–19. MacMillan Expedition. R. E. Byrd, leader of aviation section; F. Bennett, pilot. Reconnaissance flights over Ellsmere Island.

1926   March 31–April 30. Detroit Arctic Expedition. G. H. Wilkins, leader; C. B. Eielson, pilot. Ferrying flights in Alaska, from Fairbanks to Point Barrow.

April–May. M. Babushkin. First plane landings on pack ice.

May 9. R. E. Byrd, expedition leader; F. Bennett, pilot. Takeoff and landing point, Kings Bay, Alaska. Officially recognized as the first aerial attainment of the North Pole.

May 11–14. *Norge* flight from Kings Bay, Spitsbergen, to Teller, Alaska. First transpolar intercontinental crossing in a dirigible.

1927   March 29–April 15. G. H. Wilkins, leader; C. B. Eielson, pilot. Exploratory flight over the Arctic Ocean with landings on pack ice.

1927–
1928   Hudson Strait Air Expedition and Survey. Commander of flight personnel: T. A. Lawrence.

1928   April 15–21. G. H. Wilkins, leader; C. B. Eielson, pilot. First transarctic intercontinental flight in a plane from Point Barrow, Alaska, to Green Harbor, Spitsbergen.

May 11–25. Arctic flights of the *Italia*. U. Nobile, expedition leader and pilot.

May 26–September 6. Rescue operations for survivors of the *Italia* and Amundsen.

August 18–19. B. R. J. Hassell and P. D. Cramer. First attempt to scout a commercial transarctic route from America to Europe. Takeoff at Cochrane, Ontario; emergency landing near Sondre Strom Fjord, Greenland.

1929 June 9–July 11. A. Ahrenberg. Unsuccessful attempt at a transarctic flight from Europe to America. After intermediate stops in Iceland, reached Ivigtut, Greenland, where flight was abandoned.

July 4–9. R. H. Gast and P. D. Cramer. Unsuccessful attempt at a transarctic flight from America to Europe. Takeoff at Sault Ste. Marie, Ontario; aircraft destroyed by ice at Port Burwell, on Hudson Bay.

1930–
1931 British Arctic Air Route Expedition. H. G. Watkins, leader; N. H. D'Aeth and W. E. Hampton, pilots.

1930 August 18–23. W. von Gronau. Transarctic flight from Europe to America. Takeoff at List on Sylt, Germany; landing at Cartwright, Labrador. Intermediate stops in the Faroes, Iceland, and Greenland.

1931 July 24–31. H. Eckener. Arctic flight of the dirigible *Graf Zeppelin*.

August 1–5. P. D. Cramer and O. Paquette. First aerial crossing of the Greenland icecap. Takeoff from Wakeham Bay, Hudson Strait; landing at Angmagssalik, Greenland. Intermediate stop at Pangnirtung, Baffin Island.

August 15. W. von Gronau. First aerial east-west crossing of the Greenland icecap. Takeoff at Scoresby Sound; landing at Sukkertoppen.

1933 July 5–12. I. Balbo. Arctic section of mass flight from Europe to America. Takeoff from Lough Foyle, Ireland; landing at Cartwright, Labrador. Intermediate stop at Reykjavik, Iceland.

July–August. Aerial survey of Greenland by C. Lindbergh and A. Morrow Lindbergh.

1937 May 5. P. Golovin. Flight from Franz Josef Land to North Pole and back.

May 21. O. Schmidt, leader; M. Vodopyanov, pilot. First landing near the North Pole, preliminary to establishment of a drifting weather station.

June 18–20. V. Chkalov, G. Baidukov, A. Belyakov. First transpolar plane flight from Europe to America. Takeoff in Moscow, U.S.S.R.; landing near Vancouver, Washington.

July 12–14. M. Gromov, A. Yumashev, S. Danilin. Transpolar long-distance record flight from Moscow, U.S.S.R., to San Jacinto, California.

August 12. S. Levanevsky. Takeoff in Moscow, U.S.S.R., on a transpolar flight in an aircraft suitable for commercial purposes. Plane and crew vanished without trace.

1941–
1942 Construction of landing sites and auxiliary facilities in Greenland and Labrador.

1942   April. M. Arnold. Test flight in a *Liberator* bomber along the Northern Air Route from Presque Isle, Maine, to Prestwick, Scotland. June 26. Start of Operation Bolero.

1942–
1943   Development of the Alaskan Air Route.

1942   September 29. Start of Operation Alsib.

1949   September 17–18. F. Armstrong, B. Balchen. Nonstop transarctic flight from Fairbanks, Alaska, to Oslo, Norway.

1951   May 29. C. Blair. First transarctic solo flight from Bardufoss, Norway, to Fairbanks, Alaska.

1952   May 3. W. Benedict. First landing at the North Pole.

1952   November 19–20. P. Jensen. First transarctic commercial flight. Takeoff in Los Angeles, California; landing in Copenhagen, Denmark.

1953   May 23–24. M. Aschim. First transarctic flight from Oslo, Norway, to Tokyo, Japan.

1954   November 15–16. Inaugural SAS passenger flights from Los Angeles to Copenhagen and from Copenhagen to Los Angeles.

1960   June. Inauguration of transarctic jet service between Europe and America by SAS.

APPENDIX 3

AIRCRAFT USED IN PIONEER ARCTIC FLYING

Year	Leader(s)	Type of Aircraft	Name	Engines
1897	Andrée	Free balloon	*Eagle*	None
1907	Wellman	Dirigible	*America*	One 80-hp Lorraine
1909	Wellman	Dirigible	*America*	One 80-hp E.N.V.
1914	Nagursky	Maurice Farman		50-hp Gnome
1920	U. S. Army Air Service	De Havilland DH-4		400-hp Liberty
1923	Hammer	Junkers J-13	Icebird D-260	185-hp B.M.W.
1924	U. S. Army Air Service	Douglas DT-2	New Orleans Chicago	400-hp Liberty
1925	Amundsen-Ellsworth	Dornier Wal	N-24 N-25	Two 350 Rolls Royce Eagle IX
1925	Byrd	Loening amphibian	N-1 N-2 N-3	400-hp inverted Liberty
1926	Wilkins	Fokker Fokker	Alaskan Detroiter	400-hp Liberty Three 220 Wright Whirlwind
1926	Byrd	Fokker	Josephine Ford	Three 220-hp Wright Whirlwind
1926	Amundsen-Ellsworth	Dirigible	*Norge*	Three 240-hp Maybach
1927	Wilkins	Stinson		220-hp Wright Whirlwind
1928	Wilkins	Lockheed *Vega*		220-hp Wright Whirlwind
1928	Nobile	Dirigible	*Italia*	Three 240-hp Maybach
1928	Hassell & Cramer	Stinson	Greater Rockford	220-hp Wright Whirlwind
1929	Ahrenberg	Junkers W-33		300-hp Junkers
1929	Gast and Cramer	Sikorsky amphibian	Untin Bowler	Two 425-hp Pratt & Whitney Wasp
1930	Watkins	De Havilland *Gipsy Moth*		85-hp De Havilland Gipsy
1930	von Gronau	Dornier	Amundsen Wal	Two 500-hp B.M.W.
1931	Eckener	Dirigible	*Graf Zeppelin*	Five 330-hp Maybach
1931	Cramer	Bellanca *Pacemaker*		225-hp Packard Diesel
1931	von Gronau	Dornier	Grönland Wal	Two 700-hp B.M.W.
1933	Balbo	Savoia Marchetti S-55X		Two 750-hp Isotta Fraschini Asso
1933	Lindbergh	Lockheed *Sirius*	Tingmissartoq	710-hp Wright Cyclone

Year	Leader(s)	Type of Aircraft	Name	Engines
1937	Schmidt	ANT-4		Four 940-hp AM-34
1937	Chkalov	ANT-25		950-hp AM-34
1937	Gromov	ANT-25		950-hp AM-34
1937	Levanevsky	ANT-4		Four 940-hp AM-34
1937	Wilkins	Consolidated *Catalina*	Guba	Two 1,000-hp Pratt & Whitney
1937	Wilkins	Lockheed *Electra*		Two 600-hp Pratt & Whitney
1949	U.S.A.F. Armstrong	Douglas DC-4		Four 1,250-hp Pratt & Whitney
1951	Blair	*Mustang* P-51	Excalibur III	1,700-hp R.R. Packard Merlin
1952	U.S.A.F. Benedict	Douglas DC-3		Two 1,000-hp Wright Cyclone
1952	SAS—Jensen	Douglas DC-6b		Four 2,500-hp Pratt & Whitney Double Wasp

Aircraft used during *Italia* rescue operations.

Year	Leader(s)	Type of Aircraft	Name	Engines
1928	Guilbaud-Amundsen	Latham flying boat		Two 600-hp Lorraine
1928	Maddalena	Savoia Marchetti		Two 600-hp Isotta Fraschini
1928	Penzo	Dornier	Marina II	Two 375-hp Rolls Royce
1928	Riiser Larsen Lützow-Holm	Hansa Brandenburg	Maake 37 Maake 36	185-hp B.M.W. 185-hp B.M.W.
1928	Sarko	Junkers F-13	Turku	185-hp Junkers
1928	Chukhnovsky	Junkers Trimotor	Krasny Medwed	Three 300-hp Junkers
1928	Babushkin	Junkers	J-13	300-hp Junkers
1928	Tornberg	Heinkel He-5s		450-hp Bristol Jupiter
1928	Lundborg	Fokker 4-D		450-hp Bristol Jupiter
1928	Schyberg	De Havilland *Cirrus Moth*		80-hp Cirrus II
1928	Nilsson	Junkers	Uppland	Three 300-hp Junkers

APPENDIX 4

GREENLAND-ICELAND TRANSATLANTIC AIR ROUTE (BRIEF TO PAN-AMERICAN AIRWAYS BY CHARLES A. LINDBERGH)

The main advantage of the Greenland-Iceland Transatlantic air route consists of the comparatively short distances between land. The main disadvantages are the short days in winter and the variable weather both in relation to season and latitude. The high mountains and lack of flat country along much of the route also make the problem of scheduled operation more difficult. Another factor to be taken into consideration is the additional distance over the great circle route between the United States and Europe. In view of these conditions the northern route must lay its strongest claim on the basis that the larger payload which can be carried when refueling bases are comparatively close together will compensate for other disadvantages. It might also be argued that the ability to install more fixed radio stations and emergency landing facilities would constitute a safety advantage. As aviation advances the problem of short winter days and variable weather will undoubtedly decrease in importance. On the other hand the need for frequent refueling and landing facilities will also decrease.

This paper is for the purpose of discussing the establishment of an air route through Greenland and Iceland rather than the relative merits of different transoceanic routes. It seems rather certain that the Arctic will eventually be crossed by air routes wherever time and distance can be saved by northern flying. With every year that passes more aircraft are used in the Arctic for local services; and the very fact that ground and water transport is so difficult makes their use relatively more advantageous.

A scheduled transatlantic air service could probably be operated through Greenland and Iceland during the summer months with a high degree of regularity and without encountering great difficulties. Such a service could be established with seaplanes without the need of very extensive organization and preparation. However, a successful transatlantic service must operate on a year-round schedule. If a temporary seasonal service is established it should be only as a step toward a permanent service. Consequently the problem to consider is that of operating during the worst months of the year.

During all but a few weeks in summer, water landings are impossible in Greenland because lakes and harbors are either frozen over or filled with floating ice. Planes could be equipped with skis for landing in winter when the ice is sufficiently thick. However, there would be two periods each year in late spring and again in early fall when there would not be enough ice for ski landings, yet too much ice for pontoon landings. Another complication would be the great difference in climate along the route both with latitude and season. Frequently when skis could be used advantageously in Greenland they could not be used at all in Iceland. During most of the year there would be a line north of which ski operation would be desirable and south of which it would be impossible. This line would of course move north in summer and south in winter and thus cause an additional complication. However, as Dr. Stefansson brings out, this period can be shortened wherever it is possible to have a base near which there is a fresh water lake and also a sheltered arm of the sea which differ in such a way that in the spring the ice leaves one considerably earlier than the other and conversely in the autumn forms earlier on one than on the other. The entire operation might be carried on with land planes on wheels. This would require the construction of landing fields and a comparatively high original expenditure. Accessible landing field locations are particularly hard to find in Greenland and on the coast of Labrador. The problem of removing or rolling the snow on the runways would also arise. Planes might be used with ski-pontoons or possibly a combination of all three landing devices—skis, pontoons and wheels. However, it must be remembered that the primary advantage of the northern route lies in the increased pay load which can be carried. The use of such amphibians would materially decrease that payload both because of their greater inherent weight and their lowered cruising speed with consequent reduction of mileage per gallon of fuel. From the standpoint of forced landings, it is true that it is desirable for a plane to be able to land under the largest possible range of conditions. On the other hand from the standpoint of all-around safety it is desirable for a plane to reach its objective before landing. In meeting the latter requirement speed and range are among the most important factors. This again brings up the old issue of whether it is better to design a plane to have less possibility of a forced landing or to have a greater possibility of surviving a forced landing. I believe that, within reason, the greater safety lies in attempting to eliminate forced landings. As aviation develops we will fly through practically all weather conditions, over mountains at night and in fog, over the ocean in storm, and above the fog-covered ice packs. Under these conditions it seems that safety lies in airworthiness and that there is little use in attempting to build aircraft which could make a forced landing without damage. These conditions make the elimination of mechanical failures essential. Consequently it seems that multi-engined planes must be used. Probably a bi-motored plane would be most satisfactory and economical at least until enough traffic is developed to warrant the use of larger planes.

Unusually high wind velocities are reported in Greenland during part of the year. This would make high cruising speeds desirable to combat head winds. It would also make a high wind loading desirable for handling the plane on the ground or water. A full cantilever monoplane with flaps or other similar devices would probably meet the requirements of northern flying better than any other type. It is inherently less subject to winds when on the ground. It is more adaptable to the installation of flaps. The wing is less affected by the accumulation of ice and is more adapted to the installation of deicers.

Probably the plane best suited for operating the northern route is the Douglas or Lockheed type of bi-motored monoplane. This type can easily be equipped with wheels, skis or pontoons.

It seems probable that eventually wheels only will be used on all but local services. A plane equipped with wheels which can be retracted into the wing has the great advantage of higher cruising speed and lower weight empty. However, in starting operations it would be conservative to use pontoons with retractable wheels, and to being as early as possible in summer. These pontoons should be so designed that they could be used as skis if necessary. Careful consideration should be given to replacing the wheel-pontoons with wheel-skis in winter. If winter operation with wheel-pontoons is costly in maintenance or unsatisfactory from other standpoints; and if there is not enough open water along the route to warrant the pontoons from a safety standpoint in winter then it may be desirable to change to wheel-skis. The development of a pontoon which is a satisfactory ski would materially simplify northern operations. This problem has already arisen in connection with the Pan American Airways Alaskan operation and is now being studied by the technical department. Later, as experience develops, the skis and pontoons may be eliminated and wheels only used. In making this recommendation I want to point out that there is a large portion of the year when there will be too much ice to permit water landings along most of the route. Consequently pontoons alone could not be used. There is also a large portion of the year when there is too little ice and snow to permit the use of skis along portions of the route and at the same time too much ice to permit water landings. Consequently, under these conditions, a ski-pontoon would not be a solution. Wheels alone would be the best answer if we could be sure that the plane would always reach its destination or an emergency field and that the snow on the runways could be kept rolled or cleared away sufficiently to permit wheel landings. A wheel pontoon seems the best single solution for starting the operation of a northern route because in emergency it can also be used as a ski with probably little or no damage. Also such a combination would instill the greatest possible confidence in the personnel while they are gaining experience in northern flying. During summer, landings could be made in any protected water if the destination could not be reached. In winter emergency landings could be made on pontoons with safety anywhere they could be made on skis alone. It would not matter if fields became covered with several feet of snow. And if by some chance a plane was forced down in open ocean it would have the maximum possible chance of rescue.

It is more difficult to operate airways by night than by day. Consequently the long winter night of the Arctic again adds to the problem. If a satisfactory schedule could be maintained without flying twenty-four hours a day this difficulty might be lessened by scheduling the planes to take off several hours before sunrise so that they could reach their destination and land during the daylight hours. This might be an advisable procedure in beginning operations but eventually it will be necessary to fly the entire twenty-four hours with as little loss of time on the ground as possible. On more southerly routes it might be advisable to fly overnight nonstop, but to do this on the northern route would completely eliminate its main advantage of frequent refueling bases. Consequently it is necessary to plan for night landing facilities. Obviously it is impractical to install beacon lights across Davis Strait or over the Greenland icecap. I believe that in general plans should be made only to light the terminal and emergency bases. The navigation between these points should be by a combination of radio and dead reckoning. Probably the personnel should also be trained in celestial navigation.

In the few weeks we spent on the Greenland–Iceland route last summer it was possible to obtain only a very general knowledge of the problems and conditions which would be encountered in operating an airline. Final decisions should not be made until meteorological and other data covering a period of years are assembled and studied. After we had spent a short time along the northern routes several facts became apparent. As usual, in a country where little flying has been done, the difficulties have been greatly exaggerated. There is bad weather, strong winds and low temperatures, but by no means to the extent commonly believed. If the only problem was to carry on an air service to northern points, it would not be difficult of solution. Boats are infrequent in summer, and there are none in winter. Mail and passenger schedules are measured in months when there are any at all. Airlines through Labrador or Greenland would be practically without competition in carrying passengers, mail or express where time was of any importance.

From our observations and inquiries it seems that the weather improves with increasing latitude north of Newfoundland. Our observations tend to confirm Dr. Stefansson's belief in the advantages, from a weather standpoint, of a route considerable north of Julianehaab. We found on our trip, and we were informed by people who have spent many years in the north, that it was frequently clear at Hopedale and Hebron, while the weather was bad at Cartwright; also that Godthaab and Holstensborg were often clear while it was foggy or raining at Julianehaab. There seemed to be little comparison between the weather at Scoresby Sound and Angmagssalik. Scoresby Sound was practically always clear, while the weather at Angmagssalik was usually poor. However, Dr. Rasmussen informed us that the weather at Angmagssalik had been exceptionally bad that summer (1933). Subject to confirmation by a tabulation of recorded weather over a period of years, I believe that the best weather on the Labrador Coast lies just south of the fog area of Hudson Strait, probably between Hopedale and Hebron. Reports indicate that the weather in the Northwest River area is better than at Cartwright. A study of weather conditions in Baffin Land would be very interesting. We flew from Holstensborg across Davis Strait to Cape Dyer, but we were not able to reach the interior, due to a large storm area which caused little or no visibility and rain at freezing temperature. Consequently, our knowledge of Baffin Land consists only of a flight along a few miles of coast line under conditions of very poor visibility.

In laying out a northern air route I believe the coast should be avoided wherever possible. Locations inland seem to be comparatively free of fog and, certainly, operations can be carried on with greater regularity from inland bases in the majority of cases. I believe Major Logan's suggestion of placing a base in northern Maine should be studied carefully. Subject to much more detailed study, I suggest laying a tentative northern transatlantic route along the west coast of Newfoundland to the vicinity of Botwood; from Botwood to the vicinity of Northwest River; from Northwest River to a point between Godthaab and the icecap, and from there to Iceland. If a fog-free base is placed in the general vicinity of northern Maine, or possibly in Canada, a little north of Maine, planes could be routed to Botwood as the next stop or, if weather there was too bad, they could fly direct to Northwest River. Probably an inland base north of Northwest River and just south of the Hudson Strait fog area would be preferable. However, the inaccessibility of more northern bases may make Northwest River the best base for beginning operation. Hopedale would be a good base for flying boats during a short period of the year when the ice conditions permit. There are large and well-sheltered areas for takeoff and good mooring locations.

Hebron is probably a better location, but the ice-free period is apparently extremely short. At both Hebron and Hopedale the coasts are rugged and mountainous. We saw no locations nearby where it would be practicable to construct a landing field. We were informed by the Eskimos that there was comparatively flat country about fifty miles west of the coast.

From Northwest River I believe the route should go to Godthaab, where a base should be established between the coast and the icecap. We located several places where fields might be constructed close to water which is ice free in summer and accessible by boat. I suggest Godthaab, because it is closer to Northwest River than Holstensborg and because the winter daylight is longer. Also it is north of the worst fog area. I understand that Dr. Hobbs observations indicated the weather conditions near his base, east of Holstensborg, to be considerably better than those farther south and possibly enough better to warrant the additional distance. This is apparently also the conclusion of Dr. Belknap both from his studies for Pan American Airways on his 1933 expedition and from his experience on previous expeditions. A comparative study of inland weather at both locations would be of value. A comparison of weather records at Godthaab and Holstensborg would not be satisfactory in this respect, as both places are seriously affected by sea fog and weather which does not extend far inland. Dr. Hobbs has located several places where fields could be constructed in the Holstensborg vicinity, and Major Logan found a valley where a two-way field a mile or two long could apparently be constructed without great difficulty. These would be accessible by water in summer. From Godthaab, I believe, the route should go directly to Iceland via the Angmagssalik area, but with the intention of passing over Angmagssalik when the weather prevents landing. From our observations and inquiries it seems that Angmagssalik has the worst weather of any point on the route I have outlined. Angmagssalik has a good harbor for landing when ice permits. However, there are only a few weeks when the ice would permit flying boats landing at all. There is a large lake near Angmagssalik where a base could be established. The lake is large enough for landings and takeoffs but is surrounded on three sides by mountains, and under storm conditions the air is very rough. Lake Fjord would make an excellent emergency landing base. The reports of the Watkins' expedition indicate that serious consideration should be given to making it the main base in the Angmagssalik vicinity. A base close to Angmagssalik would have an advantage in being accessible to the settlement and in that boats already stop there. The air in the vicinity of Lake Fjord is extremely rough at times. Only comparative local observations can decide whether Angmagssalik or Lake Fjord or some point northwest of Angmagssalik is most suited for a base. It seems possible that weather would be better farther inland to the northwest of Angmagssalik. Lake Fjord is quite narrow and slightly curved, but could be used for the operation of either seaplanes in summer or ski-planes in winter. It is very close to the sea and also the icecaps, but is well sheltered by mountains.

The route I have suggested can undoubtedly be improved upon after more information has been assembled. Very little is known about year-round weather conditions away from the coasts, and accurate, comparative meteorological information may make a more northern route advisable, or a more southern route feasible.

The weather at Julianehaab appears to be materially worse than farther north. Operations could be carried on, but, I believe, with much less regularity, as long as aircraft are dependent on their pilots' being able to see, in order to land. Water landings can be made in summer, either in the fjord or on the lake. Apparently the country southeast of Julianehaab is less subject to fog. Governor Ibsen suggested the lake at Greenland Forest as a fog-free area. Our observations supported this. The lake is large enough, but surrounded by mountains on three sides. In this respect it should be borne in mind that there are very few level areas in Greenland, and most of these in places impracticable for a transatlantic airline. We took off from Julianehaab in a broken fog, which was thick at sea, broken at the coast and extended only part way to the icecap. The most fog-free area at this time was in the vicinity of the Greenland Forest and south of it. The fog extended as far as we could see to the south of Cape Farvel. However, the land north of Cape Farvel, the sea east of Greenland, and the icecap were all clear. Here again can be seen the importance of accurate and comparable meteorological information from the inland areas of Julianehaab, Godthaab, Holstensborg and, possibly, a point between Julianehaab and Godthaab.

Our observations indicated that the best weather area on the east coast, with the exception of more northern points, exists northwest of Scoresby Sound. Dr. Koch, of the Danish expedition in that area, informed us that the best location for water operation was at Ella Island. There are a number of locations in this general area where landing fields could be constructed easily. While it seems too far north for a regular transatlantic operation, I believe that it would be an excellent emergency base, where a plane could land if caught in bad weather between Godthaab and Iceland.

Flying conditions over the icecap were usually good when we had an opportunity to observe them. Ordinarily the visibility was unlimited and the sky clear, except for a few scattered cirrus clouds. At one time, however, we saw storm clouds over the icecap in the north. These were part of a large storm area. On both of our flights across the ice we encountered completely overcast weather during a portion of the time. Also we found that when the sky was overcast there was usually a haze over the snow, which extended upward as much as one thousand feet at times. This haze was like a thin fog or drifting snow. However, there did not seem to be enough wind to cause so much drifting snow, and whenever the sun broke through the cloud layer, the haze largely disappeared. The temperature was between $-6°$ and $-13°$ centigrade. At one time the haze and clouds blended together so that there was no horizon. Without the amber glasses, which we had carried on Dr. Stefansson's advice, it was not possible to see the snow through the haze, and the light was very hard on our eyes. With the use of amber glasses, however, we were able to see through the haze at all times.

I believe that, with the exception of the crevassed area, a landing could usually be made on the icecap without serious damage and, possibly, no damage to either skis or pontoons. The surface was quite level in most places. The small ridges set up in the snow by the wind would make landings rough at times. On the west side along our route the crevassed area extended in forty or fifty miles, but the large crevasses were only near the edge of the ice. On the east coast the snow extended almost to the land, and, with the exception of the active glaciers, there was comparatively little crevassed area visible.

It is not possible to lay too much stress on the necessity of an adequate radio organization along the northern route. Nothing will contribute more to the safety and efficiency of operations. It will be as necessary to have accurate reports from all bases which are open for landing as it will to have planes which are capable of reaching those bases regardless of intermediate conditions.

As long as possible in advance on the actual start of operations the most experienced meteorologist obtainable should be sent to the various bases and to any additional points from which it is advisable to have advance weather information. The fact that so little is known about weather along the northern route makes it essential to stress the meteorological organization.

The establishment of landing fields in Labrador and Greenland is of importance if the route is to be flown regularly during the entire year. From the air it seemed that a field location would not be difficult to find at Northwest River. In the vicinity of Hopedale and Hebron it might be extremely difficult. There seemed to be several possible locations east of Holstensborg and east of Godthaab. Even these may prove expensive to develop after a ground survey. It would be easy to locate a field between Ella and Clavering Islands. The Norwegians have already operated land planes in that vicinity. It might be very difficult to locate one in the Angmagssalik area. The problem of location is made much more difficult in each instance by the necessity of being near navigable water. The need for fields is emphasized by the fact that the period when it is neither possible to land on ice with skis nor on water with pontoons will vary with different localities along the route. Consequently it must be measured from the time of the first ice break-up at any essential base to the time of sufficiently open water at every essential base in the spring of the year, and vice versa in the fall.

The question of where bases should be located in Iceland will require further study. Fortunately a great deal more meteorological information exists in Iceland than in Greenland. Stefansson has already stated that one side of Iceland is frequently clear even though the other is covered with fog. Our experience and inquiries tended to confirm this. It seems that at least two bases should be located in Iceland. The conditions we encountered in the short period we were there can only be used to average in with observations over several years. However, they are of interest. These would indicate the desirability of three bases. One in the northwest; one in the southwest, and one in the southeast. The northeast coast seemed to be comparatively foggy. It is not difficult to find sheltered water in almost any section of Iceland. However, we were informed that there are Föhn winds of high velocity at times. It appears that in both Greenland and Iceland one of the problems is to find a means of protecting aircraft from high winds while they are on the ground or water. Also to permit the mechanics to work on them.

The harbor at Reykjavik is entirely unsuited for seaplane operation. It is too small for landing or taking off and the water outside is too exposed in the case of a north wind. However, there is sheltered water a few kilometers to the east. During the time we were at Reykjavik there was usually a gale blowing across the harbor, both night and day, while a short distance to the east the wind was very light. At Harna Fjorda on the southeast coast, there is a body of water, sheltered from the sea, which would be suitable for seaplane operation. The disadvantages of this location are that it is quite exposed to the wind and that the entrance is not good for ships. Eskifjordur, on the other hand, is well sheltered both from storm and sea but may be subject to strong Föhn winds. The fjord is too narrow for cross takeoffs. Possibly Horna Fjorda would be less subject to fog.

In contrast to Greenland there are many natural landing areas in Iceland and comparatively little difficulty would be encountered in constructing airports in almost any section.

Planes used on the northern route should be capable of flying nonstop from Iceland to Europe. The Faroes and the Shetlands can be used if desired whenever the weather is suitable, but there seems to be so much fog that they should not be relied upon as regular stopping points. It seems that the fog in the vicinity of these islands frequently exists in patches and that one part of the islands may be covered while another part is comparatively clear.

Until radio and other devices are developed to a point which permits landings to be made without seeing either ground or water it seems that the successful operation of the far northern route will lie in the knowledge of where clear weather exists and the ability to reach these points regardless of intermediate conditions.

APPENDIX 5

PURPOSE OF DRIFTING STATIONS IN THE ARCTIC

In general, because both the magnetic and geomagnetic poles are located in North America, the most important geophysical aspects for study in northern North America are undoubtedly the electromagnetic sciences. A few of the many problems are the location and movement of the auroral zone, the morphology and propagation of geomagnetic storms, the mechanism underlying ionospheric disturbances, the intensity and changes of low energy cosmic rays, the magnitude and meaning of ionospheric "drifts" and, in particular, integration of the fields of ionospheric physics, geomagnetism, auroral physics, and cosmic rays. In the Arctic Ocean, however, the climatological sciences—meterology, glaciology, oceanography and climatology—probably are of greater importance, with secondary but still important studies in the electromagnetic sciences. In the latter group, for example, many important questions still remain unanswered regarding the existence of an inner auroral zone, the cause of the geomagnetic anomaly over the Arctic Ocean, possible solar control over the high latitude "knee" of the cosmic ray intensity distribution, etc.

On the Arctic Ocean, studies of the climatological fields can scarcely be overemphasized. Interrelatedly they determine the thickness of the ice pack over the ocean; the drift or movement of ice floes; and the age, lifetime and firnification of the sea ice. On a long-term basis their study should provide an insight into the future of the Arctic within the next century—will the ice mainly disappear? Will the ocean become a navigable sea to very high latitudes? What is the interrelationship between the Arctic Ocean and the climate of the neighboring continents? And how can short-term predictions on ice conditions be improved?

In short, a study of the Arctic is vital to the future of the northern hemisphere. If appreciable warming occurs, new large Arctic ports may be opened with widespread influence on rail and water transportation patterns, population growth and the economic development over appreciable regions of Eurasia and North America.

LIEUTENANT COLONEL DONALD A. SHAW

APPENDIX 6

SOVIET DRIFTING STATIONS 1937 - 1965

Station	Principal Station Commander	Established	Abandoned	Coordinates When Established	Coordinates When Abandoned	Distance Traversed (NM) Net	Distance Traversed (NM) Total	Length of Drift (Days)	Mean Daily Speed (NM)
NP-1	I. D. Papanin	21 May 37	19 Feb 38	89.3°N 78.4°W	70.5°N 19.2°W	944	1106	274	4.0
NP-2	M. M. Somov	2 Apr 50	11 Apr 51	76.0°N 166.4°W	81.5°N 163.5°W	345	1403	374	3.7
NP-3	A. F. Treshnikov	9 Apr 54	20 Apr 55	85.6°N 178.0°W	86.0°N 24.0°W	451	1005	376	2.7
NP-4	E. I. Tolstikov	8 Apr 54	19 Apr 57	75.5°N 178.3°W	85.5°N 00.0°	1139	3762	1108	3.4
NP-5	N. A. Volkov	21 Apr 55	8 Nov 56	82.1°N 156.5°E	84.2°N 63.2°E	583	1959	536	3.6
NP-6	K. A. Sychev	19 Apr 56	14 Sep 59	74.2°N 177.0°W	82.1°N 03.6°E	1572	4670	1246	3.7
NP-7	V. A. Vedernikov	23 Apr 57	11 Apr 59	82.1°N 164.1°W	85.1°N 33.0°W	669	1900	721	2.6
NP-8	V. M. Rogachev	27 Apr 59	18 Mar 62	76.2°N 164.4°W	83.2°N 132.6°W	540	1644	1055	1.5
NP-9	N. I. Blinov	14 Apr 60	9 May 61	77.2°N 163.7°E	85.8°N 176.4°W	540	1204	376	3.2
NP-10	N. A. Kornilov	20 Oct 61	29 Apr 64	75.5°N 176.4°E	88.6°N 92.3°E	862	2847	922	3.1
NP-11	N. N. Bryazgin	1 May 62	18 Apr 63	77.5°N 166.1°W	81.1°N 139.2°W	374	1036	353	2.9
NP-12	L. Belyakov	30 Apr 63	23 Apr 65	76.8°N 165.2°W	81.1°N 146.8°W				
NP-13	A. Busuyev	2 May 64	1 July 65	73.9°N 167.7°W	80.5°N* 157.0°E *	Continuing			
NP-14	——	2 May 65	——	74.7°N 175.5°W		Continuing			

* Last position.

APPENDIX 7

U. S. DRIFTING STATIONS 1954-1965

| Station | Principal Station Commander | Established | Abandoned | Coordinates When | | Distance Traversed (NM) | | Length of Drift (days) | Mean Daily Speed (NM) |
				Established	Abandoned	Net	Total		
T-3	J. Fletcher	3 Apr 52	14 May 54	87.9°N 156.5°W	84.5°N 80.7°W	305	1470	771	2.0
T-3	A. P. Crary	1 May 55	21 Sep 55	83.6°N 188.0°W	82.3°N 98.0°W	100	—	144	—
T-3 (BRAVO)	LeBlanc	7 Mar 57	14 May 60	82.8°N 99.0°W	71.8°N 159.7°W	—	—	1163	—
ALPHA	N. Untersteiner	8 Jun 57	3 Nov 58	80.8°N 160.3°W	86.2°N 113.1°W	440	1580	512	3.0
CHARLIE (ALPHA 2)	K. O. Bennington	2 Jun 59	7 Jan 60	76.7°N 161.2°W	76.9°N 169.1°W	115	1125	219	5.1
ARLIS I	K. O. Bennington	10 Sep 60	16 Mar 61	74.7°N 141.1°W	75.0°N 169.8°W	485	744	187	4.0
ARLIS II	Arctic Research Laboratory Staff	23 May 61	10 May 65	73.2°N 156.1°W	66.7°N 27.0°W	— —	— —	—	—
T-3	Arctic Research Laboratory Staff	19 Feb 62	26 June 65	73.0°N 161.0°W	76.1°N 142.1°W	Continuing			
ARLIS III	V. P. Hessler	10 Feb 64	10 May 65	73.0°N 161.0°W	72.8°N 154.0°W	50	—	96	

APPENDIX 8

RUSSIAN EXPEDITIONS TO ARCTIC DURING POSTWAR PERIOD

Year	Stations established
1948	8
1949	33
1950	39
1954	103
1955	136
1956	208
1957	12
1958	16
1959	?

NOTES

(Full information on titles and authors referred to in these Notes will be found in the Bibliography.)

I. PIONEERS (1896–1924)

1. Nansen started his career as a zoologist and curator of the Bergen Museum. Later, he made a voyage into Greenland waters and wrote some scientific papers dealing with zoology and histology. In May 1888 he left Norway for Greenland, where he started the ascent of the inland ice on August 16 together with Otto Sverdrup, K. K. Trana, Captain O. C. Dietrichson and two Lapps. The party reached Greenland's west coast on September 8 and returned to Norway in May of 1889. This was the first successful crossing of Greenland. Nansen then became curator of the Oslo Museum and devoted himself to the preparation of the *Fram* expedition.

2. As quoted by Kirwan, p. 219.

3. Greely led a 26-man expedition to the Arctic which lasted from 1881 to 1884. Although a great deal of valuable information was gathered, the expedition was marred by dissension, insubordination and rebellion. When Greely's party was finally rescued by W. S. Schley, only seven men were still alive, the others had died of starvation, exposure, drowning or disease. One man had been ordered shot.

4. As quoted by Kirwan, p. 220.

5. The *Fram* left Oslo on June 24, 1893, and became icebound on September 22, at latitude 78° 50′N., 133° 37′E., north of the New Siberian Islands, to begin her historic drift. When it became evident that the drift would not carry the ship across the Pole, Nansen decided to try to reach the North Pole on foot. Leaving the *Fram* in charge of Sverdrup, Nansen and H. Johansen started out northward on March 14, 1895. On April 8 they reached latitude 86° 14′N. and had to turn back, toward Franz Josef Land. Nansen thus reached a spot only 224 nautical miles from the North Pole, 160 miles farther north than anybody else had ever come. Nansen and Johansen wintered on what was later named Fred Jackson Island. The following year they met Fred Jackson of the Jackson-Harmworth Expedition, which had gone to Franz Josef Land in search of a land route to the North Pole. They boarded Jackson's ship and returned to Norway on August 13, 1896. The *Fram* managed to break out of pack ice northwest of Spitsbergen after a drift of 35 months. She then returned, undamaged and under her own power, to Tromso. The drift of the *Fram* is of historic significance not only because it inaugurated a new exploratory technique but also because scientific research was continued aboard the vessel throughout the drift.

Nansen then became Professor of Zoology at the University of Oslo. In 1905 Norway gained her independence, and a year later Nansen went to England as her diplomatic representative. He returned in 1908 and resumed scientific research in oceanography. In 1917, he headed Norway's Government Commission to the United States, and in 1918 he headed a Commission of the League of Nations, which was responsible for the repatriation of some 5 million prisoners of war. In 1921 he signed an agreement with Russia's Foreign Minister in regard to large-scale famine relief and as a result of his efforts more than 1.6 million people were fed and clothed. He was awarded the Nobel Prize for Peace in 1923 and died in 1930 at the age of 68.

6. Speech made on February 15, 1895, quoted in Andrée, p. 29–39.

7. As quoted in Andrée, p. 40.

8. The air expedition was to be made by Andrée, Strindberg, and Nils Ekholm. The latter was a meteorologist and astronomer who subsequently withdrew and was replaced in 1897 by Fraenkel.

9. Andrée, p. 58.

10. This account of the Andrée expedition is based on the written record left by Andrée and Strindberg, as published in Andrée, except where otherwise indicated.

11. Andrée's balloon was somewhat elliptical and had a capacity of 170,000 cubic feet.

12. Andrée, p. 66.

13. Stefansson, *Unsolved Mysteries,* p. 201. (Here local time is given.)

14. Stefansson, *Unsolved Mysteries,* p. 202.

15. Andrée planned to have the lines drag along the ice to regulate the height and flight direction of the balloon. When carried to a greater height, the increased weight of suspended rope would increase the total weight of the balloon, thus causing a descent. Whenever the balloon came down, the length of suspended rope would be shortened, the total weight would be decreased and the balloon would have a tendency to rise again.

16. This buoy was found at Logletten on September 27, 1900, after having remained in the water presumably for 1,142 days.

17. Buoy No. 7, thrown out at 10:55 P.M. on July 11, 1897, was found on May 14, 1899, in Kalla Fjord, Iceland.

18. No shorthand message was found in the cylinder.

19. Strindberg's letter to his fiancée, dated July 24, 1897.

20. It does not appear from the written record that Andrée was anxious to go ashore. It seems rather that the men intended continuing their drift. The decision to land on White Island was probably made only after the floe broke up.

21. White Island was visited on July 9, 1930, by the *Hanseat* Expedition, which searched for survivors of the *Italia*. On that occasion Andrée's snow-covered camp was not discovered. On August 5, 1930, a Norwegian expedition aboard the *Bratvaag,* headed by Gunnar Horn, went ashore on White Island. Horn's men found a boat and a sled, as well as the remains of Andrée and Strindberg. The latter was lying in a grave made of rocks, an indication that he had died first. Subsequently, on September 5, 1930, the Swedish journalist Knut Stubbendorff arrived on White Island aboard the *Isbjörn* as head of a privately organized expedition. He recovered Fraenkel's remains and more relics of Andrée's party. The Swedish Government appointed a scientific committee to investigate the find and prepare for publication documents recovered at Andrée's camp. This committee had a Norwegian section which included Professor Adolf Hoel, Norway's leading authority on Spitsbergen. Among the material found on White Island were photographs taken by Strindberg, which had remained undeveloped for some 33 years. They were processed with meticulous care and represent the graphic documentation of Andrée's expedition.

The cause of death of Andrée and his men has never been determined. It was not starvation, because adequate food stores were on hand. Stefansson believed that Andrée and Fraenkel died of carbon monoxide poisoning, a theory which was supported by Prof. Sverdrup. As to Strindberg, Stefansson assumed that he died "by drowning or through some quick illness." Prof. Hoel, on the other hand, is convinced that Andrée and his men died of trichinosis. (Personal communication.) Trichinosis is a systemic disease caused by ingestion of inadequately cooked meat infested with *Trichinella spiralis.* Bears sometimes are reservoir hosts for this parasite in its encysted larval form and some bear meat so infested was found on White Island.

22. Clements Markham, President of the Royal Geographical Society, summed up this view when he said: "Since Nansen's discovery that the Pole

is an ice-covered sea there is no longer any special object to be attained in going there."

23. Cagni advanced to within 220 miles of the Pole, 22 miles farther than Nansen.

24. Peary was getting too old for exploratory work and was finding it increasingly difficult to obtain financial support.

25. Hayes, p. 87. According to this author Peary turned back at a point 103 miles short of the Pole.

26. Amundsen received his B.A. degree from the University of Oslo and began to study medicine in 1890. He did not finish the course, but instead during the period 1894–1903 he prepared himself with an incredible tenacity of purpose to become an explorer. From 1894–1896 he signed on as a sailor; in 1897–1899 he was on DeGerlache's *Belgica* expedition in the Antarctic; in 1900 he obtained a skipper's license. After studying the theory and practice of magnetic observations, he bought a small ship and made oceanographic observations in the North Atlantic, passing his results on to Dr. Nansen. After having collected funds and bought supplies, Amundsen and six carefully selected men hurriedly left during the night of June 16, 1903, to escape an angry creditor who was threatening to attach Amundsen's ship, the *Gjoa*. Amundsen took his vessel to Godhavn on Disko Island and from there made the historic traverse of the Northwest Passage, by sailing past Beechey Island, through the Straits of Peel, Rae and Simpson. Past Herschel Island, rounding the coast of Alaska at Point Barrow, passing across Bering Strait, the *Gjoa* finally reached San Francisco in October 1906. Amundsen fixed the position of the magnetic North Pole and then obtained from Nansen the *Fram* for an attempt to reach the North Pole.

27. The irony of it is that it was Nansen's fondest dream to go to the Antarctic aboard the *Fram* himself.

28. Von Zeppelin was born at Constance, Germany, on July 8, 1838. He served in the American Federal Army as a volunteer, and while in the United States made his first balloon ascent. After returning to Europe he participated in the Austrian War of 1866 and the Franco-German War of 1870. He retired from the army with the rank of general.

29. July 4, 1900, as quoted by Toland, p. 40.

30. As quoted by Mark Sullivan, Vol. I, p. 366.

31. Mark Sullivan, Vol. II, p. 593.

32. Most facts concerning the history of aviation as quoted here were obtained from Fraser, Sinclair, The American Heritage History of Flight, and Ellis, as cited in the Bibliography.

33. Toland, p. 51.

34. Mittelholzer, p. 33–34.

35. After graduating from the University of Iowa, Stefansson studied theology and anthropology at Harvard. In 1904 and 1905 he made two archeological voyages to Iceland; in 1906–07 he was ethnologist for the Leffingwell-Mikkilsen expedition; in 1908–12 he headed his own Arctic expedition.

36. Thomas, p. 62.

37. Sources used for biographical data on Wilkins are: Grierson, *Sir Hubert Wilkins,* Thomas, and Wood.

38. Grierson, *Sir Hubert Wilkins,* p. 17.

39. Shackleton was Scott's lieutenant during the 1901–04 Antarctic expedition. In 1908 he led his own expedition, reaching a point some 97 miles from the South Pole; he returned to the Antarctic aboard the *Endurance* during 1914–17.

40. This account of Stefansson's expedition is based on Stefansson, *The Friendly Arctic.*

41. Bob Bartlett was a member of Peary's 1908–09 North Pole expedition.

42. Thomas, p. 67.

43. The men aboard the *Karluk* eventually reached Wrangel Island and were later rescued.

44. The men with Stefansson were Ole Andreason and Storker Storkerson.

45. Stefansson, *The Friendly Arctic,* p. 272.

46. The biographical sketch of Amundsen is based on Amundsen, *My Life,* and Partridge, *Amundsen.*

47. Amundsen had received a "private flying certificate" in 1912.

48. Samoilovich in *Vozdushnyie Puti,* p. 16ff.

49. Sources for Ellsworth biographical data are: Ellsworth, *Search,* Ellsworth, *Beyond Horizons,* and Wilkins, *Under the North Pole.*

50. After this expedition Stefansson retired from active exploratory work. In 1932 he became adviser to Pan American Airways and during World War II he was arctic adviser to the U. S. Government. He surveyed defense conditions in Alaska and prepared reports as well as manuals for the Armed Forces. He died on August 26, 1962, at the age of 82.

51. Kirwan, p. 321.

52. Biographical details on Riiser-Larsen were obtained from Riiser-Larsen, from personal letters and interviews.

53. Sources for Byrd's early life are Byrd, *Skyward,* and Murphy.

54. Account of Bennett's life as given by his wife Cora Bennett.

55. Eielson's biography appears in Rolfsrud.

56. Account of Balchen's life is based on his autobiography, *Come North With Me*, Knight and Durham, and personal communications.

57. Dietrichson became one of Amundsen's pilots in 1925.

58. The *Bodensee* was turned over to Italy after World War I and became part of a fleet of airships commanded by G. Valle, then a lieutenant colonel.

59. Wilkins's chances for success were slight to begin with, because a competing team was already ahead. The prize was, in fact, won by Keith and Ross Smith, who arrived in Port Darwin, Australia, two days after Wilkins came down on Crete.

60. Nordenskiöld was first to sail this route in 1878–79 aboard the *Vega*. In 1913–14 Vilkitski's expedition, consisting of two ships, the *Taimyr* and *Vaigatch,* passed along this waterway.

61. Belov, *Istoriia*, Vol. III, p. 46.

62. Belov, *Istoriia*, Vol. III, pp. 70–71.

63. Armstrong, *The Northern Sea Route,* App. I, p. 120.

64. Cope was a member of Shackleton's 1914 Antarctic Expedition.

65. This course was organized especially for Riiser-Larsen and gave him an opportunity to establish close personal relationships with many outstanding aviators of that time, including Commodore Maitland, Chief of Britains's Airship Service.

66. Amundsen's plan was to have the *Maud* drift across the Arctic Ocean. The ship left Tromso on July 15, 1918; the decision to go to Nome rather than enter pack ice off the New Siberian Islands, as originally planned, was made for several reasons. The *Maud* arrived in Nome in August 1920.

67. Belov, *Istoriia*, Vol. III, p. 450.

68. Hanson, p. 193.

69. This episode is described by Hanson and in Stefansson, *Adventure on Wrangel Island.*

70. Sutherland was a delegate to Congress from Alaska, then a Territory which could not actually elect Congressmen.

71. Amundsen purchased the plane in the spring of 1922. As it was being flown to Seattle, the pilot, Oscar Omdal, had to make an emergency landing and the plane was wrecked. A new one arrived in Seattle by rail and was taken aboard the *Maud*. In Kotzebue Bay, Alaska, Amundsen, Omdal and

the plane were transferred to a schooner which went to Wainwright, Alaska, while the *Maud* set out for her drift, carrying aboard the *Oriole*. The *Oriole's* pilot, Odd Dahl, and Captain Oscar Wisting, made two short arctic flights. The plane was then badly damaged and could no longer be used.

72. Mittelholzer, p. 13 and p. 99.

73. A full account of Hammer's expedition is given in Mittelholzer. During these flights parts of Spitsbergen were photographed from the air for the first time.

74. In 1924 George Binney headed another flying expedition to Spitsbergen. His seaplane stayed in the air a total of 11 hours, during which time approximately 70 miles of North East Land's coast were photographed. The plane was eventually wrecked and had to be abandoned.

75. The *Roma* was an Italian dirigible built by Nobile and others.

76. New York *Times,* January 10, 1924.

77. Belov, *Istoriia*, Vol. III, p. 231.

78. Eielson was to receive $2.00 per mile for the first five flights and $1.50 for subsequent trips.

79. The history of the Northern Sea Route for the period 1919–32 is based on Armstrong, *The Northern Sea Route,* and Belov, *Istoriia,* Vol. III.

80. Belov, *Istoriia,* Vol. III, p. 280.

81. Original telegram at Oslo University Library.

II. QUEST (1925–1926)

1. Ellsworth, *Search,* p. XII, of introduction by H. T. Clark.

2. Ellsworth, *Search,* p. 76.

3. Ellsworth, *Beyond Horizons,* p. 125–127.

4. Ellsworth, *Beyond Horizons,* p. 128.

5. The aircraft industry in Germany was restricted under the terms of the Versailles Treaty. Some German planes were therefore manufactured in Italy.

6. Murphy, p. 131–132.

7. The story of the Amundsen-Ellsworth expedition is based on Amundsen, *My Life;* Amundsen and Ellsworth, *Our Polar Flight;* Ellsworth, *Beyond Horizons,* and Riiser-Larsen.

8. Amundsen and Ellsworth, *Our Polar Flight*, p. 107.

9. In 1906, Walter Wellman, a journalist who had been to the Arctic on two previous occasions, tried to make a dirigible flight to the North Pole in a semirigid 165-foot airship. The attempt was called off because of defects in the dirigible. In September 1907 Wellman managed to fly a short distance from his base on Dane Island before the ship came down. A final attempt, made on August 15, 1909, aboard a newly constructed airship ended only a few miles from Virgo Bay.

10. Amundsen and Ellsworth, *Our Polar Flight*, p. 271.

11. On that day the elder Ellsworth died.

12. Amundsen and Ellsworth, *Our Polar Flight*, p. 331.

13. Ellsworth, *Beyond Horizons*, p. 191.

14. Feucht, who had been chosen to go with Amundsen only because of his mechanical abilities, was not interested in exploratory work. Dietrichson did not want to participate in another expedition because he had no faith in dirigibles.

15. Amundsen, *My Life*, p. 134.

16. Byrd, *Skyward*, p. 143.

17. Sources for Byrd's expedition, are Byrd, *Skyward*, Byrd, "The First Flight to the North Pole," *Natl. Geogr.*, and Murphy.

18. MacMillan, *Natl. Geogr.*, p. 505.

19. Murphy, p. 150.

20. Murphy, p. 151.

21. The first was Cope's 1920 expedition. The second was Shackleton's 1921 expedition aboard the *Quest*. Wilkins went as far as Rio de Janeiro, where the ship had to undergo repairs. Then he left for South Georgia to do some biological research. When he arrived in Grytviken Harbor, to rejoin the expedition, Shackleton was dead. The *Quest* eventually returned to England without having completed the work Shackleton had planned.

22. Wilkins tried to buy Amundsen's N-25, but the plane was sold to a German aviation school for the use of Wolfgang von Gronau.

23. The account of Wilkins's arctic flights is derived from Wilkins, *Flying the Arctic*.

24. Nobile, *In Volo*, p. 109.

25. Valle, p. 100–101.

26. Wilkins, *Flying the Arctic,* p. 15.

27. General M. Patrick, Chief of Army Services, refused to allow military personnel to participate in the expedition without Congressional approval. Doolittle therefore could not go with Wilkins. Lanphier was on leave, however, and was free to go.

28. Riiser-Larsen, personal communication.

29. Amundsen, *My Life,* pp. 193 ff.

30. Valle, p. 101. The sentence remained suspended and less than a month later Valle was appointed Commandant of a newly established Academy of Aeronautics in Caserta. He became an airplane pilot and eventually was appointed Undersecretary for Aviation to succeed Balbo.

31. Nobile, *In Volo,* pp. 58 ff.

32. More than eleven years later, on December 10, 1937, in an unpublished letter addressed to Valle, then Mussolini's Undersecretary for Aviation, D'Annunzio wrote: ". . . I cherish forever the memory of your spirited presence . . . and of our old polar dreams, when dying alone in the desert of ice seemed to me to be supreme glory . . ."

33. Amundsen, *My Life,* p. 158.

34. Insurance was a last-minute demand, but firmly insisted upon by the Italian Government.

35. Nobile, *In Volo,* p. 146.

36. Wilkins, *Flying the Arctic,* pp. 56–57.

37. Description of Byrd's expedition is based on Byrd, *Skyward,* and Murphy.

38. Statement made by Amundsen in *My Life,* and confirmed in personal communication by Riiser-Larsen.

39. Riiser-Larsen, personal communication.

III. CONQUEST (1926–1928)

1. Sources for the *Norge* flight are Amundsen's *My Life,* Amundsen and Ellsworth's *First Crossing,* Nobile's *In Volo,* and Quattrini.

2. Balchen, personal communication.

3. Balchen, *Come North,* p. 26.

4. The plane was so named after Edsel Ford's daughter.

5. Balchen, personal communication.

6. Amundsen, *My Life,* p. 169.

7. A seaman named Kontor still managed to hide a ukulele aboard the plane.

8. Balchen, pp. 43 ff.

9. Nobile, *In Volo,* pp. 137 ff.

10. Riiser-Larsen, personal communication.

11. Balchen, personal communication.

12. Byrd, *Skyward,* p. 197.

13. As quoted by Cora Bennett, p. 85.

14. Byrd, *Skyward,* p. 200.

15. Liljequist, personal communication, confirmed by Balchen. The film of Byrd's landing shown in U. S. theaters was actually made a day after the polar flight.

16. Byrd, *Skyward,* p. 203.

17. Riiser-Larsen, personal communication, supporting Amundsen's statement in *My Life,* p. 173.

18. Olonkin had been aboard the *Maud.* He developed an ear infection on the eve of the *Norge* flight and had to be left behind.

19. On April 15, 1924, the N-1 was hauled out of its hangar on Ciampino Airport by a ground party of 200 men. Hit by a strong wind, the dirigible tore loose and three men who did not release their grip on the ropes fast enough were carried upward. They fell from an altitude of 200 feet and were killed. Cecioni was one of nine men aboard the dirigible. He took command and brought it to a landing. The maneuver was supervised from the ground by Valle. Nobile, who had ordered the dirigible taken out, was "impassive and stood at a distance." Valle, p. 100.

20. Amundsen and Ellsworth, *First Crossing,* p. 141.

21. Amundsen, *My Life,* p. 184: "For a few moments the *Norge* looked like a circus wagon of the skies, with great banners of every shape and hue fluttering down around her."

22. Riiser-Larsen, personal communication. Because of extreme fatigue Riiser-Larsen had a visual hallucination and thought he was seeing the Russian cavalrymen who had come to view the *Norge* at Gatchina.

23. Originally meant to be preserved and exhibited in a museum, the *Norge* was actually scrapped. One propeller, mounted on a wall in Cecioni's house, remained a conversation piece for several decades.

24. Riiser-Larsen, personal communication. It was then decided that all members of the expedition would go ashore just the way they were dressed, wearing ordinary outfits bought in Alaska.

25. Grove Karl Gilbert (1843–1918) was a geologist.

26. New York *Times,* June 19, 1926.

27. Amundsen, *My Life,* p. 212; repeated orally by Riiser-Larsen, and described by Ellsworth, *Beyond Horizons,* p. 230.

28. Nobile, personal communication.

29. Nobile, *Im Luftschiff,* p. 383.

30. New York *Times,* July 19, 1926. This rally sparked street fights between Fascists and anti-Fascists.

31. New York *Times,* July 20, 1926.

32. New York *Times,* November 17, 1926.

33. New York *Times,* November 15, 1926. In his book, *Posso dire,* p. 15, published in 1945, Nobile said that the contribution of the Fascist Government to the *Norge* expedition was absolutely nil. By that time Nobile had rediscovered a socialist "patrimony of ideas and convictions" and successfully ran for parliament on the Communist ticket (April 17, 1946).

34. Amundsen, "Rows," and Nobile, "More rows," both magazine articles.

35. Speech by Representative Roy O. Woodruff, quoted by Cora Bennett, pp. 108–110.

36. Liljequist.

37. New York *Times,* November 12, 1926. On December 20 Nobile triggered an anti-Fascist demonstration in Paterson, New Jersey, involving about 2,000 people. New York *Times,* December 21, 1926.

38. Balchen, *Come North,* p. 60.

39. In addition to his savings, Wilkins contributed $5,000 in fees collected for 107 lectures given at an average of five a day in different Detroit schools over a six-week period.

40. Ellis, p. 233.

41. Wilkins, *Flying,* p. 141.

42. Wilkins, *Flying,* p. 147.

43. Wilkins, *Flying,* pp. 150–151.

44. At Ver-sur-Mer.

45. In 1928 German fliers of the *Bremen* received this decoration, although they were neither American nor naval officers.

46. Trojani, personal communication.

47. Trojani, pp. 222–223.

48. Nobile, *Im Luftschiff,* p. 11.

49. Trojani, personal communication.

50. King Haakon expressed his displeasure that Balchen had been slighted by not being given a decoration for his part in the flight of the "America."

51. The *Samson,* renamed *City of New York,* became Byrd's base ship on his first Antarctic Expedition. Amundsen also recommended that Byrd use the Bay of Whales as a base.

52. This letter, dated February 20, 1927, was first published on September 21, 1961.

53. Mayor Belloni was removed from office on September 5, 1928. The American firm of Dillon, Read & Co. had loaned the city of Milan 30 million dollars. "Under his (Belloni's) rule almost every cent of the thirty millions was stolen." (Seldes, p. 222.) Trojani is under the impression that Belloni undertook to finance the *Italia* expedition in order to further confuse the financial account of the city of Milan. (Personal communication.)

54. New York *Times,* April 22, 1928.

55. There had been an unsuccessful attempt to fly the "Bremen" across the Atlantic in 1927.

56. Initial stages of the *Italia* flights are described on the basis of Behounek, *Siehen Wochen;* Nobile, *Im Luftschiff* and Trojani.

57. Nobile pointedly omitted consulting Italy's arctic veteran Umberto Cagni.

58. Behounek had unsuccessfully tried to be taken abroad the *Norge* in 1926.

59. Pontremoli was considered an outstanding physicist with a brilliant future.

60. Trojani, p. 259.

61. Trojani, p. 263.

62. The *Italia* was originally the N-4 and was to have been insured for 2.7 million lire (Trojani, p. 243). Nobile made an agreement to that effect with Balbo. However, when he returned to Balbo the contract covering the

loan of the *Italia*, the clause concerning insurance was omitted. Balbo, having received from Nobile assurance that the papers were in order, signed the document without reading it (Trojani, p. 258).

63. Wilkins, *Flying*, p. 283.

64. The landing was made on Dead Man's Island. The flight was so remarkable because navigation was by dead reckoning.

65. Wilkins, *Flying*, p. 331.

66. New York *Times*.

67. Returning from the *Hobby*, Kings Bay's lone radio operator got lost in the snow and perished. His body was recovered only later in the year.

68. Trojani, p. 280.

69. One of these planes was piloted by the then Lt. Einar P. Lundborg.

70. New York *Times*.

71. The *Italia* remained precariously moored to the mast for more than seven hours.

72. Trojani, personal communication.

73. Nobile, *Im Luftschiff*, p. 95.

74. Trojani, p. 299.

75. This way Nobile made sure that a representative of Mussolini's own paper would come along on the following polar flight.

76. According to Nobile a geographically significant result of the flight was that Gillis Land was not seen where it was marked on the maps then available.

77. Trojani, p. 309.

IV. DISASTER (1928)

1. The literature on the flight of the *Italia* is so vast that no attempt has been made to present it in its entirely in the bibliography. Two books on the subject have recently appeared in English: Cross, *Ghostship*, and Nobile, *My Polar Flights*, a translation of *Gli Italiani*. (A condensed version of the author's previous writings on the *Norge* and *Italia* flights.)

Primary sources for this chapter are the books by Behounek, Biagi, Giudici, Lundborg, Maddalena, Nobile (*Im Luftschiff* and *Posso dire*), Samoilovich, Sora, Tomaselli, Trojani, Van Dongen, Viglieri, Vorontsova, and Wiese—all listed in the bibliography.

Secondary sources were books by Albertini (*Alla ricerca*), Arnesen, De Geer, Hildenbrandt, Houdenak, Katz, Meyer, Mindlin, Parajanine, Pochod Krassina, and Tandberg, all listed; as well as magaine articles by the following authors: Albertini, Bartoli, Hoel, Marini, Notarnicola, Pariset, Pillon, Simoni, Tomaselli, Torelli, Trionfero and Zanetti.

Scientific results of the expedition have been reported by Behounek, Amadeo Nobile, and Romagna-Manoia. Two biographies of Malmgren exist, only the one by Lazzazero has been consulted.

2. Trojani, p. 311.

3. Trojani, p. 317. (The reference is to Mussolini's advice not to make this expedition.)

4. Biagi, personal communication.

5. Cecioni, personal communication.

6. At one time Nobile tried to say that Malmgren's leaving the controls contributed to the crash. Behounek reacted strongly to this implication, stating unequivocally that the dirigible at that moment was already hopelessly out of control.

7. Cecioni had a compound fracture; Nobile's fractures were simple ones.

8. This particular sack had been lying on the roof of the gondola; it was not the only such sack aboard.

9. Biagi, personal communication.

10. It is assumed that Pomella, trying to get out of his cabin, was thrown on the ice at the moment of impact and killed instantly.

11. Throughout that day the base ship listened for Biagi's messages, but. according to Baccarani, atmospheric conditions made reception impossible.

12. Viglieri, p. 39.

13. New York *Times*.

14. In 1920 the icebreaker *Malygin,* then known as *"Solovei Budimirovich"* was icebound in the Kara Sea with 85 people aboard. The Soviet Government solicited Norway's help. Nansen organized the rescue operation, which was conducted with the *Krassin,* known at that time as *"Sviatogor"*, in command of Sverdrup.

15. Behounek, *Sieben Wochen,* p. 123, repeats same statement in *Tragedia.*

16. New York *Times*.

17. Riiser-Larsen, personal communication.

18. Giudici, personal communication.

19. Nobile, *Im Luftschiff*, p. 175.

20. Trojani, p. 341.

21. Nobile, *Im Luftschiff*, pp. 177 ff.

22. After a spectacular flight to South America, which was very valuable for Mussolini's propaganda, De Pineda had been appointed Balbo's Chief of Staff.

23. Trojani, p. 486.

24. New York *Times*.

25. For simplicity's sake the term "Arctic Institute" has been retained throughout this account, although the name has been changed several times since the institute was founded. At present it is called: "Arctic and Antarctic Scientific Research Institute." See Armstrong, *The Arctic Institute*.

26. Survivors of the *Italia*, other than the two officers concerned, are quite unanimous on this point.

27. Nobile, *Im Luftschiff*, p. 200.

28. Nobile, *Im Luftschiff*, p. 203.

29. Nobile, *Im Luftschiff*, p. 204.

30. Finnsko is a boot made of birch-tanned reindeer skin, with the hair on. Usually worn with stuffed dry grass over heavy stockings.

31. Behounek, *Sieben Wochen*, p. 142.

32. Reference is to Dr. Harold Sverdrup, who had been with Malmgren aboard the *Maud*.

33. Behounek, *Sieben Wochen*, p. 143.

34. Behounek, *Sieben Wochen*, p. 147.

35. Viglieri, p. 88.

36. Behounek, *Sieben Wochen*, p. 149.

37. Riiser-Larsen, personal communication.

38. Giudici, p. 18.

39. The ship used by Shackleton on his last expedition.

40. New York *Times*.

41. Not all these ships were engaged in the search for Nobile's men only.

42. As quoted by the New York *Times*.

43. Chukhnovsky, personal communication.

44. Babushkin was an experienced arctic pilot. It is believed that he was the first man to land a plane on drifting ice, in 1926, while flying in support of seal hunters.

45. These two men lived in Spitsbergen and came to volunteer their help.

46. *Corriere Della Sera,* June 14, 1928.

47. Trojani, personal communication.

48. Wilkins chose to be called Sir Hubert rather than Sir George because at that time the British monarch was called George.

49. Biagi, personal communication.

50. Giudici, p. 30.

51. No effort was made to co-ordinate the flights of these four planes.

52. Vorontsova, personal communication.

53. Maddalena did not see the camp even when he was flying over it. Sunlight reflected by the improvised mirror of one of the men on the ice finally attracted his attention.

54. Arnesen, p. 109.

55. Sora, pp. 143–149.

56. So named for Prof. Michael Sars, father-in-law of Nansen.

57. Claims have been made repeatedly that Lundborg insisted on Nobile's early departure because of life insurance involved. Such claims have not been substantiated. More simply, Lundborg wanted to capitalize on the greater publicity value inherent in Nobile's rescue as compared to that of another man. Although Nobile may have thought that his presence aboard the baseship was desirable, it obviously was not. He had no information which he could not have transmitted by radio or conveyed by another member of his party.

58. The 16 dead or missing: Amundsen's group of 6; Mariano's party of 3, Pomella and the 6 carried away with the dirigible.

59. Baccarani, personal communication.

60. Samoilovich. This and many other documents pertaining to the *Krassin's* trip are reprinted by Mindlin.

61. Lundborg, original telegram, as reproduced on p. 148.

62. Nobile, *Im Luftschiff*, p. 335.

63. Behounek, *Sieben Wochen*, p. 215.

64. New York *Times*.

65. Ekman, personal communication.

66. Viglieri, personal communication.

67. This text was passed on to the press; the actual telegram sounded less dramatic.

68. The basic plan of Sora and Van Dongen was to locate Nobile's group and then to transport the *Italia* men to one of the nearby islands. However, having abandoned dogs and sled, Sora had no longer the means to do so.

69. This report was erroneous. What was taken for a third man was actually a pair of pants laid out to dry.

70. Trojani, p. 451. For many years these clothes were part of a permanent exhibit at Leningrad's Arctic Museum.

71. Giudici, pp. 100 ff.

72. Trojani, p. 448, brings out the following facts: When the three men left, they carried 121 pounds of food. The caloric value is not known, but there were 72.6 lbs. of pemmican, 39.6 lbs. of chocolate, 6.6 lbs. of condensed milk, and 2.2 lbs. of butter. According to Zappi, each man got three meals daily from May 31 to June 12 (total: 39 meals). After Malmgren was abandoned on June 12, the two Italians had two daily meals from June 13 through June 28 (total 32 meals). If Zappi's account is correct, each of the meals averaged 1.7 lbs.

73. In a letter dated May 26, 1961, Giudici said: "I omitted a sentence from Zappi's account . . . because I was afraid the censor might find it too dramatic. . . . The sentence was: 'At a certain point Malmgren covered his head with his jacket and begged that an end be made to his life with an axe which Zappi had.' "

74. Giudici, personal communication.

75. Sora's book, ghost-written in the chauvinistic style of the period, may not actually reflect the captain's personality. He is said to have been a simple and unassuming man who rose from the ranks to become a colonel during World War II.

76. July 14, 1928.

77. A national committee of ten prominent Swedish citizens collected 35,000 kr. (approximately $9,350, then) for the erection of a monument to Malmgren. The statue, 6.4 feet high, was unveiled on November 1, 1931, **and**

surplus money was set aside for a scholarship fund. The first award, roughly worth $500, was made in 1953. In 1956 the award went to Prof. Liljequist.

78. New York *Times.*

79. The implication is that Malmgren was abandoned against his will, otherwise he would have turned the letters over to the Italians.

80. De Long's *Jeannette* was caught in ice and began a drift which was to last almost two years. On June 13, 1881, the ship was crushed by the ice and sank. Of the 32 men aboard, all but two died. Articles belonging to the *Jeannette* expedition were found in 1884 off Greenland, proving the existence of a polar ocean current.

81. Trojani, p. 466.

82. Mariano wrote his motto: "Ubi nec aquila" (Where not even the eagle flies.)

83. This is Nobile's version. Tomaselli doubted that Mariano has made such a request. Trojani thinks it is quite likely.

84. New York *Times.*

85. Baigi, personal communication.

86. From a letter of Dr. Fagerstein dated July 1, 1961. ". . . in my opinion Malmgren died a natural death. I have talked that matter over so many times . . . with Mariano that I am firmly convinced that his account . . . is true . . . my wife shares my opinion. . . . I cannot say that Nobile made a very favorable impression on me . . ."

87. New York *Times.*

88. When Nobile was received by Mussolini, shortly after his return to Italy, he complained that he had not been given the full support of the Italian Government. Mussolini dismissed him curtly. On August 28, 1928, Nobile arrived in Milan, ostensibly to visit the families of some of the men who disappeared with the dirigible, but actually to see Mussolini's powerful brother, Arnaldo, whose aid he sought in forwarding to Il Duce a list of complaints against Captain Romagna. He was also intent on starting a behind-the-scenes intrigue, designed to bring about the ouster of Italo Balbo as Undersecretary for Aviation.

Smarting from attacks against Mariano and Zappi in the foreign press, and further antagonized by Nobile's accusations of Romagna, the Italian Navy pressed for an investigation designed to clear all naval personnel involved. Balbo, who considered Nobile a politically unreliable opportunist, was furious at Nobile because he had deceived him by deliberately failing to have the *Italia* insured and made no move to protect his subordinate.

On September 14, 1928, Mussolini appointed a seven-man commission to investigate "all aspects of the *Italia* disaster." The commission was headed by Umberto Cagni, Italy's famous arctic expert, whom Nobile had deliberately slighted by failing to consult him prior to the *Italia* expedition, although he had asked advice from several foreigners. Included in the commission was Balbo's Chief of Staff, General de Pinedo and an outstanding dirigible pilot, Denti Amari di Pirajno, openly hostile to Nobile.

Appearing as an expert witness, General Valle pointed out that Nobile was not a qualified dirigible pilot, that the crew of the *Italia* was numerically inadequate for such a long trip, and that the men could not have performed their functions properly because of extreme fatigue.

On March 4, 1929, after 60 sessions, the commission presented its findings, highlights of which were briefly published in the Italian press. The report was highly critical of Nobile, who thereupon hastily but voluntarily resigned his commission in the Army. He retained the professorship at Naples University, which had been conferred upon him after the *Norge* flight.

On January 29, 1930, following the publication of Nobile's self-righteous account of the *Italia* expedition in book form, Undersecretary for the Navy, Sirianni, authorized the publication of a more detailed account of the commission's findings. It was a 138-page pamphlet, complete with 11 maps, selling at the equivalent of 20 cents, of which 60,000 copies were printed. In it the disaster itself was described in 8 pages and its causes analyzed by an "expert" in 18. The conclusion was that the accident was avoidable and had been caused by an erroneous maneuver by Nobile, who, the report says, "is endowed with only limited technical ability and lacks completely the prerequisites of a commander."

The Zappi-Mariano episode required 23 pages, 8 of which related what was presented as a true, complete and factual account; 15 were required to justify their actions. Mariano was extolled for having brought "honor to the Italian Navy." Zappi was praised ("The Navy can be proud of what he . . . has done."). Viglieri, on the other hand, was said to have "given proof of not having firmness and independence of character," and Biagi was censored for having sold pictures taken on the floe.

Of the 29 pages dealing with rescue efforts, 9 were given to the *Braganza*, which had done little more than shuttle between Kings Bay and Beverly Sound, while the *Krassin* was disposed of in 112 words. Both the Swedish and Norwegian rescue efforts rated one page each, while Maddalena was accorded 3.

Nobile was severely censored for having acted "contrary to the tradition and law of military honor." His leaving the floe as the first, the commission said, "could only be explained, but not justified."

In conclusion, the report declared: "All that could be done, was done as fast as possible to locate, aid and rescue the survivors, as well as to search for the dirigible, considering the means available and the weather conditions. This work, accomplished with the initiative of Italians and competent co-operation of foreigners, constitutes a remarkable example of human solidarity, culminating in the lucky trip of the *Krassin* and the chivalrous and generous sacrifice of Amundsen."

89. The Italian Air Force awarded some medals to members of rescue crews. Maddalena received a cash award of 40,000 lire. Maddalena's copilot, Cagna, turned his own cash award of 25,000 lire over to a charitable institution. This gesture so impressed Balbo that he made Cagna his adjutant. Cagna subsequently rose within 12 years from lieutenant to general. He was killed early in World War II off Majorca, when his plane was attacked by a British warship.

90. On its way to Norway, the *Krassin* intercepted SOS messages from a German vessel, *Monte Cervantes,* and went to its assistance. This work further delayed the projected resumption of the search for Alessandrini's party.

91. Urged on by Pontremoli's mother, Albertini organized another expedition in 1929 and returned to Spitsbergen to look for survivors of the *Italia.* Giulio Guidoz, a member of this expedition, was fatally shot when mistaken for a polar bear. The number of victims in the *Italia* disaster therefore actually stands at 18.

V. MILESTONES (1929–1935)

1. This survey was made primarily to establish a sea route, shorter than that along the Great Lakes and the St. Lawrence River, which could be used to export Canadian grain to Europe. The expedition consisted of 44 men and 7 aircraft. Three bases were established, from which more than 200 routine patrol flights and many special sorties were made.

2. This account is based on Swenson.

3. For convenience the term "Cape North" is retained throughout this account, although the correct name is Severny Cape (*Severny* is Russian for "North."). It is now known as Cape Schmidt.

4. This episode is based on Rolfsrud Slepnev, in *Vozdushnyie Puti,* pp. 301–324, and Swenson.

5. The altimeter of the Hamilton registered 1,000 feet.

6. Charles Lindbergh, in Anne Morrow Lindbergh, *Flying around the North Atlantic,* p. 259.

7. The arctic portion of this flight, covered on the way back to the U. S., was Scapa Flow (Scotland)–Honafjordur (Iceland)–Reykjavik (Iceland)–Fredricksdal (Greenland)–Hawkes Bay (Newfoundland).

8. Italian Major Antonio Locatelli, whom Amundsen wanted to engage for the abortive 1924 expedition, made an arctic flight. Leaving Pisa, he flew via Marseilles, Rotterdam, Brough, Thorshavn (Faroes), Hafnarfjordur (Iceland), and Reykjavik (Iceland). On the next lap, a flight to Greenland, Locatelli had to make an emergency landing. He and his crew were rescued, but the plane could not be saved and had to be sunk.

9. Carlson, pp. 12–21.

10. Ellis, pp. 272–273.

11. Ahrenberg's route was: Stockholm, Bergen, Skaftaros (Iceland). From there the plane had to be towed to Vestermannaeyjar (Iceland), before it could fly on to Reykjavik. From Reykjavik, Ahrenberg made a 900-mile,

14½-hour-long flight to Arsuk (Greenland), and then arrived in Ivigtut (Greenland).

12. von Gronau.

13. Sources for Watkins's expedition are Chapman and Lindsay.

14. An implication that Watkins's rescue party was lost as well.

15. Johannesson was to come from Iceland.

16. Lindsay, p. 82.

17. The official name of this expedition was "British Arctic Air Route Expedition."

18. Chapman, Appendix I, pp. 265–275.

19. Chapman, p. 4.

20. Kirwan, p. 324.

21. This project had had to be abandoned partly because both planes were badly damaged, partly because of frequent storms, which made flying too dangerous. Furthermore, the planes were inadequate for such a flight.

22. von Gronau.

23. This moutain range was later named Gronau Nunatakker.

24. A year later von Gronau made an around-the-world flight in the same plane and used Ivigtut (Greenland) as an intermediate landing site.

25. Stefansson, *Discovery,* p. 312.

26. Balbo flew via Iceland. After this flight he was appointed governor of Libya. The post of Undersecretary for Aviation went to Balbo's Chief of Staff, General Giuseppe Valle, who was relieved of his office in 1939 after opposing Italy's entry into World War II.

27 Anne Morrow Lindbergh.

28. Dr. Lauge Koch mapped from the air Greenland's eastern coast north of Scoresby Sound.

29. Pan American classified the report "confidential" until 1964. It is reproduced in Appendix 4.

30. Carlson, p. 50.

31. Grierson, *High Failure.*

32. This expression is said to have been coined by Balchen.

33. Sources used for this account of Wilkins's submarine expedition are Grierson's *Sir Hubert Wilkins,* Thomas, and Wilkins's *Under the North Pole.*

34. Sinclair. Among those killed in this crash was Major George Scott.

35. "Aeroarctic" was founded in 1924 on the initiative of Fridtjof Nansen, who became its first president. The society had its headquarters in Berlin. Its program envisioned arctic exploration by means of dirigibles.

36. There was prohibition in the United States at that time.

37. Submarine voyages had been predicted by Bishop Wilkins of Chester (1614–1672), an ancestor of Sir Hubert.

38. Nobile, *Addio Malygin.* Subsequently Nobile returned to Russia, with a staff which included Felice Trojani, to start an unsuccessful dirigible construction program.

39. Description of Eckener's arctic flight is based on Asberg, "Dirigible in the Arctic," in *Vozdushnyie Puti,* pp. 80–103; Eckener; Ellsworth, *Beyond Horizons;* and Vaeth.

40. The crew was German, except for Ernest Krenkel, a Russian. He was one of the three radiomen. Among participants from Germany were L. Weickmann, a meteorologist, Captain Bruns, Secretary General of Aeroarctic, a physician, four photographers, and a reporter. Russia was represented by Prof. Samoilovich, Prof. Moltshanov, and Mr. Asberg, an engineer. From the United States there was, in addition to Lincoln Ellsworth, E. H. Smith of the United States Coast Guard. There was also a Swedish physician.

41. Ellsworth, *Beyond Horizons,* p. 248.

42. Nobile could have made this discovery had the weather been better during the second arctic flight of the *Italia.* Later it was determined that Severnaya Zemlya is an archipelago, composed of four main islands.

43. Ellsworth, *Beyond Horizons,* pp. 248–249.

44. Vaeth, p. 119.

45. Ellsworth, *Beyond Horizons,* p. 250.

46. As quoted in Grierson, *Sir Hubert Wilkins,* p. 144.

47. Belov, *Istoriia,* Vol. III, p. 222 and pp. 408 ff.

48. In his authoritative work, *The Northern Sea Route,* Armstrong gives a comprehensive history of the Northeast Passage.

49. Schmidt was born on September 30, 1891. He studied physics and mathematics. In 1918 he became a member of the Russian Communist Party and was in close touch with Lenin, who entrusted to him the organization

of book publishing in the Soviet Union. He then headed the editorial staff of the Soviet Encyclopedia. Schmidt went to the Arctic for the first time in 1929, leading an expedition to Franz Josef Land aboard the icebreaker *Sedov*. Voronin was captain of the ship and Professors Samoilovich and Wiese were Schmidt's deputies. In 1930 Schmidt headed an expedition to Severnaya Zemlya, where a wintering party led by Ushakov was left. In the same year Schmidt replaced Samoilovich as Director of the Arctic Institute in Leningrad.

50. Belov, *Istoriia*, Vol. III, p. 411.

51. Belov, *Istoriia*, Vol. III, p. 405; according to Carlson, p. 241, there was a total of 94 stations, so that presumably there were only 2 non-Russian stations in operation.

52. Belov, *Istoriia*, Vol. III, p. 413, footnote. The pilot was saved.

53. Belov, *Istoriia*, Vol. III, pp. 410–423.

54. In a speech made in March 1939, as quoted by Armstrong, *The Northern Sea Route*, p. 59.

55. von Rauch, p. 220.

56. Glavsevmorput was established on December 17, 1932.

57. As quoted by Belov in *Severny Morskoi Put*, p. 48.

58. Armstrong, *The Northern Sea Route*, p. 62.

59. Armstrong, *The Northern Sea Route*, Appendix IV, p. 122.

60. The *Chelyuskin* episode is based on diaries published in *Dnevniki Chelyuskintsev, Pochod Chelyuskina,* and *Kak my Spasali,* reminiscences of the flying personnel involved. An abridged version of the latter three books was published as *The Voyage of the Chelyuskin*. Some elements were obtained in personal conversation with Prof. Gakkel.

61. *The Voyage of the Chelyuskin*, p. 10.

62. *Pochod Chelyuskina*, Vol. I, p. 129.

63. In this group was a scientist named J. Gakkel. Together with others he discovered, in 1948, the underwater Lomonosov Ridge, which extends through the Polar Basin, separating the Arctic Ocean into an Atlantic and a Pacific part.

64. *Pochod Chelyuskina*, Vol. I, opposite p. 328.

65. *Pochod Chelyuskina*, Vol. II, opposite p. 10.

66. These were all outstanding Soviet pilots at that time, but they did not get a chance to participate in actual rescue operations.

67. Reproduced in *Pochod Chelyuskina,* Vol II, opposite p. 168.

68. *Pochod Chelyuskina,* Vol. II, pp. 78 ff.

69. Ushakov had been in charge of the first Russian group to winter on Wrangel Island and had done extensive exploratory work in the Soviet Arctic.

70. *Pochod Chelyuskina,* Vol. II, p. 245.

71. *Dnevniki,* pp. 185 ff.

72. *Kak my spasali,* pp. 91–92.

73. Neither the icebreaker nor the dirigibles were eventually needed.

74. *Kak my spasali,* p. 361.

75. *Dnevniki,* pp. 189 ff.

76. *Pochod Chelyuskina,* Vol. II, p. 358.

77. *Pochod Chelyuskina,* Vol. II, p. 387.

78. Vodopyanov, *Wings over the Arctic,* p. 54.

79. Belov, *Istoriia,* Vol. III, p. 405.

80. Armstrong, *The Northern Sea Route,* Appendix IV, p. 122.

VI. TRANSFORMATION (1936–1963)

1. Vodopyanov, *Wings over the Arctic,* pp. 96 ff.

2. This account is based on Brontman, Papanin, and Vodopyanov, *Wings over the Arctic.*

3. The orange color was used to make the planes visible against a white background.

4. Each plane needed 1,600 gallons of gasoline for the polar flight.

5. Vodopyanov, *Wings over the Arctic,* pp. 205 ff.

6. Brontman, p. 98.

7. Vodopyanov, *Wings over the Arctic,* pp. 208 ff.

8. Brontman, p. 115.

9. Vodopyanov, *Wings over the Arctic,* p. 225.

10. Vodopyanov, *Wings over the Arctic,* p. 229.

11. Brontman, p. 118.

12. Vodopyanov, *Wings over the Arctic,* p. 231.

13. Vodopyanov, *Wings over the Arctic,* p. 236.

14. Brontman, p. 120.

15. Brontman, p. 128.

16. Brontman, p. 142.

17. Brontman, p. 147.

18. Vodopyanov, *Wings over the Arctic,* p. 250.

19. Vodopyanov, *Moscow–North-Pole–Vancouver,* p. 11.

20. This account is based on Baidukov.

21. The actual distance flown was 7,100 miles by air.

22. Gromov.

23. The official distance, as given by the National Aeronautic Association, is 6,305.66 miles, somewhat at variance with several printed accounts.

24. Stefansson, *Unsolved Mysteries,* p. 324.

25. Vodopyanov, *Wings,* p. 271.

26. Wilkins, *Our Search,* p. 141.

27. Stefansson, *Unsolved Mysteries,* p. 327.

28. Vodopyanov, *Wings,* p. 271.

29. This account is based on Stefansson, *Unsolved Mysteries,* pp. 322–369, and Wilkins, *Our Search.*

30. The pilots were Air Commodore Herbert Hollick-Kenyon, who in 1935 had made the first trans-antarctic flight in Ellsworth's *Polar Star* and Silas Alward Cheesman, a member of the Second Hearst-Wilkins Antarctic Expedition. Also aboard was Raymond E. Booth, a radio operator, and Gerald D. Brown, an engineer.

31. An unfounded rumor, still persistent in the Soviet Union, has it that Levanevsky defected to the West.

32. Brontman, p. 310.

33. Brontman, pp. 311–312.

34. Brontman, p. 319.

35. Brontman, p. 330.

36. Belov, *Severny Morskoi Put,* pp. 66 ff.

37. Badigin, pp. 85 ff.

38. Armstrong, *The Russians in the Arctic,* p. 30.

39. An excellent account of the drift of the *Sedov* is given by Armstrong, *The Russians in the Arctic,* pp. 17–51.

40. Badigin, pp. 145–148.

41. Badigin, p. 168.

42. Armstrong, *The Northern Sea Route,* pp. 58–59.

43. Vorontsova, personal communication.

44. Armstrong, *The Northern Sea Route,* Appendix I, p. 120.

45. Speech made in March 1939, as quoted by Armstrong, *The Northern Sea Route,* p. 114. Reference is being made to the Russian defeat during the Russo-Japanese War.

46. Laktionov, pp. 294–298.

47. Trojani, pp. 558 ff.

48. Nobile, *Posso dire,* pp. 114–115.

49. Riiser-Larsen, personal communication.

50. Davis, p. 390.

51. Carlson, pp. 53 ff.

52. Liversidge.

53. After the war, Hoel was imprisoned as a collaborator.

54. Lützow-Holm had lost a leg in an airplane accident in Italy.

55. Hobbs.

56. Liversidge.

57. Vodopyanov, personal communication.

58. In 1930, relics of Andrée's expedition and Fraenkel's body had been brought from White Island aboard the *Isbjörn*.

59. Liversidge, p. 83.

60. The *Northland* was commanded by Admiral E. H. Smith, who had participated in the arctic flight of the *Graf Zeppelin*.

61. Balchen, *Come North,* pp. 215 ff.

62. Carlson, pp. 58 ff.

63. Riiser-Larsen, personal communication, Ole Arntzen-Lützow-Holm, a student at Oslo University, was executed.

64. Riiser-Larsen, p. 242.

65. Belov, *Severny Morskoe Put,* pp. 84 ff.

66. Motter, Appendix A, p. 481.

67. Carlson, pp. 139 ff.

68. Eisenhower, p. 49.

69. Balchen led some daring rescue operations in Greenland.

70. The Army Air Forces in World War II.

71. 7,835 planes were actually delivered to Soviet Russia.

72. Belov, *Proval operatsi "Wunderland."*

73. Germany displayed considerable interest in Greenland during the early thirties, supporting the expedition of Professor Alfred Wegener and the flights of von Gronau. Ernest Udet, a popular pilot who during World War II was a high-ranking officer in charge of German aircraft production, was a Greenland enthusiast, having flown there while starring in a motion picture called *SOS Iceberg.*

74. Liversidge.

75. Victor, p. 266.

76. Operation Highjump involved the participation of some 4,000 men, planes, amphibious vehicles, and a fleet of 13 ships which included aircraft carriers, icebreakers, and a submarine. Sixty-four mapping flights produced approximately 70,000 photographs. It is estimated that some 350,000 square miles of antarctic territory was surveyed from the air.

77. Nobile, *Posso dire,* pp. 120–121.

78. Valle, pp. 268–269.

79. Valle, p. 263.

80. *Il Polpolo D'Italia,* June 29, 1927.

81. July 23, 1946.

82. Laktionov, pp. 299–302.

83. As quoted by Carlson, pp. 191.

84. A bibliography on ice islands was published by Dunbar in *Arctic,* July 1952.

85. During the postwar period the United States has undertaken a great number of arctic projects, many of which were tagged with intriguing code names such as "Operation Frostbite, "Operation Frigid," "Operation Musk Ox," etc.

86. Shaw, "Mint Julep," and Project Mint Julep.

87. Laktionov, pp. 303–305.

88. Laktionov, pp. 306–315.

89. Vodopyanov, *puti otvazhnych,* pp. 110–112.

90. This was a GAZ-67.

91. According to Laktionov, p. 343, footnote, T-1 was first sighted by Cherevichny and Akkuratov in March 1941 at latitude 74°, by Kotov at latitude 76°N., 165°W. in March 1946, and later by Kruze. According to the same source, T-2 was sighted by Mazuruk at 82°N., 170°E. in April 1948, and again in August 1950 at 87°N., 155°E. Similarly, T-3 is said to have been sighted by a pilot named Perov in April 1950 northeast of Gerald Island.

92. Carlson, pp. 237–238.

93. Carlson, pp. 196–197.

94. The Danish explorer, Knut Rasmussen, established a trading post at this site in 1910.

95. The first occupation of T-3 is described on the basis of Rodahl.

96. On May 3, 1952, Fletcher, Crary and Cotell made a one-hour flight in a C-47 from T-3 to the North Pole. There they took a gravity reading, sounded the depth of the ocean and determined the thickness of the ice. The party then flew on to T-1, where two ice cores were obtained which on subsequent examination resembled closely those taken from T-3. Flying on to the Ellsmere Ice Shelf, Fletcher's group determined that surface relief and dirt layering of both T-1 and T-3 were very much like those of the ice shelf, thus proving quite conclusively the origin of the two ice islands.

97. *Aviation Week,* Vol. 57, No. 22, Dec. 1, 1952, p. 75.

98. Riiser-Larsen became a general when the Norwegian Air Force became independent of the Navy.

99. Project 572.

100. October 16, 1963.

101. *Greenland.*

102. Thule's Ballistic Missile Warning System itself is a group of seven special buildings arranged along a 6000-foot-long semicircle and connected by an enclosed passageway which carries utility lines and is wide enough to permit vehicular traffic required for maintenance purposes. Each of the four giant detection radars whose reflectors are the size of a football field, measuring 165 by 400 feet, has a range of 3,000 miles and sweeps steadily an azimuth sector of 30 degrees, constantly on the alert for an incoming missile. Data gathered by these vigilance screens about any target are automatically fed to especially constructed electronic computers, which transmit them to three huge tracking radars. Mounted on top of the 30-foot-high roofs of special transmitter buildings, the tracking radars trace a missile's trajectory, determine its point of impact, and transmit such information to Defense headquarters located inside the United States.

The project involved some 165,000 cubic yards of excavation, the use of some 40,000 cubic yards of concrete, and more than 1.2 million square feet of prefabricated panels to provide approximately 700,000 square feet of useful floor space. Some 5,000 tons of structural and 800 tons of reinforcing steel, all of which had to be brought from the United States, were needed to build this Thule-based surveillance unit designed to withstand the force of extremely high winds.

Power needed for operation of the radar units is provided by a floating steam-electric plant installed aboard a 350-foot ship, originally named *Duval,* which is now being referred to as the *YFP-10.* It is covered with a coat of special insulation up to three inches thick, which permits machinery installed inside the ship to operate normally even when outside temperatures drop to 50° below zero. The vessel was towed 2,800 miles, to be berthed near Thule, some 680 miles north of the Arctic circle in a basin maintained ice-free artificially. There it floats, capable of producing more than 30,000 kilowatts of electricity and 100,000 pounds of steam an hour, enough to satisfy the requirements of a fair-sized modern city.

BIBLIOGRAPHY

BOOKS

Albertini, Gianni. *Alla ricerca dei naufraghi dell'Italia*. Libr d'It., 1929.
———. *La "Heiman-Sucai" nei mari artici*. Firenze, 1932.
Allen, Frederick L. *Only Yesterday. An informal history of the twenties*. Harper & Bros., New York, 1931.
Amundsen, Roald. *My Life as an Explorer*. Doubleday, Doran & Co., Garden City, N. Y., 1928.
——— and Ellsworth, Lincoln. *Our Polar Flight*. Dodd, Mead & Co., New York, 1925.
———. *First Crossing of the Polar Sea*. Doran Co., New York, 1927.
Anderson, William R. *Nautilus go North*. New Am. Libr. of World Lit., New York, 1959.
Armstrong, Terence. *The Northern Sea Route. Soviet exploitation of the North East Passage*. University Press, Cambridge, 1952.
———. *The Russians in the Arctic. Aspects of Soviet exploration and exploitation of the Far North 1937–1957*. Essential Books, Fair Lawn, N. J., 1958.
Army Air Forces in World War II, edited by W. F. Craven and J. L. Cate. University of Chicago Press, Chicago, 1950.
Arnesen, Odd. *The Polar Adventure. The Italia tragedy seen at close quarters*. Gollancz, London, 1929.
Babushkin, Mikhail. *Zapiski letchika*. Moscow, 1941.
Badigin, Konstantin. *Tri zimovki vo ldakh arktiki*. Sovetskaya Rossiya, 1960.
Baidukov, Georgi. *Over the North Pole*. Harcourt, Brace & Co., 1938.
Balbo, Italo. *Stormi d'Italia sul mondo*. Mondadori, 1938.
Balchen, Bernt. *Come North with Me*. E. P. Dutton & Co., 1958.
———, Ford, C., La Farge, O. *War Below Zero*. Houghton Mifflin Co., Boston, 1944.
Behounek, Franz. *Sieben Wochen auf der Eisscholle. Der Untergang der Nobile Expedition*. Brockhaus, Leipzig, 1929.
———. *Tragediia v ledovitom okeane*. Izdatelstvo innostr lit., Moscow, 1962.
Belov, M. I. *Severny morskoi put*. Morskoi Transp., Leningrad, 1957.
———. *Istoriia otkrytiia i osvoeniia severnovo morskovo puti. Vol III, Sovietskoe arkticheskoe moreplavanye 1917–1932*. Morskoi Transp., Leningrad, 1959.
———. *Proval operatsii "Wunderland."* Morskoi Transp., Moscow, 1962.
Bennett, Cora. *Floyd Bennett*. Wm. T. Payson, 1932.
Biagi, Giuseppe. *I miracoli della radio nella tragedia dell'Italia. Biagi racconta*. Mondadori, 1929.
Blagodarov, V. *V arktike*. Gosudarstv. izd. Moscow, 1959.
Brontman, Lazar. *On Top of the World. The Soviet expedition to the North Pole 1937–1938*. Covici Friede, New York, 1938.
Brown, A. (translator). *Voyage of the Chelyuskin, by members of the Expedition*. Macmillan Co., New York, 1935.
Burkhanov, Vasily. *New Soviet Discoveries in the Arctic*. Foreign Lang. Publ. House, Moscow, 1956.

————, Editor. *Cherez okean na dreifuyushchikh Idakh.* Gosud. Izd., Moscow, 1957.

Byrd, Richard E. *Skyward.* G. P. Putnam's Sons, New York, 1928.

————. *Little America. Aerial exploration in the Antarctic. The flight to the South Pole.* G. P. Putnam's Sons, New York, 1930.

————. *Discovery. The story of the second Byrd Antarctic expedition.* G. P. Putnam's Sons, New York, 1935.

Calvert, James. *Surface at the Pole. The extraordinary voyages of the U.S.S. Skate.* McGraw-Hill, New York, 1960.

Carlson, William S. *Lifelines Through the Arctic.* Duell, Sloan and Pearce, New York, 1962.

Chapman, F. Spencer. *Northern Lights. The official account of the British Arctic Air-route Expedition.* Chatto and Windus, London, 1932.

Cross, Wilbur. *Ghostship of the Pole.* Sloane Assoc., New York, 1960.

Davis, Kenneth S. *The Hero. Charles A. Lindbergh and the American dream.* Doubleday & Co., New York, 1959.

Dnevniki chelyuskintsev. Compiled by M. A. Dlakonov and E. B. Rubinchik. Gosud. Izd., Chud. Lit., Leningrad, 1935.

Eckener, Dr. Hugo (D. Robinson, transl.). *My zeppelins.* Putnam & Co., New York, 1958.

Editors of American Heritage. *The American Heritage History of Flight.* American Heritage Publ. Co., 1962.

Editors of Year, 1953. *Flight. A pictorial history of aviation.* Am. Heritage Publ. Co., 1962.

Eisenhower, Dwight D. *Crusade in Europe.* Doubleday & Co., New York, 1948.

Ellis, Frank H. *Canada's Flying Heritage.* Univ. of Toronto Press, 1954.

Ellsworth, Lincoln. *Search.* Brewer, Warren and Putnam, New York, 1932.

————. *Beyond Horizons.* Doubleday & Doran, New York, 1938.

Flury, Arthur. *Statistik über sämtliche Ozeanflugversuche.* Bern, 1932.

Fokker, Anthony H. G. and Gould, Bruce. *Flying Dutchman. The life of Anthony Fokker.* Henry Holt & Co., 1931.

Fraser, Chelsea. *Heroes of the Air.* Thomas Y. Crowell Co., New York, 1940.

Gakkel, Y. Y. *Nauka i osvoenie arktiki.* Morskoi Transp., Leningrad, 1957.

Gallian, Marcello. *I segreti di Nobile.* Roma, 1928.

Geko, Yuri. *50 dnei. Gibel dirizhablia Italia.* Privoi, Moscow, 1928.

Giudici, Davide. *The Tragedy of the Italia. With the rescuers to the Red Tent.* Appleton & Co., New York, 1929.

Global Logistics and Strategy, 1940–1943, Richard M. Leighton and Robert W. Coakley. Office of the Chief Military History. Dept. of the Army, Washington, D. C.

Grierson, John. *High Failure. Solo along the Arctic Air Route.* Hodge & Co., London, 1936.

————. *Sir Hubert Wilkins. Enigma of exploration.* Robert Hale, London, 1960.

————. *Challenge to the Poles. Highlights of Arctic and Antarctic aviation.* Archon Books, Hamden, Conn., 1964.

Gromov, Michael. *Across the North Pole to America.* Foreign. Lang. Publ. House, Moscow, 1939.

Gronau, Wolfgang von. *Weltflieger.* Deutsche Verlagsanst., 1955.

Gruber, Ruth. *I Went to the Soviet Arctic.* Viking Press, New York, 1944.

Hanson, Earl P. *Stefansson. Prophet of the North.* Harper & Bros., New York, 1941.

Hayes, J. Gordon. *Robert Edwin Peary. A record of his explorations 1886–1909.* Grant Richards & Humphrey, Toulmin, London, 1929.

Herlin, Hans. *Udet. Eines Mannes Leben und die Geschichte seiner Zeit.* H. Nannen, Hamburg, 1958.

Hildenbrandt, Fred. *Nobile. Die Tragödie im Polareis.* Verl. d. Sternb., Hamburg, 1955.

Hobbs, William J. *An Explorer-Scientist's Pilgrimage. The autobiography of William J. Hobbs.* J. Edwards Inc., Ann Arbor, 1952.

Hoel, Adolf. *Et oppgjør med landsmenn.* Minerva, Oslo, 1951.

Houdenak, Gunnar. *Roald Amundsens siste ferd.* Oslo, 1934.

Katz, Otto. *Neun Männer im Eis. Dokumente einer Polartragödie.* Universum, Berlin, 1929.

Kenney, William. *The crucial years 1940–1945.* McFadden, New York, 1962.

Kirwan, L. P. *A History of Polar Exploration.* Norton & Co., New York, 1960.

Knight, C. and Durham, R. *Hitch Your Wagon. The story of Bernt Balchen.* Bell, Drexel Hill, 1950.

Kudenko, O. *Teplaia arktika.* Sovetskaya Rossiya, Moscow, 1960.

Laktionov, A. F. *Severny polius.* Morskoi Transport, Moscow, 1955.

Lazazzera, Rocco. *Finn Malmgren. L'Eroe polare.* Roma, 1931.

Lindsay, Martin. *Three Got Through. Memoirs of an arctic explorer.* Falcon Press, London, 1946.

Liversidge, Douglas. *The Third Front.* Souvenir Press, London, 1960.

Lundborg, Einar. *The Arctic Rescue. How Nobile was saved.* Viking Press, New York, 1929.

Maddalena, Umberto. *Lotte e vittorie sul mare e nel cielo.* Mondadori, 1930.

Meyer, Willy. *Der Kampf um Nobile. Versuch einer objektiven Darstellung und Wertung der Leistungen des italienischen Luftschiffers.* Radetzki, Berlin, 1931.

Mindlin, E. M. *Krasin vo ldakh.* Gosud. Izd., Moscow, 1961.

Mirsky, Jeannette. *To the North. The story of arctic exploration from earliest times to the present.* Viking Press, New York, 1934.

Mittelholzer, Walter and others. *By Airplane towards the North Pole.* Houghton Mifflin Co., New York, 1925.

Molokov, Vasili. *Soviet Civil Aviation.* Foreign Lang. Publ. House, Moscow, 1939.

Murphy, Charles J. W. *Struggle. The life and exploits of Commander Richard E. Byrd.* Frederick A. Stokes Co., 1928.

Nansen, Fridtjof. *Farthest North.* Harper & Bros., New York, 1897.

Nobile, Umberto. *In volo alla conquista del segreto polare. Da Roma a Teller attraverso il polo nord.* Mondadori, 1928.

———. *Im Luftschiff zum Nordpol. Die Fahrten der Italia.* Un. deutsche Verlagsges., Berlin, 5th edit., n.d.

———. *Posso dire la verità. Storia inedita della spedizione polare dell'Italia.* Mondadori, 1945.

———. *Quello che ho visto nella Russia sovietica.* Atlantica, Roma, 1945.

———. *Addio Malygin.* Mondadori, 1948.

———. *Gli Italiani al polo nord.* Mondadori, 1959.

Novikov, V. D. *Pokorenie arktiki.* Izdat. Akademi Nauk, Moscow, 1962.

Owen, Russell. *South of the Sun*. John Day Co., New York, 1934.

Paderin, G. *Siberia, past, present, future*. Foreign Lang. Publ. House, Moscow, 1961.

Parijanine, Maurice (L. Brown, transl.). *The Krasin*. Macaulay Co., New York, 1929.

Partridge, Bellamy. *Amundsen, The splendid Norseman*. Frederick A. Stokes, New York, 1929.

Peary, Robert E. *The North Pole*. Frederick A. Stokes, New York, 1910.

Quattrini, Antonio. *Col Norge sulla via del polo*. Firenze, 1926.

Rauch, Georg von. *A History of Soviet Russia*. Fred A. Praeger, New York, 1958.

Riiser-Larsen, Hjalmar. *Femti år for Kongen*. Gyldendal Norsk Forl., Oslo, 1958.

Rodahl, Kaare. *North. The nature and drama of the polar world*. Harper & Bros. New York, 1953.

Rolfsrud, Erling N. *Brother to the Eagle. The story of Carl Ben Eielson*. Lantern Books, Alexandria, Minn., 1952.

Roosevelt, Franklin D. *Nothing to Fear. The selected addresses of Franklin D. Roosevelt*. Popular Libr., New York, 1961.

Samoilovich, Rudolf. *Sovietskaia arktika*. Izd. vsesoiusn. arkt. inst., Leningrad, 1934.

————, and others. *Pochod Krassina*. Zemlya i Fabr., Moscow, 1930.

Samoilowitsch, Rudolph. *S.O.S. in der Arktis. Die Rettungsexpedition des Krassin*. Un. deutsche Verlagsges., Berlin, 1929, 3rd edition.

————, I. L. Baievsky and Mechlis, L. E., Eds. *Pochod Chelyuskina. Geroitcheskaya epopeya*. Pravda, Moscow, 1934.

Seldes, George. *Sawdust Caesar. The untold history of Mussolini and Fascism*. Harper & Bros., New York, 1935.

Shirer, William L. *The Rise and Fall of the Third Reich. A history of Nazi Germany*. Simon & Schuster, New York, 1960.

Sinclair, J. A. *Airships in Peace and War*. Rich & Cowan, London, 1934.

Smith, Dean C. *By the Seat of My Pants. A pilot's progress from 1917 to 1930*. Little, Brown & Co., Boston, 1961.

Sora, Gennaro. *Con gli Italiani all 80° parallelo*. Milano, 1930.

Stefansson, Vilhjalmur. *The Northward Course of Empire*. Harcourt, Brace and Co., New York, 1922.

————. *Unsolved Mysteries of the Arctic*. Macmillan Co., New York, 1939.

————. *The Friendly Arctic. The story of five years in polar regions*. Macmillan Co., New York, 1943.

————. *Great Adventures and Explorations*. Dial Press, New York, 1947.

————. *Discovery. The autobiography of Vilhjalmur Stefansson*. McGraw-Hill, New York, 1964.

Sullivan, Mark. *Our Times*. Chas. Scribner, New York, 1935, Vols. 1–3.

Sullivan, Walter. *Quest for a Continent*. Secker & Warburg, London, 1957.

Swenson, Olaf. *Northwest of the World. Forty years trading and hunting in northern Siberia*. Robert Hale, 1951.

Thomas, Lowell. *Sir Hubert Wilkins. His world of adventure*. McGraw-Hill, New York, 1961.

Toland, John. *Ships in the Sky*. Henry Holt & Co., New York, 1957.

Tomaselli, Cesco. *L'inferno bianco. Racconto della spedizione Nobile*. Unitas, 1929.

Trojani, Felice. *La coda di Minosse*. Mursia & Co., Milano, 1964.

U. S. Army in World War II: The Middle East Theater; The Persian Corridor and aid to Russia. by T. H. Vail Motter, Office of the Chief of Military History, Dept. of the Army. Washington, D. C.

Ushakov, G. A. *Po Nekhozhenoi zemle.* Molodaia gvardiya, 1953.

Uvachan, V. *Peoples of the Soviet North.* Foreign Lang. Publ. House, Moscow, 1960.

Vaeth, J. Gordon. *Graf Zeppelin. The aerial adventure of an aerial globe-trotter.* Harper & Bros., New York, 1958.

Valle, Giuseppe. *Uomini nei cieli. Storia dell'aeronautica Italiana.* Centro edit. Naz., 1958.

Van Dongen, Sjef. *Vijf jaar in iis en sneeuw. Mijn leven in het noorpoolgebied.* Amsterdam.

Victor, Paul-Emile (S. Sullivan, transl.). *Man and the Conquest of the Poles.* Simon & Schuster, New York, 1963.

Viglieri, Alfredo. *48 giorni sul "pack."* Mondadori, 1929.

Vodopyanov, Mikhail. *Moscow–North Pole–Vancouver.* Foreign Lang. Publ. House, Moscow, 1939.

————. *Outstanding Flights by Soviet Airmen.* Foreign Lang. Publ. House, Moscow, 1939.

————. *Puti otvazhnykh.* Gosudarstv. izdatelstvo, Moscow, 1958.

————. *Wings over the Arctic.* Foreign Lang. Publ. House, Moscow, n.d.

Vorontsova, Lyubov. *Na 81° shirote. Zapiski uchastnika expeditsii Krasina.* Krasnaya Gaz., 1929.

Vozdushnye puti severa sbornik statei posviashennykh voprosam osvoyenya severa. Edited by J. J. Anvelt and others. Izdatelstvo sov. Asia, 1933.

Weems, John E. *Race for the Pole.* Henry Holt & Co., New York, 1960.

Wilkins, George H. *Flying the Arctic.* G. P. Putnam's Sons, New York, 1929.

————. *Under the North Pole. The Wilkins-Ellsworth Submarine Expedition.* Harcourt, Brace & Co., New York, 1931.

Yatsyn, E. *Na ldinie cherez polius.* Molodaya gvardiya, 1957.

Zapiski o neobyknavennom na krassine i Malygine. Wiese ,V., and others. Gosud. Izd., Moscow, 1929.

MAGAZINES AND PUBLICATIONS

Amundsen, Roald: "Inside story of the rows aboard the *Norge.*" *The World's Work,* Vol. 54, No. 4, 1927.

Armstrong, Terence: "The Arctic Institute in Leningrad." *The Polar Record,* No. 33, 1947.

Aviation Week: "Log of SAS's Transpolar Flight." Vol. 57, No. 22, p. 75, Dec. 1, 1952.

Bandini, Franco: "Ricostruiamo integralmente la grande avventura del dirigibile *"Italia."* A series of articles in *L'Europeo,* Nos. 551–560, 1956.

Bartoli, Domenico: "Nobile non fu un eroe nè un vile." *Epoca,* Vol. 12, No. 536, 1961, p. 14.

Behounek, Frantizek: "Atmospheric-electric researches made in 1928 during the Nobile expedition in collaboration with Prof. A. Pontremoli (Milan) and Prof. F. Malmgren (Uppsala)." *Terrestrial Magnetism and Atmospheric Electricity,* Washington, Vol. 34, No. 3, 1929, pp. 173–198.

————: "Die im Luftschiffe *"Italia"* zur Beobachtung der atmospaerischen Elektrizitaet angewandten Methoden und Apparate. *Arktis,* Gotha, 2. Jahrg., 1929, pp. 69–76.

Buscaroli, Piero: "Anche Nobile fa brodo." *Il Borghese,* January 5, 1961, pp. 13–14.

Byrd, Richard E.: "Flying over the Arctic." *Nat. Geogr. Mag.,* Vol. 48, No. 5, 1925, pp. 519–532.

————: "The first flight to the North Pole." *Nat. Geogr. Mag.,* Vol. 50, No. 3, 1926, pp. 356–376.

Cadwalader, John: "Arctic drift stations." *U.S. Naval Institute Proc.,* April 1963, pp. 70–75.

Fusca, James A.: "Army Reveals *BMEWS* Site Details." *Aviation Week,* July 28, 1958.

"Going up: New line to aid DEW Line." *Engineering News-Record,* July 17, 1958.

Gordienko, P. A.: "Aktivny metod izucheniia prirody tsentralnoi arktiki." *Izv. vsesoyuz. geogr. obshchestva,* No. 4, 1960, pp. 293–307.

"Greenland Ice Plateau," *Air Univ. quart. Rev.,* Maxwell Air Force Base, Ala., Vol. 7, No. 4, Spring 1955, pp. 78–90.

Grierson, John: "Evolution of Arctic Airways." *Journ.* of the Roy. Aeron. Soc. Vol. 59, Jan. 1955, pp. 15–29.

Hoel, Adolf: "La spedizione polare del dirigible *Italia.*" *Nuova antologia,* No. 1841, 1954.

Liljequist, Gösta: "Did the 'Josephine Ford' reach the North Pole?" *Interavia,* No. 5, 1960, pp. 589–591.

Locatelli, Luigi: "Nobile si è messo nei guai." *Il Giorno,* December 22, 1960.

MacMillan, Donald B.: "The MacMillan Expedition Returns." *Nat. Geogr. Mag.,* Vol. 48, No. 5, 1925, pp. 477–518.

Malmgren, Finn: "Bericht ueber den Flug nach Nordland." Petermanns Mitt., Ergaenzungsheft, No. 205, Gotha 1929, pp. 63–65.

Marini, Italo: "L'eroica vita di Natale Cecioni: Un Capitolo della nostra aeronautica." Series of 2 articles in *Scienza e Vita,* Dec. 1960 and January 1961.

Ministero della Marina. "Commissione d'indagine per la spedizione polare dell' aeronave *Italia.*" Supplement to *Rivista Marittima,* Roma, 1930.

Morrow Lindbergh, Anne: "Flying the North Atlantic." Nat. Geogr. Mag., Vol. 66, No. 3, 1934, pp. 261–337.

Nobile, Umberto: "More rows about the *Norge.*" *The World's Work,* Vol. 55, No. 3, 1928.

Notarnicola, Vittorio: "Mio marito non era un gangster." *L'Europeo,* Vol. 7, No. 5, 1961, pp. 29–35.

Pariset, Dante: "Il dramma della tenda rossa," a series of 21 articles, *Il Tempo,* Vol. 15, No. 249–269, 1958.

Pillon, Giorgio: "Lettera aperta a un trasvolatore del Polo." *Candido,* Vol. 16, No. 52, December 25, 1960.

————: "Ancha alla TV ha sbagliato la manovra." *Candido,* Vol. 17, No. 3, January 15, 1961.

"Project Mint Julep. Runways beyond Greenland's icy mountains." *Air University Quart. Rev.,* Maxwell Air Force Base, Alabama, Winter 1954–55, Vol. 7, No. 3, pp. 96–106.

Romagna-Manoia, Giuseppe: "La R. Marina Italiana nella spedizione artica 1928." *Riv. Maritt.,* Vol. 62, No. 6, 1929.

Shaw, Donald A.: "Mint Julep." *Contact.* Air University, USAF Institute of Technology, Wright-Patterson AFB, Ohio, June 1954, Information Bulletin, P 3–6.

Simoni, Gastone: "La tragedia dell'aeronave *Italia.*" *Candido,* Vol. 15, No. 11, 1959.

Tandberg, Rolf S.: "Med hundespann på effersokning efter '*Italia*' folkens." *Norsk. Geogr. Tidsskr.,* Oslo, Vol. 2, Nos. 2–3, 1928.

Tomaselli, Cesco: "Tornai dal Pole portando a casa la pelle." *Oggi,* February 18, 1960, p. 8.

————: A series of 7 articles in *Domenica del Corriere,* Vol. 63, Nos. 2–8, 1961.

Torelli, Giorgio: "Si è salvato per prima anche alla TV." *Candido,* Vol. 7, No. 2, January 8, 1961, p. 6.

Trionfero, Renzo: "Processo al processo." *L'Europeo,* Vol. 7, No. 4, 1961, pp. 17–23.

Wilkins, Sir Hubert: "Our Search for the Lost Aviators." *Nat. Geogr. Mag.,* Vol. 74, No. 2, 1938, pp. 141–172.

Wood, Walter A.: "George Hubert Wilkins." *The Geogr. Rev.,* Vol. 49, No. 3, 1959.

MANUSCRIPTS AND OFFICIAL MATERIAL

(The) Andrée diaries being the diaries and records of S. S. Andrée, Nils Strindberg and Knut Fraenkel written during their balloon expedition to the North Pole in 1897 and discovered on White Island in 1930, together with a complete record of the expedition and discovery. Authorized translation from the official Swedish edition by Edward Adams-Ray. John Lane and the Bodley Head Ltd., London, 1931.

Arctic terrain research 1959, geophysics research directorate, Air Force Cambridge Research Center. Air Research and Development Command, Bedford, Mass., 1960.

Brochure covering visit to Thule Air Base, Greenland, by Maj. Gen. Minton and party. USAF North Atlantic Civil Engineer Region, New York, December 1959.

Geophysical data from U. S. Arctic Ocean drifting stations 1957–1960. G. H. Cabaniss, editor, Terrestrial Science Laboratory Project 7628, Air Force Cambridge Laboratories, office of aerospace research, U. S. Air Force, Hanscom Field, Mass., July 1962.

Greenland. By the press department of the Ministry for Foreign Affairs in association with the Greenland Department of the Ministry of State and the national travel association of Denmark, edited by Kristijan Bure, translation by Reginald Spink and A. Anslev, third edition, 1961.

Project 572, the use of ice for aircraft landing strips. Arctic, Desert, Tropic Information Center, Research Studies Institute, Air University, Maxwell Air Force Base, Alabama.

Project Mint Julep. Investigation of smooth ice areas of the Greenland ice cap, 1953. Part 1. (Introduction, narrative, and general reports.) Arctic, Desert, Tropic Information Center, Research Studies Institute, Air University, Maxwell Air Force Base, Alabama. (ADTIC publication A-104a, May 1955.) Scientific studies at Fletcher's Ice Island, T-3, (1952–1955) Vol. I, Geophysical research papers No. 63, Geophysics Research Directorate, Air Force Cambridge Research Center, Air Research and Development Command, United States Air Force, Bedford, Mass., September 1959.

INDEX

Abbruzzi, Prince Luigi, Duke of, 20
Acosta, Bert, 107
Advent Bay, 56, 57, 147, 158, 159, 175, 247
Aero-Arctic Society, German, 166
Aeroarctica, 43, 215, 243
Aero Club, Italian, 96
Aero Club, Norwegian, 65, 69, 109
Ahrenberg, Captain Albin, 230–233
Air Force,
    Free Norwegian, 310
    Italian, 323
    Norwegian, 26, 29, 143
    Royal (British), 189, 231
    Swedish, 156
    United States, 32, 230, 316, 320
Airplanes
    Alaskan, 67, 68, 71, 72, 76, 78, 227
    ANT-25, 292
    "Arctic Truck," 327
    B-29 weather plane, 327
    B-58, 335
    Bellanca seaplane, 234
    Blackburn *Kangaroo,* 33
    Bleriots, 22
    C-47, 329, 330, 333
    C-54, 330, 331
    C-124, 333
    Catalina J-240, 314
    Curtiss, 39
        Oriole, 38
        Standard Model J, 32
    DC-6B, 331
    De Havilland, 41
        Moth, 183, 191–193, 195, 231, 233, 239
        "Robert Bruce," 239
        "Rouge et Noir," 239
    "Detroit I," 103, 105
    "Detroit II," 103, 107
    Detroiter, 67, 68, 76, 78, 79
    Dornier seaplanes, 39, 156, 161, 164, 235
    Dornier-Wal, 48, 145, 175, 230, 235
    Fairchild, 227
    Farman, 22, 26
    Flamingo, 192
    Fokkers, 22, 66, 71, 84, 86, 89, 103, 108, 110, 175–177, 179–184, 191, 195, 207, 215, 227
    F-7, 109
    Fokker-31, 157, 158
    "Josephine Ford," 86–89, 91, 92, 94, 101–103

Airplanes (Cont'd.)
    tri-motor "America," 107
    Ford tri-motor, 109, 110, 112, 113, 116
    Gorbunov factory, 283
    Guba, Consolidated PBY, 296–298
    Hamilton, 225, 226, 227
    Hansa, 157, 172, 174, 177, 179, 191, 193
        Hansa 255, 180, 183, 193
        Hansa 257, 173, 195
    Heinkel III, 310
    Junkers, 35, 38, 88, 110, 195, 199, 200, 225, 227, 310
        Junkers-13, 159, 175, 183, 186, 187
        "Bremen," 113, 116, 118
        Icebird D 260, 39
    Latham, 47, 169, 170, 171, 174, 175, 178, 201, 202, 220
    Liberator bombers, 322
    Loening
        NA-1, 60–63
        NA-2, 61, 62
        NA-3, 61–63
    Lockheed *Vega* (X 3903), 110, 114–116
    Maake, 157, 162, 183
    Marina II, 169, 172, 182, 183, 196, 220
    N-24, 49, 51, 53
    N-25, 49–51, 53–58
    N-209, 295, 297, 298
    NC class seaplane, 32
    P-5, 301
    "ptarmigan," 327, 331
    RD 25-1, 294
    Savoia 55, 157, 159, 161, 171, 172, 182, 183, 196
    Seaplane S55, 163
    SH-2, 303
    Sikorsky amphibian, 230
    Sopwith fighters, 29
    Stearman, 227
    Stinson, 103, 110, 225
    Tingmissartoq, 235
    Turku, 170, 171, 182, 183, 186, 187, 209, 212, 215
    U-2 (Russian), 287
    Uppland, 157, 168, 169, 174, 183, 187, 193, 201, 212, 215
    USSR N-2, 296
    USSR N-166, 285, 286, 287
    USSR N-169, 290, 291, 308

Airplanes (Cont'd.)
  USSR N-170, 285, 287, 288, 289, 297
  USSR N-171, 290
  USSR N-172, 290, 292
  Viking Hjalmar, 333
  Waco, 227
Aklavik, 298
Alaska, 22, 24, 27, 28, 36–41, 48, 64,
  66, 71, 75, 84, 96, 97, 113, 114,
  119, 130, 223, 225, 227, 261–
  265, 270, 274, 295–297, 299,
  318, 320, 326, 329, 349
  Aerial Transportation Company, 41
  Air Route, 320
  Airways, 224
Albertini, Gianni, 150, 156, 171, 173,
  175, 178, 180, 196, 211, 213, 350
Alessandrini, Renato, 87, 95, 111, 127,
  134, 137, 187, 194, 197, 200, 210,
  211, 216
Aleutians, 318, 321, 333
Alexeiev, A. D., 284, 290, 292, 296
Alpini Island, 175
Alpini, Italian, 150
Amos, Clyde, 160
Amsterdam Island, 158, 201
Amundsen, Major General, 156, 160
Amundsen, Gustav, 93, 94
Amundsen, Roald, 20, 26, 27, 29, 30,
  33, 35–41, 43, 47–59, 64–75, 83–
  103, 108, 109, 119, 139, 142–
  145, 152, 156–158, 161, 165,
  168–171, 174–180, 183–185, 189,
  190, 193, 200, 201, 205, 212,
  213, 216, 220, 223, 230, 235,
  242, 246–248, 251, 278, 286,
  311, 349
Amur River, 266
Anadyr, 223, 255, 262, 268–272, 274
Anchorage, 321
Anderson, Rudolph M., 24, 26, 28
Anderson, Ryst, 145
Andrée, Salomon August, 4–12, 14–
  19, 51, 70, 122, 349
Angioletti, 143, 154
Angmagssalik, 231, 233, 234, 239, 316
Antarctic, 3, 20, 24, 26, 34, 35, 63,
  109, 120, 223, 230, 311, 313,
  322, 323, 334
Archangel, 42, 159, 161, 164, 216,
  244, 246, 249, 250, 252, 304,
  307, 317
Arctic, 3–7, 14, 20, 24, 26, 27, 33, 34,
  36, 42, 43, 49, 62, 63, 79, 86, 97,
  101, 119, 122, 132, 142, 149, 207,
  215, 223, 227, 243, 247, 254, 256,
  259, 261–263, 310, 311, 316, 317,
  322–324, 332, 334, 337, 349, 350

Arctic (Cont'd.)
  Canadian, 22, 63
  Circle, 227, 244, 299
  Institute, Leningrad, 168, 244, 248,
    249, 251, 252, 253, 256, 306
  International Society for Aerial Ex-
    ploration of the, *see* Aeroarctic
  Ocean, 38, 40, 50, 51, 63, 69, 72,
    84, 89, 107, 119, 148, 248, 255,
    298, 299, 306, 308, 326, 333. *See
    also* Polar Sea
  research, 308, 309
  Soviet, 34, 41, 248, 251, 255, 290,
    307, 321
Arduini, Ettore, 95, 111, 127, 130,
  136, 137
Armistead, Claude, 270
Arneson, Odd, 174
Arnold, General Henry H., 323
Assur, Andrew, 333
Atlantic Ocean, 32, 36, 227, 243, 248,
  292, 309, 313, 318, 321
Australia, 22, 23, 28, 32, 33, 39, 63,
  64, 67
Axel Heiberg Land, 49, 61

Babushkin, Michael, 165, 174, 175,
  180, 182, 184, 186–191, 253,
  254, 256, 262, 272, 273, 275,
  277, 284, 285, 288, 290, 299, 307
Baccarani, Ugo, 139, 140, 151, 172,
  181, 211, 350
Baffin Bay, 36
Baffin Island, 234, 239, 316
Badygin, Captain Constantin, 305, 306
Baidukov, Georgi, 292, 349
Balbo, Italo, 103, 108, 109, 114, 147,
  169, 239, 350
Balchen, Bernt, 29–31, 56, 58, 84, 87–
  92, 98, 102–104, 107, 109, 112,
  113, 116, 118, 223, 248, 316,
  318, 322, 326, 329, 332, 350
Balloon, 4–11, 14
Balzan, Eugenio, 145
Banks Island, 25, 294, 297
Barentsberg, 314, 315
Barents Sea, 26, 33, 146, 157, 158
Barents, Willem, 251
Barter Island, 28, 297, 329
Bartlett, Robert A., 22, 24, 43, 49, 99
Bassein, F. I., 283, 288
Bastanzhiev, Pilot, 267–269, 271, 272
Bay Fjord, 61
Bear Island, 170, 185, 219, 322
Beaufort Sea, 22, 25, 329
Beechey Point, 106

Behounek, Frantisek, 112, 130, 136–142, 144, 147, 149, 151, 154, 155, 158, 162, 172, 176, 178–181, 184, 350

Beistad Fjord, 61

Belyakov, Alexander, 292

Bennett, Floyd, 29, 59, 62, 63, 66, 71, 84, 86, 87, 89–94, 98, 99, 103, 107, 112, 113, 116, 118

Berge, 56, 86, 89, 92

Bergen, 142, 147, 156, 168–171, 175, 180, 181, 232, 243–247

Bering Strait, 24, 33, 36, 38, 97, 224, 225, 244, 250, 251, 255, 256, 270–272

Berlin, 33, 158, 161, 194, 196, 246, 313, 321

Beverly Sound, 166, 170, 171, 192, 196, 197, 201

Biagi, Giuseppe, 127, 130–142, 144, 146–153, 155, 158–161, 167–169, 172, 173, 175, 176, 178–180, 184, 188, 191–194, 196, 198, 201, 207, 209, 210, 217, 350

Bialack, Charles E., 145

Biscay Hook, 160

Bjerknes, Jacob, 50, 57

Blackjack, Ada, 37, 40

Blue Detachment, 263–267

Bluff Point, 150

Bluie West One, 313

Bluie West Eight, 316, 318, 324

BMEWS, 329, 334, 335

Bobrov, A. N., 274, 275, 276

Bolshoi Shantar, 267

Borland, Earl, 225–227, 268, 274

Borup, George, 27

Bowman, Dr. Isaiah, 73

Brandy Bay, 58, 161

Brazy, Gilbert, 170

Brennan, Captain Mike, 75, 87, 88

Bressanone, 217

Brinegar, Captain Mike, 329, 330

Britain, 35, 37, 309. *See also* England

British, 29, 32, 40, 239, 310
  Air Ministry, 189
  Air Route Expedition, British, 231, 233, 239

Broch Island, 122, 148, 174, 175, 185, 186, 192, 194, 203, 205

Brontman, Lazar, 288, 291

Brooklyn Navy Yard, 73, 243

Brower, Charley, 24

Brun, Eske, 321

Bruns, Walter, 166, 215

Bryant, Roy, 73, 75

Bundefjorden, 109

Byrd, Richard Evelyn, 29, 31, 32, 38–40, 42, 43, 49, 50, 59–63, 65, 66, 71–73, 83, 84, 86–94, 96, 98, 99, 101–103, 107–110, 116, 119, 143, 322, 324, 349

Cache Lake, 104

California, 28, 227, 331, 332

Cambridge Bay, 333

Camp Schmidt, 259, 261–269, 271–276

Canada, 27, 36, 40, 103, 104, 230, 234, 294, 296, 297, 299, 314, 333
  Canadian Arctic expedition, 28
  Canadian Defense Commands, 333

Canon Fjord, 60, 62

Cape Bruun, 175, 194, 195

Cape Chelyuskin, 254

Cape Cloven, 171, 178

Cape Columbia, 27

Cape Farewell, 234

Cape Flora, 15

Cape Leigh Smith, 178, 180, 184, 186, 187, 205

Cape Mokkorik, 59

Cape Morris Jesup, 90, 91

Cape North, 153, 159, 162, 168, 173, 182, 186, 193, 224–227, 265, 274. *See also* Cape Schmidt and North Cape

Cape Platen, 166, 171, 173, 174, 190, 192, 210

Cape Prince of Wales, 97

Cape Sabine, 60

Cape Schmidt, 296

Cape Serdtse Kamen, 256

Cape Thomas Hubbard, 60

Cape Wrede, 170, 212

Caratti, Attilo, 95, 111, 127, 130, 137

Carli, Mario, 214

Carnegie Institution, 242, 245

Cartwright, Labrador, 235, 239

Cecioni, Natale, 95, 111, 127, 130, 133–138, 140–142, 146, 147, 149, 150–152, 154, 155, 160, 172, 176, 178–182, 180–192, 196, 198, 207, 209, 211, 350

Cendali, Dr. Guido, 157, 212, 213

Charcot, Jean Baptiste, 150, 189, 201

Charles Island, 199

Charles XII Island, 141, 146, 148, 194, 201

Cheesman, Al, 104

Chelyuskinites, 261, 263, 264, 268, 273–277, 290, 291, 295, 305

Cherevichny, Ivan, 303, 307, 308, 318

Chicago, 234, 235, 309
   Tribune, 230, 234, 235
Chkalov, Valery, 292, 294, 307, 350
Christanshaab, 239
Christell, Lt. Einar, 157, 177, 181,
   182, 350
Chukchi Peninsula, 224, 225, 254–
   256, 262, 264–272, 277, 295
Chukchi Sea, 257, 259, 260, 278
Chukhnovsky, Boris, 42, 194, 196–
   199, 201, 210–213, 216, 226,
   249, 318, 350
Churchill, Winston, 313
Ciampino Airfield, 65, 71
Ciocca, Calisto, 111, 127, 130, 137
Clavering Island, 239
Cloven Cliff, 147
Coile, Commander Emory, 32, 38
Collinson Point, 25
Congressional Medal of Honor, 99,
   118
Continental Air Defense Command,
   337
Coolidge, Calvin, 42, 93, 99, 102, 108,
   131
Coolidgeland, 40
Cope, John Lachlan, 34
Copenhagen, 148, 151, 216, 217, 252,
   298, 331–333, 349
Coronation Gulf, 25, 298
Corriere della Sera, 122, 145
Corriere d'Italia, 137
Courtauld, August, 231–233
Cramer, Parker, 230, 234, 235, 349
Crocker Land, 27, 42, 65, 324
Crosson, Joe, 226, 227, 266, 297
Curtiss Airplane Company, 38
Czech Word, 269
Czechoslovakia, 114

D'Aeth, N. H., 231, 233, 349
Dagebladet, 212
Dahl, Odd, 38, 349
Dane Island, 5, 7, 15, 121, 122
Danenhower, Sloan, 242, 243, 246
Davis Strait, 36, 230, 239
Delag, 22
De Long, Lt. George Washington, 3,
   214, 243
De Lucca, Frank, 84
Demirov, Pilot, 267–269, 271, 272
Denmark, Danish, 111, 218, 231, 310,
   311, 312, 322, 332, 335
   Strait, 239, 311, 312
De Pineda, General Francesco, 147
Der Abend, 211

Det Norske Luftfartselskap (DNL),
   248
Detroit, 64, 66, 67, 101, 103, 110,
   112, 113, 116
   Arctic Expedition, 64, 66, 67
   News, 66, 103, 110
DEW, 333
Dickson, Baron Oscar, 5
Dietrichson, Leif, 32, 48–51, 53–55,
   58, 109, 158, 161, 170, 185, 349
Dietrichson, Major General Olaf, 30
Dikson Island, 249, 296, 321
Dirigible, 21, 28, 32, 33, 38, 40–43,
   50, 58, 59, 65, 70, 73, 76, 87, 95,
   100, 108, 113, 114, 120, 121, 134,
   144, 148, 155, 174, 187, 215, 266,
   309
   Graf Zeppelin, 243–246, 259
   Los Angeles, 145, 166
   N-1 (*Norge*), 49, 59, 64, 65, 68–
      71, 73, 75, 83, 84, 87, 88, 90,
      93–98, 100, 102, 108, 110, 111,
      115, 120, 217, 311
   N-3, 102, 111
   N-4 (*Italia*), 110–114, 116, 120,
      121, 122, 127, 128, 130–134, 136,
      138–143, 145, 147–151, 156, 157,
      159–162, 179, 184, 209, 210,
      212–217, 244, 245, 289, 309,
      334, 350
   R-31, 166
   R-36, 35
   R-38, 37, 40, 59
   R-100 (British), 242
   R-101 (British), 242
   Roma, 40, 59
   semi, C-5, 32
   Shenandoah, 40, 42, 73, 143
   T-3 (*Bodensee*), 33, 59
   Zeppelins, 22, 34, 194
Distinguished Flying Cross, 108
Donets Basin, 251
Doolittle, James, 64, 102
Doronin, Ivan, 263, 266, 267, 269,
   272, 274–277, 349
Drifting Polar Weather Station, 278,
   279, 283, 291
   Alpha, 334
   Arlis I and II, 335
   Charlie, 334
Duranty, Walter, 212, 213
Dzerdzeyevsky, B. L., 286

Eagle, 8–12, 14, 19
Eckener, Dr. Hugo, 194, 243, 245
Eggi, Captain Carl, 165, 189, 209,
   213, 334, 350

Ehrensvard, Count C., 6, 7
Eielson, Ben C., 29, 31, 32, 37, 39,
    40, 49, 66–68, 72, 73, 76, 78, 79,
    84, 101, 104–107, 110, 112–115,
    118–122, 142, 143, 148, 150, 189,
    223, 225–227, 268, 274, 307
Eisenhower, General Dwight D., 320
Ekman, Erik, 183, 185, 191
Ella Island, 239
Ellsmere Island, 60, 61, 323, 329
Ellsworth, James W., 47, 48
Ellsworth, Lincoln, 27–29, 31, 35, 39,
    41, 47–51, 53–56, 58, 69–71, 75,
    84, 92, 93, 95, 97, 99–101, 119,
    143, 148, 157, 223, 242, 244–
    246, 286, 349
Elson Lagoon, 113, 114
Endicott Range, 72, 113
England, 23, 28, 33, 35, 36, 38, 75,
    157, 183, 234, 239, 242, 249,
    310–313, 316–318, 320, 321, 329.
    See also Britain
Eredia, Professor Filippo, 120, 143
Erhart, Captain Lew, 329, 330, 331
Escadrille, Lafayette, 30
Eskimo, 22, 24, 37, 60, 67, 72, 106,
    113, 297, 312, 321
Eskimonaes, 239, 322
Esmark Island, 195, 199
Etah, 20, 43, 60–62, 90
Eureka Sound, 61
Explorers Club, 296

Fairbanks, 37, 40, 41, 49, 67, 71–73,
    76, 78, 101, 103, 224–226, 263,
    266, 270, 295–297, 318, 320
    News-Miner, 39, 41
Farikh, F. B., 226, 227, 261, 266
Faeroes, 230, 234, 310
Forthest-North Airplane Company, 39
Feodorov, Eugene, 284, 291, 299, 300,
    303, 350
Feucht, Ludwig, 50, 53, 56, 349
Finland, 31, 32, 121, 164
Finnish, 183, 190, 209
    Rescue Mission, 170, 174
Fitzgreen, Hugh, 60
Flagler Fjord, 62
Fletcher, Lieutenant Colonel Joseph,
    330, 331, 350
Flying Dutchman, 250
Fokker, Anthony, 65, 66, 102, 103
Ford, Edsel, 43, 64, 65
Ford Museum, 103
Foyn Island, 122, 148, 151, 155, 158,
    160, 169, 170, 175, 176, 184, 185,
    190, 192, 196, 198, 201, 206, 209

Fraenkel, Knut Hjalmar, 6–10, 15–18,
    122
Framlin Bay, 161
France, 29, 30, 33, 47, 75, 108, 164,
    168, 169, 175, 214, 243, 309
    French Air Service, 30
Frankfurter *Zeitung,* 21
Franz Josef Land, 14–16, 18, 122, 123,
    158, 188, 244, 245, 283, 284, 307,
    308, 322
Fredericksdal, 230
Freuchen, Peter, 190
Friedrichshafen, 33, 156, 164, 244, 246
Fuehrer, Der, 318
Fugloe Island, 219

Gagarin, Yuri, 277, 335
Galyshev, Boris, 263, 265–271, 274
Gast, Robert H., 230
Gatchina Airfield, 70, 76, 84, 87
Geographic Society
    American, 64, 73, 120, 244
    National, 49, 93, 99
    Norwegian, 3
    Royal, British, 234
    Royal Italian, 109, 112, 148
Geophysical Institute, Norway, 242
Germania Harbor, 321
Germany, German, 22, 29, 33, 143,
    156, 169, 215, 217, 235, 251, 309–
    313, 315, 316, 321
Ghiziga, 262
Gillam, Harold, 226, 227
Gillis Land, 123
Giornale d'Italia, 213
Giudici, Davide, 145, 148, 151, 157,
    168, 172, 182, 188, 202, 203, 205,
    206, 109, 211, 212, 350
Glavsevmorput, 251, 252, 276, 278,
    304, 306, 307, 318
Glenn, John, 335
Godthaab, 235, 239
Gold Medal of Honor, Italy, 215
Gold Medal for Meritorious Services,
    Norway, 95
Golovin, Peter, 285, 286, 287, 292, 296
Goose Bay, 316, 320, 349
Goteborg, 157
Gottwald, Birger, 95, 97, 349
Gould, L. M., 84, 87
Government,
    British, 231
    Canadian, 22, 36, 296
    Czarist, 37
    Czech, 196, 217
    French, 166
    German, 189, 230

Government (Cont'd.)
Italian, 114, 143, 144, 147, 157,
160, 161, 164, 189, 216, 217
Norwegian, 3, 35, 114, 143, 148,
150, 156, 157, 164, 166, 180, 183
Soviet, 160, 224, 266, 284, 292, 296,
297
Swedish, 6, 183, 196, 201
Graham, Alger, 103, 107
Graham Land, 34
Gran, Major, 143
Grand Tork Pacific Railway, 27
Grant Land, 115
Great Island, 193
Greely, General Adolphus, 3, 61, 296
Green Harbor, 119, 120, 138, 147,
165, 183, 314
Greenland, 11, 20, 36, 43, 49, 54, 59,
63, 65, 102, 110, 115, 128, 130,
161, 201, 227, 230, 231, 233,
234, 239, 242, 299, 300, 302,
306, 309–322, 326, 329, 330,
332, 333, 335
Greenland Sea, 36
Greenly Island, 116, 118
Grierson, John, 239
Grinnell Land, 62
Gromov, General Michael, 226, 294,
295, 298, 307, 321, 350
Guilbaud, René, 166, 167, 168, 169,
170

Haakon, King of Norway, 95, 100,
109, 311
Halifax, 231, 235
Hammer, Haakon H., 38, 39, 41, 213
Hampton, W. C., 231
Hansen, Captain Ole, 15
Harding, Warren, 38, 40
Hassell, Bert, 230, 349
Hatton, North Dakota, 32, 227
Haugesund, 234
Hayes, Isaac Israel, 60
Hayes Sound, 62
Herald Island, 105
Hero of the Soviet Union, 277, 292,
295, 335, 349
Herschel Island, 24
Hinlopen Sound, 191
Hinlopen Strait, 160, 161, 173, 177,
179, 180, 181, 183, 184, 209
Hoare, Sir Samuel, 76
Hobbs, William H., 239, 311, 312
Hoel, Professor Adolf, 111, 182, 185,
217, 218, 311, 350
Holland, 66, 108
Hooker Island, 244

Hooker, Sir Joseph, 3
Hope Island, 165, 170, 171, 189, 191
Horgen, Lieutenant Emil, 50, 94, 349
Horten, 29, 56, 58, 109, 145, 150, 157
Höver, Lieutenant J., 69, 90, 94, 109
Howden Air Station, 35
Hubbard Medal, 99
Hudson, Henry, 251
Hudson Strait, 223, 230, 234
Hull, Cordell, 312
Humber River, 37
Hungary, 114
Hutchinson, Palmer, 67
Hydrogen for balloons, 4, 9, 11

Ice islands, 323–325, 327–331, 334
Fletcher's Ice Island, 331, 332
T-2, 327
T-3, 325–331, 334
Ice, pack, 14 ff.
Ice pedestals, 327, 328
Ice station, drifting, *see* Drifting polar
weather stations
Iceland, 232, 234, 239, 310–314, 316,
322
Icelandic Aviation Company, 309
Il Popolo d'Italia, 137
Institute for Public Nutrition, 284
International Polar Year of 1882, 5
International Polar Year, 1932, Sec-
ond, 248, 278
International Geophysical Year, 334
Island X, 312. *See also* Jan Mayen
Island
Italian, 88, 90–92, 94, 98, 99, 101,
137, 143, 144, 148, 157, 162, 209,
210, 212–215, 217, 230
Italy, 23, 33, 41, 47, 49, 58, 59, 69,
71, 96, 102, 103, 109, 112, 137,
145, 157, 159, 161, 163–166,
176, 181, 182, 189, 209–211,
213–215, 218, 239, 309, 310,
322, 323
Ivanov, Sima, 202, 209, 244, 275,
276, 290
Ivigtut, 230
Izvestia, 284, 290

Jacobssen, Lieutenant Bengi, 157, 172,
177, 191, 193, 209, 350
Jan Mayen Island, 310, 312, 322
Japan, 36, 102, 108, 188, 225, 227,
251, 267, 318, 323, 349
JATO, 330
Jensen, Marius, 321
Johannesson, Professor Alexander, 232
Jugoslavia, 114

Kainergin, 269, 271, 272
Kamanin, General Nikolai, 262, 263,
    266–275, 278, 335, 349
Kamchatka, 262, 263, 265, 266
Kamenev, S. S. (Chief of the Soviet
    General Staff), 156, 187, 215,
    259
Kamenskoie, 269, 271
Kara Sea, 42, 249, 252, 253, 321
Kauffman, Henrik de, 312, 332
Khabarovsk, 262, 263, 265–267, 270
Khrushchev, Nikita S., 292, 304
King Charles Land, 180
Kings Bay, 50, 56, 58, 65, 69, 75, 83,
    84, 86–93, 95, 97, 98, 101, 114,
    120, 121, 130–132, 134, 140,
    141, 144, 145, 153, 157–159,
    161–163, 169, 172, 174, 175,
    180, 183, 189, 190, 196, 197, 209,
    212–214, 216, 218
Kitty Hawk, 21
Koch, Dr. Lauge, 239
Kolyma River, 42, 224, 250, 252, 255,
    292
Kolyuchin Bay, 225, 226, 265, 271,
    272, 274
Kolyuchin Island, 255, 265
Komseverput, 34, 42
Kopusov, Ivan, 252, 256, 278
Korean War, 329
Kramer, 150, 160
Kranklin, Ivan, 262
Kremlin, 284, 296
Krenkel, Ernest, 249, 259, 275, 276,
    284, 289, 290, 291, 299–303
Krenkel, Natasha, 301
Krylbo, 216
Kuibyshev, V. V., 259, 261–263, 268,
    270–272

Labrador, 113, 116, 235, 313, 316,
    318, 322
Labrador Sea, 36
Lacey, Major J. K., 309
Lachambre, Henri, 5
Ladd Field, 320, 321, 323
Lago, Ugo, 122, 127, 130, 132, 137
La Guardia, Fiorello, 148
Lake Fjord, 231, 239
Lake, Simon, 242, 243
Langley Field, 59
Lanphier, Major Thomas C., 66–68,
    78
Lavory, Bill, 271
Lavrentiya Bay, 226
Lavrov, Professor, 150
Legion of Honor, France, 101

Le May, General Curtis, 323
Lena River, 249, 252
Leningrad, 70, 75, 76, 84, 87, 88, 95,
    120, 163, 165, 175, 189, 244, 246,
    252, 253, 266, 304, 334
Levanevsky, Sigismund, 255, 263, 266,
    268–272, 277, 295–297, 299,
    304, 349
Lewis Holy Name School of Aeronau-
    tics in Chicago, 309
Lihr, Pilot, 170, 209, 350
Liljequist, Gösta H., 102
Lindbergh, Charles, 107, 227, 234,
    239, 294, 309, 311, 350
Lindbergh, Anne Morrow, 239
Lindsay, Martin, 233
Lomme Bay, 160
Lomonosov Ridge, 326
London, 28, 33, 63, 114, 167, 232,
    233, 310, 316, 335
    Daily Chronicle, 23
    Daily Mail, 33
    Naval Treaty, 242
Long Lake, 235
Long Year City, 191, 314, 315
Los Angeles, 294, 295, 332, 349
Lufthansa, 151, 161
Luftwaffe, 310, 311, 322
Luleo, Sweden, 169
Lundborg, Anne, 181, 189
Lundborg, Lieutenant Einar Pal, 157,
    158, 160, 170, 175–185, 187,
    188, 190–197, 200, 201, 210,
    214–216, 350
Lützow-Holm, Lieutenant Finn, 56,
    58, 145, 147, 150, 156, 158, 160–
    163, 166, 169–171, 175, 180,
    182, 184, 189, 310, 311, 316,
    317, 350
Lützow-Holm, Ole Arntzen, 316
Lyapidevsky, Anatol, 255, 256, 262–
    265, 271, 274, 276, 277, 349
Lyons, 163

Machuron, Alexis, 8
MacMillan, Donald B., 27, 49, 54,
    60–63
Maddelena, Major Umberto, 157–159,
    161–164, 166, 168–175, 178, 182,
    186, 196, 210, 214, 218, 350
Madison, Jim, 73, 75
Maina Pylgin, 268, 269, 271
Malmgren, Finn, 35, 38, 75, 87, 94,
    112, 121, 122, 130, 132, 134,
    136–139, 142, 143, 146, 147,
    149, 150–153, 155, 188, 190,
    199–203, 205, 206, 209, 210,
    212–214, 216, 242

Malmslatt, 157, 158, 160, 183
Mariano, Lt. Commander Adalberto,
111, 127, 131, 133, 135, 137–
141, 144, 146, 147, 149–151,
153–155, 166, 170, 171, 174,
186, 190, 192, 194, 198, 200,
202, 203, 205, 206, 210–216, 350
Marina di Pisa, 41, 48, 49
Markov, Michael, 258, 261, 262
Marseilles, 31, 163
Matochkin Shar, 249
Matteoda, Sergio, 150, 156, 178
Mattern, James, 255, 268
Mayo, William, 64
Mazuruk, Ilya, 287, 290–292, 321,
327
Meisterlin, 158, 161, 165
Meteorological Society, Royal, of
England, 34
Milan, 102, 109, 112–114, 145
Milan, University of, 112
Military Order of Savoy, Italy, 101
Milovzorov, Captain P. G., 224, 226,
266
Missile, intercontinental ballistic, 334
Nike, 337
Mitchell, General Billy, 102, 103
Moffen Island, 140, 161–163
Mogilevich, Boris, 258
Molokov, Vasili, 263, 267, 268, 272–
274, 276, 277, 284, 290, 296, 349
Molotov, V., 251, 259, 307
Morse, Samuel Finley Breese, Medal,
120
Morwinkel, J. L., 156, 212
Moscow, 150, 156, 158, 160, 163, 184,
195, 212, 215, 251, 259, 261,
262, 268, 271, 274, 276, 277,
283, 285, 292, 294–297, 300,
304, 308, 310, 335, 350
Evening, 212
Mossel Bay, 150, 159, 161, 162
Munich, 217
Murchison Bay, 173, 176, 184, 201
Murmansk, 212, 248, 251, 253, 278,
306, 317
Murray Bay, 118
Mussolini, Benito, 59, 69, 71, 75, 99,
103, 108, 109, 127, 128, 131,
137, 147, 148, 150, 156, 157,
164, 168, 210, 213, 215, 217,
309, 310, 323
Mys Chelyuskin, 321. *See also* Cape
Chelyuskin

Nagursky, Lieutenant Jan, 26, 309

Nansen, Fridtjof, 3–7, 14, 20, 26, 35,
43, 111, 157, 230, 247, 278, 285,
306, 308, 349
Naples, 101
Narsarssuak, 313, 316
Narvik, 49, 50, 168, 169, 183, 185,
215, 216
National Relief Organization, Russian,
150, 159
Navy,
German, 322
Norwegian, 48, 98, 185, 247, 309
Royal Italian, 151, 173, 202, 206,
210
Soviet, 317
Swedish, 156
United States, 32, 49, 83, 214
Nelson, Erik H., 230
Neva River, 165
Newcomb, Simon, 21
Newfoundland, 32, 235
New Friesland, 159, 161
New Siberian Islands, 3. *See also*
Novosiberian Islands
New York, 26, 35, 47, 66, 71, 93, 95,
97–102, 107, 108, 113, 143,
157, 189, 231, 243, 263, 296,298
Times, 64, 69, 70, 96, 97, 99,
100, 119, 128, 131, 141, 143,
145, 147, 157–159, 164, 174,
187, 200, 210, 212, 214, 233, 310
World, 116
Nikolaievsk, 262, 266, 267, 292
Nilsson, Sergeant, 157, 168, 172, 215,
350
Nizhne Novgorod, 26
Nizhne-Tambovsk, 267
Nobile, Amadeo, 120, 174
Nobile, Carlotta, 95, 131
Nobile Relief Committee, 156, 158,
184
Nobile, Umberto, 49, 50, 58, 59, 64,
65, 69–71, 75, 76, 83, 84, 87–91,
93–95, 98–103, 108, 109, 111–
114, 116, 120–123, 127–141,
144–149, 151–155, 157, 158,
160, 162–166, 168–187, 189,
190, 197, 203, 209–213, 215–
217, 231, 244, 245, 259, 309–
311, 320, 322, 350
Nogaievo Bay, 267, 268, 296
Noice, Harold, 40
Nois, 165, 166, 171, 178
Nome, 22, 24, 27, 35, 48, 96, 97,
223, 225, 262, 268–271, 295, 321
Daily News-Miner, 49
Nordenskiöld, Baron Nils A., 5, 230,
248, 251

Norfolk, Virginia, *Virginian Pilot,* 21
North American Newspaper Alliance,
                64
North Cape, 147, 250. *See also* Cape
                North
North Pole, 3–5, 11, 12, 16, 19, 20,
        26–28, 34, 40, 43, 49–51, 53,
        55, 57, 59, 70, 71, 73, 84, 89,
        100–102, 108, 109, 115, 128,
        130, 131, 230, 242, 244–247,
        279, 283, 285, 286, 289, 294,
        295, 304–306, 308, 323, 326,
                329, 331, 334, 349
    NP-1, 290, 300, 303
    NP-2, 326
    NP-3, 332
    NP-6, -7, -8, 334
North Sea, 234
Northeast Land, 122, 140, 146
Northeast Passage, 5, 26, 35, 36, 248,
                249
Northern Air Route, 227, 230, 320
Northern Sea Route, 249–252, 254,
        278, 279, 283, 304, 306–308,
        317. *See also* Northeast Passage
Northwest Passage, 20
Norway, 29–32, 35, 36, 38, 39, 41,
        48, 49, 56, 58, 59, 65, 95, 100,
        109, 111, 143, 145, 156, 159,
        164, 168, 174, 175, 182–184,
        212–216, 220, 234, 247, 310,
                311, 314, 326, 331, 334, 349
    Free, 311, 312
Norwegian, 15, 69, 70, 86, 88, 91, 93,
        99, 100, 121, 147, 159, 161, 164,
        166, 170, 171, 185, 213, 216,
                220, 312, 314–316
    Air Line, 247
    Air Transport Company, 165
    Defense Department, 56
    Flag, 95
    Rescue Mission, 176
    Sea, 36
Nova Scotia, 31, 231, 235
Novaya Zemlya, 26, 36, 42, 130, 158,
                159, 246, 308, 317, 322
Novosiberian Islands, 308
Ny Alesund, 92, 120–123, 128

Ob River, 42
Okhotsk, 262, 267
Old, General William, 329, 330
Olonkin, G., 38, 95
Olsen, Rudolf, 247
Olyutorsk Bay, 266, 267
Omdal, Oscar, 38, 48, 50, 53, 54, 56,
                95, 96, 109, 349

Operation
    Alsib, 320, 321
    Banso, 314
    Blue Jay, 329
    Bolero, 320
    Bravo, 334
    Gauntlet, 314
    Highjump, 322
    Mint Julep, 324
    Sonnie, 326
    We Do It, 326
    Wonderland, 321
    Zitronella, 315
Opukha River, 269
Oras, Paul, 165, 199, 209, 350
Oscar, King, 3, 5
Oslo, 29, 58, 59, 69, 70, 75, 76, 95,
        97, 109, 138, 141, 145, 148, 150,
        154, 161, 169, 172, 310, 312
    Aftenposten, 142, 214
    Dagbladet, 164
    University, 311
Ostrov Kostenlny, 305
Oumansky, Constantine, 296
Owen, Russell, 93

Pacific Alaska Airways, 266, 268
Pacific Ocean, 36, 248, 256, 292, 294,
                309
Pan American Airways, 235, 239, 350
Pangnirtung, 234
Papanin, Ivan, 245, 284, 288, 291,
        294, 296, 298–304, 306–308,
                318, 350
Paquette, Oliver, 234
Paris, 5, 26, 30, 150, 310
Patrick Island, 28
Pearce Point, 294
Pearl Harbor, 318
Peary, Robert E., 20, 22, 27, 28, 35,
        42, 43, 49, 51, 90, 91, 115, 230,
                324
Pechora, 33, 34
Pedretti, Ettore, 133, 140, 151
Penzo, Major, 164, 166, 168, 170,
        172, 175, 178, 182, 186, 196,
                210, 214, 220
Permafrost, 337
Pilot's Dream, A, 283
Pine Tree System, 333
Pivenshtein, Boris, 267, 268, 272
Pogossov, A., 275
Point Barrow, 24, 38, 40, 49, 64, 66,
        68, 72, 73, 76, 78, 79, 96, 101,
        103, 105, 107, 110, 112, 114,
                116, 296, 297
Point Hope, 24
Poland, 309

Polar Basin, 37, 256
Polar Sea, 6, 11, 14, 36, 244, 295,
    303. *See also* Arctic Ocean and
                      Polar Basin
Pomella, Vincenzo, 95, 111, 127, 130,
    140, 141, 153, 154, 162, 168
Ponamarev, Paul, 165, 197, 206, 334,
                                  350
Pontremoli, Aldo, 112, 130–132, 137
Pope Pius XI, 71, 112, 131, 144, 309
Popolo di Roma, 211
Port Burwell, 230
Port Harrison, 235
Povungnituk, 235
Prague, 154
Pravda, 252, 263, 284, 291
Pravda, Young Communist, 212
Prince Patrick Island, 294, 297
Project 572, 333
Project Icicle, 329, 330
Provideniya Bay, 225, 226, 256, 265,
                      271, 272, 277

Radio Relay League, 145
Ramm, Frederick, 50, 54, 56–58, 349
Randall, Robert, 296, 297
Ravazzoni, 175, 176, 185
"Red Tent," 162, 169, 170, 172, 182,
    192, 195, 197, 198, 200, 201,
                      206, 207, 210
Relative Inaccessibility
    Area of, 294, 307, 308
    Pole of, 307, 308
Rescue Squadron, Tenth, 326, 329
Reykjavik, 230, 233, 235
Riiser-Larsen, Hjalmar, 29, 32, 33, 35,
    36, 38–41, 48–51, 53, 55–58, 70,
    76, 87, 88, 90–92, 94, 95, 97, 98,
    100, 103, 108, 109, 139, 145,
    148, 157, 158, 161–164, 166,
    168–172, 175, 180, 182–184,
    189, 223, 233, 247, 248, 286,
    309–311, 316, 317, 331–333,
                                  349, 350
Rips Bay, 173
Rips Island, 174
Ritenbenk, 239
Rockaway Beach, 32
Rockefeller, John D., Jr., 43, 65
Rodahl, Dr. Kaare, 330, 331
Rodenbauch, Jim, 41
Romagna-Manoja, Commander, 112,
    120, 128, 140, 141, 162, 163,
    166, 170–173, 178, 181, 184,
    185, 186, 190, 196, 197, 203,
    206, 207, 210, 212, 214–216, 350
Rome, 49, 58, 71, 75, 95–97, 101,
    108, 110, 112, 137, 142, 144,

Rome (Cont'd.)
    145, 147, 150, 155–157, 160,
    163, 164, 173, 176, 201, 210, 217
Rommel, General Erwin, 318
Roosevelt, Franklin D., 309, 313, 315
Rosendahl, Lieutenant Commander,
                                  143, 148
Rosensvärd, Lieutenant Ivan, 157,
                      172, 177, 193, 350
Rote Fahne, Die, 212
Royal Yacht Club, Oslo, 142
Rudolf Island, 245, 283–285, 287–
                      290, 292, 296, 297
Russ Island, 179, 181
Russia, Russian, 26, 31, 33, 36, 40,
    42, 43, 120, 158, 162, 164, 170,
    197, 209, 211, 213, 215, 224,
    251, 283, 292, 309, 310, 313,
    317, 318, 320, 321, 323, 334.
                      See also Soviet Union
    Revolution, 224, 225, 248

Sabine Island, 321
Samoilovich, Professor Rudolf, 33, 34,
    36, 37, 148, 150, 159, 163, 165,
    171, 183, 185, 188, 190, 195,
    198–200, 202, 203, 207, 209–
    212, 215, 244, 245, 249, 306, 350
San Francisco, 292, 294, 317
San Jacinto, California, 294
San Paolo (IDO 32), Rome, 155, 159,
                                  161
Sarko, Pilot, 170, 182, 190, 350
SAS, 331, 332, 333, 349
Sassoon, Sir Phillip, 189
Sawyer Fjord, 62
Scandinavia, 31, 33, 35
Schmidt, Nicholas, 159, 160, 161
Schmidt, Otto Yulevich, 248–252,
    255–258, 261, 272, 274, 275,
    278, 283–286, 288–292, 296,
                      302, 304–306, 350
Schyberg, Birger, 158, 191, 193, 195,
                                  350
Scoresby Island, 171
Scoresby Sound, 235, 312, 322
Scott, Major George, 32, 35, 75, 76,
                                  227
Scott, Robert Falcon, 20, 27
Sea of Laptev, 321
Sea of Norway, 302
Seattle, 22, 26, 27, 35, 38, 41, 66, 67,
    98–100, 103, 224, 227, 294, 295,
                                  317
Seddin hangar, 116
Sedov, Georgi, 26, 283, 306
Sesto Calende, 163
Settinelli, Emilio, 214

Seven Islands, 7, 16–18, 188, 200
Severnaya Zemlya, 122, 123, 245,
      254, 308
Shackleton, Sir Ernest, 23, 24, 35, 99,
      231
Shafran, Arkadi, 258, 264
Shaw, Donald A., 324, 334
Shelkovo Airfield, 292
Shetland Islands, 235
Sheveleo, Mark, 284, 296
Ships
 Adak, 329
 Admiral Scheer, 321
 Alaska, 24
 Bergensfjord, 100
 Bismarck, 311
 Bowdoin, 59
 Braganza, 147, 157, 166, 168–171,
  173, 175, 180, 182–184, 189,
  190, 194, 196, 197, 200, 201,
      210–213
 Brood, 219, 220
 Busko, 316
 Cattaro, 192
 Chantier, 71, 73, 75, 83, 84, 86–
     88, 92, 93, 98
 Chelyuskin, 252–261, 263, 266,
    271, 276, 278, 284, 285
 Città di Milano, 112, 113, 120, 121,
  128, 132, 133, 134, 139–142,
  144, 147, 150, 151, 159–164,
  166, 169–172, 174, 178, 179,
  181–186, 188, 192, 196, 197,
    209, 211, 213–216, 218
 Conte Biancamano, 101
 Dragon, 335
 Durance, 220
 Elisif, 224
 Empress of Canada, 314
 Farm, 48, 50, 54, 56, 57
 Fram, 3–5, 20, 26, 247, 306, 309
 Fridtjof Nansen, 311, 312
 Gustave Adlu, 218
 Heimdal, 57, 83, 88
 Heimland, 58, 164, 201, 217
 Hermann, 321
 Hobby, 48, 50, 114, 120, 122, 143,
  145, 147, 150, 156, 158–165,
  168, 171, 183, 189, 194, 200, 218
 Ingefire, 157
 Ingerto, 185, 191
 Isbjörn, 315
 Jeannette, 3, 243
 Karluk, 22, 24, 37, 43
 Krasny Oktiabr, 42
 Krassin, 163–166, 168–172, 174,
  175, 180–192, 194–203, 206,

Ships (Cont'd.)
 207, 209–216, 219, 244, 247,
    252, 255, 261, 266, 350
 Litke, 225, 226, 250, 255, 257, 261,
     278, 304, 305
 Malygin, 159, 161, 164, 165, 169–
  171, 175, 180, 182–184, 189,
    191, 212, 216, 244, 245
 Marita, 174
 Mary Sachs, 24, 25, 26
 Maud, 33, 35, 38, 94, 248, 251
 Michael Sars, 164, 175, 220
 Morsecock, 244
 Munargo, 316
 Murman, 300, 302, 303
 Murmanets, 300, 302
 Nanuk, 224, 225, 226, 266
 Nautilus, 242–244, 246, 247, 334
 North Star, 25, 26, 28
 Northland, 316
 Odinn, 232, 233
 Olympia, 263
 Peary, 59, 62, 63
 Pechora, 26
 Persei, 158, 164, 174
 Pourquoi-Pas?, 150, 164, 176, 189,
      201
 Prince of Wales, 313
 Quentin Roosevelt, 164, 175, 183,
      201
 Quest, 157, 158, 164, 170, 171,
  173, 176, 182, 183, 201, 206,
     209, 216, 231
 Roosevelt, 43
 Rusanov, 249, 284
 Sachsen, 311
 Saint Anne, 26
 Saint Foka, 26
 Samson, 109
 Sargo, 334
 Scharnhorst, 315
 Sedov, 159, 164, 305–307
 Selis, 315
 Sibiriakov, 249–253, 321
 Siøliv, 58
 Skate, 247, 334
 Smolensk, 262, 263, 265, 266, 277
 Soejint, 235
 Soviet, 263, 271
 Stalin, 305–307
 Stalingrad, 263, 271
 Stavropol, 42, 224–226, 266
 Strasbourg, 164, 175, 176, 183,
      201, 218
 Submarine, Soviet, 302
 Svalbard, 175
 Svensksund, 6, 7
 Taimyr, 158, 301–303

Ships (Cont'd.)
  Tanja, 157, 164, 171, 182, 183, 191
  Tirpitz, 315
  Tordenskjold, 164, 175, 183
  U-boat, 315, 317
  Ussurnetz, 250
  Vega, 248
  Veslekari, 217
  Victoria, 98, 99
  Viking, 109
  Virgo, 5, 6
  Wyoming, U.S.S., 244
  Yermak, 301, 302, 304, 305
Shirshov, Peter, 249, 264, 265, 267,
    269, 272, 291, 299–301, 303, 350
Sholokov, M., 258
Shrader, Ludmilla, 259, 263, 264, 272
Shchukin, Anatol, 206, 211
Siberia, 5, 33–35, 37, 223–227, 248–
    251, 259, 263, 271, 276, 295,
                304, 317, 321, 335
Signehamma Bay, 315
Sirianni, Admiral, 111, 181
Slepnev, Commander Mavriki, 226,
    227, 261, 263, 266, 268–277, 350
Smith, Lowell H., 230
Smith Sound, 60
Somov, Michael, 321, 323, 326, 327
Sondre Strom Fjord, 230, 239, 313,
                316, 320
Sora, Captain Gennaro, 120, 157,
    159, 163, 166, 170, 173–175,
    180, 182, 183, 186, 190, 192,
    196–198, 202, 206, 209, 215, 350
South Gate, 144, 147, 160
South Pole, 20, 23, 27, 38, 94, 95,
                99, 102
South Pond, Maine, 235
Soviet Union, Soviet, 227, 278, 294,
    296, 298, 304, 324, 326, 332–
                334. *See also* Russia
  Embassy, Washington, 296, 298
  Fur Trust, 224
  Relief Committee, 216
Spaatz, General Carl A., 102, 323
Spain, Spanish, 70, 157, 158, 230
Spirin, Ivan, 284, 288, 289, 301
Spitsbergen, 5–7, 9, 11, 15, 18, 22,
    33, 38–40, 50, 54, 56, 57, 64, 68,
    69, 71, 75, 76, 83, 84, 90, 91, 93
    99, 100, 113, 115, 116, 118, 119,
    122, 123, 131, 134, 138, 142–
    145, 147, 150, 154, 156–158,
    161–166, 168–170, 175, 176,
    178, 183, 185, 187, 189, 191,
    192, 196, 201, 216, 243, 246,
    247, 306, 310, 311, 313–315, 322
Srednevsky, Dr., 202, 203, 206, 212

St. John's, Newfoundland, 235
St. Paul, Alaska, 96
Stalin, J., 248, 277, 307
Stefani, 156
Stefansson, Vilhjalmur, 22, 24–28,
    35–37, 40, 42, 43, 63, 66, 99,
        119, 235, 242, 294, 307, 349
Stockholm, 7, 97, 121, 168, 196, 215,
                216, 230
  Aftonbladet, 7, 8, 12, 15
Stolp, 114, 116
Storkerson, Storker, 28, 278
Strindberg, Nils, 6–10, 15–18, 122
Styhr, Lieutenant, 56, 58
Sukkertoppen, 235
Sullom Voe, 314
Sutherland, Dan A., 37
Svalbard. *See* Spitsbergen
Svedenborg, Lieutenant, 7, 17
Sverdrup, Colonel Einar, 314, 315
Sverdrup, Professor Harold, 35, 38,
    111, 139, 145, 154, 242, 243, 246
Sverdrup Island, 249
Sverdrup, Captain Otto, 3, 143
Sweden, Swedish, 4, 5, 88, 154, 156,
    157, 160–162, 164, 200, 201,
        212–214, 216, 230, 310, 326
  press, 211
  Rescue Mission, 169, 179, 191, 192,
                194, 195, 215
  War Department, 212
Swenson, Olaf, 223–226, 266
Sylt Island, 176, 230

Taimyr Peninsula, 246, 254
Tandberg, R., 165, 171, 178
Teller, 24, 27, 97, 100, 108, 226, 227,
                271, 272
Teplitz Bay, 284, 285, 289
Territorial Defense Organization, 150
Thommessen, Dr. Rolf, 65, 69
Thompson, Bill, 39, 41, 49
Thule, 326, 329, 330, 335–337
Tidens Tegn, 65
Tikhaya Bay, 245, 285, 292
Tiksi Bay, 304, 305
Tiros I, 334
Tiros II, III, IV, 335
Tishkov, 261
Tokyo, 333, 335
Tomaselli, Cesco, 122, 123, 141, 157,
                162, 350
Tornberg, Captain E., 156, 157, 168–
    170, 173, 174, 176, 180, 182,
    184, 191, 196, 200, 201, 206,
        209, 212, 214, 216, 350
                212, 214, 216, 350

Torp, Oscar, 247, 248
Tours, 30
Trangisvaag, 235
Transamerican Airlines Corporation,
    234, 235
Trans-Siberian Railroad, 251
Trapani, 49
Trepassey Bay, 32
Troianovski, Mark, 255, 284, 288
Trojani, Felice, 69, 102, 108, 111,
    113, 121, 123, 127, 130, 131,
    133, 134, 136–138, 144, 147,
    149, 152, 154, 158, 167, 172,
    176, 178–181, 188, 192, 194,
    196, 198, 207, 209, 211, 212,
    214, 215, 309, 350
Trojani, Marta, 113, 148
Tromso, 122, 127, 128, 143, 145,
    147, 150, 154, 157, 158, 169,
    170, 176, 183, 189, 216, 219,
    220, 312, 314

Udet, Ernest, 189, 192, 194, 196
Uelen, 250, 255, 259, 261–265, 270–
    273, 296
United States, 21, 29, 30, 34, 37, 38,
    41, 47, 49, 54, 64, 65, 70, 98,
    100–102, 108, 148, 166, 239,
    242, 253, 265, 268, 292, 294,
    296, 298, 309–313, 316, 317,
    320, 321, 323, 324, 331, 333,
    334, 337
University of Michigan, 230, 239
University of Naples, 309, 320
University of Uppsala, 102
Unshlikht, I. S., 150, 156, 163, 195,
    250
Urals, 251
Ushakov, Georgi, 263, 270, 273, 274

Vadso, 70, 75, 88, 121, 166, 168, 170
Valavin, G., 272, 277
Valette, Emile, 170
Valkalten, 272
Valle, Giuseppe, 65, 69, 71, 103, 322,
    350
Vancouver, 36, 294
Van Dongen, Joseph, 165, 166, 170,
    174, 175, 180, 182, 183, 186,
    192, 196, 201, 206, 217, 350
Vankarem, 265, 268, 270–277
Varming, Ludwig, 165, 166, 170, 174,
    192, 196, 198, 201
Venice, 114
Verne, Jean Jules, 243
Viglieri, Alfredo, 112, 127, 128,
    130, 133, 136–143, 147, 149,
    152, 153, 155, 172, 173, 175,

Viglieri (Cont'd.)
    178–190, 192–198, 200, 203,
    206, 207, 209–211, 216, 217, 350
Vilensky, E., 284, 290
Vilkitski Strait, 246, 254
Virgo Bay, 7, 8, 10, 122, 170–172,
    178, 181–183, 186, 187, 189, 191
Vladivostok, 42, 225, 226, 248, 249,
    252, 261–263, 266, 317
  Far Eastern University, 145
Vlasov, Gennady, 301
Vodopyanov, Michael, 263, 266–269,
    272, 274–277, 283, 285–290,
    296, 297, 313, 327, 349
Vogelsang Island, 8
Von der Lippe, Commodore, 109, 143
Von Gronau, Wolfgang, 230, 231,
    235, 349
Voronin, Captain Vladimir Ivanovich,
    249, 253–258, 275, 276
Vorontsova, Ljubov Andreevna, 171,
    182, 185, 212, 350
Voyage of the Jeannette, 214
Voznesenye, 159, 160

Wahlenberg Bay, 165, 166
Wainwright, 38, 96
Wakeham Bay, 234
Walker, Jimmy, 98
Warnemünde, 217
Warsaw, 309
Washington, D. C., 27, 37, 40, 41,
    108, 145, 296, 298, 309, 311, 321
Watkins, Gino, 231–233, 242
Wellman, Walter, 51, 70
Welt Am Abend, Die, 211
Whalen, Grover, 98
White Eagle. See Amundsen, Roald
White Island, 18, 19, 349
White Sea, 244, 251
Wiese, Professor, 150, 161, 165, 244,
    249
Wijdenfijord, 140
Wilbur, Curtis Dwight, 49, 63, 93,
    108, 145, 166
Wilkins, George H. (Sir Hubert), 22–
    26, 28, 32–35, 37–39, 63, 64,
    66–68, 72, 73, 76, 78, 79, 84, 96,
    99, 101, 103–107, 110, 112–116,
    118–122, 138, 141, 142, 148,
    150, 189, 223, 231, 242–244,
    246, 247, 278, 296–299, 307,
    322, 334, 349
Wilkins, Suzanne Bennett, 242, 243
Willoughby, Sir Hugh, 250, 251
Wisting, Oscar, 38, 94, 95, 169, 217,
    349
Wood, Dick, 39

Wood, Robert, 230
World War I, 26, 28, 29
World War II, 309–322, 323, 332,
335, 349
Wrangel Island, 37, 40, 42, 250, 252,
308, 326
Wright brothers, 21, 99

Xenia, 182

Yenisei River, 42

Young, Ed, 226, 227
Yudikhin, Ivan, 199, 200
Zappi, Lieutenant Commander
Filippo, 111, 127, 130, 133, 135,
137, 138, 140, 142, 144, 146,
147, 149, 151–155, 190, 202,
203, 205, 206, 209–211, 213,
214, 216, 350
Zeppelin, Count Ferdinand von, 20–
22, 315, 335
Zurich, 163